The Americas in the Modern Age

The Americas in the Modern Age

Lester D. Langley

Yale University Press New Haven & London

Published with assistance from the Louis Stern Memorial Fund.

Set in Walbaum type by Integrated Publishing Solutions.
Printed in the United States of America by Vail-Ballou Press.

Library of Congress Cataloging-in-Publication Data
Langley, Lester D.
    The Americas in the modern age / Lester D. Langley.
    p. cm.
    Includes bibliographical references and index.
    ISBN 0-300-10008-6 (alk. paper)
    1. America—History—1810– 2. North America—History. 3. Latin America—History 4. North America—Relations—Latin America. 5. Latin America—Relations—North America. I. Title.
    E18.83.L36 2003
    970.05—dc21

                                                    2003001157
A catalogue record for this book is available from the British Library.

The paper in this book meets the guidelines for permanence and durability of the Committee on Production Guidelines for Book Longevity of the Council on Library Resources.

10 9 8 7 6 5 4 3 2 1

For my parents,
Lester Langley *and* Lona Jane Clements Langley,
Who were born in the last decade of the nineteenth century and died in the last decade of the twentieth.

Contents

Maps

Acknowledgments

Although this book was written in the closing years of my academic career at the University of Georgia, my interest in the history of the Americas commenced during my graduate study in both U.S. diplomatic and Latin American history under Ray O'Connor and Charles Stansifer at the University of Kansas in the early 1960s, years of crisis for the Western Hemisphere. In much of my early work, I viewed hemispheric history through the distorted lens of U.S. policy toward Latin America in the cold war. In the 1980s, however, my perspective broadened, even as I acknowledged that the militarization of U.S. relations with Latin America, the continuing hostility toward the Cuban revolution, and especially the pursuit of a covert war in Central America validated that approach. I became convinced that not only political and economic but especially cultural dynamics were critical to understanding Western Hemispheric history. With the support of Malcolm Call and Karen Orchard of the University of Georgia Press I took on the challenging role of editor of a series, The United States in the Americas, and wrote the general volume in the series, *America and the Americas: The United States in the Western Hemisphere.* I have relied on the excellent books in this series throughout this study. I have also benefited from the comments of other scholars: Bill Stueck, Peter Hoffer, and Thom Whigham, former colleagues; Ralph Lee Woodward, Jr., Michael Conniff, Jeremy Adelman, Charles Stansifer, Thomas Benjamin, and William Walker.

My thanks also to those graduate students in my Inter-American Relations class at the University of Texas in fall 2000—Emily Berquist, Julie Blase, Michelle Fontanez, Emily Forrington, Jeff Hooper, Daryl Maas, Walter Pineda, Lockett Pitman, Aaron Schuelke, Keith Sims, David Stiles, Kerry Webb, and Jackie Zahn—and in a similar class at Texas A&M University in spring 2002— Clay Baird, Brandon Mitchell, David Nelson, Brian Neumann, Angela Spoede, and Jennie Stuhrenberg. They made my brief postretirement teaching as pleasant and challenging as it was when I began my academic career at TAMU in the fall of 1965.

And, finally, a special note of gratitude to Lara Heimert and the editorial staff of Yale University Press.

The maps were prepared by Krysia Haag of Campus Graphics and Photography of the University of Georgia.

A Note on Usage

The use of *America, North American,* and especially *American* becomes more confusing with every generation, and it is not likely to be cleared up anytime soon. Throughout this study I have followed the Library of Congress definition for America as "the Americas" or the "Western Hemisphere," although the LC distinguishes between Americas (lands) and Western Hemisphere (lands and waters). I have not followed the (to me) peculiar LC subject definitions for "Americans" to mean citizens of the United States who are living outside the United States but instead have employed "North American" rather than "United Statesian" to identify what most residents of the United States and Europeans call Americans. Mexicans commonly use North American to refer to people from the United States and, occasionally, to Canadians. Some of the latter share the Latin American and Caribbean resentment of the use of "Americans" by residents of the United States but persist in identifying themselves as "not Americans."

Dictionaries often define *American* as an Indian of North or South America, an inhabitant or native of North or South America, or a citizen of the United States—and not always in that order. Clicking on "American" on the Library of Congress Web page will ultimately lead to more than 140 definitions under the Authority Record's "narrower terms," including the familiar African Americans, Asian Americans, and Mexican Americans as well as Belarusian Americans, Hmong Americans, and Bengali Americans. In the early twentieth century, *Americanization* referred specifically to the movement to assimilate immigrants to U.S. ideals, traditions, language, and ways of life. In our time it has retained that meaning but has also acquired hemispheric and even global implications.

There may be less controversy about the definition of *Latin America* than *America,* but the term, first used by French diplomats in the mid–nineteenth century, is also imprecise. There is no uniform Latin American culture but a mosaic of cultures incorporating African, Amerindian, European, Asian, North American, and even Middle Eastern peoples and traditions. Anglo-America, French America, Portuguese America, Spanish America, Iberoamerica, African America and Indoamerica are sometimes used to identify the differing major historical ethnic and racial groups in the Americas. In recent years, it has become commonplace for social scientists to distinguish between the independent states and dependencies of the insular Caribbean, some of which are linguistically and culturally a part of Latin America, and those of mainland Latin America, a few of which are not. Some might exclude Belize, Surinam, Guyana, and French Guiana from a definition of *Caribbean* because none is an island, though the history and culture of each are closely linked to the insular Caribbean. Throughout this study I have commonly used *Latin America* to refer to the mainland and *the Caribbean* to refer to the islands. When I refer not only to the islands but to those mainland states and dependencies that border the Caribbean Sea, I have used *greater Caribbean* or *circum-Caribbean.*

I have Anglicized the spelling of some Latin American, Caribbean, and francophone Canadian place-names: Havana not La Habana, Mexico City not México, D.F., Panama not Panamá, Peru not Perú, Bogotá not Santafé de Bogotá, Montreal not Montréal, and Quebec not Québec.

1. The Americas in the Mid-Nineteenth Century

Introduction

This book represents part of a continuing effort to understand the evolution of the Americas from the breakdown of colonial empires and kingdoms that commenced with the political crisis in British North America in the 1760s to the Western Hemisphere of our times. In some respects, the narrative deals with many of the issues and themes I explored in *The Americas in the Age of Revolution, 1750–1850*, a comparison of the American, Haitian, and Spanish-American revolutions, struggles that began under different circumstances and for different reasons but that culminated in the creation of independent states. The emphasis in that book lay primarily in the contrasting experience of these wars and what they portended for the future of these new states and for the hemisphere. There were few commonalities in these revolutions, and when they were over virtually none of the revolutionary leaders were satisfied with the outcome or the kind of society left in their wake. The political upheavals and civil wars of midcentury served as tragic reminders of their fears.

In these formative years in the history of the Americas, it is generally acknowledged, two presumably incompatible visions of the Western hemispheric future took form. The first is associated with the position taken by President James Monroe in his message of December 1823 to Congress, in which he acknowledged the reality of Spanish-American independence and stated his government's opposition to future European territorial expansion in the Americas. The second is identified with one of the revolutionary era's most controversial and brilliant figures, Simón Bolívar, the Venezuelan who commanded armies that liberated northern Spanish America and whose calls for unity among his victorious comrades prompted the first formal gathering of hemispheric delegates at Panama and then Tacubaya, Mexico, in 1826. These two variations of the Western Hemisphere idea bequeathed two competitive and presumably irreconcilable concepts: the Monrovian tradition, that is, the belief that democracy, development, and security in the Americas have always depended on U.S. power and guidance; and the Bolivarian tradition, which rejects that notion by calling for cooperation in the face of a common threat.

In the nineteenth and early twentieth centuries, the Bolivarian view weakened under widespread doubts about the compatibility of such diverse societies and cultures and then withered before an aggressive U.S. territorial expansion and a hemispheric policy based on domination and intervention rather than cooperation and "good neighborliness." The contrived unity of World War II collapsed before U.S. cold war priorities, the challenge of the Cuban revolution, the inadequacies of the Alliance for Progress in the 1960s in meeting the pressing political, economic, and social demands of a rapidly changing hemisphere, and the invasion of Santo Domingo in spring 1965 in order to prevent "another Cuba." In the two decades that followed, inter-American harmony suffered. President Jimmy Carter won the admiration of most hemispheric governments for his willingness to return the Panama Canal to Panama and is still widely admired among the peoples of Latin America for his promotion of human rights; but U.S. policy toward the Socialist government of Chile in the early 1970s, U.S. intervention in Central America in the 1980s, and U.S. drug policy in the Americas persuaded a generation of Latin Americans and Canadians that this country remained the biggest obstacle to hemispheric cooperation. The Christmas invasion of Panama in December 1989—Operation Just Cause—confirmed in many minds that little had changed in U.S. policy toward the Americas in the twentieth century.

Yet the story of the Western Hemisphere in the 1990s and the relation of the United States to the other nations and peoples of the Americas sounds very different. In May 1998, a report of the prestigious American Assembly of Columbia University observed that "no region in the world has a more direct impact on the everyday lives of U.S. citizens than does the rest of the Western Hemisphere itself."[1] In a decade when the United States seemed more preoccupied with dramatic events in Europe and Asia, such a statement appeared unwarranted, yet it was premised on the fact that at the turn of the twenty-first century, this country's greatest economic opportunities lie with its two most important trading partners, Canada and Mexico. By 2010, it is estimated, U.S. exports to Latin America will exceed those to Japan and the European Union. Brazil and Chile are already more important trading partners than China and India. For its energy sources, the United States depends more on Venezuela, Mexico, and Canada than on the Persian Gulf. The importance of the Western Hemisphere is also expressed in the "Latinization" of the United States. In recent years, this term has become a familiar refrain, as our culture and domestic politics, particularly in such key states as Florida, New Jersey, New York, Illinois, Texas, and California, reflect the influence of Spanish-speaking peoples, most of whom are Mexicans, Puerto Ricans, and Cubans. According to the 2000 census, the number of Hispanics in the United States reached 35 million, equaling the size of the historically "majority-minority" population of African Americans and scheduled to surpass it early in the twenty-first century.

A hemisphere whose governments and peoples nowadays seem committed to not only an economic but also a common political and even social agenda appears to be more achievable than at any time in the history of the Americas. At the turn of the twenty-first century, North Americans express fewer doubts about Latin America's economic, political, and social prospects than they did at any time since World War II. In two Summits of the Americas in the 1990s (in 1994 and 1998) and a third in early 2002, representatives of hemispheric governments assessed proposals for the economic integration of the hemisphere, the strengthening of democracy and human rights, the eradication of poverty and discrimination, and plans for sustainable development. Phrases such as "enterprise of the Americas" and "liberal pacific union" are now part of the hemispheric vocabulary.[2]

Certainly such lofty proposals about the future of the Western Hemisphere must be measured against the historical record of more than two centuries of fundamental political and cultural divisions among the governments and peoples of the Americas. Appeals for hemispheric unity and even formal agreements binding the governments of the continent are not new; indeed, they go all the way back to the age of independence in the Americas. But critics of any notion of "common history" of the Americas have always been able to offer examples that belie evidence of unity or commonality. Beginning with the earliest expressions of U.S. designs on Spanish Cuba in the 1820s to the confrontation with the Cuban and Nicaraguan revolutions during the cold war years, they point out that the real menace to a liberal pacific union and to democracy in the Americas has always been the United States. Others retain fundamental doubts that democracy has taken hold south of the Rio Grande or that Latin Americans and most Caribbean peoples subscribe to those cultural values required of any society that wishes to modernize. Still others contend that the cultural role of the United States has been largely beneficial, its military interventions necessitated by legitimate security concerns, its imperial record comparatively more benign than that of other European powers, and its commitment to fostering democracy genuine. Curiously, all three may acknowledge what is called American exceptionalism, in the differentness of the United States both quantitatively and qualitatively. But despite the end of the cold war they harbor fears that political and economic uncertainties and instability in the Americas may jeopardize the future of this country.

These are old debates, not new ones, and each has already prompted a contentious literature. My purpose here is to place them within a broader context of the history of the Western Hemisphere since the wars of independence. That generation experienced varying kinds of revolution, from the rebellion of thirteen English colonies against the most powerful European nation of the age to the slave uprising on French Saint Domingue in 1791, which culminated in the creation of the second independent nation of the New World in 1804, and then to the upheaval that erupted throughout Spanish America in 1810. In those tumultuous years, notions of a common struggle against European monarchy appeared to strengthen the eighteenth-century idea of America as a unity; "American" was commonly invoked by the rebellious and disaffected throughout the Western Hemisphere to distinguish themselves both culturally and politically from Europeans.

In the 1820s, however, as the revolutions in Spanish America came to an end, these sentiments rapidly dissipated. Some U.S. leaders, it is true, still believed that national unity and security mandated a policy of good neighborhood and closer ties with the new governments to the south. But to more outspoken nineteenth-century U.S. leaders, Spanish America was either the wretched offspring of declining European empires or, conversely, a vastly diverse region with enormous potential if its leaders would only follow the example of their counterparts in the United States. For their contemporaries in Latin America, the United States stood, paradoxically, as both menace and example—threatening because of its rapid and dynamic expansion on the North American continent and into the Caribbean and Central America, yet a model of economic and political development, even to those who believed its culture to be shallow and materialistic. Those contradictory sentiments seem as relevant in our time as they were in the early nineteenth century.

At the onset of the twenty-first century, people in the United States are experiencing a parallel sense of triumph and insecurity that their forebears of the 1820s would have understood: a belief that U.S. exceptionalism, a faith in the nation's immunity from the travails of the world and especially those of Latin America, is imperiled by what lies to the south and at the same time a belated recognition that the U.S. economic future and even cultural identity are intimately linked to the nations and peoples of the Western Hemisphere. The debates about that relation are no less intense today than in the early nineteenth century, when a generation of U.S. political leaders believed the prospects for the political and economic development of the new republics (and one empire) of mainland Latin America were considerably less promising than those of the United States, a judgment largely seconded by Alexis de Tocqueville in his classic account *Democracy in America*. One who expressed such a somber view in the early 1820s was Edward Everett (the other speaker at Gettysburg), who believed that Anglo- and Spanish-Americans were "sprung from different stocks" and because of that ethnic and cultural divide it would be impossible to make "their [Simón] Bolívars into [George] Washingtons." Everett lived long enough to witness a succession of domestic political crises and civil war that most of his contemporaries in the 1820s believed lay in Latin America's future, not in that of the United States.[3]

A history of the Western Hemisphere must necessarily consider the broader issues and forces that have impacted the politics, economies, societies, and cultures of the Americas in such a way as to prompt beliefs that the nations and peoples of the Americas have a common destiny or at least relate to one another in distinctive ways. The quest for cultural unity has found expression in such myriad episodes as the efforts of the American Philosophical Society to promote inter-American cultural understanding during the Spanish-American wars of independence and the call for a hemispheric commitment to democracy and human rights in the Summit of the Americas meetings in the 1990s. Political leaders, most of them from the United States, have often invoked sentiments of hemispheric unity to advocate trade agreements, for example, Secretary of State James G. Blaine's promotion of a continental customs union at the Pan-American Conference in 1889 and President George Bush's Enterprise for the Americas proposal a century later). In the twentieth century, particularly since World War II, the dominating concerns of security and development prompted collective efforts in the Organization of American States (the successor to the Pan-American Union) to address issues of hemispheric importance: revolution, communism, immigration, environmental damage, trafficking in drugs, police, labor, health, and the electoral process, among others.

The history of the Western Hemisphere is unarguably an integral part of Atlantic and global history, but the governments, economies, cultures, and societies of the Americas do relate differently to one another and especially to the United States than to the rest of the world. I am not suggesting that the Americas have a common history but that belonging to a common hemisphere has made a difference. This claim, I believe, has been validated by the persistence of political, economic, social, and cultural patterns that acquire their most persuasive meaning when viewed in a hemispheric context. From the age of revolution and the formation of newly independent states until the present, these linkages in the Americas have been ideological—the "idea" of the Western Hemisphere as something distinct from the Old World—as well as material. Among the first U.S. emissaries to the Spanish-American revolutions were Yankee traders who ferried copies of the Declaration of Independence and George Washington's farewell address along with the wares they were peddling. In our times, the cultural and commercial exchanges continue. The ties with the Old World were not severed, of course; indeed, in many important respects, they were strengthened. Yet the concept of a hemisphere with a past and especially a future distinct from those of the rest of the world took hold and continues to this day.

The fact that the encounter between several hemispheric nations and cultures has often been conflictual rather than harmonious justifies one of the arguments that I shall make in this book: the Americas have not a common but an uncommon history, a history unlike that of any region of its size and diversity in the world. The nations and peoples of the Americas are linked by formal economic and political agreements as well as through cultural exchange and especially human encounters. Issues that have historically divided hemispheric peoples have also united them. They dispute the meaning of revolution but express common professions about the right of self-determination and sovereignty; their governments are divided over the degree of intrusion in the national economy but linked by beliefs that regional or hemispheric economic agreements will better shield their national economies from the uncertainties of global economic and political currents.

Modernization has failed to bring about a convergence of social and cultural values in the Americas, as some sociologists were predicting in the 1950s and 1960s, but middle classes throughout the hemisphere have begun to express a common apprehension—in some quarters, a fear—over the fragmentation of contemporary society and the estrangement of political systems from the citizenry. Anti-Americanism in this hemisphere sometimes displays features found elsewhere. One can find anti- and pro-American sentiments in the same person among many of the world's peoples, undeniably, yet the anti-Americanism in the Americas is rarely fueled by religious beliefs, and it is sometimes more virulent among conservatives than among those on the left. Few could deny the hostility of Latin America's twentieth-century revolutionaries toward this country, yet these same Marxist revolutionaries, while rejecting the racist and exploitative values of North American corporate culture, often absorbed much of that culture's beliefs about material prosperity and political democracy.[4]

The history of Greater North America—Mexico, the United States, and Canada, each of which considers itself exceptional—is riddled with disharmony, confrontation, and violence, yet something more than economic imperative is necessary to explain the crafting of the North American Free Trade Agreement (NAFTA), an economic consortium that was in the making since the late nineteenth century. Similarly, the history of U.S. policy toward the Caribbean and Central America, a troubled story written largely by U.S. economic and military power and the intrusion of large multinational companies, must incorporate the human bonds and cultural exchanges that have also shaped that history. Cuban revolutionary traditions in the late nineteenth century, for example, drew their antipathy as well as their strength from North American linkages. Since 1959 Cuba has been the most defiantly anti-United States nation in the hemisphere, yet in terms of cultural preferences Cubans are arguably the most Americanized of Latin American and Caribbean peoples, even more Americanized than Puerto Ricans, who have been our "colonial charges" since 1898. And perhaps the most humorous example of anti-Americanism in this hemisphere is the persistence of Canadians in identifying themselves as "Not Americans." These are but a few examples of the symbiotic nature of inter-American relations that I explore in this book.[5]

Although the peoples of the Americas nowadays may share a sense of optimism that economic development and a parallel convergence of political values will lay the foundation for a prosperous twenty-first century, they also express a frustration over the inability of government to resolve the most pressing social issues of the age. Despite more than a century of efforts to balance the twin dynamics of the increase in wealth through capitalist economic development and efforts to mitigate the sometimes harmful social impact of development in market economies, hemispheric governments today seem no closer to resolving the social question than they were a century ago. Political leaders throughout the Western Hemisphere (except, of course, in Cuba) laud the privatization of economies and the prospect of a liberal pacific union, but everywhere in the Americas, including the United States and Canada, there are disturbing indicators that the putative triumph of the market economy has exacted a very heavy social price and that the end of the cold war has neither provided the security hemispheric governments have sought nor significantly improved the material well-being of the hemisphere's most disadvantaged peoples. Why those inequities have persisted will be another theme of this book.

Somewhere between the history of the nation-state and global history lies hemispheric history, and that is what I propose to explore in this book. How I have gone about that task requires some explanation. Virtually every topic of relevance to the history of the Americas since the nineteenth century—expansion, continentalism, nationalism, imperialism, colonialism, and revolution, among others—has prompted a rich, often contentious literature, yet to impose any one theory—modernization, diffusion, Marxism, dependency, or convergence—on that history often fails to capture its complex and often chaotic nature. To alter an old bromide, the whole is not greater than but different from the sum of its parts.

To get at these complexities I have stressed not only general patterns but also specific features. For example, the character of U.S. intervention in the Caribbean and Central America in the first third of the twentieth century often looks similar from place to place, yet to understand the inner history of U.S. empire in the "American Mediterranean," to use a contemporary phrase, requires a closer look at two particular places—Cuba and Puerto Rico—in order to fathom what that intervention really meant for subject peoples. Some periods (the late nineteenth and early twentieth centuries) and especially some countries and regions (Mexico, Canada, and the Caribbean, particularly Cuba) may appear to receive an inordinate amount of attention in these pages. In the late nineteenth and early twentieth centuries, the Americas experienced the dynamic changes associated with the second industrial revolution—rapid economic growth, heightened social tensions, cultural conflicts, and abnormal strains on political systems—and the creation of an empire that contemporaries believed rivaled that of Rome in its power and sweep.

Virtually every major issue hemispheric peoples and governments currently confront was familiar to the generation that came of age at the dawn of the twentieth century. The strains placed on the hemisphere in the half century from the election of Woodrow Wilson to that of John F. Kennedy and from the dual strategic and social crisis of the 1960s to the present cannot be understood outside the context of the pre-World War I history of the Americas. Similarly, my distortion of the hemispheric story to place more emphasis on Greater North America and the Caribbean, particularly Cuba, has less to do with the fact that I am writing largely for a North American audience than with the belief that the relations between these countries and cultures since the late nineteenth century offer fundamental insights about the history of the Americas today. From the time Herbert E. Bolton proclaimed the essential unity of the Americas in the early 1930s, many U.S. and most Mexican historians have scoffed at the idea. Yet by the end of the century one of the early skeptics, the eminent Mexican philosopher Leopoldo Zea, acknowledged that "at the end of the [twentieth] century and of the millennium we can no longer speak of two Americas, our Latin and their Anglo-Saxon. . . . The history that once divided us nowadays unites us."[6]

Zea's comments referred more specifically to the presumably unifying role that a multiracial and multicultural Caribbean provides for a hemisphere in which cultural exchanges in everything from literature, art, movies, dance, and music—a significant portion of which is south to north—and such diverse issues as biodiversity, deforestation, conservation, pollution, popular culture, cultural diplomacy, gender, labor, and agriculture, among others, warrant inclusion or at least more consideration. The fact that I have given less attention to these issues, as well as to Latin American, Canadian, and Caribbean linkages to Europe, Africa, and Asia, and have chosen to focus on the political and economic dynamics of inter-American relations and U.S. relations with other hemispheric countries and regions is has to do with choice of emphasis—the contrast of Cuban revolutionary José Martí's America with Theodore Roosevelt's America and their intertwined histories in the twentieth century.

For some contemporary observers of the hemispheric condition, of course, the Americas of the early twenty-first century continue to display the same fundamental differences they exhibited at the turn of the twentieth. North Americans still retain their admiration for TR's reaffirmation of the Monroe

Doctrine and for his blustering nationalism; their Latin American, Caribbean, and Canadian neighbors still hearten to Martí's warnings about the U.S. menace to its neighbors. Too often what is forgotten about these human embodiments of the Two Americas at 1900 is their relevance to the hemisphere of 2000. Whatever their differences in thought and deed, they shared values and beliefs that retain their primacy for understanding the hemisphere of our time. Roosevelt and Martí shared a belief in the centrality of political and economic considerations in governance and in the relations between governments, the historical necessity of the liberation of New World nations from the confining grip of the Old, the worldwide vision of their respective nations and their specific obligations in the Americas. They had sharp differences about race and ethnicity—Roosevelt worried about "race suicide"—but they had in common the conviction that each must be subordinated to unity and nation. Both admired Abraham Lincoln for his commitment to national unity. Neither was antimilitary, though both were antimilitaristic. They condemned privilege, despaired over the growing chasm between rich and poor and the condition of labor, and believed in the purposeful role of government in society and in the economy to shield against special interests. They understood the importance of respect between nations and the danger that the scorn of the strong portended for the weak.

My selection of Roosevelt and Martí and their Two Americas as a more appropriate contrast for gaining insight into the contemporary hemisphere than, for example, the Uruguayan José Enrique Rodó or Woodrow Wilson requires a brief explanation. In his classic 1900 book *Ariel,* Rodó drew sharp distinctions between the model of a spiritual, European ideality for Latin America and the vulgar material culture of the United States. Though an admirer of U.S. prosperity and achievement, he feared that not only Latin American leaders but also ordinary people would succumb to the mystique of the North American example. What was even more frightening to Rodó was an imperial power intent on a moral conquest of its weaker southern neighbors even as its leaders voiced their belief in self-determination and diversity or, as did Wilson, employed the military in the name of nation building. Undeniably, as contemporary observers attest, the judgments Rodó and Wilson made about such diverse issues as immigration, culture, race, politics, economics, and especially the extension of U.S. power, resonate in discussions of the hemisphere's modern condition.

Martí and Roosevelt, I believe, expressed beliefs about these and related topics of importance to the Americas that speak more directly to the Americas of our times. Unlike Rodó, Martí had a deep appreciation of the diversity of Latin American and Caribbean culture and ethnicity, lauded the democratic spirit of the United States, and was certainly less disdainful of its material culture. Both were fearful of the U.S. role in the Americas, but Martí did not refrain from subjecting Latin America to a probing critique. In what some may regard as a curious logic, Martí regarded his America as superior to that of Roosevelt not for its estimation of cultural elegance over material advancement but for its greater suffering in gaining independence and its nineteenth-century political ordeal. Roosevelt, who is often compared with Wilson, sensed more acutely than his famous political adversary the diversity of Latin America and the lingering effects of its nineteenth-century disorders on its efforts to unify. Ultimately, he came to respect certain Latin American countries and leaders for their achievements in ways that acknowledged at least a degree of equality with the United States. Roosevelt did not always project the U.S. role in the Americas as part of a global mission. Like Martí, with whom he should be compared, Roosevelt could think in hemispheric terms, and in the troublesome and unsettled conditions of the contemporary Americas, North Americans often invoke his spirited rhetoric about national interest and singularity of purpose. They would do well to remember his doubts about the limits of U.S. power as well as Martí's admonitions about its threat.

Most important, Roosevelt and Martí understood that the Two Americas were intertwined in distinctive ways.

Part *I*

I

Theodore Roosevelt's America

In February 1912 four hundred distinguished literati and guests, among them President William Howard Taft, gathered at Sherry's in New York City for a birthday dinner in honor of the renowned realist writer William Dean Howells, aged seventy-five. Their host was Colonel George Harvey, editor of *Harper's* and owner of the restaurant. Most of the guests recognized that Howells's literary reputation was in decline. Within a few years, he would become a symbol for a generation that largely rejected what he had stood for: a nineteenth-century civilization predicated on universal moral values, a belief in progress, and the conviction that truth and goodness were the same thing. Presumably, these credos had enabled the nation to weather the perilous course of political, economic, and social change after the Civil War. Injustice and hardship had been a part of the country's industrial transformation in the late nineteenth century, Howells conceded, but these were small problems when measured against the moral and material achievement of a generation. Yet Howells harbored troubling thoughts about the experience. "It was all, all wrong and unfit," he wrote to his friend Henry Adams shortly after the dinner, "but nobody apparently knew it, not even I till that ghastly waking hour of the night when hell opens to us."[1]

The hell Howells referred to was the nation's tumultuous experience of the previous half century: civil war and reconstruction, the Indian wars of the West, industrialization, urbanization, successive waves of immigration, labor convulsions, turbulent reform movements, war with Spain, racial strife, and the imperial ventures of Theodore Roosevelt's America. Within one generation, the economic growth of this era had created unprecedented opportunities but also widespread confusion and uncertainty. Unregulated trusts, labor strife, and the rapidly changing ethnic and racial makeup of the nation's industrial cities prompted doubts about the compatibility of social peace and economic growth. The chaos of the age jarred the confidence of persons throughout society, certainly, but especially alarmed those at the highest and most influential levels. For some—certainly for Roosevelt—such threats to nation and civilization required those who led to act, not reflect.[2]

Conquest of the West

One place to confront such challenges and to redeem the national purpose lay in the West, which occupied a special place in the country's development, a view identified with the historian Frederick Jackson Turner and his address at the World's Columbian Exposition in 1893 in Chicago, titled "The Significance of the Frontier in American History." The symbolic closing of the frontier meant the end of cheap land and thus constituted a sea change in the nation's history. Set against the backdrop of multiple crises of financial panics, growing unemployment, agrarian unrest, labor wars, and unsettling memories of the Civil War, Turner's message may have offered a reaffirmation of national history with reminders about the leveling influence of the frontier experience, but it provided no reassurance for the future. For Roosevelt, the winning of the West was less a democratic than a military and racial experience. As William F. "Buffalo Bill" Cody noted in the handout for his "Wild West" show at the Chicago Fair: "The bullet is the pioneer of civilization, for it has gone hand in hand with the axe that cleared the forest, and with the family Bible and school book."[3]

Cody's comment is an unsettling reminder about the Western Civil War of Incorporation from the 1860s to World War I, a bewildering montage of sometimes violent confrontations, pitting not only developer against settler, but rancher against farmer, white against Indian, conservative sheriffs against social bandits, "boomers" against traditionalists, and soldiers against practically everybody. In 1862, the U.S. Congress had reaffirmed the myth of the Settler's West with the passage of the Homestead Act, which provided grants of 160 acres of public land in the West but no credit to those who elected to occupy

it. But through other, more generous concessions to railroad, mining, and timber companies, Congress virtually assured that the West would be incorporated into an economy of industrial production and that its social development
would be uneven, chaotic, and violent—a world in which the railroad, not the
settler, was the colonizer, in which mining, not farming, established social
conditions that Thomas Jefferson and his contemporaries would have abhorred,
in which prostitution enabled women to gain a financial independence unknown to their contemporaries back East, in which the expressions "honest
outlaws" and "lawless sheriffs" were not oxymorons, and in which settlements
contained a disproportionate number of unsettled people.[4]

In such a world, to "civilize by force" became a mandate for those who believed in progress, a commitment dramatically and tragically embodied in the
Indian wars that raged on the Great Plains from the Sioux uprising in Minnesota in 1862 until the Ghost Dance War of 1890 and the official declaration
of the closing of the frontier. At the end of the Civil War, General William
Tecumseh Sherman set the standard by declaring that the Indian must be exterminated, and then he unleashed a campaign of search-and-destroy warfare
against the Plains Indians. By 1868, he had compelled the Indians to accept a
peace settlement which provided that they settle in two enormous reservations, one in the southern plains and the other in the Black Hills of the Dakotas. A year later, President Ulysses S. Grant solemnly noted that a policy of
disabusing Indians of the backwardness of their way of life was sufficient to
ensure the West's peaceful development.[5]

This presumably enlightened policy ran afoul of another, more fundamental credo in the European experience in the Americas: As a "savage" the Indian must not be permitted to impede the march of progress and particularly
the material development of the West. The issue became clear in 1874 with the
discovery of gold in the Black Hills, most of it on unceded land preserved as
hunting grounds for reservation Indians. Miners and prospectors flooded into
the region. In these circumstances, President Grant did an about-face. Removing the impediments to the white invasion of what was technically Indian
territory, Grant declared that Indians not on the reservation after January 1,
1876, would be considered at war with the U.S. government. The decision
made inevitable the Battle of the Little Bighorn in southeastern Montana six
months later, a clash in which 2,500 Sioux warriors led by Sitting Bull wiped
out the 275-man U.S. Seventh Cavalry commanded by Colonel George Armstrong Custer.[6]

Custer's defeat unleashed another campaign against those Indians who left the reservation and raided white settlements. Sherman's extermination policy found new advocates, but opposing them were some influential humanitarians, among them President Rutherford B. Hayes's secretary of the interior, Carl Schurz, who advocated ending the reservation system on the expedient grounds that whites hungry for Indian lands would never respect the reservation and the government could not prevent conflicts. The best policy, Schurz believed, called for phasing out the reservation by turning the Indian into a landowning farmer. Under the Dawes Severalty Act of 1887, the government held in trust allotments of 160 and 80 acres for heads of families and single persons, respectively, for twenty-five years. Very few Indians became farmers, and speculators were able to take advantage of loopholes in the law and of Indian vulnerability to gain access to the land. Senator Henry Teller of Colorado correctly predicted that the Dawes Act would turn the Indian into a vagabond. Roosevelt, who had just returned from the Dakotas, had few qualms over such outcomes: Indians who declined the offer should "perish from the face of the earth which he cumbers," as did the white trappers and hunters who killed the game in the western country![7]

Actually, Senator Teller had understated the consequences of the Dawes Act. Its purpose had been to undo the wrongs of the treaty and reservation system, or, as the bill's sponsor, Henry Dawes, put it, "[to] wipe out the disgrace of our past treatment, and lift [the Indian] up into citizenship and manhood." In the half century after 1887, Indians lost control of almost two-thirds of 138 million acres of tribal lands. Nor were they lifted up and incorporated into the larger society, despite their limited numbers and relatively small threat to a society more concerned about assimilating Asians, African Americans, and the new European immigrant. By the time Roosevelt left the presidency in 1909, the optimism over Indian incorporation had virtually disappeared, supplanted by the twin beliefs that the Indian was racially inferior and thus could never be assimilated or was little more than a reminder of a nostalgic past. Indians could not be assimilated, but Indian resources could be integrated into the national economy.[8]

The Mexican Question

Mexican national unity, also forged in civil conflict, was intricately linked to developments in the United States, especially the issue of security on Mexico's northern frontier. The nation's defeat in the war of 1846–48 with the United States exposed the country's north to a new kind of aggression. From the early days of settlement in Mexican Texas until the Civil War the intruders had been land-hungry settlers, slaveowners, muleteers, traders, soldiers, and filibusters. In the 1860s came the invading French army and empire of Maximilian, and, in the following two decades, North American developers, who were contemptuous of the "mixed-race" Mexican, save for his utility in the early years as laborer in the gold, silver, quicksilver, quartz, and copper mines of Arizona, California, Colorado, and New Mexico. The North American transformed Mexicans into a commodity, stripping them of their rights with "Greaser laws." In south Texas, they drove Mexican farmers from the land in order to found the great cattle ranches of the region.[9]

These developments made the encounter between two nations and two cultures hostile and sometimes violent, yet, curiously, conflict reinforced their symbiotic unity. Both governments expressed a concern about the importance of a secure border. Their reasons, however, were fundamentally different. The United States wanted to prevent Indian flight into Mexico. In the minds of U.S. leaders, Mexico's inability to police its northern frontier justified the dispatch of U.S. troops into Mexico. For their Mexican counterparts, from Benito Juárez to Porfirio Díaz, who seized power in 1876, a stable border policed by Mexican, not Yankee, soldiers would afford undeniable evidence that the nation was stable, united, and deserving of the North American investment and expertise required for its industrial development.

To accomplish that formidable task required a novel kind of relation with the U.S. government. Juárez set the standard for his successors shortly after the victory over Maximilian. The hero of the War of the Intervention may have held well-founded suspicions about the Yankees, but he had accelerated U.S. economic penetration of the country. And despite his liberal ideology, he understood the importance of national security to the survival of the state. In 1861, Juárez had created a national police force called *rurales,* a security force under the command of the Ministry of the Interior, as a means of dealing with civil strife. Like civil authorities in the U.S. West in the same era, Juárez recognized that budget limitations made recruitment of police difficult, so he resorted to the expedient of turning bandits into policemen. More precisely, bandits *agreed* to serve as policemen, but, as in the U.S. West, they sometimes continued their banditry and other illegal activities. When Maximilian fell before a firing squad in 1867, the victorious Juárez confronted an even greater problem with disorder and brigandage caused by embittered soldiers discharged into an economy ravished by almost a decade of continual strife.[10]

Díaz had been among those Liberal officers who had criticized Juárez for turning against the soldiers and for his failure to curb the disorder plaguing the countryside. In 1876, Díaz confronted the same problem, but unlike Juárez he suffered few constraints on his determination to use power to pacify the countryside, especially the rebellious northern frontier. He was both accommodating and defiant in his relations with the U.S. government. He readily yielded to U.S. demands for settling indemnities to its citizens who had suffered property losses in Mexico during previous wars, and he won the support of south Texas investors and ranchers who had helped him launch the Revolution of Tuxtepec and bring down the government. But he would not concede to a unilateral right of the United States to dispatch troops into Mexico in pursuit of rustlers or Indians; he accepted a plan for reciprocal border crossings. In an agreement signed in 1878, the U.S. government formally extended diplomatic recognition, and Díaz showed his appreciation by opening up the northern frontier through a duty-free zone and, more important, granting to U.S. investors the right to purchase land and pursue mining concessions in the region.[11]

In the aftermath, other forms of intervention ensured U.S. political, economic, and even cultural influence. Promoters descended on abandoned mines and tropical plantations; pamphleteers who had once written about a corrupt government and barbaric people now extolled a bountiful country with a progressive government and an intelligent populace. North American investments poured into Mexico, from only a few million dollars in 1870 to more than a billion during the early years of the twentieth century. The advance guard of railroad developers came during the last years of Juárez's presidency, but the floodtide of railroad investment did not hit Mexico for another decade. Businessmen who had built the great railroads of the United States—Collis Huntington, Jay Gould, Russell Sage, and E. H. Harriman, among others—moved into Mexican railway construction. In 1877, the first year of the Porfirian regime,, Mexico had 417 miles of railway; a decade later, 4,100 miles; and by 1901, 9,600 miles. The concessions, subsidies, and generous terms meted out to foreigners prompted inevitable criticism, but the Mexican government argued that prosperity depended on such investment.[12]

Industrialization depended on imported technology and government protection of domestic producers. By following such an agenda, Mexico's economic planners believed, the country would be able to join the North American and European club of modern industrial nations. By the 1890s an economy derided at midcentury for its backwardness boasted of factories producing glass, paper, steel, cement, soap, beer, cotton, and textiles. The approach to industrialization was capital-intensive, which appealed to Mexican manufacturers because they believed that imported technology was necessary in that it permitted them to avoid developing their own. Mexico lacked the skilled labor force for such enterprises, but Mexican manufacturers presumed that immigration would supply their needs. When unskilled Mexican workers resisted the routinization of work required by industrial labor, employers could rely on the coercive power of the state to control them. Manufacturing might be risky, but manufacturers had the benefits of monopoly and oligopoly and could rely on the protective shield of the government. In actuality these presumed advantages were debilities because they characterized an economy of high-risk, low-profit manufacturing whose producers lacked the incentive to develop new processes and products. If one measures the costs against the long-term benefits, the frenzy of railroad building during the Porfiriato was of dubious benefit to Mexico's ambitious plans for modernization, first, because railroads failed to produce significant social savings and, second, because they did not carry enough freight to repay the enormous costs entailed in constructing them.[13]

Progress carried a social price. Mexico's indigenous people, who made up almost 50 percent of the population, and poor mestizos were now mobilized as a labor force in a country whose government and Creole elites considered them dumb, fearful, and utterly useless, except of course for their labor, in building a modern nation. But the cosmetic transformation of the nation under Díaz's program of economic development and social engineering in the cities and especially in the capital impressed even North American critics. Travelers averred that the political anarchy of the old days had practically disappeared. Mexico was no longer the "sick man" of North America, but its leaders remained apprehensive about the U.S. presence. They chose to cede the nation's markets rather than its territory, a tactic as appealing to Mexican leaders in the late nineteenth century as it became in the 1990s. As Matías Romero acknowledged, "The best means of impeding annexation is to open the country to the United States . . . with the objective of making annexation unnecessary and even undesirable."[14]

Such choices help one to understand the rebellion and then the revolution that erupted in 1910; but the revolutionary impulse did not thrive simply because the Mexican government modernized the economy by crushing the political opposition catering to every demand of the foreign investor, and driving ordinary Mexicans and indigenous people into misery. Some Indian communities successfully resisted efforts to take over their communal lands. And liberals, whether of the old school that spoke of reform or the new one that espoused so-called scientific racism, sharply divided over such social programs as rural colonization with Europeans and "whitening" the Mexican "race" through immigration, as Justo Sierra suggested in 1874 in his assertion that the history of the world was the history of colonization. Tragically, these elements (and others) were symptomatic of the Mexican condition during the Porfiriato, but isolating them from other, less salient but no less critical factors distorts some of the realities of Mexico's prerevolutionary history. One of the most important features attributed to Mexico's transformation in the late nineteenth century, for example, was peace and order in the countryside. Díaz was able to impose order in the countryside not so much because he relied on a constabulary that was ruthlessly efficient in stamping out disorder but because he formed a tenuous alliance with local and regional chieftains and, just as important, turned bandits, landless campesinos, and unemployed artisans into policemen. In other words, the security of an economy predicated on order and stability depended on people whose lives had been disrupted by modernization. To describe such persons as victims is to overlook the fact that they were also opportunists. But their loyalty to the Porfirian regime was tentative.[15]

The Canadian Variation of Progress

Canada's western history in the same era displayed yet a third variation of development, linked in often nuanced ways to that of its southern neighbor. Canada's experience with western development and relations between whites and Indians seemed more humane. Most Canadian mining towns had little crime or disorder. Canadian ranchers had cartels to preserve their control and did not resort to range wars. The most striking difference lay in Indian–white relations. In the three decades after the Civil War, the U.S. army had almost a thousand military engagements with Indians; Canadian soldiers, by contrast, fought seven, and six of these took place during the Riel Rebellion of 1885. Canadians copied the U.S. model for western expansion—grants of land to the railroad (the Canadian Pacific) and to settlers, similar bureaucracies, signing of treaties, and the use of the reservation for Indians—but their approach to controlling Indians was successful because Canadian authorities focused on a closer supervision of the behavior of white people. Canadian officials were more paternalistic; they were also ill disposed to spend large sums for the purpose of killing Indians. Most of the reasons for the differences, then, lay not in fundamental disparities in law or policy but in the Canadians' approach to the West.[16]

The architect of Canada's national policy was the Conservative leader John

Macdonald, who staked the Canadian future on the development of the western country. If the Canadian prairies were united to the populated east by the Canadian Pacific Railroad (CPR), he reasoned, they would attract not only easterners but new immigrants as well. Canada's development, unlike that of its southern neighbor, would be orderly and lawful. For a few years, the western design appeared to be working. The growth in population, notably in Manitoba, was spectacular. But in the early 1880s Macdonald's grand design began to unravel under the collective pressure of the CPR's demands for more financial assistance, the impact of the world depression, and the reality that European immigrants were headed not for the Canadian prairies but for those of the U.S. West. A combination of grievances prompted a momentary alliance of white settlers, Indians, and *métis* (persons of French-Indian heritage) who in 1884 jointly appealed to Louis Riel, organizer of the first Red River rebellion, to lead them. When Riel took command of the movement, his erratic behavior persuaded his petitioners that he was insane. In the first Riel Rebellion, Macdonald's response had been conciliatory. In dealing with the second Riel Rebellion he followed a course his North American contemporaries would have applauded. He dispatched a seven-thousand-man army into the Red River country, which in two battles defeated the rebels. Riel was captured and hanged over the protests of French Canadians, who believed him to be a defender of Catholicism and minority rights.[17]

Suppression of the second Riel Rebellion and Riel's execution marked the apogee of Macdonald and the fortunes of the Conservative Party. Canada had sectional and ethnic divisions and hatreds that Macdonald's policies could no longer meliorate. Employment of French Canadians in the federal government failed to quell their bitterness about national policy in the northwest. On the provincial level, the Conservative hold began to weaken before a resurgence of the French cultural nationalism and the formation of a new party, the Parti National, with an outspoken leader, Honoré Mercier, who declared that Riel had been murdered. Mercier's call for greater provincial autonomy found kindred spirits not only among Quebecers but alienated Liberals in the English-speaking provinces. In 1887 Mercier hosted an Interprovincial Conference, at which disgruntled Liberals could be appeased with a wide range of proposals to reduce federal power and increase federal subsidies. Macdonald was persuaded to alter his allegedly heavy-handed approach to the provinces. As he aged he grew more cantankerous and outspoken. In 1891 he won the last of his political campaigns, rejecting Liberal calls for commercial union with the United States and greater provincial autonomy. Exhausted by the campaign, he died in June 1891, unrepentant over his national policy. He is generally hailed as one of the greatest of Canadian statesmen, loyal to the British Crown yet defying demands for colonial obedience.[18]

Macdonald's Liberal adversaries often spoke disparagingly about his betrayal of the Anglo and his accommodation to the imperial will—particularly in his acquiescence to the 1871 Treaty of Washington between Great Britain and the United States—in defiance of the true national interest. But, as in so many other matters, he was able to turn Liberal logic on its head. Canada could remain within the empire yet have a special relation with the Crown. Goldwin Smith, like several other prominent Liberals, gave up on the notion of independence, substituting for it a vague proposal for reunifying the Anglo-Saxon peoples of North America in a union in which Canada would become "another Scotland." This was little more than a charade for U.S. annexation, something that even the most discontented Anglo-Canadians viewed with suspicion. Macdonald survived because he understood the complexities of the Canadian experience. The political style and agenda that would have doomed a U.S. leader were often critical in a Canadian venue. Canadian "independence" was born not of revolution *against* empire but evolution *within* empire. Canada was the first of Britain's overseas empires to gain dominion status. As such, it had a special role to play as a society preserving European values rather than one fundamentally altering or even defying that tradition. The frontier experience held no central or mythmaking place in the Canadian sense of national identity because the frontier lay in every direction, as much in Nova Scotia as on the northwestern prairies.[19]

But Canadians lacked the U.S. option on numerous social issues. Outcries against the character of industrial capitalism and the condition of labor raged in Canada but did not produce the kind of militant unionism the United States experienced. The numbers of ethnics were much greater in the United States, certainly, but they also represented a much greater diversity, thus diminishing the influence of any one ethnic group. Canada's Anglo leaders did not have that advantage. Their political success depended on cooperation with their French counterparts. Indeed, some of the most vocal proponents of Anglo-Saxon superiority were successful in their ability to forge political alliances with French Canadians, believing that the French shared their loyalty to the monarchy and to a Christian society and their suspicion of liberalism and materialism. This myth of French loyalty would collapse during World War I, but it served the interests of Canadian Conservatives for a generation.[20]

The Transformation of Roosevelt's America

The Canadian way of reconciling cultural and ethnic divisions amid rapid development would not have suited its southern neighbor. The transformation of Roosevelt's America had begun in the early nineteenth century, as the old familial enterprises had slowly begun to give way to corporate organization, when machines altered the character of labor, and telegraph and railroads quickened the pace of economic change. In a fundamental respect, the U.S. Civil War was a conflict between economic systems—one based on involuntary human labor, the other on powerful new forces. Whether or not the war accelerated these changes is less relevant than the undeniable reality of a generation of industrial titans who considered themselves bound by few traditional laws or social restraints and, frankly, lacked satisfactory experience for the kind of industrial economy they would encounter. For the hallowed canons of enterprise, they substituted a new agenda and in the name of progress and order carried out a remorseless exploitation of land, labor, and resources. The political and social consequences associated with their endeavors provoked condemnation and praise, but there is no doubting their economic impact. Among their most impressive achievements lay the expansion of the country's rail network, which ended the old Atlantic empire by opening up the vast landed interior of the Americas, especially North America; and the factories, which proliferated in U.S. cities in the late nineteenth century, drawing a generation of domestic and immigrant laborers. They commanded men and machines. In the process, individualism and the republican ethic succumbed to corporate regulation and authority.[21]

By the late 1870s the U.S. economy had entered what was properly described as a buoyant decade of economic growth and technological innovation. In the following years, France and Britain doubled and tripled their steel output, respectively, but Germany and the United States *quintupled* theirs. Although the United States had played an important role in the Atlantic economy since the early years of the Republic, only after the Civil War did it assume its place among those nations of the modern world economy, joining European countries (especially Britain) in the race for new markets, astounding Europeans with its technological innovations, and, most important, profoundly altering the character of business organization and transforming the world of work through scientific management. In 1898, the president of the American Bankers' Association boasted, "We hold now three of the winning cards in the game for commercial greatness—iron, steel and coal. . . . We have long been the granary of the world," he continued, "we now aspire to be its workshop, then we want to be its clearing house."[22]

The institutional icons of those who had crafted this new industrial order were the corporation and the trust, the first exemplifying their organizational acumen, and the second their ability to dominate and control. Their human symbols were men of extraordinary power and economic cunning: in the chaotic world of the petroleum business, John D. Rockefeller; in commerce and shipping, Cornelius and William Vanderbilt; and in steel, Andrew Carnegie. In time, the driving ambition of these men for profits and expansion saturated markets, and they voluntarily made trade agreements and agreed to control production and price and to divide markets. The industrial system they contrived would survive until World War I and the momentary boom of the 1920s but ultimately succumb to powerful new controlling forces in the 1930s. At their height in the late nineteenth century, laws could neither subdue nor restrain the tycoons of the post–Civil War industrial order. As William Vanderbilt explained to a stupefied congressional subcommittee in 1879, the industrial tycoons were "very shrewd men" and no "legislative enactment or anything else" could "keep such men down."[23]

By the time of the International Centennial Exhibition of 1876 in Philadelphia, the republic of free laborers and citizens imagined by an earlier generation and articulated by Lincoln remained a chimera. The political model crafted by an earlier generation had collapsed before the onslaught of the new economic order. In an era often identified as the age of the tycoon and big business in the United States—years of undeniable display of excessive wealth amid widespread suffering and inequity—the biggest business and often the most corrupt was politics itself. Neither the Republican Party, presumably the party favoring big business, nor the Democratic Party, the putative party of reform, proved to be immune to the pathology of corruption. When government levied taxes, it did so not so much to raise revenue as to fund political machines. Political party and government served the officeholder. As James Bryce observed in his classic study *The American Commonwealth*, "The source of power and the cohesive force" among the nation's political parties "is the desire for office and for office as a means of gain."[24]

Such words did little to reassure those who held lingering beliefs about self-determination, moral restraints, and self-denial in an age that extolled consumption. From the historical perspective of a century, a more consequential social change was the emergence of a new middle class, much less homogeneous and cohesive than Veblen's but also very much preoccupied with social status. Composed of aspiring professionals, in law, administration, economics, and social work, for example, and specialists in agriculture, labor, and business, this emerging middle class was concerned about the political and social discord of the 1890s and the crumbling of the nation's "island communities," to use Robert Wiebe's apt phrase, but its solution was not a radical one. Like Roosevelt, who sensed the new class's collective apprehension over political corruption, labor unrest, and the ethnic and racial discord of the times, the members of this middle class often confronted the social issues of the day by the expedient of framing new sets of questions and a new language.[25]

The language inherited from the antebellum or certainly the revolutionary era no longer seemed adequate to explain the new industrial order or to prescribe what must be done to assure social peace yet preserve the country's political traditions. To late-twentieth-century analysts what was at stake was democracy, ordinarily defined in idealistic terms and inclusive of both political and social rights. But the salient issue was not the lack of democracy or the existence of poverty. Indeed, the depressing statistics on the late-nineteenth-century standard of living, the general lack of formal schooling beyond the primary grades, and the undeniable political corruption of the age did not retard the development of a robust political environment and an invigorated electorate. Contemporary observers seemed less preoccupied with the completeness of the democratic process than with the possible failure of the revolutionary experiment in republican government in the complex and chaotic circumstances of the times. In 1879, Walt Whitman ruefully commented that the mushrooming of "vast crops of poor, desperate, dissatisfied, nomadic, miserably-waged populations" threatened "our republican experiment."[26]

Were the ills of the Old World now visited upon the New? For the nation's political and business elites the immediate concern was not the social traumas of the Old World but the opportunities in the new industrial economy, which required capital, management, and order. To those ends, they had devised schemes to rid the marketplace of unbridled competition and the workplace of chaos. Their collective power and urging had compelled state government and sometimes even the national government to bend to their will. Although the business failures of this generation might have warranted a different judgment, those who survived these entrepreneurial wars emerged as the standard-bearers for a generic ethic, the survival of the fittest. John D. Rockefeller explained how he fashioned Standard Oil: "The growth of a large business is merely a survival of the fittest, the working out of a law of nature and a law of God. .... [Someone had to] bring order out of chaos [in the petroleum business]."27

The Embattled Republic

Entrepreneurs—those who organized, calculated, and controlled—replaced workers as models for a prosperous society. These cultural icons of the new economic order might live in the city and speak contemptuously of country rubes, but they extolled the values of large enterprise and small-town America. Industrial workers were commodities as interchangeable as the machines they operated, proletarianized wage earners in the factory system. They represented the Other America, people who were foreign, alien, and threatening because of their numbers (one-third of the population by 1900), their religion (predominantly Catholic), their concentration in cities, and their predominance in the industrial workforce. They were scarcely mentioned even in the so-called realist literature either because they were invisible or because the traumas of their daily lives were considered too alien or distasteful to those who might otherwise be sensitive to their condition. "My people do not live in America," lamented a Slavic immigrant, "they live underneath America."28

African Americans expressed a different grievance. Emancipation had freed an enormous pool of black workers, most of whom in the postwar years remained in the South; but black laborers were rarely used as a permanent labor force outside the South. In his Atlanta Exposition address of 1895, Booker T. Washington, often regarded as unrepentantly acquiescent in segregation, addressed the preferential hiring of immigrants when he declared to white employers, "Cast down your bucket where you are . . . , among the eight millions of Negroes whose habits you know . . . , who have, without strikes and labour wars, . . . helped make possible this magnificent representation of the progress of the South."29

In their confrontation with the titans of capital, laborers could depend only on their numbers and on a collective determination to sustain a cause. As prices rapidly fell from the mid-1870s until the 1890s, employers sought to reduce their costs through a transformation of labor, and laborers, particularly craft workers, became more aggressive in defending their interests. They were capable of controlling the production line—disruptively, if necessary—thus creating an unpredictability in the factory system. In an age when the national ideology no longer extolled the laborer but the industrial tycoon for making possible the wealth of the country, workers became more defensive. The socialist Eugene Debs echoed their defiance. If not for labor, he cried out, "the warehouses would stand empty, factories would be silent, ships and docks would rot, cities would tumble down, and universal ruin would prevail."[30]

Despite their weaknesses under the law and their lowly social status, workers were capable of demonstrating their strength in a series of labor strikes from the mid-1870s until the early 1890s. Two of these—a railroad strike in 1877 that virtually paralyzed traffic in the East and a widespread labor stoppage in 1886 that culminated in an anarchist rally at Haymarket Square in Chicago—shook those in power. In 1892 Henry Clay Frick's determination to break the union at Andrew Carnegie's Homestead (Pennsylvania) steel plant brought on a lockout and a shootout between union men and the state militia. Two years later, the American Railway Union, led by Debs, launched a strike against the Pullman Company. Although these strikes had differing provenances, the violence accompanying each of them revived middle-class fears of social disorder and prompted severe retaliation.[31]

Probably the most destructive struggle was the Great Strike of 1877, which erupted after a series of wage cuts provoked a local strike on the Baltimore and Ohio Railroad in Martinsburg, West Virginia. Workers took control of the yards and began obstructing traffic. Within a week the strike had spread eastward to Baltimore and westward to Saint Louis. As the violence escalated, militias and police clashed not only with strikers but with local bands of unemployed and urban poor. From the urban press came a litany of warnings about the social chaos convulsing eastern cities and the imminent threat to republican government. Inevitably, some editorialists drew comparisons with the "war between the races" that is, Indians versus whites, in the West. There were problems in equating white strikers with warring Indians, but frightened middle-class readers had few qualms about the necessary response to white workers engaged in mob action like the Great Strike. Such a threat must be met by a military trained to confront mobs.[32]

But the Great Strike also mobilized labor organizers, and in the Knights of Labor they had an organization that welcomed all workers—skilled and unskilled, ethnic, black and white, male and female—and whose leaders spoke of a common cause. Workers now struck not only as protest against working conditions and pay but also as defiant gestures of power and collective solidarity within an industrial system. The ultimate goal was to bring an end to the wage system and create cooperative factories. Before such lofty goals could be achieved the Knights campaigned for regulation of monopolies and trusts, currency reform, land distribution, and an end to child labor. In the early 1880s, with the onset of depression, their numbers soared.[33]

The Knights' moment of high triumph came on May 1, 1886, when 350,000 workers in 11,562 sites struck for the eight-hour day. Three days later in Chicago, someone tossed a bomb at police who were breaking up an anarchist rally in Haymarket Square. The explosion set off a riot in which ten died and fifty were injured. Throughout the country the reaction of local governments was swift and repressive. Chicago authorities jailed eight radicals for making incendiary speeches during the Haymarket affair. Four were executed. The irregularity of their trials and sentencing was of less concern to those who presided than the symbolic importance of what was happening in Chicago, which had a large immigrant population, and in other industrial cities of the country. The Haymarket riot and labor agitation challenged beliefs about the city and its relation to progress and modernity. Striking workers not only threatened corporate rule; they menaced the social order. Anarchists and their accusers recognized that the Haymarket trials served as high drama for expressing the true state of things in the country. This was the defiant cry from an ethnic, immigrant, and industrial laborers' social order. So pervasive was the fear of social chaos and domestic insurrection that community leaders in the nation's cities organized vigilante Law and Order Leagues, one of the first of which appeared at Harvard in 1877, and by 1890 armories stood in the nation's cities.[34]

Between 1886 and 1895, state governors called on the militias to restore law and order in the industrial workplace 118 times. But the populist rebellion from the countryside proved far more ominous for the architects of the new industrial order in the United States. Those apprehensive about labor violence might readily equate striking workers with militant Indians in the West, but what thoughtful person could look on the descendants of Jefferson's yeomanry as socialists, radicals, and anarchists? Most populists were not immigrants or ethnics or former slaves but people with a claim to the country's future as valid as that of their forebears, who had confronted British regulars in the Massachusetts' countryside in 1775. Although their economic language could sound as radical as that of socialist labor organizers, their cultural discourse evoked Jefferson's agrarian republic. Populists condemned the national government as being too intrusive and the political parties hopelessly corrupted, the banks and railroads as their oppressors, and the global marketplace as the creature of an evil capitalist system that had enslaved them. Where they gained political control, especially at the state level, populists were in the forefront in their arguments for the use of state power to intrude into the market economy. They condemned imperial ventures yet enthusiastically supported the search for markets. Southern populists like the Georgian Tom Watson called for unity among black and white farmers, yet in the aftermath of the movement they often expressed and practiced a virulent racism.[35]

Populists offered an alternative vision of industrial society and thus embodied more than a protest against hard money and high railroad rates and corrupt politics. In the South, populism was a rebellion of small farmers and tenants driven to take desperate measures by tight credit and a crop-lien system that eventually drove them from the land. In central Texas they finally took a stand by forming an alliance system, creating cooperatives to market their crops. In the plains states of Kansas, Nebraska, and the Dakotas, the cooperative system proved less popular, but even there farm families suffered from low grain prices and tight credit. In Russia and Spain, populism took on anarchical as well as anticapitalist traits, but in the United States the movement was never so radical: the family farm constituted a unit of production linked to the world economy through the commercialization of agriculture. The struggle by U.S. populists was not to restore a folkloric past but to shield themselves against the uncertain future of the new economic order.[36]

The populist moment proved sufficiently broad in its appeal to mobilize large numbers of activists, not only disgruntled farmers, certainly, but small-town people: doctors, lawyers, merchants, bankers, and schoolteachers. Populists held strong religious and cultural traditions and related to farmers and farm families in ways that urbanites could not understand. In a time when corporate values eroded the community credo of the small town, the populist movement served as a standard for those who believed that a fundamental battle over the future of the nation lay at hand. On July 4, 1892, the Peoples', or Populist, Party held its first convention at Omaha, Nebraska, and nominated James B. Weaver as its candidate for president. Its platform called for the secret ballot, the income tax, one-term presidential terms, direct election of senators, public ownership of railroads and telegraph, and prohibition of alien ownership of land. The indebtedness of country people and alien ownership of land were explosive issues, but the conflictual character of the movement cut across ethnic, class, and regional demarcations. Modernity challenged the Jeffersonian myth of a republic founded on the cultural ideals of a rural yeomanry and the endurance of community values. The new agroindustrial order had heightened expectations but had also brought restrictions on admission into the core culture and limitations on social mobility for immigrants, African Americans, laborers, and farmers. Populism evoked a sense of unity among those who shared the frustrations of a putative unfairness and uncertainty in the new corporate order. Their collective claim to social justice inspired not only political outcries but literary responses.[37]

Capitalism in the United States had created wealth and hardship, to be sure, but it had not fashioned a class society that divided along economic lines; neither had industrialization created a revolutionary society. Rural and urban peoples may have suffered from similar economic conditions, but they rarely shared the same religious or cultural values. Confronted with a unified corporate order above them, they crafted a collective agenda of protest against the evil of property and the subjugation of labor, but very few espoused Marx's prescription for social justice and progress through revolution. At the bottom rungs of late-nineteenth-century society were disparate groups of people who stood no chance of being incorporated into the larger society and only a marginal opportunity of finding a meaningful role in the presumably unifying protest movement of the age. Among those with a justifiable claim to such inclusiveness—farmers, skilled workers, and the inhabitants of communities under siege—were political activists and organizers, of course, but they had to be willing to create a truly different *national* political movement crafted to favor mass participation. Populist leaders, men and women, often employed the rhetoric of unity and mass participation, but as political organizers they comported themselves like elitists. The fraternity of protest had its own habits of exclusivity: native-born from recent immigrant, farmer from laborer, country from city, male from female, white from black, black males from women suffragists, and so on. Populism never really threatened capitalism, for it had only individual adherents, not a mass base.[38]

Even so, the economic titans were not going to take a chance on somebody like William Jennings Bryan, who advocated the populist agenda and won the Democratic nomination for president in 1896 after railing against the new economic order in a riveting convention address. Bryan campaigned by train across the nation's heartland, denouncing the evils of the economic system. His Republican opponent, William McKinley, welcomed ordinary people to his Ohio home and reassured them with platitudes. In the final tallying McKinley triumphed, indisputably because the moneyed interests stood solidly behind him but, in addition, because Bryan's rhetoric alienated Catholic voters in the pivotal Great Lakes states. As Henry Adams somberly noted, "Nothing could surpass the nonsensity of trying to run so complex and so concentrated a machine [as the capitalist system] by Southern and Western farmers in grotesque alliance with city day-laborers."[39]

Empire

Two years later, the United States plunged into a war with Spain. Though brief, it had a devastating impact on the reformist impulses generated by the Populist revolt. Some of the more outspoken political activists would find emotional solace in the crusade to liberate Spanish Cuba in 1898. "Populists, Democrats, Republicans are we," Senator Ben Tillman of South Carolina declared in a jingle he composed for his colleagues in the U.S. Senate, "but we are all Americans to make Cuba free." His fellow southern populist Tom Watson was more sanguine when he lamented, "The Spanish War finished us. The blare of the bugle drowned the voice of the reformer."[40]

Neither Tillman nor Watson proved correct, but their observations about the popularity of war with Spain in 1898 help one understand why contemporaries were swept along by the passions identified with a conflict so brief in duration yet so portentous as regards the nation's role in Latin America and above all in the Caribbean in the twentieth century. Certainly, the vigorous economic expansion of the United States in the Western Hemisphere in the late nineteenth century (which I explore in more detail in the following chapter) may have provided a material and even cultural justification for "informal empire" and reinforced the arguments of those who called for the building of a modern navy. But the extracontinental empire created in the aftermath of the war with Spain had its most durable roots not in the post–Civil War hemispheric expansion but in the succession of continental empires fashioned in the transappalachian region after the American Revolution, in the Mexican War, and in the U.S. West after the Civil War. To Roosevelt, who had witnessed the violence and chaos accompanying the Second Industrial Revolution and the pacification of the West, these were the experiences that had shaped the national character and must necessarily serve as a guide for the nation's role in a chaotic world.[41]

For Roosevelt and other leaders of the nation, there was no alternative path for the Republic, but the suddenness of the nation's plunge into the "business of empire," as a few wiseacres remarked, probably contributed to the ambiguous and often divided public reaction to what was happening. After all, within the short span of two years, the United States had intervened in Cuba and Puerto Rico, dispatched its soldiers into the Philippines backcountry to quell the insurrectionist challenge to the U.S. annexation of the archipelago, and joined European powers in the suppression of the Boxer Rebellion in China. Strategic issues seemed peripheral to the discussions, except, of course, among the military. Annexation of the Hawaiian "republic" in the summer of 1898 came as a virtual afterthought. Keeping Puerto Rico, which had been "liberated" in a secondary campaign in July 1898, as war reparations roused few concerns, even among some of those with serious reservations about taking on the "burdens of empire" elsewhere, particularly in the western Pacific.[42]

In the heat of the debate over the necessity for such a course, the arguments of national security and economic necessity seemed no longer sufficient, for despite the popularity of the war with Spain, critics and naysayers could dredge up some distressing evidence that the experience of imperial rule would be detrimental to the nation's republican character. Empire had destroyed the inner fiber of the Roman republic by incorporating alien peoples, Senator George Frisbie Hoar importuned his colleagues during the Senate's discussion of Philippine annexation. To civilize and uplift the Filipinos was no more a persuasive argument for empire than the notion that the Indian must be taught to be less savage. Congress must not be corrupted with the messy questions identified with empire. Senator Albert Beveridge responded in words Roosevelt would have endorsed: "Rebellion against the authority of the flag must be crushed without delay, for hesitation encourages revolt. . . . Law and justice must rule where savagery, tyranny, and caprice have rioted."[43]

Senator Charles Sumner had invoked arguments similar to Hoar's in his fiery speeches opposing annexation of the Dominican Republic during the Grant administration. Sumner and like-minded senators had won the day in that debate, but in 1900 expansionists could marshal powerful arguments that the course of empire posed no insurmountable burden. Rome had drawn vitality and strength through conquest, Brooks Adams wrote, and the United States was an inheritor of its mission. Adams forgot or omitted the fact that Rome was an assimilationist empire, and few in the echelons of power in the United States were seriously considering extending the benefits of the Constitution or the principles of the Declaration of Independence to Puerto Ricans or Filipinos. There was a more purposeful calling to the nation's pursuit of empire. Anti-imperialists could lament that the so-called Indian problem or Negro problem was really a white problem, but Roosevelt could cite the lessons of history: "During the past three centuries," he had written in *The Winning of the West*, "the spread of the English-speaking people over the world's waste spaces has been . . . the most striking feature in the world's history."[44]

The United States might be the exemplar of the progressive sensibility because it had managed to blend traditional values into the creedal requirements of the new industrial society. A generation of elites from Roosevelt's

America had redefined civilization and progress according to the revolutionary agenda of industrialism. They had transformed the merchant republic into corporate America. They had assimilated eastern and southern Europeans and Chinese immigrants into the mix of Irish, Germans, and British who had arrived earlier in the century by creating a multiracial and multiethnic but not a miscegenated society. One could never be altogether sure if the eight million people of color in the nation's oceanic empire would be absorbed in the same way as African Americans and Plains Indians or follow the nineteenth-century pattern of incorporation as territories and ultimately as states. In the late nineteenth century, jurists had reconfigured constitutional precepts to meet the needs of those who ran the new industrial economy by providing a legal buffer to the reformist political challenges of organized labor and farmers. Years before he became president, even Roosevelt pondered the implications of what he would later call race suicide. As did most old stock North Americans, he regarded the English-speaking as a white race, and he harbored concerns about the decline in their fertility patterns in comparison with the new immigration, particularly after he took a close look at the census of 1890. Such doubts did not make him an anti-imperialist, however.[45]

Yet empire offered a novel kind of challenge, and the anti-imperialists were alert to its uncertainties. In 1898 Andrew Carnegie, who opposed Philippine annexation, urged President McKinley to heed a warning from the editorial pages of the British periodical *The Spectator* about the world's future hinging on the political character of North Americans and their ability to absorb large numbers of diverse peoples. Would the experience of the previous thirty years serve the nation in an unstable world with a capacity for self-destruction, a world in which history and civilization might crash and in which the use of power to prevent such calamities would not only be dangerous but exacerbate the chaos? Would empire transform ruler into parasite?[46]

At this critical juncture in the nation's history, those who advocated the imperial course had to persuade the doubters that the United States could indeed become a colonial power without violating the Constitution or suffering the racial and ethnic debilities that came with insular expansion. Elites had already laid the cultural foundations for such a mission in the World's Columbian Exposition, which celebrated the latest achievements in urban planning and architecture and introduced the skeptical to evolutionary ideas about race, ethnology, evolution, and progress in ways that reinforced the authority of a ruling class. In 1901, as Latin American suspicions of U.S. policy in the hemisphere increased, promoters anxious to open up hemispheric markets launched the Pan-American Exposition in Buffalo. The exposition was marred by the assassination of President McKinley by an anarchist, but the exhibits served to remind foreign visitors of the essentially peaceful intent of the United States in world affairs and at the same time to reassure domestic spectators of U.S. dominance in the hemisphere.[47]

Such cultural reassurances regarding what the contemporary British writer Rudyard Kipling called the "white man's burden" could not adequately address the political and legal implications of the country's insular empire. The United States had a continental but not a transcontinental expansionist tradition. Would the populations of Hawaii, the Philippines, and Puerto Rico, which had become U.S. possessions either during or as a consequence of the war with Spain, become citizens? and would these territories ultimately become states? Until 1901, neither the Constitution nor Congress, the branch of government constitutionally mandated to legislate for the territories and admit new states, made a distinction between incorporated and unincorporated territories. The former status carried an implicit promise of ultimate statehood. Even the most fervent imperialists had their doubts about such a course. Secretary of War Elihu Root stated in his 1899 report that the peoples of territories acquired under the Treaty of Paris, that is, Puerto Rico and the Philippines, were not entitled to the historical constitutional privileges of territorial inhabitants or of states. In a series of important decisions between 1900 and 1905, the Supreme Court by very narrow votes concluded that Alaska and Hawaii were incorporated territories but that Puerto Rico and the Philippines fell into the novel description of unincorporated territories. Although in each region Congress tolerated a process of self-government, the distinction ultimately proved critical: peoples of incorporated territories were entitled to the benefits of "domestic citizenship" and the prospect of statehood; those in unincorporated territories were not. In the case of the Philippines, despite the grisly suppression of the insurrection of 1899–1902, the United States did not intend to make the islands over into a colony in the European tradition. Puerto Rico was a different matter. Even the anti-imperialists proved to be ambivalent about the future of the U.S. role in the island.[48]

Empire was less troublesome for Roosevelt, in large part because he believed such a choice would strengthen the national character and, just as important, persuade his class of its continuing responsibilities to lead. But it deeply troubled some of his contemporaries—Howells among them—and not because Howells and his kindred spirits lacked Roosevelt's convictions about the nation's accomplishments. They had a nagging fear that the qualities that had enabled the nation's industrial and political leaders to bring order out of chaos at home were not those virtues usually identified as the hallmarks of advanced societies and civilizations. Roosevelt's America embarked on an imperial course in the belief that the perils, violence, and contradictions that often accompany the transition to modernity belonged to the nation's recent past. That may have been a usable past for Theodore Roosevelt—"Unless we keep the barbarian virtues," he boasted, "gaining the civilized ones will be of little avail"—but it was not reassuring to some of those who remembered it.[49]

José Martí's America

In the 1890s, as Roosevelt's America poised to assume the tutelary rule of an insular empire made up largely of people of color from the Caribbean to the Philippines in the western Pacific, the "other America" found its most articulate voice in José Martí, the Cuban revolutionary, poet, and essayist. In his essay "Our America" (1891), Martí imagined a continent whose leaders responded to the inner strengths and needs of their peoples rather than imposing alien political and cultural institutions on them, incorporated indigenous peoples into the civic body, and rejected the political debilities inherited from the Spanish colonizer.

"Our America" was also an appeal for cultural unity and a warning about U.S. designs on Latin American sovereignty, a threat Martí perceived in the proposal of U.S. Secretary of State James G. Blaine (1881, 1889–92) for a customs union and arbitration system in the hemisphere. During his abbreviated tenure in 1881, Blaine broached the idea of a Pan-American conference as part of his effort to mediate the War of the Pacific (1879–83) between Chile and Peru and Bolivia. That goal fell through, although a few years later Blaine's successor, Frederick T. Frelinghusen, organized a South American Commission that continued attempts to promote closer commercial ties between U.S. business and Latin American markets. In 1889, Blaine resumed the post of secretary of state and promptly revived his plan at the First International American Conference, which convened in Washington, D.C. Touting the promises of hemispheric development and progress through closer economic ties, Blaine proudly escorted the visiting Latin American delegates on a tour of the nation's eastern industrial plant.[1]

In the end, Blaine got much less than he wanted. Led by the Chileans, the victors in the War of the Pacific and opponents of arbitration, and the Argentines, who believed the customs union would be of little economic benefit, Latin American delegates gutted Blaine's plans. Later, some of them celebrated at a party in New York City, where they exulted in their victory and hailed the Argentine delegate, Manuel Quintana, for his eloquent defense of the Latin American stand. Martí, who chronicled the conference proceedings for the Buenos Aires newspaper *La Nación*, quoted Quintana's response: "I accept this kindness on behalf of my country! We in America are but one single people!"[2]

"Our America": The Perspective from South America

The Latin American representatives' sentiments of solidarity apparently did not incorporate Martí's vision, as the delegates, especially those from South America, failed to address the issue of Cuban independence and to take a forthright stand against U.S. annexation of the island. This may explain the ambiguity of Martí's position toward his putative compatriots in "Our America" and his belief that the continent's cultural and political elites regarded him as a foreigner when he believed he spoke for them as a peer. Latin Americans who rejected Blaine's grandiose proposals for a hemispheric customs union and a Pax Americana crafted in Washington, D.C., did not always see the Cubans as kindred spirits. Cuban revolutionaries and exiles who of necessity used the United States as a place to plot their conspiracies and raise monies for the liberation of the island sometimes inspired but occasionally disturbed South Americans. If the United States failed to serve them as a cultural model, neither could revolutionary Cuba provide reassurance for a generation determined to rid themselves of the political and social chaos Simón Bolívar had condemned as being a plague on his generation.[3]

Martí invoked the Bolivarian rhetoric of national liberation and voiced his warnings about the menace from the north at a time when his intellectual and political contemporaries in mainland Latin America, among them the Argentines Juan Alberdi and Domingo Sarmiento, were exalting immigration, science, education, steam, electricity, and railroads. Sarmiento urged his countrymen to imitate the United States in order to benefit from the progress and liberty of the age. There was a racial construction to Latin American elites' views about development. Martí blamed Latin American backwardness and disunity on those Latin Americans who increasingly espoused a racial pessimism. When questioned about such choices, of course, elites could always point to the industrialized North Atlantic countries, which were expanding even more rapidly. Latin Americans had only to visit Europe or the United States to see the widening gulf between those countries and their own, graphic reminders that the nations whose economies and political stability they so admired were peopled largely by whites.[4]

Perhaps Martí refused to acknowledge that South America's incorporation of foreign ideas was less slavish imitation than calculation and adaptation. In New Granada (renamed Colombia in 1863), Liberals commenced their renovation of the nation not by rejecting foreign ideas but by eagerly adapting them to local circumstances. In the spirit of the French revolutionary tradition, Liberals insisted that notable people be addressed as citizen, and the constitution of 1853 endorsed freedom of the press, introduced universal male suffrage, and abolished slavery (with compensation to the slaveowners). These measures conformed to Martí's thoughts, undeniably, but their purpose was not to incorporate those from below into a modern nation but rather to assure the free play of economic laws, particularly in the supply of labor. The severity of these measures plunged the country into civil war. Unlike what happened in the United States and in Mexico in the 1860s, however, the form of liberalism that triumphed in Colombia with the constitution of 1863 severely limited the power of the central government and permitted unbridled individual liberty.[5]

Despite these problems, the Colombian economy experienced a slow if erratic growth. U.S. private investment, notably in railroad and telegraph construction and mining, had begun to appear, though it was already clear that the principal U.S. interest lay not so much in the populated highlands as in the commercially and strategic important Panamanian isthmus, which in the reform era of the 1850s had gained more autonomy. In the late 1860s representatives of the two governments drew up a hasty agreement providing for the construction of an isthmian canal by U.S. interests; the suspicious Colombian senate, however, balked at any concession of national sovereignty over the proposed route. Even as they chafed under insistent pressures from the U.S. government over the canal issue, Colombians were impressed with its resolve. As one of them remarked, "If there is one nation that satisfies all the aspirations of those who seek the indefinite progress of mankind, then it is the North American people."[6]

As the first Liberal era in Colombia came to an end in 1884 with the seizure of power by a former doctrinaire Liberal, Rafael Nuñez, the costs of Liberal economic progress were painfully apparent. Nuñez was in the Bolivarian tradition, frustrated by Colombia's fragmented society yet determined to bring order out of chaos. In 1885, the government regained control over the rebellious Panamanian isthmus when U.S. forces, acting under an 1846 treaty, landed troops to suppress a revolt led by a dissident Liberal, Pedro Prestán. Nuñez took his revenge on the province by pushing through a new constitution that granted the executive broader powers and enabled him to legally end Panama's privileged status in the Colombian federal structure. He restored centralism to the political system, the church to its privileged position, and boasted about bringing a "scientific peace" to Colombia. But the discordant and occasionally violent features of national political life remained.[7]

Argentina's path to modernity after midcentury proved similarly fractious. The first presumptive leader of the new Argentina was the federalist Justo José de Urquiza, formerly governor of Entre Ríos province and leader of the forces that overthrew the dictator Juan Manuel de Rosas in 1852. When Urquiza tried to fashion a national organization, he confronted the revived hostility of Rosas's old adversaries, the Unitarios, who regained control of Buenos Aires city and province. The two groups quarreled for a decade. Urquiza and the federalists had powers in the new constitution that Rosas had never wanted or required—relative autonomy for the provinces but a national government with the *constitutional* authority to intervene in a province if it fell into anarchy or its politics menaced republican institutions. In the beginning, Buenos Aires arrogantly resisted the new federalist regime, so Urquiza established the federal capital at Paraná in Entre Ríos province.[8]

Urquiza opened the Paraná River to foreign commerce, which deprived the federal government of much-needed customs duties but at least assuaged the merchants and consumers of the littoral cities, especially in Rosario, who had long chafed under the older restrictions. Inspired by the arguments of his advisor, Juan Bautista Alberdi, who had affirmed that "to govern is to populate," Urquiza launched an ambitious immigration policy designed to import not only European settlers but European ideas, attitudes, and "blood" into the country. Promoters arranged to bring in European families who would be settled on public lands to found colonies of small farms. Despite its estrangement,

Buenos Aires prospered even more than the rest of the country, but such progressive measures were not enough to ensure its peaceful incorporation into the federation. In two brief civil wars between Buenos Aires and the confederation in 1859 and 1861, Buenos Aires emerged victorious when in 1862 Bartolomé Mitre, governor of Buenos Aires province, declared himself provisional president of the country and then assumed a six-year presidential rule. The federal capital was moved to Buenos Aires, and Mitre and his successor, Domingo Sarmiento, an admirer of Abraham Lincoln and the public education system of the United States, launched the *porteño* program for progress and national unity. However noble their agenda, they sometimes employed the methods of the "barbarian" Rosas—repression of troublemakers and the use of military force to stamp out armed resistance—choices that sometimes troubled Mitre but not Sarmiento.[9]

Argentina's liberals in the age of Mitre and Sarmiento constituted an intellectual aristocracy bent on spreading their ideas throughout the provinces. They were committed to the rule of law, to education, to material and political progress, and to ridding the nation of the barbarism Sarmiento and the Generation of 1837 had identified with the interior and gaucho culture. But they remained doubtful about the place of the Argentine gaucho in the nation's future. Though glorified in the epic poem *Martín Fierro*, the gaucho had no claim to a special place in the new Argentina, whose future would be built on exports from the land and investment and immigration from abroad. In the 1860s British investors began opening up joint-stock operations, mostly in banking and railways. A trade once dominated almost exclusively by textiles expanded to include iron, steel, metal manufactures, and coal. With considerable British assistance, the Argentine government constructed more than twelve hundred miles of track in the interior. Argentines seemed to be following the North American pattern of using the railroad to foster development of the interior and to populate its prairies with farmers. Few U.S. leaders would have dared to adopt Sarmiento's 1850 dictum for progress: "We are not industrialists or navigators, and Europe will provide us for long centuries with its artifacts in exchange for our raw materials."[10]

Even the similarities between Argentine and North American development could be deceptive. Argentine politics during the presidencies of Mitre, Sarmiento, and Nicolás Avellaneda—who gave Rosas's gauchos their last moment of glory in the 1879 Desert Campaign against the Indians on the southern frontier—was riddled with fraud and coercion. North American politics was similarly plagued, certainly, but it is difficult to imagine any nineteenth-century

U.S. ex-president seriously contemplating a military revolt because he lost office in a fraudulent election, as did Mitre. The United States modernized in the late nineteenth century with foreign investment and foreign labor, but its leaders did not try to remake the country through immigration. In the United States, the impact of the immigrant and the foreign landholder lessened in that the newcomers, both as laborers and landowners, constituted a smaller percentage of the general population than in Argentina. Argentina drew its immigrants mostly from Spain, Portugal, and Italy. In 1850 the population of Argentina approached 1 million; twenty years later it reached 1.7 million. In the same period the city of Buenos Aires doubled its population, from 90,000 to 178,000, half of them foreigners. In the United States, immigration fed the labor force. In Argentina, immigration fueled population growth. Under the Argentine constitution of 1853, foreigners had most of the rights of Argentines but few of their civic obligations. Before long, the provinces began encouraging immigrant settlers for agricultural colonies. Sarmiento, who admired the tradition of small farms in the United States, spoke expansively about the peopling of the Argentine countryside in a similar fashion, but the dream perished with the government's encouragement of the use of land as a commodity and of powerful landowners who believed that land should be reserved for sheep and cattle raising and had more political clout than immigrant farmers.[11]

Chile had not suffered a rule as despotic as that of Rosas, but the nation had experienced its own variation of strongman rule in Diego Portales, who never held the presidency but whose authoritative influence shaped Chilean civil and military culture in the 1830s. In the aftermath of Portales's assassination in 1837, Chilean radicals became more defiant, and at midcentury they had a brilliant but erratic voice in Francisco Bilbao, a founder of the Society of Equality, who organized street demonstrations in protest against the rigged electoral system. The Chilean president, Manuel Bulnes, promptly dissolved the society and proceeded to fix the upcoming election of his successor, Manuel Montt. Rebellions of protest in 1851 and 1859 weakened but did not break the grip of familial land concentration in the central valley and in the mining districts of the north. Migration to the California goldfields, to Chilean cities, and to Peru for work on the railroads permitted the Chilean elite to export the country's surplus labor. But they could not export the nation's social conflicts. Chile had one of the most stable social and political systems of nineteenth-century Latin America, but its route to modernity was no less troublesome than that of its neighbors. As one of its most distinguished men of letters, Benjamín Vicuña, warned at midcentury, the rebellion of 1851 had been necessary to "rescue our rural classes from abject servitude." A contemporary reminded an arrogant elite that Chilean rural society had "two rival classes, almost two races, that are becoming increasingly antagonistic."[12]

Paraguay followed a distinctive path to modernity in the nineteenth century. Historians who recite the dreary collapse of much of the continent into political chaos, economic dependency, and betrayal of the revolutionary promise often point to Paraguay's autonomous development under the Creole Dr. José Gaspar Rodríguez de Francia. From 1811, the date of Paraguay's declaration of independence, until 1840, Francia exercised a personalist rule in the name of the people, often meting out harsh punishment to his enemies, whether Spanish or Creole, and, most important, ensuring the elimination of the upper classes through decrees requiring intermarriage with Indians, mestizos, and mulattos. Francia's social revolution incorporated a crude but unmistakable state socialism. He transformed seized private property into government estates to provision the military or leased it to individuals for a generous return to the state. Slavery ensured that there would be an adequate labor force. Francia's successor, Carlos Antonio López, came from one of the few Creole elite families to survive Francia's purge, but he retained El Supremo's personalist style. López built schools, founded the country's first newspapers, and commenced the policy that ended slavery. With the assistance of British advisors, Paraguay enjoyed a limited modernization: the government built an iron foundry, a railroad, and a shipyard. At midcentury, then, Paraguay seemed on the verge of taking its place among the rapidly modernizing nations of South America, a continental Prussia.[13]

In reality these changes were plunging Paraguay toward a war with its neighbors, Argentina, Brazil, and Uruguay. Francisco Solano López's accession to the dictatorship in 1862 coincided with a political crisis in Uruguay, a crisis precipitated by the machinations of a wealthy Brazilian entrepreneur and ambitious politician, Irineu Evangelista de Sousa, the Baron de Mauá. The baron made his first fortune with an iron foundry. By the early 1860s his diverse interests included food processing, banking, land speculation, transportation, construction, and colonization in his native Brazil and in Argentina and Uruguay. He belonged to a generation of risk-takers and opportunists committed to the modernization of the country through industrialization and capitalism. To that end, he was willing to serve (and to manipulate) those who held power in order to transform a country in which traditional values and disdain of the value of work permeated society. Mauá was perhaps the most aggressive Brazilian entrepreneur of his times. His influence among a generation of ambitious Brazilians and foreigners coincided with the slow absorption of Brazil into the international economy, years when the coffee regions of the south began to supplant in economic importance the older sugar plantation zones of the northeast. The end of the slave trade in 1850 and the expanding export trade in the following fifteen years prompted changes in the commercial code and the appearance of corporations to serve the needs of an export economy. Foreigners, principally British, French, and North American, dominated the commercial houses and played a critical role in roadway and railroad building. Adopting European ways of thinking was the only realistic means of assuring Brazil's proper place in Western society. As one discontented Brazilian wrote, "We must change our customs. . . . And I know of no better way than to open freely the doors of the Empire to the foreigner."[14]

In Uruguay, the measure of Mauá's influence was such that when the opposition Blancos (Whites) rebelled against his Colorado (Red) friends in 1854, threatening his investments, four thousand Brazilian troops intervened. Mauá took no chances. He made friends among influential Blancos, and when they gained power six years later his holdings seemed secure. Uruguay's new Blanco rulers were vulnerable. In 1860 Mitre became Argentine president; the following year a Liberal convert, Zacarias de Góis e Vasconcelos, became prime minister of Brazil. They were united in their disgust with the Uruguayan Blancos. And they were leaders of two governments with historic claims to Paraguayan territory. As the political crisis thickened, the younger López built up the Paraguayan army and confirmed his government's commitment to the Uruguayan Blancos (the liberal party), who began seizing property of rebellious Colorados and their Brazilian friends and relatives who crossed the border to help them. This was a situation made to order for Zacarias and Emperor Dom Pedro II, who needed to distract attention from the increasingly contentious issue of Brazilian slavery following Lincoln's Emancipation Proclamation (which took effect on January 1, 1863) and the abolition of slavery in the Dutch West Indies the following year. Brazil delivered an ultimatum to the defiant Blancos to restore confiscated property; when it was rejected, the Brazilians invaded Uruguayan soil in September 1864. Solano López waited two months to respond: he ordered the seizure of a Brazilian steamboat on the Paraguay river and then dispatched troops into the Brazilian province of Mato Grosso. Early in 1865 he sent troops across Argentine territory to relieve his Blanco friends. In May 1865, Brazil, Argentina, and the new Colorado government signed a war alliance against Paraguay.[15]

Thus commenced the War of the Triple Alliance, Latin America's costliest war, in which the Paraguayans won the initial battles but after six months of fighting were pushed back. For five years the Paraguayans managed to stave off the invading armies, although by 1868, when the Brazilians overran the fortifications around the capital of Asunción, Paraguay's defeat was inevitable. Solano López would have accepted a truce if his adversaries had promised to evacuate the country, but the aggressive Brazilians would not hear of such concessions. In the last two years of the struggle, he resorted to the drafting of teenage males. The madness continued until Solano López died in battle on March 1, 1870. The devastated nation had lost half its 1864 population of four hundred thousand. Most of the survivors, of course, were women, children, and the aged. There were territorial losses, too, as the victorious Brazilians took lands lying northeast of the Paraguay River; and their Argentine allies, the province of Misiones. Paraguay's strategy had ended in defeat and humiliation, "a total waste of effort, money, and lives," proving, wrote John Lynch, "that it was impossible to create a Prussia in South America."[16]

For the Brazilians, the Paraguayan war was an ambiguous triumph. In the early months of the fighting, the Brazilian army had driven Paraguayans from national soil, yet the early victories had not reaffirmed national identity. If Paraguayans were racial hybrids—barbaric, uncivilized, and suffering from tyrannical rule—then what were Brazilians? Those who had calculated that the war would divert the attention of Brazilians from the internal contradictions of the society and its convoluted politics were also proved wrong. From midcentury Brazilians had prided themselves on consensus among those in the upper rungs of political power, yet the Paraguayan war had worsened partisan feelings and exposed the enormous differences between the rhetoric of Brazilian political elites and the grim reality of the society. In the years after the war, Conservatives, inspired and occasionally intimidated by the farsighted José María Paranhos, later viscount of Rio Branco, recognized that to survive they should respond to the growing criticism of slavery from a younger generation. At the same time he persuaded the slaves that continuing obedience would ensure their freedom. Liberals seemed satisfied with his solution: order, progress, and reform. But Rio Branco's essentially moderate course was deceptively simple and potentially dangerous because it demonstrated that the stability so valued by Brazilian elites depended not on political institutions but on the social exchange of favor and protection. The state derived the necessary benefits from the impressive growth in foreign trade to assume a paternalistic status among Brazilians, preserving its legitimacy and the social order. It was the empire that stood exposed to an enlightened hemisphere. In

1870 a band of disaffected Liberals issued the Republican Manifesto. One of its statements, clearly inspired by the collapse of Maximilian's empire in Mexico, boldly declared, "We are Americans. . . . Our monarchical form of government is in its essence and practice contrary and hostile to the rights and interests of the American States."[17]

Martí's views about the decadence of monarchy, the promise of republican government, the imperative of ending slavery, and especially his beliefs about the ignominy of race should have found kindred spirits in late-nineteenth-century Brazil. In its final twenty years, the Brazilian monarchy displayed many of the same debilities Martí identified with Spain, particularly the weakness of its monarchical institutions in the face of modern social and economic realities. But there were significant differences in the two societies. For one thing, antipathy toward monarchy ran deep among Brazil's Republicans, but their feelings about abolition were lukewarm. In São Paulo state, slaveholding planters flocked to the Republican standard. The color question resonated differently among Brazilians than among Cubans. Brazilians developed their own myth of racial democracy within an intellectual atmosphere that demonstrated increasing acceptance of scientific racism and a parallel belief that national progress depended on a so-called whitening of society. Parallel strains of such thinking appeared in nineteenth-century Cuba, certainly, but few Brazilian thinkers harbored fears about whether Brazilian society would be European or African or whether the slaves, once set free, would rise and kill the whites, as in Haiti. In Brazil, the military vowed to modernize by recruiting more and more from the emerging middle classes. In Cuba, contrastingly, the army waging a war for independence in 1868–78 and again in 1895 was a multiracial force integrated at all levels.[18]

Nowhere in South America, then, did the cause of *Cuba Libre* appear to evoke the sympathies and commitments Martí identified as those of our America. He praised the Argentines for their steadfast opposition to the North American peril, yet his descriptions of the inadequacies in the Indian policy of the United States make the reservation system seem humane when compared with the devastation wreaked upon Indians in Argentina during the Desert Campaign of 1879. Martí wrote with compassion about moral renovation of Indians and the masses through sacrifice and education; in Peru, the most Indian country of South America, the nation's first civilian president, Manuel Pardo, preached a similar message but believed the way to achieve it lay in railroad building and the whitening of the republic through immigration. Some Andean Americans doubtless heartened to Martí's warnings about the cultural peril from the north and subscribed to his belief about a United States in decline and a Spanish America in ascendance. But others, notably those liberals disdainful of the southern continent's economic and political backwardness, readily absorbed North American thinking about economic self-interest, progress, and the need for order.[19]

The Greater Caribbean in the Age of Martí

Would the smaller states and colonies of the Caribbean and Central America respond to the revolutionary message of Cuba Libre? In the 1790s, the insular Caribbean had been the center of a vigorous mercantilist empire of such staples as sugar, coffee, tobacco, and indigo and boasted a slave labor economy that seemed invulnerable to the revolutionary torrents sweeping the region. A century later, the social and economic landscape of the region had changed dramatically. Slavery had disappeared, the plantation economy had weakened, and peasant and subsistence economies had taken root in some islands and withered in others. Urban and rural workers began to challenge the social and political influence of the planter class. Deprived of a slave labor force and frustrated in their efforts to create a wage-labor rural proletariat, planters increasingly turned to contract labor, especially from China and India. Although the transition from slave to free labor was problematic everywhere in the insular Caribbean, the real challenge to sugar producers was the uncertainties identified with technological modernization in the industry, particularly the increasing need for more complex, costly machinery. Planters often used, first, their considerable political power to deny or restrict access to land in an effort to compel rural people into a wage-labor economy and, second, their financial leverage to promote worker indebtedness. These severe labor strategies proved successful in the British Leeward Islands, Puerto Rico, and Danish Saint Croix but provoked resistance in other Caribbean islands, as the Morant Bay rebellion of 1865 in Jamaica tragically demonstrated. The rebellion that followed was short-lived and, frankly, no threat to the existing social order, but it was ruthlessly suppressed.[20]

By the end of the century, the sugar industry in the British West Indies had diminished before the dual competitiveness of European beet sugar and the rapid growth of the sugar industry in the Greater Antillean islands of Hispaniola, Cuba, and Puerto Rico. A more persuasive reason for the decline of the industry in the British isles was the determination of the Colonial Office and planter alliance to preserve the plantation mode of production in an era of rapid technological and economic change, thus inhibiting diversity and advances in the export sector. Curiously, in 1897 the West Indian Royal Commission, or Norman Commission, lauded peasant landholding as the most reliable means of support for the seventy-two thousand Jamaicans (half of the population) that lived on holdings of ten acres or less and participated in the fledgling banana industry. But Jamaica's white elites had little intention of sharing political power with people they had once denounced as savages and now described as black entrepreneurs essential to the island's economy. Diverting the attention of small plotholders from the protected plantation was another way of reinforcing the racial and class structure of the island.[21]

Another potential ally of Cuba Libre lay in the Dominican Republic. In the late 1860s, one of the more opportunistic Dominican politicos, Buenaventura Báez, responded to a U.S. proposal for a naval base concession on the Bay of Samaná by offering to cede the entire republic! Both Seward and Báez had questionable connections with the speculator William L. Cazneau, whose American West India Company had gone broke trying to promote U.S. colonization in the republic in the 1850s. With his partner, Joseph W. Fabens, Cazneau organized the Santo Domingo Company and began promoting the commercial and investment possibilities of the republic among some powerful businessmen, who along with Báez stood to benefit financially if the annexation scheme succeeded. Both the Andrew Johnson and Ulysses S. Grant administrations responded favorably, although the antiforeign sentiment in the Dominican Republic prompted Seward to shift his interest to the Danish West Indies. Grant's secretary of state, Hamilton Fish, renewed the efforts at Dominican annexation. When a treaty finally reached the Senate, Charles Sumner denounced it on the grounds that such a step was little more than prelude to further territorial acquisitions in the Caribbean. Fearing that Grant's policies would also lead to the acquisition of Haiti, he invoked a geographical imperative, declaring that "San Domingo, situated in tropical waters and occupied by another race, never can become a permanent possession of the United States."[22]

Following the failed annexation, treaty politics stabilized, and the basic character of Dominican society and economy took shape. Modern sugar plantations in the southeast created a new financial and agrarian elite who soon rivaled the old landowning class in the Cibao. The population, reckoned at approximately 150,000 in 1865, more than tripled over the next three decades. Railroads were built between Moca, Santiago, and La Vega, the major towns of the Cibao, and the northern port of Puerto Plata. New towns appeared, invigorating urban cultural life. There was a disturbing social price in this dramatic transformation, of course. The old social families had lived in a virtual barter economy. With the new wealth of the late nineteenth century came sharper social divisions. As the price and value of land increased, a new monied elite rose to occupy the highest positions in the social pyramid. Wedged beneath this aristocracy and the army of hired laborers and migrants on the bottom was the nearest thing to a middle sector—*los de segundo,* a layer of second-class people who possessed sufficient skills, education, income, and even physical traits to set them apart from the masses beneath them. Within this sector, even the darker-skinned Dominican found sufficient opportunity to move up a bit. By the end of the century, however, as the gap between rich and poor noticeably widened and the lines of social demarcation sharpened, lighter-skinned Dominicans became increasingly resistant to accepting people of color as equals. Ironically, Ulises Heureaux, the dark-skinned general who had pacified the country for this new bourgeoisie and monied class, became an anachronism even as his power was at its height. As Martí observed, within the military that protected the economic and social elites a color line prevailed: mulatto officers, black soldiers. Under the Heureaux dictatorship, as under Rafael Trujillo three decades later, some cities prospered, others languished. Cuban and Puerto Rican immigrants joined North Americans in developing the Dominican sugar industry.[23]

In neighboring Haiti, development followed another pattern. Haitian peasants participated in a cash economy by cultivating tree crops—coffee was the principal cash crop and the major source of government revenue—but they persistently resisted growing those crops that competed with foodstuffs. A small group of Haitian and foreign mercantile and banking houses dominated a tightly controlled commercial trade with the outside world. Foreigners could not own Haitian land—a constitutional provision that lasted until the U.S. occupation during World War I—thus providing the Haitian people a shield against alienation of the national domain in an era when foreign landholding became an explosive political issue in the United States. In Haiti the foreigner might prosper, but he did so not in the countryside but in the city. Country people instinctively resisted any effort by governments to increase agricultural production by creating a rural proletariat. Throughout the British West Indies, the plantation economy had survived by vagrancy laws that restricted the mobility of rural labor, severe restrictions on access to public lands, and immigration of foreign labor. In Haiti none of these measures proved successful. Haitian peasants were ignorant, but they remembered stories about the resistance to the slaveholder and the foreign invader during the revolution. Haiti was underdeveloped, but the reasons for its backwardness in the late nineteenth century lay not so much in the oft-cited prohibitions against foreign, that is,, white, ownership of property but in the increasingly desperate condition of country people denied access to land and unable to mobilize a populist revolt with clear political goals. Many of the dispossessed became *cacos,* soldiers who embodied a "peasant consciousness brutalized and deformed, looking for a road, a guide, a cause."[24]

Central America in the late nineteenth century offered yet another example of the distortions of political and economic development, yet, in an apparent denial of Martí's prescription, the revolution that mattered was not the anticolonial rebellion but the coffee revolution. Coffee had not only shaped the social structure of Central America but gave isthmian Liberals the opportunity to transform politics. When the Liberals took power in 1871, they moved quickly. They seized church property and sold it with the condition that the land be used for coffee production. Under special laws, they compelled those who held land in common to purchase it; when the occupants could not produce the necessary cash to buy the land, the law required its sale at public auction. The state sold public lands to coffee growers. In Guatemala, the economic transformation was not so harsh as late-twentieth-century chroniclers have described, but its social consequences were traumatic.[25]

In neighboring El Salvador, where the indigenous population was much smaller, the dramatic changes in landownership in the decades of the 1870s and 1880s were even more traumatic for country people. In the 1830s El Salvador's indigenous people lived relatively secure lives on communal lands. Fifty years later, they were practically serfs, as a succession of land laws in effect wiped out communal landholding rights. Honduras followed yet another economic progression. By almost universal consensus the Honduran government was the weakest in shielding its citizenry from the economic changes sweeping the isthmus. In the twentieth century, Honduras would become the quintessential banana republic, but in late 1870s and early 1880s the nation enjoyed its Golden Age, a laudatory reference to the presidency of Marco Aurelio de Soto, who declared that mining, not agriculture, was the promise of the nation's future. At the New Orleans Exposition of 1884, Hondurans joined other Central American representatives in promoting the many and varied isthmian products.[26]

Perhaps the least dramatic social changes wrought by the coffee revolution occurred in Costa Rica, where the expansion of coffee production reinforced rather than undermined small landholding. Costa Rican farmers did not exploit their indigenous labor force because they were relatively poor and had few Indians to exploit. They were labor poor; land was scarce and overpriced. Ensconced in the central highlands, the nation's political leaders lacked both the power and the resources to use coffee as a means of transforming the social structure. When they needed finance, they relied on London banks. In the early 1870s, as the historic port of Puntarenas on the Pacific coast declined in importance, they began looking to the east coast. In 1870 Puerto Limón was founded. A year later, President Tomás Guardia signed an agreement with the U.S. promoter and railroad builder Henry Meiggs, whose nephew Minor Keith began laying track for a rail line connecting the Atlantic coast with the capital of San José. "If the Costa Rica R.R. should go through," predicted a U.S. émigré who had lived for many years in Panama, "the country will become one of great importance as it is valuable in products, and mines, and only requires Anglo-Saxon brains to make order out of chaos."[27]

In one Central American country, Nicaragua, the Liberal revolution brought about a direct and dramatic confrontation with the great powers. In 1893, José Santos Zelaya became president. The following year, he confronted the British on their de facto protectorate over the vast area of eastern Nicaragua known as the Mosquitia. Technically, the issue was a question of British influence versus Nicaraguan sovereignty. Zelaya's challenge was not only arrogant but stupid, yet it was a portent of the defiance he later exhibited toward the United States in the early years of the twentieth century.[28]

North American and European entrepreneurs neither played a central role in the coffee revolution in Central America nor were directly responsible for the growing social inequities often attributed to these economic transformations by modern historians. But the coffee revolution formed only one aspect of Central America's immersion in the global economy in the late nineteenth century and its dependence on foreign capital, expertise, and technology. Although the success of each in dealing with foreign powers and especially with foreign entrepreneurs varied considerably, by the end of the century they were rapidly becoming vulnerable in ways not even their midcentury forebears could have imagined. Even as the Liberal political triumph in the 1870s appeared to herald a new era, the parallel development of agroexport economies and the opening up of isthmian economies provided opportunities to a new generation of immigrants. They were not numerous but they were very different from those Francisco Morazán had welcomed a half century before, for they were not settlers but ambitious and creative entrepreneurs who crafted special arrangements with isthmian governments or mercenaries who fought in Central America's wars. At the turn of the twentieth century, several isthmian Liberal leaders began to challenge the power of the U.S. government and the growing enclaves of foreign entrepreneurs and companies—the most aggressive was United Fruit Company, formed in 1899—by articulating a more nationalistic agenda for modernizing the nation. Unlike their predecessors of the 1850s, however, they did not unite against the intruder but divided, sometimes violently, over the most appropriate route to modernizing the isthmian economy.[29]

In the Colombian province of Panama, by contrast, the foreign presence prevailed from the 1840s. In 1856 occurred the first landings of U.S. troops under the curious provisions of the 1846 treaty with Colombia (then called Nueva Granada), which granted the United States the right to protect the "neutrality" of the transit route. The North American impact was social as well as strategic. During the construction of the railroad from the late 1840s until 1855, the Panama Railroad Company imported thousands of workers from the West Indies, Africa, Europe, North America, and even China to supplement the local labor force. Panama was an international, multiracial, and multilingual commercial venue a half century before achieving its independence in 1903. Panama's educated elite disdained the kind of labor and the imported laborers who did the work, yet they were also dismissive of any efforts by national authorities in the capital of Bogotá to direct the course of isthmian affairs.[30]

Decades before Panama's independence in November 1903, the U.S. government and especially local North Americans played a critical role in isthmian economic development. North American entrepreneurs established what became known as the Yankee strip, the transit route across the isthmus, ran many of the transit establishments that catered to migrants to the California goldfields, and even exercised local police power. Panama City's population grew from five thousand to thirteen thousand during the heyday of transisthmian California traffic from the mid-1840s until the mid-1860s. Although the Panama Railroad gave it the advantage, Panama did not have an exclusive edge on transisthmian traffic, of course, as the Nicaraguan route up the San Juan River, across lakes Nicaragua and Managua, and from there by horse-drawn carriage to the Pacific remained a viable alternative and potential threat to Panama. Nonetheless, Panamanian elites were resentful and exploited: resentful over their dependence on Colombian authorities in Bogotá and over decisions made in Washington, D.C., and New York that affected their interests. Thousands crossed the isthmus every month, yet the benefits appeared to go elsewhere, principally to the foreign community. Here, as elsewhere in Martí's America, the Americanization of local society and culture was everywhere evident yet very deceptive. The United States was both a foil to use against an intrusive national government in Bogotá and the putative enemy of local interests.[31]

In the 1880s, a third foreign nation, France, jolted Panamanian Liberals and their domination of local politics. After the Civil War, U.S. official interest in an isthmian canal increased, but a French group headed by Ferdinand de Lesseps, who had directed the building of the Suez Canal in the 1860s, proved more aggressive. In 1881, over strenuous objections from the U.S. government, the French company commenced to dredge a sea-level canal across Panama. In the beginning their efforts proved rewarding. The prosperity identified with the 1850s returned but so did the problems—a shortage of labor, speculation in real estate, inflation, high food prices, and social unrest attributed to the rapid growth of the immigrant workforce, fifty thousand West Indians and several thousands more from Europe, the United States, and Africa. At the height of construction the payroll of the canal company nearly equaled the population of Panama City in 1880. The French had wrangled their concession with the timely assistance of Bogotá's Liberals. They had little use for Panama's Liberals, military men whose habits had been acquired not in literary salons but in saloons and in the barracks. Liberals in the capital were white, cosmopolitan, and progressive; those in Panama were racially mixed, nationalistic, and sometimes violently antiforeign. Little wonder, then, that the French more readily identified with local Conservatives, descendants of older families who prided themselves on their light skin, made their money in commerce, and invested heavily in real estate.[32]

For these and other reasons the French welcomed Colombian president Rafael Nuñez's efforts to reassert national control over the province in 1885, a policy that precipitated the Prestán revolt and the U.S. military intervention that crushed it. In the aftermath, the ambitious French effort began to collapse, the victim of poor planning, financial problems, and disease. With it the image of France and French technology as the lodestar for Panamanian development also rapidly declined. But there was no doubting the resolve of the U.S. naval officers who ordered the landing of troops when the desperate Prestán set fire to the wooden buildings of Colón and his followers began ripping up railroad track and cutting telegraph lines. Marines disembarked from the *Shenandoah* and *Wachusett* to restore order along the railroad. They marched into Cathedral Plaza in Panama City. When a fight erupted among locals, the North Americans raked the tops of buildings with fire from a Gatling gun. Years later, some of the Panamanians and North Americans who witnessed or participated in the events could still recall the emotional impact of the U.S. presence.[33]

Throughout the second half of the nineteenth century, Liberals in Central America and Panama formed ambivalent views about the foreign connection and these countries' often ambitious plans for development. On one hand, Liberals wished to profit from the heightened international interest in the isthmus as a passageway. On the other they were quite conscious of the political and cultural costs of relying too much on foreign governments and the foreign entrepreneur. They could ill afford to sever their connection with foreign governments and especially foreign entrepreneurs who appeared to share their view of the promise of capitalism and their vision of development. As nationalists and developers, their commitment to the nation and to growth seemed always qualified by their deference to foreign philosophies, foreign cultural models, and foreign ways of looking at labor and the role of the state in national progress. The coffee revolution in the late nineteenth century presumably enabled these elites to consolidate their hold on the countryside, and the dramatic growth of the banana industry that followed the coffee revolution permitted foreign (principally U.S.) companies to exercise enormous political and economic influence in these societies. Yet the notion that the local economies and folkloric cultures immortalized by successive generations of historians and anthropologists could have been modernized without foreign capital or technology was a chimera. There was always a foreign connection to development in Central America. The essential question was the degree and character of that relation and the social and political price it exacted.[34]

The Cuban Shock

What mattered just as much as development were the revolutionary dynamics in Martí's America and what they meant for Roosevelt's America. The first shock occurred not in Central America but in Cuba.

In the nineteenth century Cuba became one of two pivotal places in Latin America—the other was Mexico—for U.S. interests; it was critical not only for strategic and economic but for political, social, and even cultural reasons. By the 1890s Mexico appeared to be thoroughly integrated into the North American economic system. The professed values of its ruling political elites sometimes reflected European rather than North American norms, to be sure, but Mexican social and cultural preferences no longer conveyed that noticeable anti-Anglo harshness of earlier years. More important, Mexico had achieved remarkable political stability and economic growth. Cuban Creoles had been

adopting North American social and cultural credos since the American Revolution. By an understandable inference from Cuba's behavior and its relative
weakness, most U.S. leaders assumed that the island, as John Quincy Adams
had prophesied in the 1820s, could be incorporated into U.S. hemispheric designs in ways that accommodated Washington's timetable and agenda.[35]

Cubans themselves contributed to such beliefs by adopting North American
cultural values and insisting on maintaining a color line in society even as
their commitment to slavery weakened. Others called for an end to slavery, al-
beit with compensation to the slaveholders, and the formal recognition of
social equality. Even after seventy-five years of intermittent rebellion and
struggle, Cuba's revolutionary cadres had not resolved their often bitter conflicts over the incorporation of blacks and colored in the kind of society they
envisioned and over the relation between an independent Cuba and its powerful northern neighbor.[36]

Clearly, the revolutionary agenda Martí articulated threatened not only
Spanish rule but also the imperial pretensions of the United States. To some
North American observers, doubtless, Martí represented little more than one
of the marginal views of the Cuban separatist movement after the disaster of
the Ten Years' War, yet, more than any of the exiled patriots in the Cuba Libre
movement, he spoke for the aspirations of Cubans who dreamed not only of
independence but of a republic shorn of the militarism that had plagued so
much of Latin America in the nineteenth century. When Martí arrived in New
York City in January 1880 he found revolutionary cadres whose members
heartened to tales of military adventurism and the belief that the just cause
would inevitably triumph. In 1884 these views brought Martí into immediate
conflict with veterans, among them the Dominican Máximo Gómez, who
wanted to launch a new rebellion that would be organized and dominated by
the generals. Martí denounced the militarism of the separatist movement. He
was also adamant about rapidly expanding U.S. influence in Cuba. "Once the
United States is in Cuba," he prophesied, "who will get her out?"[37]

Estranged from the veterans of Cuba Libre, Martí left New York and headed
for Florida. Among the militant cigar workers in the Cuban communities of
Tampa, Key West, Ocala, and Jacksonville he met Cubans who shared his vision of a liberated Cuba and his suspicions of the U.S. connection. Their views
were not likely to reassure those North Americans who had always looked
upon the intermittent Cuban rebellions against Spanish rule as the efforts of
Cuban Creoles to *encourage* U.S. annexation of the island as a way of breaking the economic and political grip of the Spanish metropolis over the island's

ambitious planters and merchants and, more important, of ensuring the continuation of slavery. After the U.S. Civil War made that choice more problematic, Creoles persisted in their beliefs that armed struggle would eventually prompt the U.S. government to act and, if necessary, annex the island to protect their property interests.[38]

Others saw the continuation of empire as the best guarantee against revolution, independence, and especially the prospect of not having to share political power and social status with the island's majority black and colored population. These were not Martí's views, of course. At the outset of the 1868 war, he believed that the participation of the island's black and colored population would be critical to the success of the revolt. The fragile peace of 1878 certainly doomed slavery, and in the postwar years the colored population of the cities dramatically improved their social status. But the lot of black Cubans in the countryside did not noticeably change. The experience of war also had a profound impact among eastern Cuban rebel leaders. To sustain morale among their guerrilla bands of whites, blacks, and mulattos, rebel leaders had to follow through with promises of freedom. In the chaos of war, the slave system of eastern Cuba weakened as runaways and freedmen joined the cause. In the perilous peace that followed, they did not return to the plantations but found sanctuary in mountainous communities.[39]

The condition of western Cuban planters had never been as precarious as that of their counterparts in the more rebellious eastern region of the island. Ambitious Cuban Creoles from the west readily identified with North American notions of development and cultural (and racial) preferences. Martí the revolutionary rejected those harsh racial beliefs increasingly associated with the United States in the nineteenth century, of course, and he was uniformly suspicious of U.S. motives about the island. But his expressed views about the prospects for Cuban (and Antillean) development, his indictment of Spanish backwardness, and his apprehensions about the island's subordination to a dominating U.S. economy echoed those beliefs of revolutionary British Americans in 1775 who spoke ominously about the North Atlantic colonies becoming "another Ireland," a metonym for impoverishment and dependence. In one of his final letters, Martí wrote about living "inside the monster," to be sure, but he found the "other America" in the United States, in its rebellious workers, farmers, and ordinary people and in its traditions of revolutionary defiance. He may have been naive about the support for Cuba Libre among these people, but he was never taken in by the expressions of commitment from U.S. leaders. When some Cubans spoke about the benefits of annexation to the United States, he replied, "No honest Cuban will stoop to be received as a moral pest for the sake of the usefulness of his land in a community where his ability is denied, his morality insulted, and his character despised."[40]

The revolution thus confronted two adversaries. The first was the Spanish government, its army, and those Spaniards and Cubans determined to keep the island within the Spanish empire and, that failing, to advance the rapidly withering cause of U.S. annexation in order to prevent the triumph of Cuba Libre. The second lay in Cuba's vulnerability to the powerful structural changes in the island's sugar economy and the ability of native sugar producers to control those changes. During the Ten Years' War, ambitious sugar planters occupied lands abandoned or seized from separatist collaborators and partici-pants. Their aggressive expansionism continued after the war ended. U.S. in-vestors, missionaries, and promoters poured into the island, transforming its economy and even its culture in ways that few Cubans could have anticipated. They joined Cuban planters frantically trying to adjust to the rapidly changing sugar industry and its myriad contradictions—improved transportation by rail prompted planters to expand their areas of cultivation, driving out smaller farmers. As specialization dictated a shift in production strategies, Cuban sugar entrepreneurs had to choose between cultivation and manufacturing, between growing and harvesting the cane and milling it. Increasingly, they chose to become growers, which meant they needed more land and a labor force to work it. Some growers, Cuban and North American, profited by these changes, but the social and economic distortions of such dramatic changes in the island's economy had a devastating impact on many Cubans. Cigar pro-duction, which alone counted for the employment of one hundred thousand Cubans, rapidly declined with the closing of factories, throwing workers into marginal employment or forced migration. In the last three decades of the century, a hundred thousand Cubans left the island.[41]

Cuba remained Spanish for another generation, but Cubans continued to absorb North American cultural forms (baseball among them) and transmit-ted these values through Cuban migration elsewhere in the Caribbean, Cen-tral America, and Mexico. Most emigrating Cubans went to the United States, where they became investors, manufacturers, workers, and even local public officials. They admired U.S. political culture, industry, and the promise of up-ward mobility and material progress. And when the war against Spanish rule revived in 1895, some of them revived older notions about annexation and then statehood. They would accept nothing less. But Theodore Roosevelt's America would not have contemplated such a choice. As a traveler to Cuba wrote after visiting the island, "A large majority of the native population of Cuba have negro blood in their veins. Practically one hundred percent of the people confess the Roman Catholic faith and Spanish is the mother tongue of the same proportion. Would the American nation agree to the construction of a sister state out of such material?"[42]

These judgments of white, essentially Anglo-Saxon, superiority reflected the prevailing racial sentiments of the 1890s, paralleling the U.S. South's efforts to keep blacks in a permanently inferior status and Congress's passage of laws discriminating against Chinese immigrants. North Americans had once characterized Mexico as an unprogressive and backward society, Mexican males as racially degenerate, Cuba as the Queen of the Antilles and Cubans as "white maidens" who must be saved from the ravaging Spaniard. From these twin images they now began to conjure up yet a third, the Latin "black child," a hybrid of the male racial degenerate and the hapless female dependent. This was a creature who must be rescued from Spanish oppression but could not be entrusted with self-governance nor taken on as mate. Occasionally, racial considerations could be as important as strategic and cultural imperatives in deliberations over the country's role in Latin America and the Pacific, though race might serve as justification for a cautious policy or, conversely, for a more assertive one. In 1893, white planters overthrew the Hawaiian monarch and quickly applied for annexation to the United States. To their chagrin, the Grover Cleveland administration rebuffed their offer and restored the Hawaiian monarch to power, a decision explained in part by Cleveland's suspicions about the entire affair, but, just as important, by the reluctance of Congress to incorporate large numbers of nonwhites who could never be assimilated or rise to citizenship. In the war summer of 1898, when the strategic importance of the Hawaiian Islands seemed obvious, such arguments weakened before other imperatives.[43]

During the sometimes intense prewar debates over intervention in Cuba, newspapers, especially those owned by William Randolph Hearst, had routinely described Cuban rebels as mostly white males fighting a conventional war for their freedom. In March 1898, Senator Redfield Proctor of Vermont assured his colleagues that 75 percent of Cubans were lighter in color than Spaniards, an observation reinforced by comments from Frederick Funston, a Kansas soldier of fortune in the rebel cause, and Congressman Joseph Wheeler, both of whom referred to Cubans as brethren. That image quickly vanished after the first U.S. troops, composed of both black and white soldiers, landed on Cuba's isolated southeastern coast and encountered Cuban guerrillas who were darker than those portrayed in stories about Cuba Libre in the U.S. press. Cuban guerrillas and white U.S. troops clashed from the outset. After the fighting ended, several U.S. officers commented disdainfully on the Cubans' fighting capabilities and their fitness for self-governance. The racial slurs accompanying these remarks disturbed many of the black U.S. soldiers. When talk of annexation revived, blacks in the United States held public forums in a dozen cities to remind their government of the prewar pledge not to annex Cuba. Their reasons went beyond an emotional attachment to the cause of Cuba Libre, however. The victory won, Afro-Cubans would acquire a position in government, and black Americans suffering racial discrimination would have a place of refuge in the Caribbean. When U.S. officers began treating the defeated Spaniards with more respect than their Cuban brethren, African Americans attributed the lingering bitterness between white U.S. officers and the Cubans to racial prejudices. "The whole trouble in Cuba," wrote one editorialist, "is the American stumbling block, the Negro. There are just a few more black soldiers in the Cuban ranks than [U.S. General William] Shafter cares to deal with and recognize as men."[44]

The tragedy of the revived Cuban war of independence in 1895, then, lay not in its military but in its political failure. In a relatively brief span of three years, Cuban insurrectionists effectively contained a superior Spanish force because they were united in their goal of independence. What defeated their cause was the U.S. intervention in late spring 1898, a military intrusion that effectively divided Cuban separatists and weakened the cause of Cuba Libre before a putative liberator who, in actuality, had an agenda for Spain's Caribbean empire very different from Martí's. In Caribbean history the war of 1898 may have been the last battle of the Spanish-American wars of independence that had commenced early in the nineteenth century, but it also represented the first phase of the twentieth-century counterrevolutionary interventions of the United States. The U.S. intervention effectively destroyed the cause of Cuba Libre, but the Creole and Spanish elites who both despised and feared the radical elements of the separatist movement welcomed their new ally, for the U.S. military presence provided them with the protection they desperately required to preserve their place in the island's economy and society.[45]

The Making of U.S. Empire in Martí's America

Martí had envisioned a new Cuba as the center of Antillean civilization arising from this struggle, but the reality was a devastated island and people who had suffered an enormous physical and human toll. Cuban revolutionaries who had demanded a free Cuba in 1895 now confronted an even more formidable opponent than Spain: a U.S. military headed by men intent on pacifying the island and disdainful of those Cubans who had hastily created local governments in the wake of the Spanish departure. The meaning of McKinley's comment about "ties of singular intimacy" soon became apparent to those Cubans who had never wanted U.S. intervention and reassuring to those Cubans and Spaniards who had pleaded for that intervention. Cuba's new rulers were U.S. military officers commanded by Major General John Brooke, who ran Cuba by the most expedient means. Quite probably, his determined resourcefulness kept thousands of Cubans from dying of starvation and prevented the island from collapsing into chaos. But by the end of 1899 he was gone, the victim of Cuban complaints about his decision to reappoint Spaniards to their old posts in the civilian bureaucracy—thus depriving the Cubans of the political spoils of war— and of his own subordinates, particularly Leonard Wood, the commander in Santiago, whose stern regimen impressed Secretary of War Elihu Root.[46]

Root had already defined the distinctive U.S. approach to empire in an address on the new U.S. soldier, who represented not the mercenary of imperial conquest but the citizen of a self-governing people, committed to the rehabilitation of "poor, bleeding Cuba and devastated Puerto Rico." It was only fitting, then, that Brooke's successor should be Wood, who governed in the manner of a conscientious plantation owner, keeping a respectable distance from the Spaniards, consorting with the Cuban elite, yet finding time to visit with Cuban *guajiros* (rural dwellers). He paid complaining Cuban rebel veterans seventy-five dollars a man and created a rural guard to police the countryside and the towns. Persuaded that the old practice of tossing refuse into the street explained the outbreaks of yellow fever, he imposed severe regulations on garbage disposal and called for whitewashing all public places. He dispensed with the Spanish curriculum in the schools, which Brooke had retained, and substituted the Ohio Model with its emphasis on history, civics, and vocational education. Directed to prepare Cubans for independence, he encouraged the formation of political parties and participation in local government, a promising sign to those Cubans who convened at the island's first constitutional convention in late 1900. Had they perceived the subtle shifts in U.S. thinking about the island, Cuban *independentistas* would have been justifiably troubled.[47]

Cubans charged with drawing up the island's first constitution shortly learned what their U.S. liberators intended when they spoke of guaranteeing Cuban independence. The criteria of the "special relationship" were spelled out in an attachment, the Platt Amendment, to the Army Appropriation Act of

1901, requiring the Cuban republic to respect U.S. rights in its treaties with other nations and to grant to the United States long-term naval leases and the right to intervene to protect U.S. property and lives. Cubans formally protested. A special delegation arrived in Washington, D.C., to plead their case with President McKinley, only to learn he had already signed the Platt Amendment into law. Root mollified them with reassurances that his government would respect Cuban sovereignty, but when the convention tried to modify the amendment before incorporating it into the new constitution Wood threatened to keep U.S. troops in Cuba.[48]

Under the Platt Amendment, Cuba had self-government and independence but not self-determination or the fundamental rights of a sovereign nation. The U.S. Congress had pledged to secure Cuban independence, but neither the form nor the content of that independence satisfied the aspirations of those who had fought for Cuba Libre. Although many North Americans, Roosevelt among them, persisted in believing that the decision for war in 1898 was less a question of safeguarding the nation's interest than a moral obligation to end the strife on the island, Wood recognized that the Platt Amendment made Cuban independence virtually meaningless. The Cuban revolutionary general Máximo Gómez agreed: "The Republic will surely come but not with the absolute independence we had dreamed about."[49]

Another casualty of Martí's dream of independent Caribbean nations rising out of the last of Spain's New World possessions was Puerto Rico. Spared the devastation of a long guerrilla war, the island suffered a different kind of deprivation. Puerto Rico boasted a revolutionary tradition, and when the disaffected planters of eastern Cuba raised the flag of rebellion in 1868 their Puerto Rican counterparts joined them. Puerto Rican Liberals spoke of the "embracing Puerto Rican family" in their demands, yet as sugar and coffee planters they were principally interested in the export market for their products and in autonomy for the island within the Spanish empire. In the early 1890s their most articulate spokesman, Luís Muñoz Rivera, father of Puerto Rico's best-known twentieth-century governor, Luís Muñoz Marín, wrote disconsolately about the indifference of the island's ordinary people to the political struggles of the era.[50]

So they elected the second path: a political alliance with the monarchical party in Spain and a government fighting a guerrilla war in Cuba and a secondary but critical diplomatic conflict with the United States. Their choice gained them a momentary reprieve. In 1897, the Spanish government granted the island an autonomist charter, which provided for universal male suffrage, enabling the recalcitrant landowners to win more than 80 percent of the vote. More disturbing for the island's future was the disaffection of a small but vocal group of Autonomists, mostly professionals, who represented a distinct social element in Puerto Rican society. At the time of the U.S. invasion of the island in July 1898, this division among Puerto Rican elites meant that there would be no united front to put forward an alternative plan for the island's future.[51]

The imminent U.S. triumph in the war made it clear that Spain no longer had a future in the Caribbean. But what did this portend for Puerto Ricans? In 1900, a year in which the character of the U.S. presence began to suggest both a permanence in the island's affairs and a simultaneous indifference to Puerto Rican elite sensibilities, Muñoz Rivera, who had been named prime minister of an autonomous Puerto Rico in 1897, reminded the readers of *Diario de Puerto Rico* of his 1896 warnings about the choice between independence, which would lead the island into poverty as well as civil war, and annexation to the United States, which was an absurdity because of the vast cultural, linguistic, and racial differences between the two peoples.[52]

Muñoz Rivera glossed over some of the deeper social divisions among Puerto Ricans as well as his own ambiguous position about the U.S. relation with Puerto Rico. Ordinary Puerto Ricans disdained the propertied Creole elites. The Spanish exploited these hatreds, then just as quickly began to suppress the rural social bands that sprouted from this discontent. As the Spanish grip rapidly weakened in 1898, some Puerto Rican exiles in New York joined Cuban revolutionaries in calling for U.S. intervention. Fearful of an uprising from below, Muñoz Rivera and his kindred spirits ultimately came to a similar judgment in summer 1898. Yankee occupiers, they believed, would have no more sympathy for the rural social bandits and campesinos than Roosevelt or McKinley had had for strikers and populists. Muñoz Rivera told McKinley's envoy, Henry Carroll, that the vast majority of Puerto Ricans aspired to citizenship and the benefits of statehood in the United States, but when U.S. troops landed at Guánica on the island's southeastern coast, he and Minister of Justice José de Diego asked Spanish authorities for weapons to repel the invaders! They soon abandoned any notion of resistance when they heard General Nelson A. Miles, who had led the U.S. Army's chase of Geronimo, read the proclamation about "giving the people of [Puerto Rico] the largest measure of liberty consistent with the military occupation."[53]

Miles's soothing words did not apply to those country people who had been fighting off and on against Creole landowners. In the months following the initial landings, as disaffected campesinos and social bandits revived these local struggles—what the historian Fernando Picó describes as the "war after the war"—U.S. troops fanned out into the Puerto Rican countryside to suppress them. To veteran soldiers, these Puerto Rican guerrillas were as threatening to order and progress as the Indians they had fought during the Plains campaigns. Spain had repressed these people; so did their U.S. liberators. General Brooke declared them to be outlaws and criminals. Carroll, the island's resident commissioner in 1899, had them tried in military tribunals. Such actions were inconsistent with Miles's decree but not with military practice or international law. Congress had passed no legislation forswearing any intention to annex Puerto Rico as U.S. territory. The island was acquired by right of conquest. During the armistice negotiations in Washington, D.C., in August and in the negotiations that followed in Paris, U.S. officials insisted that the island would be retained as war reparation and governed as conquered territory.[54]

As in Cuba, the island's first experience with Americanization was military rule—benign in intent, perhaps, but often harsh in practice. The Liberal Party, which enjoyed majority status under the Spanish grant of autonomy, tried to promote "Puerto Rico for the Puerto Ricans," but the new U.S. military governor, Major General Guy Henry, quickly undermined the Liberal hold by appointing U.S. military officers as mayors and bringing the Liberal-dominated cabinet under his control. Some Puerto Ricans sought to accommodate the new regime by forming the Puerto Rican Republican Party, announcing that their ultimate goal was statehood. The party's manifesto also called for making English the official language. But even they were quickly disillusioned by the character of U.S. military rule. As José Hanna, one of the early advocates of U.S. intervention, testified before Congress in 1900, "The occupation has been a perfect failure. We have suffered everything. No liberty, no rights, absolutely no protection, not even the right to travel. We can not travel today because we can not get passports. We are Mr. Nobody from Nowhere. We have no political status, no civil rights. That can not go on very long."[55]

The uncertainty over status continued. But the U.S. Congress soon made clear to Puerto Ricans what it would and would not do for the island and its people. Confronted in 1900 with a question about the applicability of U.S. tariff law to the island, Congress established in the Foraker Act—named for Senator Joseph Foraker, with President McKinley an early advocate of U.S. citizenship for Puerto Ricans—the island's first organic law. The law called for a governor appointed by the U.S. president, an executive council composed of six department heads and five Puerto Rican citizens, and a house of delegates made up of thirty-five members elected for two-year terms. Laws passed by this lower chamber, for example, the extension of universal male suffrage, could be annulled by the executive council and governor, and, if that proved insufficient, by the Congress. Puerto Ricans could elect a resident commissioner to represent islanders before the executive council, but they would have no elected voice in the U.S. Congress. Puerto Ricans lost most of the rights and liberties they had gained with autonomy in 1897. They were citizens of Puerto Rico but not of the United States. U.S. laws, unless found locally inapplicable, would apply to Puerto Rico, but not the U.S. Constitution. The liberated had lost the right of self-determination.[56]

Part *2*

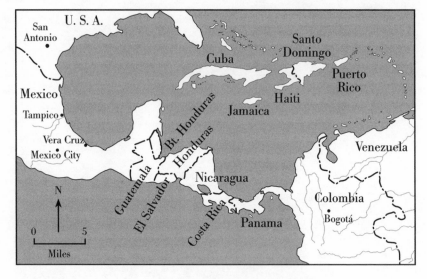

2. The Caribbean and Central America on the Eve of World War I

3

The End of the Long Century

In 1900 the America of Roosevelt and the America of Martí displayed contradictory features. Even in the most advanced countries, social commentators routinely described the ill effects of uneven social and economic change attributable to industrialization. Although reform movements and rebellions had challenged entrenched interests, political leaders continued to represent the propertied rather than the laborer and the dispossessed. In some places, the result of these confrontations was social revolution, as in Mexico after 1910, or a millenarian movement, as in the rebellion in the Brazilian backlands in the 1890s. More often, violent protest became the organized and occasionally spontaneous uprisings of laborers in the industrial workplace. In this hemispheric portrait, the United States, as Martí had warned, served as the willing ally of unpopular and repressive governments and the violator of national sovereignty and self-determination in the name of order and stability and civilization and progress.[1]

A contradictory but equally plausible image is a hemisphere of enormous cultural vitality, with dramatic changes in transportation, technology, and communication and extraordinary improvements in health and sanitation, local governments more attentive than ever to the pressing demands for urban planning and beautification as well as municipal services, state and national governments more responsive to the needs for regulation and reform, and urban social workers and volunteers committed to human development and the amelioration of the quality of life for urban workers and immigrants. The political and social literature of the age exhibited strong tones of racial pessimism, undeniably, but more often it could be powerful and compelling in its indictment of social injustice. Perhaps the most dramatic changes had occurred in the cities. At 1870, despite the growth of technology and trade, the quality of urban life, especially in Latin America's capital cities, lagged behind that of western Europe. By 1900, the integration of Latin America more fully into the global economy enabled middle-class residents of its capital cities to enjoy many of the amenities common to European and North American cities.[2]

The most impressive economic growth in the hemisphere had occurred in the United States, where the value added by industrial production had tripled and that of agricultural output had almost doubled in the last two decades of the nineteenth century. Its domestic corporate empire had grown not so much by territorial expansion and government aid as by the accumulation of investment capital from securities markets, banks, and insurance companies, by technological and scientific achievements that kept down costs and increased productivity, and especially by the acquisition of a labor force from natural increase and foreign immigration. Latin America's experience after midcentury did not reach these standards, of course, but the economic changes were impressive, particularly when compared with the continent's dreary political and economic conditions at independence. From midcentury and above all in the last quarter of the nineteenth century, Latin America rejoined the world economy. Its population doubled from thirty to sixty million, and some of its capital cities, Mexico City and Buenos Aires, for example, evolved into modern metropolises rivaling Paris, London, and New York. Its exports of primary products fueled an economic growth that brought unparalleled wealth to a small elite and the promise of a better life to an emerging middle class, the primary beneficiaries of the resurgence of European lending—principally British in South America and, later, French, German, and North American—and the demand for Latin American natural resources and agricultural products.[3]

Although a generation of poets and essayists disdained the material—but not the technological—culture of North America, the continuing lag of the continent's economy remained an embarrassment. Scholars point to the reflexive character of Latin American economies, noting the critical role of foreign trade and dependence on exports for income; the concentration of landownership, a problem attributed less to an unfavorable person/land ratio than to the difficulty of access to land and a system of land tenure that discouraged smallholdings; and the reluctance of employers to permit real wages to rise. Fundamentally related to this trend was the survival and even strengthening of "notable family" networks despite the growth of the national government bureaucracy, changing cultural expressions that often denigrated the traditional values identified with the old families, and the growing sense that social relations were shaped less by familial and obligatory ties than by the discourse of the public realm. Domestic economies were intentionally permitted to lag behind, thus releasing more of the available capital for the use of the foreign sector and, except in southern Brazil and the River Plate area, keeping wages low. In many rural areas, subsistence agriculture coexisted with large haciendas and plantations. In the sugar zones of the British Caribbean, including British Guiana, the situation was acute after the 1880s, when the lowering of subsidies and the dumping of European beet sugar drove smaller and less efficient producers into poverty or bankruptcy. Wages dropped precipitously amid complaints about labor shortages from the surviving plantations and the competing peasant farms. Importation of mostly Indian agricultural laborers ameliorated this condition to some degree, and after 1904 opportunities for West Indians in the construction of the Panama Canal provided labor opportunities for significant numbers of British West Indians. Yet the reality for both the British and French Caribbean was an uncertain economic future. The most aggressive economic and political player in the region after 1900 was the United States.[4]

The Liberal Predicament

Liberals had played a critical if controversial role in the shaping of this new hemispheric economic and social order, and in the early years of the twentieth century they confronted some disturbing predicaments about the disruptive forces unleashed by the second industrial revolution. One tenet of liberalism, especially as the doctrine developed in the United States, held that capitalism would act as a stabilizing force in society because it offered opportunity to the community of talents, yet exercised subtle but effective coercive pressure on the industrial labor force. In actuality, a market economy could be socially destabilizing and often chaotic, prompting unsettling reminders of the uncertainties of the revolutionary age. In the process, liberalism underwent a substantive transformation, but the changes assumed differing forms and nuances throughout the Americas and sometimes even within a single country. They were most pronounced in the United States, where the protean character of liberal thinking could incorporate not only those who called for political non-interference on social issues, respect for property rights, white supremacy, and the use of police and perhaps even the military to bring order to the industrial workplace but also those who wished to preserve the existing order but who recognized the strategic importance of adapting to their own needs the values of middle-class reformers and even socialists. Although middle classes recognized the social inequities of modern industrial society, they also harbored genuine fears about the disruptive forces of socialism and the collective power of labor, whose ranks expanded from 500,000 to 2.5 million from 1898 to 1915 and whose behavior became increasingly radical. Socialists played a critical role in mobilizing labor, both within and outside the American Federation of Labor. In 1909 the most militant socialists helped to organize the International Workers of the World, the Wobblies, who decried the "wage slavery" of capitalism and exhorted workers of the world to unite.[5]

Presumably, the adaptability and flexibility of the new politics would offer a means of developing the twin concepts of social efficiency and social engineering together with the corporate gospel of industrial engineering and efficiency into the transforming political force of Progressivism. Those most concerned with social justice at the local level, particularly in the industrial cities of the northeast and upper midwest, looked across the Atlantic to England and especially to Germany for inspiration. Within the United States, then, the models of liberalism ranged across the political spectrum, from the provincial laissez-faire and racist variety identified largely with the South to those grassroots Progressives who were kindred spirits of European social democrats. In the post-1898 evolution of U.S. relations with the other countries of the Americas, however, the ideology of liberalism was shorn of its diversity and readily lent itself to what Emily Rosenberg has aptly described as "liberal-developmentalism," a phrase that encompassed not only such traditional notions as free trade but also the belief that "other nations could and should replicate America's own developmental experience."[6]

In the early years of the twentieth century North Americans pursued these goals with a determination rivaling that of the British. In November 1906, following his return from the Third International Conference of American States at Rio de Janeiro, Secretary of State Elihu Root outlined the reasons for a more aggressive trade policy in a speech at the Trans-Mississippi Commercial Congress in Kansas City. After more than a century of pouring energies and resources (and the capital and labor of the world) into national development, the United States had arrived at a point where its surplus energy and its surplus capital required an outlet. South America seemed a logical place for U.S. attention. At a time when both editorial cartoons and serious commentary often made little distinction between the political and economic conditions of Argentina and Nicaragua, Root argued that South America had followed the U.S. example in its evolution from militarism to industrialism. What was now required was an expansion of U.S. banking facilities in the region to afford not only a basis for enlarging trade with South America but also to better serve those North American entrepreneurs who had already established businesses there, and especially to serve as an alternative to the European banking establishments. The United States, more advanced industrially than its European rivals and with as many goods to sell, suffered from the lack of U.S. branch banks in South America. "We are living in a world not of natural competition" Root noted, "but of subsidized competition."[7]

Despite persistent Latin suspicions about U.S. motives in the Caribbean and Central America, Root believed that enhanced trade with South America coupled with recognition of its achievements would lay the foundation for hemispheric unity. He was certainly alert to the importance of distinguishing between South and Central Americans. In this articulation of Pan-Americanism, South Americans would acquiesce and perhaps even support U.S. intervention in the Caribbean and Central America because they would see the hemisphere as North Americans saw it: a vast culturally and politically differentiated continent in which some countries had reached a stage of development that warranted respect and full admission into the hemispheric fraternity but in which others lagged behind and required tutelage or even force to be brought into line. This was the destiny of a continent.[8]

No other liberalism in the Americas displayed such a militant character. Under the influence of Wilfred Laurier, who acquired the sobriquet "the first Canadian," liberalism in Canada assumed an unusual tolerance in the cause of economic development and national unity. From 1896 to 1911, Canada enjoyed a wheat boom. The resulting prosperity in turn fueled immigration and investment and thus refuted earlier predictions of the inevitable disintegration of the Canadian nation. Yet Laurier came increasingly under fire from those who believed his nineteenth-century brand of liberalism was becoming irrelevant. Small farmers and labor leaders were especially outspoken. In the first decade of the century, Canadian labor unions, 90 percent of which were affiliated with the conservative U.S. American Federation of Labor, grew phenomenally and participated in more than a thousand labor disputes. There were other complainants as well: French-Canadian nationalists wary about the future of their "distinct society" at a time of increased migration from central and eastern Europe; women demanding the vote; urban social reformers alarmed over the mushrooming of slums. Like liberals in the United States, Laurier began to sense that the inequalities and materialism of the new era required new social policies, but he was too much a product of nineteenth-century thinking to adapt his philosophy to fit contemporary political fashions.[9]

Liberals in Latin America exalted material improvement, pluralism, and rationalism, though more often than not they followed the trends in Europe rather than those in the United States. In the final decades of the nineteenth century, the older liberal belief that the small property holder and those who embodied the work ethic formed the foundation for economic progress and social harmony withered before the reality of a countryside made up of large landholders and dispossessed rural peoples who persistently and sometimes effectively challenged their authority. As the export economy regained strength, liberals who railed against large landholding (latifundia) sought to achieve the "natural" economic order by ridding society of the inherited privileges from colonial days. In some countries, notably Argentina, they called for colonization of the countryside by immigrant farmers. But the effect of much of their labors was to undermine the communal landholding of indigenous people and, when colonization schemes failed to work out as planned, to accelerate the rural tendency toward larger estates. As Argentina became more a European and less a Latin American nation, those who speculated on its future agreed that the persistence of large landholdings tarnished its progress, yet they were reluctant to do anything about it.[10]

The once-sacrosanct liberal antagonism to a strong central state weakened as the commitment to laissez-faire economics gained more liberal adherents. In Peru and Bolivia, two countries that had suffered a humiliating defeat in the War of the Pacific and in which the indigenous population was too large to be ignored, the liberal revolution followed yet a different course. With the timely assistance of Aymara Indians, Bolivia's liberals took advantage of a political crisis to gain power and then, in the cause of modernizing the country, betrayed their promises to restore the federal system. When the Aymaras revolted against the new regime, they were crushed. Liberals ruled Bolivia essentially unchallenged for the first two decades of the twentieth century, years when the rapid development of tin mining and railroad building persuaded some U.S. observers that Bolivia's more progressive leaders readily accepted North American cultural values. For a brief time at the end of the nineteenth century, Peru under Nicolás Piérola vigorously pursued a modernization strategy based on autonomous development and incorporation of the Indian into national life. By the time Augusto B. Leguía became president in 1908, however, U.S. companies and North Americans had assumed a place in national life that would have been unthinkable a generation earlier.[11]

From the U.S. perspective, the most promising changes in hemispheric relations were not political or cultural but economic and commercial. From the 1880s until the onset of World War I, U.S. exports to Latin America and the Caribbean soared by 600 percent, and direct investments grew from a comparatively modest $300 million on the eve of the war with Spain to $1.2 billion by 1914. In some countries, above all Cuba and Mexico, and in some industries, such as sugar, bananas, mining and petroleum, North American investments and companies constituted a presumably necessary force for the economic development of the nation. In the early years of the century, two-thirds of these investments and the majority of the trade lay with Mexico and the Caribbean Basin, the territorial domain of the postwar informal U.S. empire. But a far more impressive change in the U.S. economic presence occurred in South America. From 1897 to 1914, when the Panama Canal opened, U.S. investments in South America had surged from $38 million to $323 million, modest by comparison with the British stake but crucial to the surge in U.S. investments in the southern continent after World War I.[12]

Yet almost everywhere in the Western Hemisphere that U.S. capital and companies penetrated, liberals often divided over their benefits not only to the nation but to their own political future. Some believed that a close identification with either the U.S. government or North Americans might prove not only politically embarrassing but risky. For others, cultural differences were crucial. Some hemispheric liberals responded to those credos North Americans exalted, certainly, but others heartened to *Hispanismo,* a branch of Spanish liberalism that stressed social unity and solidarity. In its acceptance of social hierarchy, Hispanismo reinforced the values of traditional society, emphasized education, supported labor unions and the rights of women, and disdained the vulgar materialism a generation of Latin American writers often identified with the United States while expressing admiration for its industrial advances and presumed ability to reconcile equality with liberty. On the eve of World War I, the Peruvian Francisco García Calderón expressed the dilemma confronting a generation of Latin Americans wanting to modernize economies without yielding too much of their soul or their sovereignty.[13]

The implications of the North American connection differed from country to country. Central Americans might agree about the role of the state in the

economy, but in Nicaragua and Honduras they divided sharply and often violently over the impact of U.S. entrepreneurs and companies, particularly the
banana companies—United Fruit and, later, Standard and Cuyamel. By far the
largest and most controversial of these companies was the United Fruit Company (UFCO), formed in 1899 by Lorenzo Baker, a sea captain and trader, Andrew Preston, a New England banker, and Minor Keith, a railroader who had
started growing bananas in Costa Rica. In Costa Rica, political elites believed
they had effectively neutralized UFCO's impact by a mutually beneficial con-
tractual arrangement permitting the company to have considerable authority
in the sparsely populated Caribbean coastal plain but not in the interior. National politics did not focus on the banana enclaves.[14]

In Nicaragua and Honduras, on the other hand, the banana companies profoundly disrupted the political, economic, and social landscape. There were
predictable disputes in national assemblies over the granting of concessions
and tax policy; the companies, in turn, complained ceaselessly about discrim-
inatory practices favoring nationals and about forced loans to political aspi-
rants. Not surprisingly, the companies plunged into local politics by supporting (to the extent of subsidizing rebellion) those willing to give them favors. In
Nicaragua, Zelaya at first favored U.S. companies and granted North American entrepreneurs valuable concessions, but his political allies soon began to
complain that neither they nor Nicaragua benefited that much from their
operations. To make matters worse for the Nicaraguan leader, local planters
resentful of UFCO's growing domination began destroying the crops of Nicaraguans who sold to the company. Zelaya put down the movement, but in doing
so he alienated both Nicaraguans and the U.S. government, who blamed him
for his inability to maintain order within the country. As relations among
Zelaya, the banana barons, and the U.S. government worsened, UFCO began
shifting its operations into northern Honduras, where the Vaccaro brothers
had been operating banana plantations since 1899. Honduran elites proved
more hospitable to U.S. banana growers for several reasons: they had little financial interest in the banana regions of the north coast, and bananas provided the country with prospects for developing an export economy.[15]

Development of the coffee economy in the late nineteenth century paralleled
the maturation of a coffee culture, enabling the state to assert political and economic power in rural areas and to mold nations from the chaotic nineteenth-
century experience. The banana companies threatened this process. Banana
plantations functioned as business enterprises run by people who demanded
total managerial control, a compliant labor force, and little interference from

the capital in their operations. They exercised an inordinate control over local suppliers, laborers, and growers. Within the enclave they had their own hospitals, schools, social organizations, and money. They effectively dominated local markets by supplying urban services—railroads, docks, ports, and subsidiary maritime companies. They fashioned alliances with local landlords. These conditions severely limited the national development plans of the state.[16]

Economic progress in Latin America and the Caribbean posed greater dilemmas for liberals and reformers of other persuasions as well. Cultural disparities seemed the most pronounced. The Uruguayan essayist José Enrique Rodó perhaps best described the cultural dissonance between Protestant, material North America and Catholic, spiritual Latin America in his remarkably influential book *Ariel*. Rodó effectively adapted Martí's inscription of "our America" and called for a "true statue of liberty" adorned by Ariel, a character from Shakespeare's *The Tempest*, whose figure exalted spirit, beauty, and fruitful leisure. Rodó's nuanced condemnation of material culture prompted an enthusiastic response among a generation of Latin American literati, but his warning also appealed to a significant minority of U.S. cultural elites who decried the vulgarity and coarseness of the times. Democracies required enlightened aristocracies to lead them. Like Rodó, these North American Arielists remained suspicious of the beneficial effects of "economism"—the belief that potentially rebellious workers of the industrial age could be placated through material rewards—on the grounds that the continuing escalation of wants and the inability of society to satisfy the demands of ordinary people would lead to unrest and disorders that governments might not be able to control. Contrary to the prevailing wisdom, then, social stability depended on nonmaterial inducements to human betterment.[17]

By these standards, the cultural elites believed that government and laws were products of history, not reason. Thus, race and ethnicity assumed a critical place in the calculations of Arielists as well as of those who disdained the term. Roosevelt pondered the implications of "race suicide" for the progress of the United States, and the Argentine Carlos Bunge described a continental "tower of Babel" suffering from the impurities of racial miscegenation. Self-denigration was more extreme in *Pueblo Enfermo* (Sick people), the classic work of the Bolivian critic Alcibiades Argüedas, who blamed the Indian and the mixed-race Bolivian *cholo* for the country's backwardness. García Calderón echoed a similar pessimism, as did the first generation of Brazil's republican messiahs, who welcomed the waves of white European immigrants as the economic and especially the racial salvation of the nation.[18]

Pan-American Economic Union and Hemispheric Empire

Just as troubling was the realization that the chaos endemic to the nineteenth-century industrial workplace and market had persisted into the twentieth century. No one sensed this more keenly than Roosevelt, the architect of U.S. hemispheric empire and, in unappreciated ways, the kindred spirit of those Latin American and Caribbean elites who disdained his cultural values and routinely condemned his bullying tactics but shared his fears about the explosive and unpredictable forces still troubling the hemisphere. Neither his determination to dominate the weak nor his resolve to prove his manliness nor his compulsion to validate American exceptionalism concerned him as much as his belief that the chaos and lawlessness he had witnessed in the Dakotas and in the industrial workplace plagued the Caribbean and Central America.

Though a cultural elitist, Roosevelt shared with Martí an instinctive fear of the European threat in the Americas. What drove him to act in a succession of hemispheric crises—in Venezuela in 1902–03, in Panama in November 1903, in the Dominican Republic in 1904–05, in Cuba in 1905–06, and in Central America in 1906–07—was fear of what might happen if he did not act. For Roosevelt, failure to respond, especially in those regions of the hemisphere still plagued by political and social instability, served only to reward those who believed they could take power through either violent means or invited European, read German, intervention. The logic of intervention and the antirevolutionary impulses associated with it, however frustrating and dangerous the consequences, made sense to Roosevelt, particularly when he invoked the lessons of the U.S. Civil War and the price a generation of North Americans had paid to deny the Confederacy's claim of a right to revolution. Progress and unity typified the advanced societies and marked their ranking on the scale of civilizations, and it was silly to pretend that all nations were equal before the international bar of justice.[19]

An early test of Roosevelt's resolve and style occurred during the 1902–03 Venezuelan debt crisis, in which naval forces of Germany and Great Britain (later joined by Italy) blockaded the Venezuelan coast in retaliation for Venezuela's default on its international obligations and abuse of German and British nationals. In the months prior to the blockade, prominent U.S. officials, including Roosevelt and Secretary of State John Hay acquiesced in the action on the grounds that Latin American governments that did not pay their international obligations must be taught a lesson. After all, the Venezuelan miscreant, Cipriano Castro, had tweaked the noses of both John Bull and Uncle Sam with his public criticisms of Anglo-Saxon imperialism in Guiana, the venue for an earlier British–Venezuelan confrontation in 1895, and in Cuba, whose independence the Venezuelans had championed. The blockade heightened apprehensions about European political and military involvement in a region now considered vital to U.S. strategic interests and prompted reminders that both Kaiser Wilhelm and Queen Victoria had criticized the U.S. government for its harassment of Spain in 1898. Roosevelt and most of his advisors deemed Germany the greater menace because the kaiser's government in South America and in the Caribbean appeared to challenge the United States in provocative and not easily predictable ways, thus reinforcing Roosevelt's instinctive fears that if he did not act the Germans would quickly do something in the hemisphere that would "make us put up or shut up on the Monroe Doctrine." After the war with Spain, British–U.S. relations had noticeably improved when the British had acquiesced in Washington's pressures for an isthmian canal built and controlled by the United States. Relations with Germany rapidly worsened as the Germans expanded their cultural and military missions in Argentina, Chile, Brazil, and Central America and sought naval leases in the Caribbean. Germany even had a contingency plan for war with the United States, Operation Plan III, which called for an invasion of Puerto Rico and from there an assault on the mainland. In 1902, as Castro's defiance heightened, the General Board of the U.S. Navy drew up a plan for a defense of the Venezuelan coast.[20]

There was no military confrontation, and the tension eased when the contending governments agreed to adjudication of the dispute by the Hague Court. For Roosevelt, the entire affair demonstrated the need for a statement warning European powers about taking similar action while at the same time assuring them that the United States would not permit Latin American governments to renege on their international obligations. But the logic of such a policy could be turned on its head because it made the United States not only a more important participant in the international affairs of Latin American debtor countries but a player in their domestic politics and society as well. In December 1902, Foreign Minister Luís M. Drago of Argentina suggested an alternative when he proposed to the U.S. government that the use of armed force by European powers against a Western hemispheric nation to collect a debt should be prohibited. What he had in mind was not an addition to international law but an economic corollary to the Monroe Doctrine, or the Pan-Americanization of what had always been a unilateral policy.[21]

Two years later, embroiled in yet another Caribbean debt crisis with both domestic and international political implications, Roosevelt gave Drago his

answer. In October 1903, the Dominican Republic collapsed in civil war after a falling out between General Carlos Morales and his political mentor,
Juan Isidro Jiménez. When Morales declared himself chief executive, Jiménez
promptly responded by launching his own rebellion. Harassed by political enemies as well as foreign lenders—the republic had a foreign debt of $32 mil-
lion, two-thirds of it owed to European creditors—Morales turned to the only
benefactor in sight, the U.S. government. Roosevelt assured a correspondent
he had no intention of annexing the beleaguered country, but because it was
"drifting into chaos" the United States must assume a protective role over the
smaller countries of the Caribbean.[22]

In the same month Roosevelt wrote those words, February 1904, a special
tribunal established by the Hague convention declared that Venezuela must
pay the blockading nations *before* the republic's other lenders. The Dominican
situation was different in one important respect. In the Dominican Republic,
U.S. naval officers regularly landed troops in the coastal cities and had at their
service an experienced and usually reliable ally, the San Domingo Improvement Company, which had been operating in the republic for several generations. Roosevelt thus could be more assertive in dealing with the Dominican
Republic. But he waited until he was safely elected in November 1904 to deliver his oft-cited and still controversial corollary to the Monroe Doctrine:
"Chronic wrongdoing, or an impotence which results in a general loosening
of the ties of civilized society, may in America, as elsewhere, ultimately require intervention by some civilized nation, and in the Western Hemisphere
the adherence of the United States, however reluctantly, in flagrant cases of
such wrongdoing or impotence, to the exercise of an international police
power."[23]

In the early months of 1905 Roosevelt worked out an executive agreement
with his Dominican counterpart, establishing the Dominican customs receivership and informally establishing what would later be called dollar diplomacy, the belief that financial controls and fundamental safeguards for foreign investors would prove as effective as military intervention in achieving
political stability. The customs receivership would be encapsulated in a treaty
in 1907, approved reluctantly only after Root mollified a group of U.S. senators
with assurances that the arrangement was not the same thing as a protectorate. More serious are charges that Roosevelt used the Dominican crisis to
undermine Drago's 1902 proposal for an *economic* corollary to the Monroe
Doctrine, thus distancing the United States even farther from its hemispheric
neighbors. At the 1906 Conference of American States in Rio de Janeiro, Latin

American resentments over the Roosevelt Corollary and U.S. interference in the internal affairs of Caribbean states had become so widespread that the U.S. delegation, represented by Root, who was making an official tour of South America, tried to expunge politically sensitive issues from the agenda. With the timely assistance of the Brazilian foreign minister, Joaquim Nabuco, Root was able to assuage the ill feelings of Latin American delegates by reassuring them that the United States sought neither territory nor domination within the Western Hemisphere and believed in the juridical equality of all hemispheric states. His speech to the delegates expressed sentiments that sharply diverged from those conveyed in Roosevelt's Corollary: "We wish for no victories but those of peace; for no territory except our own; for no sovereignty except the sovereignty over ourselves."[24]

North American and Latin American students of this era often cite the corollary as yet another instance of U.S. rejection of hemispheric cooperation and even a reversal of what President Monroe had presumably meant in his famous message of 1823 in which he warned against future European territorial expansion in the New World. But neither Monroe's nor Roosevelt's generation of U.S. leaders (nor Spanish-American ones, for that matter) applied the principles of Monroe's statement to the Caribbean without qualification. Cultural historians sometimes attribute Roosevelt's pledge about taking on the role of policeman to the reaffirmation of the dictates of manliness, threat of force, and the destiny of the white race to uplift backward and childlike peoples. To these subsumed motives must be added the fear of anarchy his generation instinctively attributed to the Caribbean and the parallel belief that the United States could not expect other hemispheric governments to assist Washington in containing it.[25]

Argentine leaders, frankly, surpassed their U.S counterparts in their suspicions of Drago's proposal. At the 1889 Pan-American Conference, Roque Sáenz Peña, the Argentine delegate and future president had led Latin American delegates in their overwhelming rejection of Secretary of State Blaine's call for a hemispheric customs union. Rejecting Blaine's appeal to regionalism—"America for the Americans"—Sáenz had declared, "America for all mankind." He explained, "What I lack is not love for America but suspicion and ingratitude toward Europe." Argentina's position on the issue of Pan-American cooperation and its faith in an international system directed by Europe were less philosophical than practical: Argentine trade patterns, cultural preferences, and source of immigrant labor lay with Europe. There was an inevitable cost to such an orientation, for it meant that Argentines believed the European connection and the nation's place in the international division of labor would be sufficient to supply their needs. Argentina could remain on the margins of the international system without having to assume the responsibilities of a world power.[26]

The Chileans and the Brazilians did not make the same mistake in dealing with the North Americans. Of the two, the Chileans had the more difficult adjustment. In 1891 U.S. meddling in the Chilean civil war had created a war scare that had ended in Chile's humiliation. Chileans heartened to Washington's opposition on the Calvo Clause, which required foreigners to settle their pecuniary claims in national courts, on the grounds that some countries were too unstable, and then they just as quickly cooled when they feared the United States favored Peru in the Tacna-Arica dispute, a legacy of the War of the Pacific. Root mollified the Chileans with soothing words during his 1906 South American tour. The Brazilians rarely did such flip-flopping in their dealings with the North Americans. Indeed, an informal Brazilian–United States alliance took form in these years, owing largely to the labors of a remarkable Brazilian foreign minister, José Maria da Silva Paranhos, Jr., the Baron do Rio-Branco. Rio-Branco irritated Brazil's South American neighbors with his public comments supporting U.S. intervention in the Caribbean and the Roosevelt Corollary and at the same time managed to retain and even strengthen the vital European connection.[27]

Some welcomed the North American presence; others were apprehensive. In the Panamanian isthmus social conservatives often agreed with Liberals about separation from Colombia but did not share their convictions about a truly independent government and a canal that might be built with North American help but not at the price of Panamanian sovereignty. Both were certainly familiar with the U.S. presence in the isthmus but drew very different meanings from the experience. From the 1840s until 1902, the United States had intervened on the Panamanian isthmus more than a dozen times (the largest landing had occurred in 1885), each time relying on a clause in an 1846 treaty with Colombia permitting the use of troops to safeguard the "neutrality" of the transisthmian passageway. In 1899, as Colombia collapsed in civil conflict during the Thousand Day War, isthmian secessionists continually intrigued and plotted to create a Panamanian republic. Over the next two years, the United States obtained through negotiation with Great Britain the unilateral right to construct an isthmian canal, and rival advocates of a Panamanian and a Nicaraguan canal conducted a ferocious political battle in Washington, New York, Paris, and Panama City. Roosevelt displayed no noticeable preference for either route, but when Congress finally authorized him to move on the measure early in 1902, it stipulated that he must achieve an agreement with Colombia for the construction of a canal across Panama within a reasonable time. Failure to do so meant that the venue would shift to Nicaragua. This stipulation in effect assured that he would move aggressively.[28]

Such questions seemed trivial when compared with the troubles of Roosevelt's Colombian counterpart, José Manuel Marroquín, a Conservative who had taken power in 1900 during the early months of the Thousand Day War. By fall 1902, as negotiations with the U.S. government were under way in Washington, Marroquín's forces appeared to be winning the civil war everywhere except in Panama, where Liberal forces had been victorious save for the one place that really mattered to them—the transit zone, where the U.S. government could deny them a victory. This rebellion ended with a negotiated truce signed aboard the U.S.S. *Wisconsin* in November, but the real victor was neither the Colombian government nor those Liberals who wanted to create a Panamanian nation. Victoriano Lorenzo, an Indian from Penonomé who had commanded a guerrilla army of *cholos* (mixed-blood peoples) in the war, denounced the peace accord, was captured and executed. His death and the cause he spoke for would be forgotten in the United States and even in Bogotá, but not in Panama.[29]

The defeat of the Liberal rebellion proved to be a shallow triumph for Marroquín, as his emissaries in Washington, D.C., had spent most of the year proposing treaty drafts that were summarily rejected by Hay. And neither Marroquín nor his negotiators were a match for the indefatigable Philippe Bunau-Varilla, a lobbyist committed to persuading the U.S. government to complete the abandoned French canal project in Panama in order to recoup some of the losses and salvage French pride. Bunau-Varilla noised a variety of disquieting tales among prominent Panamanians, among them, a not-improbable story that Marroquín's dalliance would ruin Panama's chances for a canal—unless, of course, Panama became an independent country. When the negotiations concluded in early 1903, Roosevelt finally had an agreement with Colombia, the Hay-Herrán Treaty, but it was not altogether everything he wanted—transfer of the French concession, a six-mile-wide zone, a hundred-year renewable lease, a $10-million lump sum payment, a $250,000 annual rental, and shared jurisdiction and civil administration. The U.S. Senate took less than sixty days to approve the treaty. Colombia's senate waited until July to take up the measure and, following a month-long debate, unanimously rejected it.[30]

Roosevelt was skeptical about shifting to the Nicaraguan route, as the Senate legislation required him to do if negotiations with Colombia fell through. That would have meant dealing with Liberal president José Santos Zelaya of Nicaragua, who desperately wanted the canal for his country but could be as combative as Roosevelt in his dealings with foreign governments. Few in the U.S. government cared for Zelaya, who harassed his Conservative enemies, meddled in the political affairs of his neighbors, and handed out lucrative concessions to his political cronies. When it became clear to him that Roosevelt favored Panama over Nicaragua for a canal route, he called a conference of the isthmian heads of state in Corinto. All save his archenemy President Manuel Estrada Cabrera of Guatemala showed up to give their approval to Zelaya's plan for isthmian peace: compulsory arbitration of regional disputes and a parallel affirmation by the Nicaraguan president that he would refrain from meddling in the internal political affairs of his neighbors. They assented not because they trusted Zelaya but naively believed such an arrangement would forestall European intervention to collect debts. To his credit, the Corinto treaty brought the isthmus four years of a fragile peace, but it also meant that Zelaya had thrown down the gauntlet to the United States.[31]

Roosevelt would first have to find a way to make the Panama route a reality. Legally bound by the 1846 treaty to guarantee Colombian sovereignty over the transit route, he could not act, at least not until others acted. The Panamanian revolution, then, was a conspiracy hatched not in Washington, D.C., but in Panama by Conservatives who were fearful that the Yankees would build the canal across Nicaragua and that Panama would lose out on the commercial bounty the waterway would bring. Liberals bemoaned the whittling away of the province's autonomy, but the Conservative conspirators, among them, Manuel Amador, one of the founders of the republic, could act. They had help from the New York City attorney William Nelson Cromwell and especially from Bunau-Varilla, who obtained from Hay and Roosevelt something just as vital as money and weapons: a scarcely disguised acknowledgment that if the Panamanians started something the U.S. government would not let them down. The opportunistic Bunau-Varilla gave Amador everything he needed save a loaded pistol: a declaration of independence, a flag, a communications code, military plans, promises of money, all conditional on Amador's assurance that the first representative of the republic of Panama to the United States would be Bunau-Varilla.[32]

This was not the first time that Caribbean revolutionaries had been persuaded that their future ultimately depended on a powerful benefactor, but the Panamanian conspirators could not imagine what the costs of this alliance would be. A U.S. warship docked at Colón on November 2 to safeguard the transit route in the event of disturbances. The revolt came off the following day with the loss of only one person, a Chinese laundryman, and the United States formally recognized the independence of Panama on November 6. As more U.S. warships arrived, the designs of the Panamanian founders began to unravel. Like a generation of Cuban conspirators who had fashioned an alliance with Washington, the Panamanians were quickly reminded that they entered the assembly of hemispheric republics not as sovereign equals but as wards of the United States. Less than two weeks after the recognition of independence, the Panamanians had a canal treaty with their protectors, a treaty predictably more generous to the United States than the one rejected by the Colombian Senate. The Panamanian negotiator was Bunau-Varilla, a Frenchman, not a Panamanian. He readily acceded to Secretary of State John Hay's every wish. Perhaps the most damning clause from the Panamanian point of view was the grant to the United States of virtual sovereign rights in the Canal Zone. A Panamanian delegation arrived within hours after Hay and Bunau-Varilla had signed the document. Its members were aghast at the terms, but the Frenchman warned them that independence depended on prompt ratification of the treaty by Panama. In early December, the Panamanian assembly acquiesced.[33]

The loss was doubly humiliating even to those Colombians who had long anticipated the event because it had occurred so suddenly. Rafael Reyes, a moderate Colombian Conservative who became president in 1904, blamed the defeat on the ideological and social divisions within Colombia and the nation's failure to keep pace with the rapid technological changes of the age. As president, Reyes brought fundamental changes to Colombia. He professionalized the military, provided the opposition Liberals with appointments in his government, and infuriated some Conservatives by replacing the Congress (where they dominated) with a national assembly that brought the Liberals back into national political life. In the economy he emulated the Mexican model by encouraging rail construction, created a Ministry of Public Works, and reestablished Colombia's international credit rating. In this recovery, the United States played an important role, as purchaser of Colombian exports and as supplier of capital for Colombian development. "We must study to understand the exact character, position, and power of the American nation," Reyes told Colombian politicians still infuriated over the U.S. role in the Panamanian revolution. In early 1909, he submitted to the Colombian assembly two treaties of reconciliation—one with the United States, a second with Panama—by which

Colombia would receive a modest indemnity for the loss of Panama in return for recognizing its independence. The ensuing debate revived bitter memories of the nation's humiliation. In the middle of the year, Reyes stepped down and voluntarily left the country, a victim of the only unifying nationalist passion of his generation.[34]

For most North and Latin Americans, the birthing of Panama and the building of the canal became the acknowledged metonym for Americanization, encapsulating everything from the triumph over nature to the arrogant display of power. But Cuba, not Panama, perhaps best exemplified the character of U.S. empire and the North American presence in the hemisphere.

In 1902, there were two Cubas: one dreamed of the eradication of the humiliating Platt Amendment and the triumph of Cuba Libre; the other acquiesced in the U.S. presence as the only practical means of achieving independence. Those who belonged to the appeasing group moved easily among Cubans and North Americans, held U.S. passports, spoke English as naturally as Spanish, and acknowledged that the island's economic well-being and physical security depended on North American cooperation and the tutelage accompanying it. These Cubans played the most critical role in the early years of the republic because they occupied a "dual world of devotions" to the cause and values of Cuba Libre and to North American institutions. They were the hybrid nationalists, the self-appointed interpreters of the North American presence in the new Cuba. Tomás Estrada Palma, Cuba's first president, was perhaps the exemplar of this group. But they did not always speak for Cubans who decried the continuation of the old inequities and contradictions of Spanish Cuba in the republic and were prepared, if necessary, to confront the United States. In their thinking about the United States, Cubans formed contradictory values: a deep-seated resentment of the United States for its denial of their legitimate claims to self-determination and national identity and a parallel admiration of North American material culture.[35]

Of all the new imperial acquisitions, Cuba seemed the most secure because the island and its people were linked to the United States in myriad ways, not only through formal bonds such as the Platt Amendment and the Reciprocity Treaty of 1903 but through a host of economic and cultural prescriptions. To be successful a Cuban had to become *americanizado,* had not only to speak English but perhaps even to anglicize his given name. Tourists, missionaries, diplomats, and businessmen descended on the island. In the economic sphere, North Americans moved quickly into such vital areas as sugar, tobacco, trade, utilities, railroads, and banking. In some cases, to be sure, the process of Americanization required more than two decades to attain its full impact, but the impact of U.S. political, economic, and cultural power was sufficiently strong in the early days of the republic to provoke outbursts in the National Assembly against North American opportunists and even calls for a rebellion.[36]

The very degree of U.S. power and economic penetration of the Cuban polity made rebellion inevitable. Denied opportunity in the major sectors of the economy, Cubans instinctively looked to government as a place for employment and to politics as a route to advancement and power. Involvement in public life, then, was less a question of civic obligation or public service than of economic need. Because of the Platt Amendment and the commitment to intervene in Cuba's internal affairs to protect life, liberty, and property, the United States was not only an observer but a participant in the republic's distorted political system. For that reason it was vulnerable to the manipulations of the republic's calculating political contenders and the *differing* interpretations they gave to the Platt Amendment.[37]

How Cubans could use the Platt Amendment and the special relationship with the United States became clear in 1905, when Estrada Palma, the candidate of the Moderate Party, conducted an election campaign riddled with fraud and physical abuse of the Liberal opposition. Estrada believed the U.S. government would intervene to quash any rebellion against him. Liberals, however, read the Platt Amendment very differently. In their interpretation of its articles, the violence committed by Estrada's government obligated the United States to establish a Cuban government respectful of the property, liberty, and lives of all Cubans. When they were rebuffed, the Liberal candidate for president, José Miguel Gómez, sailed for New York to give speeches about U.S. responsibility for securing Cuban democracy. Throughout the remainder of 1905 and into 1906 there was sporadic violence in the island. Estrada held firm for several months, but by late summer the size and daring of rebel forces had obviously unsettled him, and he sent a frantic message to Washington requesting two U.S. warships, one at Havana and a second at Cienfuegos. The Cuban government, he explained, could no longer guarantee the safety of foreign property. Events in Cuba confirmed Roosevelt's somber judgments about the island's politics and Estrada's resolve. He privately complained of the island falling to "misrule and anarchy" because of the Liberal yet tried to conciliate both sides by dispatching Secretary of War William Howard Taft to Havana in a fruitless effort to broker a settlement. It was a mission virtually doomed from

the beginning, largely because the Liberals recognized that provoking another U.S. occupation of the island offered the best means for them to attain
political power.[38]

First, Cubans had to endure a second occupation in 1906, but the circumstances varied from those of 1898. McKinley had had no intention of transferring power directly from Spaniard to Cuban, nor did he have to because the
United States entered Cuba in 1898 not as liberator but as conqueror. In 1906
Roosevelt did not have this option, and he knew it. Although the provisional
government was made up largely of U.S. army officers, some with experience
in the Philippines, the president chose not to recall Leonard Wood as provisional governor lest he give his European and Senate critics an opportunity to
question his motives. Instead, he settled on Charles Magoon, a onetime Lincoln, Nebraska, lawyer and developer who had joined the closest thing to a
U.S. colonial office, the Bureau of Insular Affairs. Magoon had experience in
Cuba in 1899 and, later, as advisor to the Isthmian Canal Commission. One of
his tasks in Panama was to mollify Panamanian nationalists. Having these
skills, Roosevelt believed, Magoon was the ideal choice for what the president
had pledged to do in Cuba.[39]

Magoon was a good choice, particularly for the Liberal claimants to office.
As Marine contingents scurried into the countryside to disarm rebels and a coterie of U.S. army officers appointed to assist the five civilian secretaries of
government departments drafted an electoral code, advised on the reorgani-
zation of the demoralized rural guard, and handled a welter of claims for property losses, Magoon set about to accommodate the Liberals at every turn. Reforms came, but they either occurred too late or were cleverly altered to fit the
Liberals' agenda. By then, of course, most Cubans knew the occupation was
coming to an end. With every expectation of winning the political power denied them in 1905, Liberals had little incentive to abide by the provisions of the
new electoral code devised by Magoon's secretary of justice, Colonel Enoch
Crowder. As Roosevelt's presidency was ending, the new Cuban president,
José Miguel Gómez, escorted Magoon to a waiting U.S. battleship, the new
U.S.S. *Maine*. The Cuban sported a Panama hat and a broad grin. As he bade
Magoon farewell, Gómez proudly declared, "Once again we are free." His
friends knew what he meant.[40]

The triumph of Gómez opened up unprecedented opportunities for those
who sought public favor and employment. But it was not a victory for Cuba
Libre, especially not for the Afro-Cuban veterans of the war of liberation, who
found little opportunity in the restored republic. As veterans of the long

struggle for independence, Afro-Cubans became increasingly embittered over the continuing discrimination against people of color in the republic and created the Partido Independiente de Color (Independent party of color). During the almost three years of U.S. occupation, discontented Cuban veterans had won at least partial compensation for their years of service in the rebellion, but Afro-Cuban veterans still suffered from discrimination. In 1910, after the U.S. occupation ended, the Cuban government outlawed the Partido Independiente, jailing many of its followers on the grounds that the party was conspiring to wage a race war in order to seize power and create a black republic. Two years later, when Afro-Cuban leaders led an armed protest to restore the party's legality, the Cuban army crushed the revolt and killed most of the rebellious Afro-Cubans. Not since the Morant Bay uprising in Jamaica in 1865, when British officials ordered the killing and flogging of a thousand Afro-Jamaicans, had a government in the Caribbean waged such bloody retaliation against people of color. Ten years after its independence, Cubans remained racially divided and fearful of black rebellion.[41]

The Mexican Shock

Had the Cuban government not acted to deal with the Afro-Cuban revolt, U.S. leaders would have instinctively sought out someone more reliable to deal with the challenge. After all, Cuba was a U.S. protectorate, and when dissident groups, however justifiable their reasons for taking up arms, threatened to plunge society into chaos, the immediate issue was the restoration of order, not the right of rebellion or even of revolution. A generation that tolerated racial discrimination at home and sanctioned the use of force against strikers in the industrial workplace would not be unduly troubled by such severe measures.

For some liberals and many progressives in the United States, certainly, the use of force at home and even in the protectorates in the Caribbean did pose larger questions, not only about the means by which the United States exercised its controls—that is, the dispatch of troops versus the less direct but presumably no less effective method of economic influence—but the purpose of that power, particularly in those societies whose political and economic development lagged behind that of the United States and such contemporary modern hemispheric nations as Canada, Brazil, Argentina, and Chile. Herbert Croly, founder of the liberal journal the *New Republic*, believed in the necessity of a new hemispheric order. In a seminal book published in the year Roosevelt left the presidency, *The Promise of American Life,* Croly called for an

"American international system" in which the United States played a vital role as democratic nation with a legitimate colonial policy. An effective hemispheric system, Croly wrote, would inevitably confront disorder in certain states, but that "coercion should . . . be used only in the case of extreme necessity; and it would not be just to deprive the people of such states of the right of revolution, unless effective measures were at the same time taken to do away with the more or less legitimate excuses for revolutionary protest."[42]

Croly's articulation of a more purposeful imperial role for the United States in promoting democracy rather than protecting the interests of international business appealed to those progressives who were convinced that liberalism had lost its sense of democratic purpose at home and abroad, as did his belief that revolutionary discontent in the hemisphere could be contained by addressing the "legitimate excuses" that provoked people to violence in the first place. *The Promise of American Life* also offered some reassurance to those who had begun to doubt if the nation's nineteenth-century tradition of accommodating disparate immigrant cultures by the dual process of dispersal and gentler means of coercion could still work. Some social critics, Randolph Bourne, for example, exalted pluralism and spoke of a "federation of cultures," yet they did not go so far as to incorporate people of color in their vision of "transnational America" nor did they participate actively in the civic life of the country. If Croly's call for the furtherance of democracy through imperial design and economic integration sounded farfetched to those who worried about the costs of carrying out such a program, it was no less fanciful than the beliefs expressed by Norman Angell in his book *The Great Illusion* (1911). Angell contended that the new economic realities of an interdependent world made conflict for territorial gain or military rivalries among imperial European nations almost unthinkable.[43]

What neither Croly nor Angell clearly perceived was the imminent end of the nineteenth century in both Europe and the Americas. In Europe, the collapse occurred suddenly and dramatically in the guns of August 1914. In the Americas, contrastingly, the end of the nineteenth century can be attributed not to a single event but to a succession of crises that shook the political and social order that hemispheric liberals had forged to deal with the uncertainties and the opportunities created by the second industrial revolution. These crises beset the stronger and presumably more advanced hemispheric nations as well as the weaker ones.

In Argentina, conservative oligarchs who had manipulated the electoral system for a generation finally relented in 1912 to the pleas of reformers and accepted a new voting law that dramatically expanded the political power of the urban electorate. The man who pushed through the new law, Roque Sáenz Peña, made clear that its purpose was to impress the foreigner that Argentines were not turbulent and unpredictable like Central Americans. To Europeans and North Americans, Argentina had undergone a political and economic sea change in only one generation, yet on the eve of World War I it remained two nations. Buenos Aires and the east were centers of consumption and modernity and had close economic ties with Great Britain and cultural preferences for European, especially French, standards; the interior, which supplied food and raw materials, lagged far behind. Argentina's revolutionary generation had suffered civil war; the Generation of 1880 shared with liberal regimes everywhere a fear of social revolution, torn between those who wanted to change everything and those who wanted to change nothing. Though the closing of the frontier hit Argentines in much the same way as it did some North Americans, Argentines believed they might compensate for the scarcity of land by the abundant numbers of immigrant laborers. By 1912, however, the combination of poor harvests and organized rural protests of sharecroppers and tenants and the inadequacy of the state response to them called into question the liberal agenda enunciated by Sarmiento and the Generation of 1837 and recast by their successors, the Generation of 1880, in the late nineteenth century. Beneath the facade of prosperity lay a rural nation only partially integrated into the world market. Argentine liberalism and prosperity would survive for another two decades, but for those who looked closely at the national condition in 1912, there was little consolation in the myth of Argentine exceptionalism. For others, creation of the illusion of order and tradition served as reassurance against the perils of rapid change.[44]

In Brazil, similar fissures in the political culture did not always prompt similar responses. Its elites, including the coffee barons, moved into industry and commerce and fashioned alliances with immigrant industrialists. Like their Argentine counterparts, Brazilian industrialists imported their industrial workers, but in its repression of labor the Brazilian state was far more severe. Brazil's cultural elites, too, wished to project an image of progress and civilization that informed the world of the country's achievements and reminded Brazilians that the debilitating heritage of race and colonial backwardness could be overcome. Rejection of the Afro-Brazilian, as Joaquim Nabuco recognized, meant denial of the nation's only substantial culture. For Brazil's liberals, progress meant rejection of tradition, but unlike Argentina, Brazil had a tenacious rural folk who resisted incorporation into the modern economic and social order. Country people in the *sertão* (backlands), suspicious of the new republic and the secularization of national politics and culture, gathered at Canudos to build the new Zion. There was a social dimension to this conflict. As the economic situation in the sugar zones of the Brazilian northeast and the coffee plantations in the southwest deteriorated in the 1890s, rural workers began migrating to Canudos, which rapidly became a symbol of defiance to the republic. Frustrated in its initials efforts to dislodge them, the Brazilian military finally crushed the encampment at Canudos by leveling it and killing its defenders. An eyewitness, Euclydes da Cunha, justified the razing of the New Zion in disturbing phrases: "We are condemned to civilization. Either we shall progress or we shall perish. So much is certain. Our choice is clear."[45]

The years following the siege at Canudos proved relatively prosperous for Brazil, but economic development remained uneven and sporadic and the social impact often jarring to those who recalled the assurances and traditions identified with the monarchy. For one thing, Brazil experienced a rubber boom, which made millionaires of some entrepreneurs in Belém and Manaus, who paid wages of a dollar a day to an Indian rubber gatherer who in turn had to pay four times what a New Yorker paid for coffee, sugar, rice, and beans. All Brazil profited, but the neglect of other forest products and the sudden collapse of the boom in 1910 threw Brazil into a panic and the Amazonian cities of Belém and Manaus into depression. The economic crisis paralleled a political one, as Brazil selected a new president, Marshal Hermes da Fonseca, a military man and son of the republic's first president, in the now familiarly corrupt pattern of earlier elections; yet the disillusionment over the endemic corruption in the young republic, a legacy from the imperial era, differed from that of earlier years. Brazil's political reformers now discredited liberalism as an inappropriate ideology for the nation's problems and espoused a new philosophy of Brazil for the Brazilians. The old political order would still hold sway, of course, but in Brazil as well as in Argentina and Chile—countries singled out by U.S. leaders as having achieved an impressive level of political and economic development—social and cultural tensions had profoundly disturbed the political culture. Local bosses, almost always landowners, were attached to state governors and ultimately to the president in a symbiotic linking that made it possible to contain the explosive and sometimes violent forces at the local level.[46]

For Canadians and especially for the Liberal prime minister, Wilfred Laurier, the end of the old ways came with the proposed U.S. reciprocity treaty of

1911, which President Taft declared would make Canada an adjunct of the United States. In *The Promise of American Life,* Croly wrote prophetically that the incorporation of Canada into a North American continental empire would be difficult to achieve because of Canada's cultural ties to Great Britain. Even Samuel Gompers, whose views about the pursuit of empire had been tentative, endorsed continentalism as part of his dream of creating a world labor organization and defeating the Wobblies. Laurier, staking his political future on the treaty, approved the plan in the mistaken belief that Canada's principal hope for dealing with British indifference lay in developing the U.S. connection. A peaceful border, after all, would afford tremendous security to the British and constitute a unifying force within a country increasingly fragmented by regional and ethnic divisions. Canadian migration to the United States, an embarrassment for much of the nineteenth century, had diminished. North American farmers looked for the "last west" not within their own country but in Saskatchewan and Alberta, joining the larger numbers of U.S. capitalists Laurier had welcomed. Such was Laurier's dream that the twentieth century would be Canadian. Robert Borden, his opponent, won the election by reminding Canadian voters that the choice was between a future irredeemably shackled to the U.S. economy and one that preserved its historic ties with Britain. In reciprocity he sensed an even more insidious threat than formal annexation: the Americanization of the country would bring all the social ills and divisions of the United States into Canada and retard, not advance, Canadian industrial development.[47]

Canadians could defy Washington without any real fear of military retaliation. In the Caribbean and Central America, the Republican design for securing order in weak and presumably vulnerable places without the use of troops—a policy known as dollar diplomacy—actually commenced with Roosevelt in his prescription for the Dominican Republic. Roosevelt had relied on Root to persuade South American diplomats of the benign intentions of the United States in the Caribbean. For a brief time, the approach appeared to be working. In 1907, with the timely assistance of Porfirio Díaz of Mexico, Roosevelt brokered a series of Central American peace treaties that provided for a Court of Justice to resolve disputes between isthmian states and forbade the diplomatic recognition of a government that obtained power by unconstitutional means. Shortly after Roosevelt left office, however, the means to control the disruptive forces in the region began to collapse. In the Dominican Republic, Ramón Cáceres, who had killed the dictator Ulises Heureaux in 1899, was himself assassinated in 1911. His death set into motion a series of decisions and events leading to the eight-year military occupation of the republic five years later. Nicaragua experienced a different persecution. In 1910, President Taft and Secretary of State Philander C. Knox determined to rid the country of Zelaya—whom Knox declared to be a "blot on civilization" after the Nicaraguan leader ordered the execution of two U.S. mercenaries—by supporting one of the numerous revolutions that had broken out on the republic's east coast. Zelaya fled the country, first for Mexico and then, inexplicably, for the United States. When his successor, José Madriz, refused to knuckle under, Knox continued looking for someone more compliant. This approach provoked yet another civil war that culminated in a massive U.S. invasion of the populous western region of the country in fall 1912, the removal of Liberals from control of the national government, and the installation of a pro–U.S. government. In the process, the Central American treaties of 1907 had taken a beating. But order and "civilization" had been restored to Nicaragua.[48]

Critics of dollar diplomacy in both the United States and in the hemisphere might be soothed by comments that the Nicaraguan Expeditionary Force was performing a mission similar to that U.S. and European troops had carried out against the Boxer Rebellion in China in 1900 and that the intervention had been relatively short-lived. But the rebellion that erupted against Porfirio Díaz in Mexico in 1910 and the revolution that came in its wake proved far more calamitous in its impact on U.S. politics and society and on the self-appointed mission of the United States to lead the Western Hemisphere in the twentieth century.

From all outward appearances, the Porfirian regime seemed as secure in 1910 as in 1902, when Mexico City had hosted the Second Conference of American Republics, yet the fissures within the political system crafted by the aging dictator had begun to appear more than a decade before. In 1895, Wilson Luís Orozco, a jurist in Guadalajara, called on the government to arrest the growth of larger landholdings by breaking up public lands. Five years later, the Flores Magón brothers, Jesús, Ricardo, and Enrique, began publishing *Regeneración,* a Mexico City weekly that supported the liberal clubs sprouting up around the country. When Díaz cracked down on the publication, the brothers took their operation first to San Antonio, Texas, and then on to St. Louis, where they organized a revolutionary junta to bring down the Mexican government. They were arrested for violating U.S. neutrality laws but were shortly released. The Liberal Plan of 1906 did not call for toppling the regime, but it did champion many of the political and social concerns dear to U.S. progressives, such as freedom of speech and the press, educational reforms, prohibitions against child labor, eight-hour workdays, and six-day work weeks. Some objectives were too radical except for socialists: nationalization of church lands, the redistribution of uncultivated lands to those who worked them, and restoration of Indian communal lands taken illegally. Yet not even the brutal suppression of a labor strike at the U.S.-owned Consolidated Copper Company at Cananea in the border state of Sonora in 1906, which was put down with Arizona Ranger "volunteers," dissuaded moderate liberals from the belief that Mexico's problems could be addressed through political reform.

They were much encouraged when in early 1908 the old dictator told a U.S. journalist, James Creelman, that he would not seek reelection in 1910 and that he would tolerate opposition political parties. Díaz's announcement galvanized moderate liberal intellectuals and activists into believing that the nation stood on the verge of a new era, yet an acute observer would have recognized that Mexico's liberals were unified only in their opposition to the Porfirian regime and in their fears of radicalism. In *The Great National Problems,* the Yucatecan sociologist Andrés Molina Enríquez called for sweeping social reforms, especially in the Mexican countryside, in order to prevent radicals from gaining control of the disorganized groups of agrarian discontented. His contemporary, the Coahuilan landowner Francisco Madero, believed there was a more imminent political danger, and in *The Presidential Succession of 1910* warned that the nation's fundamental problems were not social but political.

Madero warned about a military takeover to keep Díaz in power and predicated his cause on no reelection. Just as Madero feared, Díaz changed his mind about continuing in office, his police threw Madero into jail, and on election day in June 1910 the old dictator and his running mate were overwhelmingly reelected. Madero lingered in prison into September, as Díaz prepared to celebrate his eightieth birthday, and Mexico the centennial anniversary of the Hidalgo revolt of 1810. For the mass of the Mexican population, the social condition of the country in 1910 appeared as desperate as it was in 1810. In October Madero got out of prison on bail and in disguise made his way across the border to San Antonio. From the sanctuary of the United States he announced the Plan de San Luis Potosí, in which he characterized the recent election as illegal and declared that he was assuming the role of provisional president of the republic. He called for an uprising on November 20. Mexicans responded but not always for the reasons Madero believed central to the cause. Yet, save in the northern border state of Chihuahua, the military seemed to hold its own against the rebellion. In May 1911, however, the rebels won a critical battle when they laid siege to the border city of Ciudad Juárez. Its fall to a combined assault from the armies of Francisco "Pancho" Villa and Pascual Orozco, Jr., spelled the collapse of the Díaz regime. Federal troops began deserting to the revolution, and before the end of the month the old dictator resigned.

Significantly, his abrupt departure came about not because of military victory but because of the failure of the federal army and the parallel willingness of Madero to negotiate a peaceful settlement. That choice disturbed some of Madero's officers, and the disagreements proved to be a portent of further trouble. Amidst the celebration of the end of one era and the onset of another, the divisions among the victors became even more uncertain. Madero had launched a political rebellion in the liberal tradition, but the triumph of his cause depended on the participation of an armed populace impatient with those who could not deliver tangible benefits. His was not a narrowly political cause, yet the brand of liberalism his movement represented proved too ideological to accommodate the myriad and often conflictive demands of a rural population with a rebellious tradition. Those liberals who believed in a prosperous and democratic Mexico and who had supported Madero undoubtedly sympathized with the condition of ordinary Mexicans, but they were understandably apprehensive about the violence in the countryside and in the city.

In less than two years, Madero confronted six rebellions—the first from the Zapatistas, who demanded immediate restoration of communal lands to Indians; another led by Pascual Orozco in the north; and the last in the terrible days of February 1913, when the capital became a combat zone between rebel forces and federal soldiers commanded by Victoriano Huerta, who in 1912 had led the defense against the Orozco rebellion. In these tumultuous and uncertain days, Huerta determined to end the fighting by signing an agreement with the rebels. The two sides worked out the details in the U.S. embassy on February 18 under the approving gaze of Ambassador Henry Lane Wilson. In the name of national unity and peace, it called for the resignations of Madero and Vice President Jesús Pino Suárez and the naming of Huerta as provisional president. Huerta went through the motions of legality by securing their resignations and having himself named in the line of succession. But this was not the greatest indignity. Three days after the infamous Pact of the Embassy, Madero and Pino were shot as they were being transferred from the National Palace to the federal penitentiary. The official story held that they died in a shootout between Madero's supporters and the *rurales* while trying to escape. Few believed the official version.

Mexico's brief experiment with liberal democracy had lasted less than two years, but the revolution survived, a revolution unlike any in the history of Mexico or Latin America. Historians have attributed its origins to the nineteenth-century experience of peasant defiance and revolt against the imposition of a liberal capitalist regime in the countryside, to a conflict of cultures, and to a nationalist rebellion against development from without. These interpretations may suffice as an overview of the Mexican condition before 1910; but they fail to explain the explosiveness and dynamics of what occurred after that date. There is no point in the trajectory of Mexican history from the mid-nineteenth to the first decade of the twentieth century at which we can locate an event or process that can explain what happened in the revolution.[49]

Simpler assessments came from contemporaries. Porfirio Díaz remarked that Madero had unleashed a tiger, but not even the crafty Díaz could have forecast what lay ahead for his diminutive adversary and those who followed him. Certainly, the mechanisms of institutional and personal power the dictator employed to tame Mexico would have been insufficient to ensure Madero's survival in the chaos of the times. At the other extreme was the view held by Woodrow Wilson, who believed that the revolution had been betrayed by Madero's successor. Two weeks after Madero's murder, Wilson took the presidential oath and steeled himself to a dual task: adapting U.S. foreign policy to the Mexican Revolution without stifling the democratic aspirations he believed it had unleashed; and forging a new hemispheric pact dominated by the United States but acceptable to Latin Americans.

The determination to accomplish the first manifestly frustrated efforts to succeed at the second. Something more consequential than the sudden, violent end of a liberal Mexican political leader was at stake, however. The Mexican Revolution ended the long nineteenth century in the Western Hemisphere.

4

The Fractured Continent

Much to the dismay of those Latin Americans who believed Woodrow Wilson might alter U.S. policy in the Americas, he would prove even more excessive than his Republican adversary in his willingness to use military force to achieve U.S. goals in the hemisphere. In the aftermath of the 1912 intervention in Nicaragua, he made clear his determination to keep U.S. warships in Nicaraguan waters as a symbol of national resolve. Roosevelt would have applauded his decision. Wilson's first secretary of state, William Jennings Bryan, negotiated a canal treaty with a virtually penniless Nicaraguan government with an agenda most dollar diplomats would have approved, a treaty that led inexorably to the collapse of the Central American Court of Justice in 1918, the year in which Wilson proclaimed the Fourteen Points as the foundation of a liberal world order. Certainly, the 1915 and 1916 interventions and subsequent occupations in Haiti and the Dominican Republic, respectively, seemed to many Latin Americans and even some North Americans a continuation of gunboat diplomacy and a fulfillment of what Herbert Croly had advocated in *The Promise of American Life* as the use of military power to deal with the centers of disorder in the hemisphere.[1]

In important ways, however, the Wilsonian decade in the history of the Americas conforms more to the dynamics of later years than to those of the

first decade of the twentieth century. Latin America and the Caribbean became more critical for Wilson than for his predecessors. In 1913, 50 percent of
all U.S. foreign investments lay in Latin America, and the domestic market, as
Wilson had warned in his 1912 presidential campaign, could no longer readily absorb what the nation's agroindustrial economy produced. Washington's
relations with other hemispheric governments and economies changed dramatically with the outbreak of World War I in 1914. The reaction of Wilson's
generation to European and especially German machinations in the Americas
proved to be similar to that voiced in the 1930s by U.S. leaders but revealed
fears that went far deeper than those expressed during the 1902–03 Venezuelan blockade. Whereas his predecessors had sensed opportunity, Wilson recognized the challenges to liberal capitalism and the political systems that sustained it from not only the right but also the left. To confront that peril, he
proposed a new political and economic agenda for the Americas, one that preserved the fundamental strategic and economic interests of the United States,
undeniably, but would also address what he correctly sensed was a common
frustration among political contemporaries in the hemisphere who were unsettled about the continuing fragmentation and disorder in society.[2]

Such a bold approach went beyond the credos of the liberal international
order whose values, particularly that of self-determination, Wilson often espoused. It mandated a new way of looking at a chaotic world and the dangers
that conflict anywhere posed for those who believed that power politics and
war must not be permitted to dictate the world's future. Traditional mechanisms for dealing with conflict, such as the balance of power, had been ren-
dered obsolescent by the horrors of World War I. Peace and progress required
a world organization—the League of Nations—and a prompt response to any
local conflict that might escalate into another world war. Although rejected by
the U.S. Senate, Wilson's reasoning about the danger of even local conflict ultimately became a signal feature of the nation's political culture. Far from being
a utopian vision, as Wilson's detractors consistently averred, his interpretation
of history and the danger of threats to a liberal world order constituted something quite unsettling, however compelling its intellectual power and ultimate
acceptance by later generations of North Americans—the apprehension, even
fear, of the nation's failure in this global quest.[3]

That fear about what might happen if he did not act bedeviled Wilson from
the beginning of his presidency. His flaw lay not in his unwillingness to use
power but in his seemingly unchangeable conviction that hemispheric governments and peoples rejected U.S. leadership because his Republican pred-

ecessors had used force to intimidate weaker governments and to advance the economic interests of select U.S. banking and industrial magnates. Power must be guided by nobler purposes. Unfortunately, chaotic situations did not lend themselves to this kind of logic, nor did the defiant discriminate between the purpose behind his actions and their results.

Pan-American Visions and Hemispheric Order

In its chaos and in the defiance of its leaders toward U.S. interference, the Mexican revolution frustrated the Wilsonian design for the hemisphere. In the aftermath of President Francisco Madero's killing, Wilson not only refused to recognize the provisional government of Victoriano Huerta in Mexico—nonrecognition was in itself an abrupt departure from the practices of big-power diplomacy—but vowed to remove him from office. He then confounded the emissaries of European governments, most of which had recognized Huerta's government, by trying to mediate a political election in Mexico with the promise that if Huerta did not interfere, the United States would recognize whatever government won. Such a course of action was not altogether incon-sistent with Wilson's approach to other Latin American governments. He had, in fact, drawn up a plan for political succession in the Dominican Republic and Haiti, but the Mexican imbroglio proved considerably more complicated. In the Haitian and Dominican case, the seeming intractability of the political sit-uation and the parallel defiance of local political elements to U.S. pressure prompted the president to turn matters over to the military. In Mexico, how-ever, Wilson took direct control of policy in the conviction that he was not only safeguarding the Mexican people and the revolution from the usurper Huerta but purposefully avoiding a military solution to the Mexican question. Media-tion was the proper course, John Barrett of the Pan-American Union assured him, for such a course would doubtless "strengthen Mexican confidence in your good intentions and gain the lasting sympathy of the rest of Latin America."[4]

Here was an opportunity to transform the Monroe Doctrine into a hemi-spheric statement, and Wilson took up the challenge. In a speech at Mobile, Alabama, in late October 1913, the president assailed European "economic aggression" and the parallel threat to "true constitutional liberty" in Latin America. In their quest for concessions and privileges, Wilson charged, Euro-peans threatened the self-determination of Latin American governments. The United States, by contrast, followed a hemispheric policy of morality, not ex-pediency. Correctly sensing that Latin American leaders might doubt his pur-pose, Wilson pledged a common cause with them to emancipate the continent from European economic vassalage and promised that the United States never again would use force to acquire "one additional foot of territory." This was not a pledge of nonintervention or even a renunciation of the use of armed force, as Wilson himself recognized. Self-determination, after all, might require intervention to shield the deserving from arbitrary rule. But Wilson's approach did place enormous constraints on his ability to use the military power at his command, particularly where rebellion, civil war, and revolution were so intertwined as to make distinguishing among them virtually impossible: his choices of action were thus never as clear as he believed them to be.[5]

Contradictions in the administration's relentless pursuit of "peace and order" with a moral purpose may have eluded Wilson himself, but others, including some of Wilson's dozen emissaries to revolutionary Mexico, recognized that such a course ultimately might require the use of armed force. The revolution that had begun as Liberal protest against bossism and *continuismo* and then erupted in mass uprisings of campesinos in the south and petit bourgeois and labor militants in central and northern Mexico had become by summer 1913 a civil war that divided Mexico into a quagmire of revolutionary factions and their leaders—among them, Emiliano Zapata in the south, and Venustiano Carranza, governor of Coahuila and First Chief of the Constitutionalist Army, with his erstwhile allies Álvaro Obregón and Francisco "Pancho" Villa in Sonora and Chihuahua, respectively, in the north. What united these groups was a common antipathy toward Huerta, who resolved to unify Mexico by first pacifying it. As the Mexican crisis spilled over into 1914, Huerta's determination to hang on to power despite the multiple forces waged against him from both within and without the country impressed even the indomitable Wilson. Try as he might, even to the point of channeling aid to Carranza's Constitutionalist Army, the president could not dislodge the Mexican "thorn" in his Latin American policy. But when his secretary of war tried to persuade him that intervention remained the president's only recourse to deal with the chaos in Mexico, Wilson curtly responded, "There are in my judgment no conceivable circumstances which would make it right for us to direct by force or by threat of force the internal processes of what is a profound revolution."[6]

What followed in Mexico over the next five years was something very different from what Wilson believed would happen when he took control of Mexican policy. In late April 1914, after a confrontation between the commander of a U.S. warship and a local Mexican official in the port of Tampico, U.S. naval forces seized the Mexican port of Veracruz. The official reason was to prevent a shipment of arms from a German vessel to the "illegitimate" government of

Mexico, but Wilson sought to drive Huerta from power without an invasion of central Mexico or, more troubling, a resurgence of unrest along the Texas border. Few of the president's predictions save that of Huerta's inevitable fall came true. Mexican resistance at Veracruz proved fierce, and the seizure of the city provoked denunciations from Zapata and Carranza, who apparently preferred to risk war with the United States rather than depend on Wilson as their surrogate.[7]

Indeed, the war Wilson swore he did not want might have occurred had not emissaries from Argentina, Brazil, and Chile moved swiftly to arrange for a May meeting between U.S. delegates and representatives of both Huerta and Carranza in Niagara Falls, Canada. The mediation averted a conflict but did not resolve the Mexican crisis, as neither Huerta nor Carranza acknowledged any interference in Mexican internal affairs. But the loss of Veracruz and the military triumphs of Carranza's Constitutionalist Army had their desired effect. In mid-July Huerta fled the country. Wilson exulted, believing that he had preserved the principle of Mexico's self-determination by deterring those who called for a full-scale military intervention (as would be the case in Haiti in 1915 and in the Dominican Republic the following year) as well as frustrating the designs of the German government to transform Mexico into a client state. For seven months a U.S. army occupation force provided Veracruz with the kind of government advocated by progressives, while Wilson continued to resist pressures from within his cabinet to deal with the Mexican conundrum with more forceful measures, as President James K. Polk had done during the Mexican War of 1846–48 when he dispatched General Winfield Scott's army into the populous regions of central Mexico.[8]

Following the U.S. departure from Veracruz, Mexico collapsed into anarchy, and the pressure on Wilson to intervene intensified. Sentiments were perhaps strongest on the Texas border, fueled by publication of a bizarre plot—the Plan of San Diego—calling on Mexicans in Texas to commence war against their Anglo oppressors with the ultimate goal of creating an independent nation of Texas, New Mexico, Arizona, Colorado, and Upper California. For Mexican and North American anarchists, however, the Plan of San Diego constituted the onset of another campaign against capitalism and the state by the radical wing of the Mexican Liberal Party, represented in the United States by Ricardo Flores Magón, publisher of *Regeneración*, and its allies, the Industrial Workers of the World. Here was the radicalism of the Mexican revolution most feared in the United States because it was occurring *in* the United States. As far as Wilson was concerned, if Carranza warranted recognition, he must, like Porfirio Díaz, prove that he could pacify the border.[9]

Carranza had to be concerned not only with the internal dynamics of the Mexican revolution and its increasingly radical course but also with his enemies Zapata and especially Villa. In April 1915, as the United States prepared to host a Pan-American financial conference to study the impact of the war on hemispheric economies, Carranza's ablest general, Obregón, won a major victory over Villa's army. The triumph did not noticeably resolve border tensions, certainly, nor did it prompt Carranza to acquiesce in the appeal of six hemispheric governments—Argentina, Brazil, Chile, Bolivia, Guatemala, and Uruguay—who joined the U.S. government in an appeal to the revolutionary factions to put aside their differences and form a provisional government. Zapata and Villa seemed favorably disposed but not Carranza, who made clear that hemispheric governments must recognize him or witness further chaos in Mexico. De facto recognition came in October 1915, but the United States insisted on conditions. In the estimation of Wilson, Carranza's tenure was probationary, and although Carranza benefited politically from the recognition, he denounced the interference of the Pan-American powers in Mexico's internal affairs. Nonetheless, Wilson exulted in his annual address to Congress in December, "We have been put to the test in the case of Mexico, and we have stood the test." Three months later, Villa's army attacked the small border town of Columbus, New Mexico. The logic of conciliation articulated by Barrett now suddenly became the imperative of action. As Secretary of the Interior Franklin Lane commented, not to respond to the attack "would ruin us in the eyes of all Latin Americans."[10]

In truth, Lane and certainly Wilson were alert to Latin American sensibilities in this crisis and held some fleeting belief that the Pan-American Pact might survive the Mexican crisis, but neither the president nor his more outspoken cabinet members could easily discount the demand for retaliation throughout the country or the appeal of a military resolution of the crisis to those who lived in the region. Senator Albert T. Fall (Rep., N.M.) called for an invasion force of five hundred thousand to occupy all of Mexico and "end the chaos on our doorstep." The U.S. response to the Villa raids was the Punitive Expedition, a force of seven thousand men (later expanded to ten thousand) commanded by General John J. Pershing, which trooped out of Columbus, N.M., in March 1916 and headed into Mexico in search of the elusive Villa. As it penetrated deeper into the country, Carranza became apprehensive that

Pershing's army would be transformed into a pacification force to clean up Mexico. There were several military encounters between U.S. and Mexican troops. Although Wilson resisted continuing pressures for a full-scale military intervention, the Mexican crisis did not abate. A few weeks after Pershing's "wet hens" crossed back into the United States in early 1917 came the dramatic revelation of a German offer of a formal alliance with Mexico and the announcement of unrestricted submarine warfare in the North Atlantic, a decision that made U.S. entry into the world war inevitable. If Carranza agreed to the alliance, the German government pledged, at the end of the war Mexico would get back the lands it had lost in the 1846–48 war with the United States.[11]

Carranza rejected the offer but accompanied it with his own plan to counter the pro-Allied course of the United States. Fearful of what U.S. participation in the war might mean for Latin America, he proposed the creation of a neutral bloc including the United States to settle the war through mediation. If that failed, the bloc would strive to limit the impact of the conflict on the hemisphere and cut off trade with belligerents. Recognizing that the resumption of unrestricted German submarine warfare made U.S. involvement inevitable, Wilson arrogantly rejected the Mexican proposal. When the United States entered the war in April 1917, ten Latin American governments, Mexico and Argentina among them, declared their neutrality, six, including Brazil, broke diplomatic relations, and two, Cuba and Panama, both U.S. protectorates, declared war. Ultimately, the combination of U.S. diplomatic and economic pressure and self-interest prompted declarations of war from six more, but Brazil was the only South American country in that group. The economic reach of the United States nonetheless increased dramatically in oil, cables, and finance capitalism as well as in the wartime demand for raw materials. Within individual nations, the distortions of the expanded commercial ties sometimes had disruptive effects. Restrictions on imports drove up prices and with budget deficits caused inflation, and the impact on real wages in cities contributed to political disturbances during and after the war.[12]

Those countries within the realm of U.S. formal and even informal empire seemingly lacked any realistic choice. The Dominican Republic had a U.S. military government, which did not declare war, thus relieving Washington of any obligation for military assistance, and the client government of Haiti declared war because U.S. troops occupied the country. Despite Wilsonian rhetoric the notion of self-determination proved a mockery elsewhere as well. Puerto Ricans, whose ambiguous status disturbed Wilson, gained a qualified

U.S. citizenship with the Jones Act, though discerning critics, among them Luís Muñoz Rivera, who did not live to see the law enacted, recognized that the intent behind such measures was to bind the island even closer to the mainland without giving its people much hope of either gaining independence or statehood. In Haiti and the Dominican Republic, the military intervention had provoked a guerrilla war and an equally severe response. Wilson persisted in believing that in both places the professed goals of creating viable political institutions and the undertaking of economic projects overshadowed the ill will these two occupations instilled among Haitians and Dominicans. Accusations of abuse and even torture of civilians began to appear in the U.S. press. These kinds of ventures, tolerated in wartime, inevitably impacted on politics. In the presidential campaign of 1920, Democratic vice presidential candidate Franklin D. Roosevelt boasted that he had written the 1918 Haitian constitution, which prompted Warren G. Harding, the Republican presidential nominee, to respond with a similarly inane remark that if elected he would not use bayonets to impose democracy on West Indians. Neither occupation figured significantly in the outcome of the election, but the cumulative charges and countercharges prompted a congressional investigation in 1921–22 that publicized most of them. The military occupation ended in the Dominican Republic in 1924, and only a token number of marines remained in Haiti.[13]

Here and elsewhere in the Caribbean, U.S. leaders now boasted to their skeptical southern neighbors, the United States was demonstrating its commitment to nurturing republican government abroad and its unwillingness to create European-style empire. The reality, of course, proved much more complicated. Since the early twentieth century, the U.S. interventions in Central America and the Caribbean had encountered considerable resistance. A succession of U.S. presidents had failed to create a political consensus to sustain these interventions either in the Congress or in the public. Organizations representing people of color were the most outspoken. This kind of opposition could be expected, as were the muted demurrals of the military about using troops to intervene in civil wars or protect the property of U.S. investors. Though such a view would not be sanctioned until the late 1920s, a few in the State Department acknowledged that policies designed to prevent the deployment of troops—for example, demanding that Caribbean governments provide adequate protection for private property—made the likelihood of U.S. intervention more, not less, probable. Not anticipated were the subtle alterations of the symbiotic relation between not only governments but economies and peoples of the United States and Mexico and the circum-Caribbean.[14]

The character of the relation seemed least clear in the case of Mexico. After U.S. entry into the war, Wilson's frustration with Carranza and with the Mexican government escalated, a frustration exacerbated not only by Carranza's opposition to Wilson's hemispheric policies but, more critically, by the undeniable challenge to nineteenth-century liberalism and foreign property interests in the 1917 Mexican constitution. Article 27 in particular alarmed U.S. interests, for it required any foreign concessionaire to abide by Mexican laws and not to appeal to their own governments in disputes. Although Wilson shared their concerns, some oil men and Republicans became convinced that he was less interested in protecting U.S. economic interests in Mexico than in propagating the virtues of liberal capitalism and democracy to a people who consistently rejected them. Unintentionally, Wilson worsened the situation in summer 1918 when he professed to a group of Mexican journalists that he believed in the principle of nonintervention in Mexico and had dispatched troops into that country for the singular purpose of assisting them in getting rid of a dictator. He then disingenuously suggested the Pan-American Pact be revived with the understanding that if any state, including the United States, violated the territorial integrity of another, the other states would unite in condemning the violator. The incompatibility of these words with the president's pointed criticism of Mexican threats to the property rights of U.S. citizens in Mexico prompted denunciations of Wilson's hypocrisy throughout Mexico. Carranza called on other Latin American governments to join Mexico in a Pan-Hispanic alternative to the Wilson Doctrine, a movement designed not only to eliminate U.S. political and economic influence in Mexico but to isolate the United States in the Western Hemisphere. Wilson now confronted the sobering prospect that he must not only rearrange peace in Europe but deal with the problem at his doorstep.[15]

Latin America occupied a special place in the U.S. preparations for the end of the war (a project titled "The Inquiry"), but hemispheric issues and countries figured only marginally in the actual deliberations at the Paris Peace Conference. Mexico did not receive an invitation, though Carranza dispatched a delegate, Alberto J. Pani, to lobby against those international oil interests calling for retaliation against Article 27 of the Mexican constitution. To the dismay of Pani and the former president of the Dominican Republic, Francisco Henríquez y Carvajal, exiled after the U.S. invasion of 1916, who had sailed to Paris to protest the U.S. occupation as a violation of Wilson's vaunted Fourteen Points, the Covenant of the League of Nations—against Wilson's wishes, it should be noted—included a formal recognition of the Monroe Doctrine but said nothing about the Pan-American Pact. Carranza kept up his hemispheric campaign against the United States, despite the efforts of the ambassador to Mexico, Henry Fletcher (then on assignment in Washington), who called for an international commission to restore the credibility of the Mexican government. Such a proposal paled in comparison with the recommendations of the Oil Producers Association and the National Association for the Protection of American Rights in Mexico and prominent Republicans, among them, Senator Albert Hall of New Mexico, who held hearings on the Mexican situation in August, whose solutions included a break in diplomatic relations and implied yet a second military intervention.

But no massive military intervention occurred, in part because of Wilson's refusal, despite his debilitating illness in fall 1919, to yield to the clamors of powerful Republican opponents and oil interests to sanction the overthrow of a man who had defied him. The Mexican revolution survived the North American challenge, Wilson's defenders insist, because he had purposefully limited U.S. power to preserve national interests yet permitted the revolution to run its course. His critics, North American and Mexican, often employing the same evidence, contend that Wilson had denied Mexico the principle of self-determination or, worse, used his power to assist the most conservative elements of the revolutionary generation in the betrayal of the social revolution symbolized by Villa and Zapata.[16]

The capitalist transformation of the prewar hemisphere—a transformation in which North American companies and entrepreneurs had played a signal role—had spawned a myriad variety of radical, revolutionary, and even reactionary movements. World War I exacerbated the social tensions inherent in these dramatic changes. Some—certainly Wilson himself but also powerful North American business interests—looked upon the outbreak of the war and especially the opening of the Panama Canal as an opportunity to advance North American financial and economic interests throughout Latin America at the expense of warring European nations. Others, such as Samuel Gompers, founder of the American Federation of Labor, Santiago Iglesias, a Puerto Rican Marxist who had helped to organize the Socialist Party of Puerto Rico, and John Murray, a U.S. Marxist revolutionary, feared that the president's Pan-American Pact would simply unleash North American and European "predatory capital" on Latin American labor. At Iglesias's urging, Gompers lent his efforts to the creation of the Pan-American Federation of Labor to advance the interests of Latin American workers.[17]

In this context, then, it is understandable why Gompers and Wilson viewed the Mexican situation as critical, for Carranza, though he became a victim of the revolution in 1920 when he tried to remain in power, proved capable of containing the power of labor as well as checking the social revolution unleashed by the Zapatista movement. The year before, as a special committee of the U.S. Senate held hearings on the Mexican situation, the Military Intelligence Division upgraded its 1911 Contingency War Plan for Mexico, which called for the seizure of oil and coal fields, a blockade of Mexico's ports, closing down of the border, and a march on Mexico City. When Carranza's death threatened to plunge the nation into yet another civil war as bloody as that of 1914–15, Obregón persuaded his rivals that the most expedient way to shield the nation from another invasion from the north was to rally behind him as president. His selection a few months later did not prompt immediate U.S. recognition, however, as haggling over the application of Article 27 to U.S. oil operations went on for another three years; tentative agreement came with the Bucareli Accords, which shielded the oil companies from Article 27 if drillers could prove they had undertaken "positive acts." Obregón received recognition just in time to purchase U.S. arms and planes (and U.S. pilots) to quell a revolt against him from a longtime political rival, Adolfo de la Huerta. The cost of this assistance, it is sometimes remarked, was the weakening of the social revolution embodied in the 1917 constitution, as the U.S. economic penetration of Mexico continued. One obvious reward was the survival of the political hold of the revolutionaries from the Mexican northern states and the parallel weakening of peasant and labor groups.[18]

The Twenties

World War I confirmed U.S. power in Central America and the Caribbean and increased its influence in South America and Canada. No European power, certainly not Germany or even Great Britain, now challenged the United States in the Caribbean, Central America, and Mexico, and the restrictions of the Five-Power Naval Limitation Treaty (1922) between the United States, Great Britain, Italy, France, and Japan indirectly acknowledged U.S. domination by granting each of the signatories naval superiority in its home waters.

But the hemisphere that evolved in the 1920s and then dramatically collapsed in the Great Depression evolved differently from the one either Martí or Roosevelt or even Wilson had envisioned. Latin Americans began to subscribe to the notion of a regional organization as Wilson's enthusiasm for such an arrangement diminished. Latin American governments began joining the League of Nations, though in most cases their action was explained more by the belief that the league would serve as a counterbalance to U.S. power than by a commitment to the universalism Wilson had espoused. At the Fifth Conference of American Republics in Santiago, Chile, in 1923, the president of Uruguay, Baltasar Brum, who had shocked his colleagues with his call for a community of interest between Latin America and the United States, proposed the creation of a Pan-American League of Nations. The move collapsed amidst denunciations of the Monroe Doctrine and the apprehension that the failure of the United States to join the league in effect negated Article X of the League Covenant, which guaranteed the political and territorial integrity of states, thus leaving the continent more rather than less vulnerable to U.S. intrusion. The fact that such a delicate political question got on the agenda of the conference in the first place constituted an achievement, as was the bemused satisfaction that Latin American delegates must have gotten from Secretary of State Charles Evans Hughes's declaration before the American Bar Association that the Monroe Doctrine was no impediment to Pan-American cooperation. Two years later, he suggested that every Latin American government should adopt a similar principle for its foreign policy! But there was one ominous remark in the explanation of what the doctrine meant: "So far as the region of the Caribbean Sea is concerned," Hughes stated in 1923, "it may be said that if we had no Monroe Doctrine we should have to create one."[19]

To some, doubtless, Hughes's words sounded eerily like those of Theodore Roosevelt in his 1904 warning that the United States might have to play the role of hemispheric policeman. They echoed as well the British editorialist W. R. Stead's prediction about the Americanization of the world, not by soldiers but by U.S. companies with their company towns exercising control as well as reforming local labor forces and economic advisors ("money doctors") inculcating sound principles of fiscal management among a new generation of hemispheric politicos. Professor Edwin Walter Kemmerer of Princeton, the most well traveled of the money doctors, probably came closest to an official view of the benefits of dispatching financial advisors southward when he noted that "a country that appoints American financial advisors and follows their advice in reorganizing its finances . . . increases its chances of appealing to the American investor and of obtaining from him capital on favorable terms." Investors might be satisfied with such logic, but the ordinary citizen needed to be reminded that material advancement and moral improvement were mutually reinforcing faiths spread throughout the hemisphere, not by soldiers but by U.S. companies in a "revolutionary mission." At home, this culture had brought order to the industrial workplace by disciplining the laborer with a combination of controls and rewards; arguably, it was capable of accomplishing the same task everywhere in the Americas.[20]

The presumed cultural transformation of the hemisphere wrought by Americanization proved more difficult to assess. Certainly, Germany's behavior during the war and the unpreparedness of France had shattered the faith of many Latin American liberals in a progressive Europe, but such changes did not always mean the United States became an alternative as a political or cultural model. University students read North American reviews, and Latin Americans and Canadians absorbed North American popular culture. High school students throughout the United States debated hemispheric issues with a knowledge that would have embarrassed later generations. Undeniably, despite the outcries against U.S. intervention, the experience of twenty years offered some evidence that North American cultural preferences had penetrated more deeply among Latin Americans and Canadians. Not unexpectedly, Yankeephobia continued to run strong in Latin American literary circles and political cultures. In Peru, where Augusto Leguía vigorously promoted an Andean brand of capitalism, thus mortgaging the nation's future to the U.S. economy, the modernist cause found a voice in Manuel González Prada. Two of his disciples, José Carlos Mariátegui and Víctor Raúl Haya de La Torre, assailed the Peruvian oligarchy for the social and economic injustices suffered by workers and Indians. Their message was hemispheric. The American Popular Revolutionary Alliance (APRA, whose followers were known as Apristas), the political arm of the movement, called for Latin American unity, nationalization of industry and land, and the inter-Americanization of the Panama Canal.[21]

Perhaps the most ambivalent form of anti-Americanism took root in postwar Canada, where the critical role of U.S. investment, especially in such key industries as pulp and paper, mining and smelting, auto manufacturing, and hydroelectricity, prompted concerns among those who charted the nation's economic development, and resentments over the unequal losses in the war persisted. "America counted her profits while Canada buried her dead," Canadians grumbled, yet increasingly their apprehensions centered not on economic dependence or annexation but on the continuing migration of Canadians southward and the fear of being overwhelmed by U.S. culture. Americanization, observed a writer in the prestigious *Canadian Forum*, is "like baldness; once caught there is no escape from it," an exaggeration, doubtless, but closer to the mark than President Harding's insipid remarks to a Vancouver audience in July 1923: "We think the same thoughts, live the same lives and cherish the same aspirations."[22]

Criticism of the U.S. role in the hemisphere also came from some unexpected places in the United States, a sign that the imperial experience had changed the nation in ways that anti-imperialist critics of 1900 had predicted. The writer Waldo Frank, in a direct rebuke of the credos of the money doctors, called on Latin Americans to redeem the United States from the corrupting values of materialism. In a provocative article entitled "Imperialist America" in the *Atlantic Monthly* for July 1924, Samuel Guy Inman, a Texas-born missionary fresh from a tour of the Caribbean, echoed familiar charges that U.S. intervention and dollar diplomacy bred resentments. He prophesied that violations of the sovereignty of weaker peoples in the Caribbean and Central America would lead to the "destruction of our nation just as surely as it meant the destruction of Egypt and Rome and Spain and Germany and all the other nations who came to measure their greatness by their material possessions rather than by their passion for justice." Inman's critique set off a firestorm of rebuttals within the Department of State. The more outspoken referred to Inman as a "parlor bolshevist," praised the benefits of commerce, and, in the rhetorical faith of dollar diplomacy, pointed out that sending money doctors southward was preferable to dispatching marines.[23]

Both assessments were exaggerations, and neither captured the complexity of the hemisphere's economic and cultural relations with the United States. From the turn of the century and especially after World War I, massive amounts of U.S. finance capital poured into Latin America and Canada, and with these funds came a concerted effort on the part of banking houses to control the process. Viewed in a narrow sense, their purpose was not so much to violate the sovereignty of nations, promote material values, or enhance U.S. power but to safeguard long-term relations between borrowers and investors. Canadian and Latin American leaders were increasingly alert to the importance of maintaining fiscal order and avoiding loan defaults—the bane of earlier governments—and South American borrowers recognized that Central American and Caribbean bonds sold better in the New York market when the money doctors exercised some supervision over them. To no one's surprise, this kind of intrusion created hostility, but there were benefits. Most of the finance capital in the 1920s went toward servicing debt, to administration, and especially to public works. None of these benefits would have qualified to satisfy the agendas of those who believed the role of the United States in the hemisphere must be the promotion of democracy and social justice, but these endeavors were important in addressing the critical need to bring fiscal order to government and political economy.[24]

Distortions of the system had already begun to appear years before the Great Depression devastated the money doctors' prescriptions for bringing sanity to the economic disorder that plagued many hemispheric governments. Money doctors naively believed their proposals would liberate economic institutions from politics. To their dismay they discovered that they were most successful when they were dealing with authoritarian governments. In Chile, for example, the military supported economic reforms, but constitutional barriers prevented their full achievement. Even within the nation's informal empire, accommodation and defiance characterized relations between the United States and its surrogates. Employing large foreign subsidies and loans from the United States, Cuban president Gerardo Machado undertook an ambitious public works program that impressed U.S. observers, but very early in his presidency he had to confront a rising chorus of criticism of the Platt Amendment as well as labor unrest and a severe economic downturn in the sugar industry. As conditions worsened, Machado responded to the outcries of Cuban businessmen for protectionist measures, which displeased the United States, and reassured both domestic and foreign investors with promises to safeguard private property. In 1928, with the tacit approval of the United States, he used bribery, intimidation, and force to get a change in the Cuban constitution permitting his reelection. By the end of the decade, U.S. leaders were so sick of Machado that they were looking for virtually any alternative. Panama's dominant political figure of the twenties, Belisario Porras, could be unrelentingly critical of U.S. domination of the country, yet Porras just as quickly reminded Panamanians that progress and order depended on the canal and the U.S. presence.[25]

Two parallel crises in the 1920s sorely tested the hemispheric system because they directly challenged U.S. power. The first came with the U.S. confrontation with Mexico when President Plutarco Elías Calles angered U.S. leaders by his decision to enforce Article 27 of the 1917 constitution, which retained subsoil rights for the nation and in effect threatened U.S. oil companies. During the revolution, the oil companies had actually increased production. From 1920 to 1925, however, the companies cut back their output by more than 80 percent and imposed draconian measures on Mexico's petroleum unions, which persisted in their demands for higher wages and greater social benefits. Calles's position appeared to the oil companies as a repudiation of the Bucareli Accords of 1923, when Obregón's government had consented that in exchange for diplomatic recognition, U.S. oil companies engaged in "positive acts" in drilling would be exempted from application of Article 27. The companies and the U.S. government expected Calles to deal with militant labor in the same way Díaz had. When he failed to do so, Ambassador James Sheffield called for a more militant policy, and President Calvin Coolidge solemnly declared that "Mexico was on trial before the world." Calles, after all, had championed the cause of labor. In the midst of a crisis between the two nations, negotiations between U.S. bankers and Mexican officials as well as the naming of a new ambassador, Dwight Morrow, produced a compromise in which Calles yielded just enough to reassure the oil companies and especially North American investors that Mexico's revolution was grounded in capitalism and liberal reformism. In any event, a military response struck most of the bankers as foolish. "There is no big stick to wield [in Mexico]," declared Thomas W. Lamont, their spokesman, "and we have no boot that could possibly reach their remote and very tough stomach."[26]

Calles had yielded, to be sure, but he had done so because of the economic and political circumstances confronting the Mexican government in the 1920s. The priorities of Mexico's first generation of postrevolutionary leaders, both of them from the northwest state of Sonora, were clear: Mexico must be made over into a modern nation but not in the way Díaz had wanted. Industry was secondary to agriculture, and despite enormous obstacles the northwest prospered during the years of Obregón and Calles. The Sonoran dynasty tamed the army, drove the church from the schoolroom, and brought warring groups to heel by fire and sword. Workers enjoyed a corporate existence. To assure the orderly transition of power in a fragmented society in which parliamentary democracy could only further disunity, Calles presided over the creation of the National Revolutionary Party, which under various names would rule the country for the remainder of the century. The building of a modern economy required placing economic and political power in the president and his advisors. The state must be responsible for creating financial institutions and those projects private enterprise could not undertake. State building and national development required a fundamental understanding and cooperation between the "revolutionary family," on one hand, and bankers, businessmen, industrialists, the Mexican labor confederation, landowners, and even foreign investors, on the other. Oil companies joined communists and anarchists in their reluctance to cooperate. Calles's acquiescence in the oil crisis did not lessen his resolve to deal with the church or with the challenge of the *cristeros* to the authority of the state. Rather, the concession in the oil controversy was a belated acknowledgment that the revolution had not basically decreased the Mexican economy's reliance on foreign investment and exports.[27]

The second crisis occurred in Nicaragua, where the United States had deployed marines in 1912 to drive the last of Zelaya's Liberal followers from power and to install a Conservative political dynasty in their place. So secure did this system appear that candidates for the Nicaraguan presidency in the years following routinely traveled north to secure Washington's informal blessing. If they returned home aboard a U.S. warship, election was assured. Nicaragua ceased to be the nemesis of the United States. In 1923, with Washington's blessing and isthmian Conservatives fearful of the spread of revolutionary nationalism from Mexico, the Central American governments signed a Treaty of Peace and Amity forbidding recognition of revolutionary governments. A Princeton University political scientist, Harold Dodds, drew up an electoral code for Nicaragua, and Secretary of State Hughes informed the Nicaraguan government of the imminent removal of the hundred-man marine legation guard from Managua as soon as Nicaragua created a constabulary to take their place. Despite these measures, the outgoing Conservative president managed to manipulate the 1924 election and thus ensure that his bitter personal rival, Emiliano Chamorro, another Conservative, would be kept out of the presidential palace. The irregularities of the election disturbed U.S. officials, but they could scarcely encourage Chamorro to contest them. Given assurances of reform by the new president, Carlos Solórzano, Washington acquiesced. In the following year the legation guard left Managua. "Peace reigned in Nicaragua," wrote the journalist Harold Denny, "for three weeks, four days, and thirteen hours after the marines departed."[28]

Convinced that the marines would not return, Chamorro commenced a campaign of intimidation, conspiracy, and bribery that culminated in the resignation of the president and the prevention of his Liberal vice president, Juan B. Sacasa, from succeeding him. In March 1926, Chamorro as first designate of the Nicaraguan Assembly assumed the office. Liberals proclaimed a rebellion on Sacasa's behalf and won their first victories on the isolated east coast, where most North American residents of Nicaragua lived. In a reprise of traditional naval policies, the commander of a patrolling U.S. warship landed a contingent of marines and declared Bluefields a neutral zone. Chamorro counterattacked and within three months drove his enemies into the interior and toward the Costa Rican border. Sacasa fled to Mexico and then to Guatemala. Lacking U.S. recognition, however, Chamorro could not continue, and in a hastily arranged conference at Corinto he agreed to resign. As it had after Zelaya's departure, Washington turned to the reliable Adolfo Díaz to serve as interim president and to sustain the war against the rebellious Liberal armies.

But in fall 1926 Díaz proved as incapable of fighting this war without U.S. troops as he had in quelling the Mena revolt of 1912. Patrolling U.S. warships continued to land more marines and bluejackets to reassure him, but in the first months of 1927 the resurgent Liberals appeared to be winning the struggle. Shortly after a Liberal army routed a government garrison at Muy Muy, the U.S. minister, George Eberhardt, solemnly noted, "It is increasingly evident that without complete intervention there is no likely prospect of an early restoration of order." A year later, the United States had five thousand marines back in Nicaragua.[29]

Although not apparent to most observers, the Nicaraguan crisis of the 1920s signaled a subtle change in the U.S. approach to the hemisphere. The shift is explained neither by acceptance of the principle of absolute nonintervention nor by a growing sensibility concerning the sovereign rights of smaller hemispheric countries, but rather by a realization that playing the role of policeman—the gravamen of the Roosevelt Corollary—was both ineffective and costly. Of course, the arrogance of the powerful did not permit such a direct disavowal. In early 1927, as the Liberal rebellion in Nicaragua appeared close to triumph, Coolidge suddenly resolved to dispatch Henry L. Stimson to settle the civil war there. Stimson's approach followed the U.S. political tradition: call the warring parties to the table, buy off the recalcitrant with sinecures and money, and promise a fair election. There would be no recurrence of 1912, the intervention that put the Conservatives in power, for this time the U.S. purpose would be not simply to crush a rebellion but to improve Nicaraguan politics. The rebels had a choice. They could put down their arms in the reasonable expectation that Liberals would win the U.S.-supervised election of 1928 and that the exiled vice president Sacasa would become president; or they could persist in the certain expectation that if successful in the war the United States would not recognize the new government. All save one of the rebel leaders took the offer. The holdout was Augusto César Sandino.[30]

As Stimson had promised, the U.S. military supervised an election, and when Sandino raised an army of men, women, and children in defiance, Coolidge dispatched five thousand marines to subdue him. But this last banana war bore little resemblance to the 1912 campaign, when the most fabled marine of the era, Smedley "Old Gimlet Eye" Butler, had told one of the rebel generals to take his rebellion into the mountains, for Sandino decided to wage his war in the formidable Nicaraguan north. With the Nicaraguan elites in disarray, Sandino was able to capitalize on latent Nicaraguan hostility to the U.S.

presence. As the marines became more frustrated in their chase, hemispheric leaders denounced the war. At the Sixth Pan-American Conference, which convened in Havana in January 1928, the Mexican and Argentine representatives, fired by anti-American sentiments among the Latin American delegations, urged a debate over the intervention in the final plenary session. When it occurred, however, the Argentine goal of an absolute ban on intervention failed when Secretary of State Hughes delivered a spirited defense of the Monroe Doctrine and then, echoing a traditional North American refrain, asked rhetorically, "What are we to do when government breaks down and American citizens are in danger of their lives? Are we to stand by and see them killed [some in the audience stated later that he had said, "butchered in the jungle] because . . . a government can no longer afford reasonable protection?" In a masterpiece of legal casuistry, Hughes described the U.S. effort in Nicaragua not as an intervention, but as an "interposition of a temporary character."[31]

Hughes's vigorous rebuttal impressed his listeners but persuaded few of them, and Hughes returned to Washington convinced there had to be a better way to safeguard U.S. interests in Central America. Two years later, the solicitor general of the Department of State, J. Reuben Clark, a devout Mormon, provided one in a memorandum that bears his name. The Roosevelt Corollary, Clark observed, ill served the nation's purposes in the hemisphere. Hard-liners denounced his report as a retreat from responsibility, and both President Herbert Hoover and (now) Secretary of State Stimson offered reassurances about U.S. commitments; but it was soon evident that even Stimson had reservations about playing the role of hemispheric policeman. In 1931, he announced that U.S. property owners in Nicaragua should look to Managua, not to Washington, D.C., for protection. Three years before, such a comment would have been heresy, but then the United States had a formidable marine force in Nicaragua, the Nicaraguan constabulary was in its infancy, and the U.S. economy was running at full throttle. When Stimson made his somber declaration, most of the troops had departed, and even the true believers in the country's role in the hemisphere conceded that the expenditure of $9 million of public moneys in Haiti, the Dominican Republic, and Nicaragua since 1915 constituted too high a price for promoting democracy and protecting U.S. interests. Besides, Stimson had the reassurance that the future commander of the Nicaraguan national guard would be Anastasio Somoza García, who had proved of inestimable value during Stimson's 1927 visit. The secretary of state had little inkling that the national guardsmen in which he had such faith

would become less the protectors of U.S. interests than the guardians of a dynasty that would rule Nicaragua for more than fifty years.[32]

The Sandino War had made nonintervention a rallying cry in the inter-
American system, yet in its wake the U.S. government found other ways of
tightening its grip on the smaller republics of the hemisphere. In the Dominican Republic, Rafael Leonidas Trujillo used his power as head of the Dominican National Guard, a creation of the U.S. military during its eight-year
occupation, to gain power in 1930. And in early 1934, following six months of
social and political crisis in Cuba, a former sergeant in the Cuban military,
Fulgencio Batista, capitalized on Washington's hostility to a five-month-old
revolutionary government headed by Ramón Grau San Martín to become the
de facto power in the republic. The United States had only an indirect role in
Trujillo's rapid ascent. In Batista's case, however, its actions proved decisive
and would precipitate an early challenge to the Franklin D. Roosevelt administration in the hemisphere. In 1906, Theodore Roosevelt had reacted to a political crisis in Havana and to a civil war by despatching an army of "pacification"
to the island. The second Roosevelt had no such intentions—a depression-era
Congress would not have tolerated such a decision—but neither could he
afford to permit the revolution to run its course, despite his critique of intervention in a *Foreign Affairs* article he wrote in 1928. He dispatched a special
emissary, Sumner Welles, to ascertain if the Grau government warranted
recognition—Welles surmised that Grau's inability to restore order meant that
it did not. Then he surrounded the island with warships, while Grau spoke
grandly about a new Cuba and a legitimacy for a revolutionary government
that sprang from the approval of the Cuban people, not from the U.S. government. Welles recommended intervention, but Roosevelt reminded his emissary about the pledge of nonintervention Cordell Hull made at the Seventh International Conference of American States, which convened in Montevideo in
December 1933.

Batista sensed U.S. priorities from the beginning. He would accommodate
the Yankees, certainly, but neither his politics nor his economic philosophy
bore much similarity to that of Trujillo or Somoza. Grau despised the Platt
Amendment. So did Batista. Grau failed to get the support of Cuba's nascent
communist party. Batista did. Many of the edicts of the failed revolution of
1933 found their way into the Cuban constitution of 1940: political democracy,
rights of labor, limits on the size of sugar plantations, and state intervention in
the economy. "Many want to forget that I am the chief of a constructive social

revolution," Batista declared in 1937, in the aftermath of a two-year purge of defiant labor leaders. "My idea of order is that of an architect rather than a policeman."[33]

The Depression

In any event, what most preoccupied the peoples and especially the leaders of the Americas in the early thirties was the Great Depression, which devastated hemispheric economies and called into question the liberal economic models created in the late nineteenth century. In the United States, a generation of political leaders who had drawn on their wartime experience to create an "associational order" to address the historic needs of controlling an economy watched their grand design collapse in the downturns that followed the stock market crash of October 1929. When Franklin Roosevelt took the presidential oath in March 1933, with factories closing and unemployment at 25 percent of the workforce, his predecessor's prediction of boundless prosperity four years before seemed like a cruel hoax. John Maynerd Keynes, the British economist, calling the depression "one of the greatest economic catastrophes of modern history," advocated deficit financing and decreased saving, and he even stood ready to reject free trade in the cause of national mass production. Consumers and producers could interact within a national, not a global, economy.[34]

Keynes ridiculed the statism of the Soviet Union, but his cure for the depression sounded like a repudiation of the economic wisdom of the early twentieth century. Neither Hoover nor Roosevelt in the United States nor Mackenzie King in Canada proved willing to go that far in their reaction to the economic calamity. In many ways, the U.S. and Canadian experiences in the early thirties appeared to follow a similar pattern—widespread hardship, radical politics and violence in the prairie states and provinces, and a federal government either unable to cope or unwilling to undertake measures sufficient to meet the challenge. But there were revealing divergences as the decade wore on. King's reaction to the economic disaster baffled most Canadians. Unlike Roosevelt and Hoover, the Canadian prime minister attributed the depression to a temporary malady and dismissed the pleas for financial assistance from provincial and municipal governments as a Tory plot to undermine the government. In fall 1930 an irate electorate turned him out in favor of a Conservative, R. B. Bennett. It was King's only political loss, but he knew the Conservatives must try to deal with the depression. Bennett threw himself into the task, gaining the reputation of being a one-man government. When the depression reached its depths in 1933 he exhibited little of the willingness Roosevelt displayed to use the organizational and administrative structures pioneered in World War I to meet the economic challenge.

Within a few years, it is true, the "broker state" crafted by the New Dealers had proved inadequate to restore prosperity, but Roosevelt, unlike Bennett, did not react with proposals so radical that his own party and even his cabinet voiced concerns about his sanity. A student of U.S. liberalism perhaps best captured the New Deal's political accommodation to the public mood by pointing out its protean character. Leftists denounced it as lacking any revolutionary character; conservatives bemoaned Roosevelt for being socialist and prolabor. Traditional liberals expressed apprehensions about Social Security and the Tennessee Valley Authority, the most socialistic of New Deal measures, yet these received the least criticism of New Deal programs. Roosevelt aroused powerful hatred in the nation's political culture, but at least he could rightly claim that the New Deal rested on broad popular support. Contrastingly, in 1935, Mackenzie King, sounding much like Herbert Hoover, required not a platform but only a slogan—"King or chaos"—to win a resounding victory.[35]

Roosevelt followed in the next year with an even more lopsided triumph over his Republican opponent, pledging a war against the unreconstructed rich of the nation. Abandoned by the titans of U.S. business, the beneficiaries of early New Deal legislation, Roosevelt shifted to the left. There were new overtures to labor and to those apprehensive about a future without a pension. Few of the early experiments in national planning survived, and the reformist legislation, even Social Security, seems in retrospect quite modest. In 1937, when federal spending dwindled, the number of unemployed shot up again, thus demonstrating that private enterprise alone could not provide enough new jobs for a growing population or distribute income to provide the people adequate clothing, food, and shelter. The notion that government must be the employer of last resort had not yet taken hold, but the entry of government into the business of housing, banking, and public utilities signified the end of one era and the uncertain beginning of another. And though the New Dealers focused on "economic man" (principally white males), a departure from the Progressive-era fascination of molding a new person, they altered the political culture by shifting the public's attention from the private to the public sector. In the process, the relation between the federal government and the states and also the cities changed. At the center of the drama stood Roosevelt himself, who more than any of his predecessors—though Theodore was more popular and certainly never hated as much—changed the way ordinary people thought about government and about the presidency.[36]

For all the political and economic drama of the depression years in Canada and the United States, the Latin American and Caribbean experience in the thirties proved far more explosive and, consequently, more significant in the continent's future. In the United States and Canada, the crash cast doubts on the prevailing economic wisdom of at least two generations and brought opposition parties into power. In Latin America and the Caribbean, however, the crash marked the end of an economic and political era, perhaps less by discrediting the export economy model crafted by successive generations of liberal political regimes than by accelerating the move toward industrialization and the role of the state in the economy.[37]

Within two years of the October 1929 debacle on Wall Street, almost every Latin American government suffered a coup or revolution. In five South American nations—Bolivia, Peru, Argentina, Brazil, and Chile (all save that of Carlos Ibañez in Chile led by civilians)—the consequences of these political upheavals for the United States and the goal of the Roosevelt administration to restore U.S. trade in South America were considerable. From 1929 until the eve of Roosevelt's inauguration, U.S. exports to Latin America declined in value by more than 75 percent, and the nation's imports from the region by almost that much. Reviving that trade without harming domestic producers, it was generally agreed in Washington, was critical to restoring the nation's commerce with the world. The architect of this foreign economic policy, Secretary of State Hull, believed the best way of succeeding in this endeavor was to begin with a lowering of tariffs (accomplished in the 1934 Reciprocal Trade Agreements Act) and negotiation of bilateral commercial treaties with Latin American governments. Expansion of U.S. exports into Latin America did not hamper domestic industry, which confronted little competition from the south, or domestic commodities because those imports permitted in at a lower tariff, such as rubber, bananas, bauxite, and platinum, did not compete with domestic producers.[38]

The depression hit the Caribbean and Central America with devastating effect, worsening conditions and tensions that had festered for two generations. In Puerto Rico, the record of three decades of Americanization had exacerbated tensions within society and done little to improve the material conditions of ordinary Puerto Ricans. If anything, they were worse off economically in 1930 than in 1900. The New Dealers would undertake a much-publicized economic rehabilitation program designed to revamp the economy, but years of neglect and political squabbling had taken their toll. In 1931, one scholar characterized the U.S. record as a "broken pledge." A decade later, the new governor, Rexford Guy Tugwell, called Puerto Rico "the stricken land." (A few years earlier, the Moyne Commission had issued an equally depressing judgment about the British Caribbean.) Even independent countries like Cuba and Panama were so intimately linked to the U.S. economy that their governments could ill afford to shield their markets. Batista's variation of Caribbean nationalism did not extend to Cuba's foreign economic policy. Cuba's dependence on sugar actually increased in the 1930s. By the end of the decade, following years of negotiation, Panamanian merchants had largely achieved their goal of getting access to the canal transit market with a modification of the 1903 canal treaty; but the economic grip of the United States on the republic had scarcely lessened. Other countries, such as Guatemala and Honduras, tried for a few years to broaden their commercial ties with European countries but ultimately succumbed to U.S. pressures. In these places, the motto of Roosevelt's Good Neighbor policy—nonintervention, noninterference, and reciprocity—and even the president's pledge about "giving them a share" masked a concerted effort to bind their economies more closely to that of the United States. A few years after World War II, as Washington pressured Latin American governments to open their markets ever wider to U.S. products, the Mexican economist Jesús Silva Herzog commented on Roosevelt's policy: "The big stick has been replaced with the white glove . . . [but] compared with the policy of [Theodore] Roosevelt, the Good Neighbor Policy is a change of form rather than content."[39]

In South America, the power of the United States to forge another Pan-American economic union lessened considerably, as the new governments coming to power in the early years of the depression had an economic agenda that did not fill Hull's prescriptions. Their political model conformed more closely to European corporatist examples, especially Benito Mussolini's Italy. This was less a matter of ingrained anti-Americanism than a need to meet the demands of the economic crisis and the rapidly changing politics of the decade. Bennett and Roosevelt gained political power in large part because of the economic crisis, but they were elected. In major countries in South America, the new governments gained power by extralegal means, and though circumstances were everywhere different, there were some disturbing parallels. Bolivia's disgruntled military officers initiated the process in May 1930 when they removed President Hernando Siles. A civilian president, Daniel Salamanca, shortly took office, but the frustration of an economic crisis and their exclusion in the settlement of the Tacna-Arica dispute between Chile and Peru, which effectively denied the nation an outlet to the Pacific, enraged Bolivia's leaders. In 1932 they provoked a crisis with Paraguay over the Chaco, a vast, sparsely populated region lying between the two countries. Victory, they believed, would ensure Bolivia's access to the Atlantic and restore prosperity. The discovery of oil in the Standard Oil concession in the eastern region of the country was an added incentive.

The war lasted for four years and ended with an overwhelming Paraguayan victory, a triumph directly attributable to the machinations of Argentina. The United States, eager to keep the League of Nations from playing any role in the crisis, clashed with Argentina over a regional solution. From the onset both combatants looked to Buenos Aires, not to Washington, D.C., for a solution. Peace did not come to the Chaco until early 1936, when the Argentines finally permitted it. Later in the year, Bolivia's army under Germán Busch and David Toro seized power, ending nearly a half century of civilian rule. Influenced by Italian fascism and the 1917 Mexican constitution, they initiated an antiliberal, corporatist regime. In 1937, the military government nationalized the properties of Standard Oil on the grounds that the company had provoked the Chaco war. In the process, Bolivians, once strong admirers of U.S. power, had found another patron and protector.[40]

Early in the depression, a parallel process appeared to be taking shape in Peru, where disgruntled colonels overthrew the pro-U.S. Augusto Leguía in late August 1930. The following year, the country was thrown into political and social crisis when Haya de la Torre and the Aprista party challenged Luis Alberto Sánchez Cerro in the presidential election. Aprista rhetoric continued to be virulently anti–United States and hostile to U.S. business in the country, although Haya himself softened his earlier views sufficiently to persuade the U.S. minister that foreign capital would be secure in Peru. Haya lost the election, but the political and social crisis did not abate, as the Aprista hard-liners, declaring the election a fraud, threatened rebellion.

In July 1932, the Peruvian army crushed a revolt in Haya's hometown of Trujillo. In retaliation, an Aprista militant assassinated Sánchez Cerro in April 1932. Four years later, Peru's new president, Oscar R. Benavides, declared the Aprista party illegal. These circumstances boded ill for the U.S.–Peruvian connection, particularly in the late 1930s, when a band of inter-Americanists in Washington labored to forge a united hemisphere. Two very different people subtly changed things. One was Haya de la Torre, whose reminders about the place of indigenous people in the Americas—Indoamérica—appealed to diverse North Americans, particularly to Roosevelt's commissioner of Indian affairs, John Collier, and the popular journalist Carleton Beals. During the Sandino War, Beals had angered the U.S. military with his reporting on the war, but after a conversion to the Aprista cause, Beals became committed to the notion of "hemispheric regeneration." There was another success story in this symbiotic union of Andean-Indian spiritualism evoked by Haya de la Torre and North American materialism. Engineers at the Grace Company, sensitive to Peru's difficulties in marketing its sugar in the United States, applied their expertise to making paper out of bagasse. That modest beginning would lead to a paper-chemical industrial complex that would market modern plastic products by the 1960s.[41]

Where historical experiences and cultural makeup *appeared* to be similar, as in the case of Argentina and the United States, ironically, the relation worsened. In September 1930, the civilian president of Argentina, Hipólito Irigoyen, suffered an even more humiliating ouster than Leguía when the military drove him from office at gunpoint. Those who followed him in power looked to the Argentine past or to continental Europe for their political philosophy and to Great Britain as a trading partner. The division between these two groups— the first wishing to return to the pre-1912 oligarchical system, and the second, to craft a corporatist state emulating European fascism—proved too subtle for most North Americans to comprehend. Time and again in the *Concordancia*— a term referring to the political coalition crafted by President Juan B. Justo, a disciple of the first group—Argentina's leaders frustrated the U.S. design for a united hemisphere. Explanations varied. In the Chaco War, certainly, Argentine ambition and jealousy of Brazil played a role.

In the economic sphere, a stronger U.S. connection ill served Argentine interests. In 1933, Argentina opted for a basic commercial treaty with Great Britain (the Roca-Runciman Agreement), which guaranteed the nation certain quotas in the British home islands market it could never obtain from Washington. These seemed minor obstacles, but they reflected more consequential differences than the oft-cited observation about Argentine determination to share with North Americans a dominating role in the hemisphere. Argentina's war of independence, its tortured nineteenth-century route to nationhood, its immigrant experience, its relation with Europe and Europeans—all varied in critical ways from the U.S. experience. Most fundamental was the role of the military. When the Argentine generals tossed out Irigoyen, few raised a protesting voice. The 1930 revolution, wrote its chronicler, "was the army transformed into people, and the people transformed into army."[42]

Military men did not triumph everywhere. Venezuela remained in the grip of Juan Vicente Gómez and thus escaped the political crisis sweeping the continent in 1930. In Colombia, Liberals at last ended thirty years of Conservative rule and commenced the *revolución en marcha,* a program of liberal reform sometimes compared with the New Deal. Chile's Colonel Carlos Ibañez, who had gained the presidency in 1927 by intimidating the civilian president to the extent that he resigned, weathered the first two years of the crash then was hounded from office during a general strike. But circumstances scarcely favored a cordial Chilean–U.S. relation. His successor, confronting a mutiny of naval officers who demanded agrarian reform and nationalization of the nitrate industry, requested U.S. military assistance, but President Hoover refused. The following year leaders of a short-lived Socialist republic blamed the United States for the depression in Chile, alarming several U.S. businessmen in the country.

Perhaps the most ominous of the coups in South America was the overthrow of Brazil's president Washington Luís, which commenced with an army coup in Rio de Janeiro and the installation of a three-man military junta and ended with the triumph of Getúlio Vargas, an ambitious politician from Río Grande do Sul, who had assumed nominal command of a revolutionary army. Fearful that the old Brazilian custom of cutting a deal at the top would deny him power, Vargas compelled the military junta to relent by pledging that he would not purge the army. Eight days after being named chief of the provisional government in early November 1930, he suspended Brazil's constitution and named intervenors for every state except Minas Gerais, where a political crony governed. It was the end of the Old Republic.[43]

Brazil shared with Argentina a desire to dominate the southern cone but did not emulate its rival in its dealings with the United States, a condition sometimes attributed to the early-twentieth-century diplomacy of Rio Branco or Vargas's decision to bring Brazil into the war when the Argentines appeared to be following a pro-Axis course. Although Brazilian–U.S. political and economic ties had always been stronger, the explanation for the Brazilian variation in the thirties lay elsewhere. When Vargas first came to power, the Department of State initially refused to recognize his government, then abruptly saw the blunder and reversed the decision. In 1932 Brazil adopted a new constitution, further evidence in U.S. eyes that Latin America's largest nation was pursuing a political course different from that of Argentina. By mid-decade, however, everything changed. Confronted with powerful adversaries on the right (the Integralistas, led by Plínio Salgado) and the left (the National Liberation Alliance, controlled by the Communists), Vargas retaliated, not by attacking both simultaneously but one at a time, beginning with the National

Liberation Alliance. The crushing of the alliance of course pleased the Integralistas, who sensed that Vargas must be one of their own when in 1937 he dissolved congress and declared the *Estado Nôvo,* a government modeled loosely on Mussolini's brand of fascism. Vargas suspended foreign debt payments, mandated a tax on exchange transactions, and declared a monopoly on foreign exchange sales. In less than a year, economic power moved from the private sector to the state. As if to symbolize the power of Brazil's central government and the power of the federal armed forces over the historically defiant states, Vargas ordered a public burning of twenty state flags.[44]

Elsewhere in the hemisphere, the mere suspicion of fascist leanings of a government could provoke Hull, but in his dealings with Brazilian leaders the secretary of state demonstrated his Tennessee political skills. At the 1933 Montevideo conference, Hull wrote later in his memoirs, the Brazilians were edgy about the prospects of a U.S.–Argentine rapprochement, and Hull tried to reassure them in the following years. The informal diplomacy began to pay off: Brazil became more supportive of Washington's efforts to counter the German trade offensive in Latin America in the 1930s and, especially, of the Roosevelt administration's position in the inter-American system. Roosevelt received a thunderous welcome in Rio de Janeiro on his way to the 1936 conference on peace and war in Buenos Aires, attributing the ovations to the "moral effects" of the Good Neighbor policy. In Vargas's mind and in Roosevelt's, too, the moral effects of policy had less to do with the matter than the somber reality that the United States needed Brazil, and Vargas sensed the opportunity. German influence in Brazil continued to mount, but the fragile bonds of the Brazilian–United States alliance remained intact.[45]

Mexico posed an altogether different problem, particularly when Lázaro Cárdenas of Michoacán became president in 1934. Like Obregón and Calles, Cárdenas had a military background and exhibited much of the same determination as Calles and Obregón in running the country. He shared their views about the necessity of modernizing the Mexican economy and taming the military, but he went about it very differently. Whereas Calles had offered reassurances to U.S. emissaries and companies about the limitations of agrarian reform, Cárdenas used the Agrarian Code of 1934 to transform Mexican agriculture, distributing during his six-year presidency almost forty-four million acres of land—more than two and a half times the land redistributed by post-1917 regimes—to *ejidatarios,* families and individuals on an *ejido* who possessed rights of usufruct in the land, and so-called small landowners, including some Mexicans and foreigners who held large amounts of land. He organized peasants into a confederation and incorporated them in the revamped Party of the Mexican Revolution. Highly publicized (and still lauded as the rejuvenation of the revolutionary pledge to the peasant), Cárdenas's agrarian program probably did just as much to ensure the survival of the large landowner, and in fact benefited him more than the peasant. In 1940, 60 percent of Mexico's arable land lay in parcels of more than twenty-five hundred acres, and two-thirds of these landholdings were more than twenty-five thousand acres. Large and even small landowners also gained from easier access to markets, capital, and technology. When Cárdenas left the presidency, less than 10 percent of ejidatarios labored on the collectives, and these often clashed with sharecroppers, migrants, or peasants who had gotten nothing. The results of the agrarian reform in Sonora and the north would have pleased Obregón, Calles, and U.S. agricultural economists. Those landlords driven out were those who had refused to modernize. Cárdenas, the "true revolutionary," had made the north into a Mexican imitation of U.S. agriculture.[46]

Unlike his predecessors, Cárdenas looked beyond the United States in charting Mexico's international course. Mexico, he believed, must not only industrialize but take advantage of the weaknesses of the great powers to chart a distinctive foreign policy among the competing political systems of fascism, communism, and liberalism. Mexico's economy was capitalist and the minister of finance (Hacienda) admired the New Deal, to be sure, but when the Roosevelt administration declared its commitment to nonintervention, Cárdenas pushed for Mexico's reinstatement in the League of Nations in the belief that the league could play an important role in settling hemispheric disputes. Perhaps nothing better exemplifies Cárdenas's realistic approach to international affairs than his belief, which he expressed as early as 1934, that war between Japan and the United States was inevitable and the parallel fear that European fascism would inspire imitators among Latin American Hispanists. A Japanese–United States conflict would compel Mexico to join a U.S. alliance; the triumph of fascism in Spain and its spread to the Americas would prompt U.S. intervention and lead to a reversal of the Good Neighbor policy. Yet these circumstances did not drive Cárdenas closer to the United States. After all, the credos of the revolution dictated another agenda. Much to the discomfiture of the Roosevelt administration, the Japanese had both a military and naval attaché in Mexico City, and, in a clear departure from the policy pursued by the west European powers and the United States, Mexico joined the Soviet Union in providing aid to the Spanish republic. In 1937, averring that both countries had a common commitment to economic independence, Cárdenas commenced discussions for a commercial agreement with German representatives.[47]

But in fall 1937 and winter 1938, Mexico's domestic and international condition changed dramatically and rapidly with three parallel crises. The first occurred in the aftermath of a strike by Mexico's national petroleum union, whose leaders demanded not only higher wages and more social benefits for the workers but control of the workplace. Increasingly, Cárdenas found himself pressured by the unions to bring the oil companies, principally British and United States, to heel; the companies, remembering how Porfirio Díaz had handled labor disputes, wanted Cárdenas to discipline the workers. The second problem was the Saturnino Cedillo rebellion in the Federal District and in a cluster of states to the west and northwest of the capital. Fueled by growing urban and particularly rural discontent with the revolution and linked ideologically to Spanish and Italian fascist groups, the Cedillo uprising and the National Sinarquista Union (those opposed to anarchy) it spawned posed as serious a challenge to the regime as the *cristero* revolt of the late 1920s. To complicate matters, the Mexican government confronted in fall 1937 an economic crisis for which there seemed to be a single solution: an appeal to the U.S. Treasury for economic assistance and an olive branch to the foreign oil companies. Again, as in the late 1920s, the Mexican government emerged from these crises stronger than ever. It got desperately needed financial assistance from Washington, D.C., because, as Secretary of the Treasury Henry Morgenthau, Jr., made clear to Roosevelt, if the United States did not respond, Germany, Italy, or Japan would. Cárdenas crushed the Cedillo revolt, and, though the *sinarquistas* continued to pose a threat for several more years, they possessed little economic or political power, and the uprising proved to be an embarrassment to the Germans, who were persuaded that civil war in Mexico could benefit only the United States.[48]

Cárdenas's handling of the dispute between the petroleum workers and the foreign companies constituted his most formidable test during these critical years. Frankly, despite his convictions about the sanctity of Article 27, he appeared reluctant to take up the cause of the oil workers. But on March 1, 1938, the Mexican Supreme Court issued a decree that effectively sided with the workers. Persuaded they had the backing of the British and especially the United States governments, the companies resisted the decree. In the following weeks, outraged oil workers began seizing foreign (principally British) oil properties. His authority challenged on other fronts, Cárdenas had to respond where his predecessors had hesitated. On March 18, he announced the ex-propriation of the foreign oil companies, explaining that "the social interests of the laboring classes of all the industries demand it." The oil companies called the decree a confiscation, brought their engineers and geologists home, and commenced a propaganda campaign against the Mexican government. In the U.S. Congress there were denunciations of "bolshevist Mexico" and calls for a boycott of Mexican silver purchases. Domestic political pressures on Roosevelt to press the Mexican government to reverse the decision or at least submit to arbitration intensified. More militant voices called for intervention. Cárdenas held firm. The growing international crisis coupled with the smash-ing of the Cedillo rebellion strengthened his position. Most of the properties expropriated were British, not U.S., holdings, a consideration of no small im-portance to Roosevelt, as were reminders from U.S. investors, manufacturers, and mining proprietors who stood to lose financially if the boycott succeeded or Mexico was forced into immediate arbitration.[49]

At the Inter-American Conference in Lima in December 1938, the Mexican delegation joined the Argentine contingent in reaffirming the principle of ab-solute nonintervention and in expressing doubts about Hull's efforts to con-demn the German political and economic onslaught in Latin America. But for Mexico there would be no reprise of the role it had played in the hemisphere in World War I. The following year, as Europe plunged into war, the Mexican government confronted its final interwar political and social crisis, continuing violence in the countryside from the sinarquistas and the launching of a na-tional opposition party, National Action, which fielded a candidate in the 1940 election. National Action could count on international as well as national sup-port, and for a few months in spring 1940 there were rumors that if the Na-tional Action candidate, Juan Andreu Almazán, could raise an army and gain control of several Mexican states, he would be recognized as the legitimate government of Mexico. Just as quickly, the Roosevelt administration made it clear that it would countenance no such takeover, and in one of the most fraudulent elections in Mexican history, Manuel Ávila Camacho was chosen as Cárdenas's successor. The presence of vice president–elect Henry Wallace at his inauguration confirmed what Cárdenas had anticipated six years before: Mexico could benefit from the international crisis and preserve the revolu-tionary state against its enemies, foreign and domestic. But the price had been high, for Mexico in 1940 remained a fragmented society linked in symbiotic fashion to its northern neighbor.

The Decade of Global War

For the Americas the decade of global war falls roughly between two bench-mark dates—1938 and 1948—both of which are seminal years in transatlantic history because of the Munich Crisis over Czechoslovakia and the announce-ment of the Marshall Plan to rebuild ravaged European economies, respec-tively. These are critical years for the Western Hemisphere as well. In De-cember 1938, apprehensions about the world situation prompted delegates to the eighth Inter-American Conference in Lima to invoke a hemispheric per-spective by approving a sweeping Declaration of American Principles, most of which Secretary of State Cordell Hull had enunciated in July 1937. The decla-ration called for peaceful settlement of disputes between nations and faithful observance of treaties and urged economic and intellectual cooperation among nations as essential to world peace. The proposal fell short of the U.S. objective to isolate the Americas from the contagion of war by affirming hemi-spheric "isolationism," though the conferees did lay some guidelines for action in the event war erupted in Europe. In spring 1948, at the Ninth Inter-American Conference in Bogotá, Colombia, hemispheric representatives ap-proved the Charter of the Organization of American States, an American Treaty on Pacific Settlement, an American Declaration of the Rights and Duties of Man, and an Economic Agreement. In the same year, Costa Rica's vote formally approved the Inter-American Treaty of Reciprocal Assistance signed at Rio de Janeiro in 1947 at the Inter-American Conference for the Maintenance of Continental Peace and Security. As had been the case at the Lima conference a decade earlier, the hemispheric meeting at Bogotá occurred during a critical time in the cold war. In both meetings, undeniably, events in Europe and Asia dramatically influenced the thinking of the delegates. Their affirmations of continental solidarity reflected their global concerns as well as their global strategies.

Presumably, these commitments signaled a new departure in the quest for a unified continent as well. Despite the fashioning of a wartime alliance that went beyond anything accomplished in World War I, the Americas seemed no closer to a sustainable unifying mission in 1948 than in 1938. Most clearly, it is generally acknowledged, cold war imperatives constituted the driving force in U.S. policy in the Americas. Fundamental differences over economic policy of the prewar years, subsumed by the wartime crisis, revived in the postwar years. Not only did the Western Hemisphere idea or the belief in a transnational cultural community lose strength, within the U.S. bureaucracy those who had championed the hemispheric connection in the interwar and wartime years (that generation's "north-southers") saw their influence rapidly erode. Yet, in often nuanced ways, the experience of these years strengthened no less important symbiotic linkages that survived the war and persisted well into the cold war era.

The Hemisphere on the Eve of Pearl Harbor
One of the familiar stories about the decade of global war in the Americas conforms to a script wherein the United States recognized the danger of the international situation to the security of the Americas as early as 1935 and began to take energetic measures in the hemisphere to address the challenge, only to be thwarted by a coalition of South American states led by Argentina. In the process, the Roosevelt administration effectively (if not explicitly) began to "panamericanize" the Monroe Doctrine with pledges of nonintervention and a parallel respect for Latin American sovereignty and culture. At the Buenos Aires Conference on Peace and War in 1936, Roosevelt urged the delegates to adopt measures to keep any European conflict out of the Western Hemisphere. Two years later, the agenda included proposals for a hemispheric league of nations and court of justice. Neither was approved, although the delegates reaffirmed their commitment to continental solidarity and their willingness to defend it. But they signed no defense treaty and made no provision for

machinery to eliminate war. The U.S. entourage departed from Lima still troubled about perceived Argentine machinations against Washington's plans for hemispheric solidarity. Predictably, U.S. delegates attributed the hesitance of their Latin American colleagues to a naivete about the dangers of war and an unjustifiable apprehension about U.S. intentions. The truth of the matter proved to be more complicated. As the Argentine Carlos Saavedra Lamas recognized, Latin Americans would be foolish to forsake the security guarantees of the League of Nations or to abandon their ties with Europe to placate the United States.[1]

Those most concerned about German and Italian influence in the Americas noted that the European fascist political and even economic impact derived largely from undeniable cultural ties, particularly the appeal of corporatist political thought identified with Nazism and especially fascism and continuing resentments over U.S. intervention. A generation of contemporary writers, some of them harsh critics of U.S. policy, pointed out that the most expedient way to overcome this Old World challenge lay in panamericanizing the Monroe Doctrine and strengthening cultural ties. The first would provide hemispheric security by making it a collective rather than a unilateral task, and the second would reaffirm the ideal of a hemisphere of "good neighbors." Modern scholars have picked up on these themes in their reevaluations of the Good Neighbor policy in peace and war, arguing that U.S. leaders grievously erred in their refusal, among other things, to approve the creation of an Inter-American Development Bank or to sustain the democratic forces unleashed throughout Latin America during the war. Put bluntly, those who subscribe to this view believe the Roosevelt administration promoted the idea of hemispheric unity largely as a means of defeating the isolationists within the country and especially in the U.S. Congress in order to lay a foundation for a global political and economic policy. That interpretation of events also warrants reconsideration.[2]

At the Lima conference, the U.S. delegation had failed to sever the cultural and economic ties between Latin America and Europe and to persuade their hemispheric colleagues to adopt a stronger declaration. A year later, at the special conference of foreign ministers in Panama in October 1939, the United States would get a stronger commitment from Latin American governments, but the reasons had less to do with what the United States wanted than with the uncertainties created by the outbreak of war in Europe. The Panama conference—the first of three special meetings authorized at Lima—is usually remembered for its sanction of Roosevelt's proposal of a hemispheric "safety belt," which prohibited the belligerents from waging war in the imaginary and admittedly indefensible "neutral waters" lying three hundred miles outside the Americas. (Canada, as a belligerent, was of course excluded.) Hull considered the plan not only impractical but a violation of neutrality. The British made it clear they could not respect the safety belt unless the U.S. Navy was prepared to enforce it by keeping German warships out of the proscribed zone.[3]

Too few observers paused to consider that in 1939 the inter-American system, whatever its flaws, proved to be the only viable international organization in the disintegrating world order. A far more critical issue for most of the delegates was the desperate economic situation confronted by Latin American governments suddenly deprived of their commercial ties with Europe. Their only recourse lay in cooperating with the United States, a commitment resting on economic necessity, not conviction. The U.S. response came in the form of a pledge to assist the republics in overcoming the ruptures in trade. Latin Americans, of course, wanted approval of an Inter-American Development Bank, and by May 1940 eight of the republics had pledged to assist in funding it. But when the administration brought the plan to Congress, conservatives balked at this proposal on the grounds that it would be harmful to the nation's economic strategies. Here, again, there was a price to be paid, for U.S. economic planners now determined that the most expedient way of meeting the problem lay in shifting away from Wilsonian free trade ideas and the reciprocal trade program and using the Export-Import Bank to finance inter-American trade. The implications of such an approach for fashioning long-lasting hemispheric economic ties were ominous. From 1938 to 1940, Latin Americans were shorn of much of their trade with Europe and deprived of the benefits of trade within the British imperial economy. They bought from and sold to the United States at an economic disadvantage.[4]

The naval battle between three British warships and the German pocket battleship *Graf Spee* off the coast of Uruguay in late 1939 made clear the vulnerability of South America's Atlantic coast, but the fall of France in June 1940 led to a far more serious crisis. Among the northern republics of South America, there were immediate concerns about German submarine patrols and the unsettling possibility that defeated France and the Netherlands might be compelled to cede their New World possessions to Germany. The State Department brought considerable pressure on the Colombian government to take over SCADTA (a joint Colombian-German airline) and replace its German and Italian pilots. In the United States, of course, apprehension about Caribbean security had prompted some (among them the Republican Frank Knox, who became secretary of the navy in 1940) to advocate seizure of European possessions in the West Indies to prevent a German takeover of the islands. Even before the collapse of France, polls in a still overwhelmingly isolationist United States revealed that two-thirds of the public favored military intervention in Latin America to prevent German takeovers. The U.S. Congress, reviving an 1811 "no transfer" statement originally applied to Spanish Florida, declared its unwillingness to recognize the transfer of any European colony in the Caribbean to another European power and gave the president the authority to enforce it. In anticipation of a German victory in Europe, which meant the United States must assume most of the responsibility for defending the Americas, the Rainbow 4 plan of the Army-Navy Board called for U.S. "protective custody" of European possessions in the hemisphere as well as protecting the Atlantic approaches to the Panama Canal.[5]

Within the United States, the fall of France in June 1940 dramatically altered thinking about the urgency of aid to the British, certainly, and also reinforced public apprehension about Hitler's designs on the Americas. In the preceding years the United States had seemed intent on severing the European, including the British, connection with the Americas. Protection of Europe's Caribbean empire from German control dominated U.S. concerns at the meeting of foreign ministers at Havana in July, though Hull was probably correct in assuming that the Germans were more interested in influencing several Latin American countries than in acquiring new territories. A few North Americans remained wary, as did several South American leaders, about the north-south connection as an effective means of achieving hemispheric security. Skeptics such as the Yale political scientist Nicholas Spykman saw the issue as a clear choice between "Fortress America," which now incorporated the notion of an impregnable Western Hemisphere, or alliance with Great Britain. For Spykman and other internationalists, unity with the rest of the Americas was as shortsighted as isolationism, for the economic future of much of Latin America depended on Britain's survival. "Hemisphere defense is no defense at all," Spykman wrote. "The Second World War will be won or lost in Europe and Asia. If our allies in the Old World are defeated, we cannot hold South America; if we defeat the German-Japanese Alliance abroad, our good neighbors will need no protection."[6]

By a curious but understandable logic some hemispheric leaders concluded that Latin Americans could not rely on the United States for security. At Havana, the Argentine Leopoldo Melo had mused to Hull about what South American nations confronted from a militant Germany. Caribbean states could rely on the United States to prevent a German occupation in the nearby West Indies, he pointed out, but Argentina lay sixty-five hundred miles from Washington. He could not have known about Rainbow 4's limitations on U.S. army and naval operations to the bulge of Brazil. In any event, Roosevelt took no chances. On the day the Havana conference convened, the president announced that he was recommending to Congress an increase of Export-Import Bank lending from $200 to $700 million with the purpose of assisting Latin American governments in marketing their surpluses. A week later, the delegates to the Havana conference approved the Act of Havana, empowering any hemispheric republic to occupy a European colony in the Americas threatened by a German takeover.[7]

Again, in a critical moment, the United States looked south for expressions of support but had to pay an economic price for them. The governments of Guatemala, Venezuela, and Argentina nurtured old territorial claims, respectively, on British Honduras, British Guiana, and the Falkland (or Malvinas) Islands. Early in September, the United States signed the "destroyers-for-bases" agreement with the British, trading fifty destroyers for ninety-nine-year leases on naval and air bases in Newfoundland, the Bahamas, Jamaica, Antigua, St. Lucia, Trinidad, British Guiana, and Jamaica. In Panama, U.S. military commanders trying to acquire sites with long-term leases for air defense installations beyond the Canal Zone were at loggerheads with a nationalistic president, Arnulfo Arias, who objected to leases that went beyond the war and insisted on economic concessions before permitting occupation of the sites. As things worked out, the situation in the French West Indies proved to be less problematical because French officials in the West Indies forestalled any unilateral U.S. military action by declaring neutrality. In Panama, contrastingly, the wrangling with Arias persisted until his ouster in October 1941 in a coup orchestrated by his minister of justice, Ricardo de la Guardia. The new president proved more cooperative, and he obtained several major economic concessions from the United States.[8]

The psychological impact of the fall of France perhaps best explained the willingness of South American representatives to the Havana conference to accept the declaration of Havana. For the United States, and particularly for Roosevelt, the drama of events in Europe posed something more ominous. Clearly, domestic isolationism was no longer defensible, but what of the appeal of the parallel argument for hemispheric isolationism? The British ambassador, Lord Lothian, feared the United States would keep its battleships and carriers in the Pacific as a deterrent to the Japanese. He overlooked a possible scenario whereby the United States pulled back from the western Pacific and concentrated on defending the Western Hemisphere. In May 1940, Chief of Staff George C. Marshall cited the defense of the Panama Canal and the uncertainties about what would happen in the Americas to reinforce his recommendation to deny Prime Minister Winston Churchill's request for forty to fifty destroyers and two hundred fighter planes.[9]

Stories about pro-German and pro-Italian fifth columnists in Argentina, Uruguay, and Brazil alarmed Roosevelt. Argentine president Roberto Ortiz was outspokenly pro-French, but he took little action against pro-Nazi elements. Two hundred thousand Germans and Italians lived in Uruguay; a million Germans, the U.S. military attaché estimated, resided in Brazil. Presumably, they were kindred spirits ready to move at Berlin's command. When Roosevelt got wind of a plot hatched by an Uruguayan Nazi, Gero Arnulf Fuhrmann, to overthrow the Uruguayan government, he ordered two cruisers to South American waters. From London came a bizarre story about six thousand German soldiers secreted in the holds of merchant vessels headed for Brazil. Over the hectic weekend May 27–28, 1940, an army/navy planning group drew up the Pot of Gold plan. If both France and Britain fell to the German war machine, the United States would occupy the Brazilian bulge with the acquiescence of the Brazilian government! Six weeks later, as the foreign ministers gathered in the sweltering heat of a Cuban summer, the War Plans Division drew up yet another scenario for German domination of South America, beginning with economic pressures, followed by either an airborne invasion or the voluntary association of several countries (Uruguay, Argentina, and Brazil) with the Axis bloc, and culminating in an attack on the Panama Canal.[10]

None of these disturbing stories about fifth columnists or prospective German invasions of South America meant that the Roosevelt administration had committed to the notion of a fortified hemisphere isolated from the war in Europe. For one thing, Canada's declaration of war against Germany in September 1939 had already indirectly linked the United States to Britain's survival. A year earlier, during the Munich crisis, Roosevelt had pledged in a speech in Kingston, Ontario, that the United States would not remain indifferent if Canada were threatened by another empire. At the time, some of King's advisors told him that he had perhaps made too much of the pledge. Canada's probable enemies lay outside the Western Hemisphere, and Roosevelt had astutely avoided making any commitment to democracies in Europe. In actuality, after the British prime minister Neville Chamberlain yielded a third of Czechoslovakia to Hitler, Roosevelt had praised Chamberlain's appeasement of Germany in a letter to King. But in mid-August 1940 Roosevelt gave substance to his words when he and King negotiated an informal executive agreement at Ogdensburg, N.Y., providing for a Permanent Joint Board of Defense and the stationing of ninety-four thousand U.S. troops near the Canadian border. At Havana, Hull did further damage to the plan for an economically self-sufficient hemisphere by killing the Inter-American Trading Corporation. A few days after the cabinet approved the destroyers-for-bases deal, Roosevelt in felicitous phrases spoke publicly about the unity of the Americas. But when Hull returned from Havana with somber reminders that a German victory over Britain would doubtless prompt the Brazilian, Argentine, Uruguayan, and even the Chilean government to move closer to Berlin, Roosevelt knew that, as Spykman had prophesied, the security of the Americas depended on Britain's survival.[11]

In September 1940, the inter-American system seemed almost as fragile as it had a year before, when Hitler had unleashed his blitzkrieg against Poland. Only Canada had gone to war against the German empire. For the rest of the Americas, whatever passed for a common commitment against the "Axis evil" rested on the fragile bonds created at the Lima conference and the acquiescence in U.S. leadership registered at Panama in October 1939 and at Havana in July 1940. Undeniably, when compared with the efforts of the First World War, the willingness of hemispheric nations to keep the European war from the Americas seemed far more impressive than it had in 1914, yet even after Havana expressions of inter-American solidarity for individual governments almost always concealed the lack of realistic alternatives and not a belief in a common history or the fear of a common peril. In such circumstances, even onetime critics of U.S. policy in Latin America like Samuel Guy Inman tried to articulate a common purpose with his vision of a continent of 275 million people spread over a land mass four times greater than that of Europe but unified by a belief in republican government. For less altruistic motives, the Office of Coordinator of Inter-American Affairs, created in 1940 and headed by Nelson A. Rockefeller, would establish as its goal the replacement of the "Axis credo" with the "U.S. credo" in Latin America.[12]

The War Years

The United States entered World War II with essentially the same hemispheric allies that had followed its lead in declaring war in 1917, small Caribbean and Central American countries with no realistic choice save to join in a declaration of war. Elsewhere, however, the situation was rife with uncertainty. Colombia and Venezuela broke diplomatic relations. Other South American governments, fearful of antagonizing Germany or Japan without any certainty of British or even U.S. protection, maintained their neutrality. When the foreign ministers met at Rio de Janeiro in January to thrash out the issue, Undersecretary of State Sumner Welles dutifully presented the case about the need for solidarity and pledged U.S. assistance to those governments willing to sever diplomatic relations. Even the Argentine and Chilean delegates seemed persuaded, but in the midst of the conference Welles learned that the Argentine president had refused to go along with his foreign minister's recommendation. Rather than abide by the State Department directive to insist on unanimity, Welles decided to support a modified proposal recommending rather than requiring severance of diplomatic relations. To Hull, the entire affair constituted a humiliation of the United States at the hands of the Argentines. In accommodating them, Welles's actions constituted disloyalty. Roosevelt wisely chose to follow Welles's recommendation, and when the Rio meeting adjourned, nineteen of the twenty-one governments represented had broken diplomatic relations with the Axis powers. In the strategic southern cone, only Argentina and Chile held back. Cynical commentators noted that the United States had achieved little, but a young Eric Sevareid, who covered the conference for the Columbia Broadcasting System, reckoned its significance differently. "In return for a unanimous agreement of twenty nations to break commercial ties with the Axis, an almost unanimous agreement to break diplomatic relations," he noted, "we [the United States] have pledged ourselves not only to help maintain the faltering economic systems by which 120,000,000 persons live . . . but, more important and more difficult, physically to protect them from attack by the Axis."[13]

The history of the Western Hemisphere in World War II was in actuality a series of parallel and interrelated stories. One was the often frustrating effort of the U.S. government to create a military and political alliance of nations committed to the Allied cause and its wartime umbrella organization, the United Nations, the successor to the League of Nations. From securing the critical declarations of war by the Mexican and Brazilian governments in late spring 1942 to acquiescing in Argentina's belated commitment to the Allied side in late March 1945, Washington undertook to mold a hemisphere of one collective mind, guided of course from the United States. Such was the official U.S. position, yet it was riddled with contradictions that inevitably created doubts throughout the Americas. During the perilous year of 1942, when Canadian leaders publicly commented that Canada's participation in the inter-American system did not interfere with its role in the British commonwealth of nations, the U.S. Department of State responded by publishing its instructions to delegates to the 1928 Havana conference opposing any such notion![14]

After the war broke out in Europe, the U.S. military began training junior Latin American offers and increased the number of its military, naval, and air missions in Latin America from only five in 1938 to thirteen by mid-1942. A modern hemispheric military would be more adept at confronting fifth columnists and pro-Axis agitators. Exploiting the media, advertisements in friendly newspapers, magazines, movies, and even cartoons, the Office of Coordinator of Inter-American Affairs (OCIA) drew on a budget that increased from $3.5 to $38 million by mid-1942 to launch its campaign of psychological warfare. Individual rights and freedom of the press suffered, predictably, and some observers apprehensive about national sovereignty and domestic control of the economy complained about OCIA's use of the Reconstruction Finance Corporation as a model to establish similar bureaucracies throughout Latin America. But OCIA also supplied assistance to local communities in building safe water systems, providing midwife services, raising healthy animals, and even training farmers how to grow more abundant crops. As suspicions about his spending priorities increased, Rockefeller was quick to remind skeptics in Congress in 1944 that OCIA was "laying foundations for economic development and the expansion of markets based on a rising standard of living."[15]

Such words sounded both noble and self-serving, and modern critics of U.S. policy toward Latin America and the Caribbean during the war sometimes indict OCIA as little more than an agency for promoting U.S. economic control, but it was only one of several agencies exercising U.S. economic influence. Through the office of Economic and Financial Control the United States oversaw financial and commercial activities between hemispheric nations and "aggressor states." The Board of Economic Warfare facilitated commodities exchanges and made quarterly allotments of steel, iron, farm equipment, and other scarce products to Latin American countries. An inter-American development commission established agencies in every hemispheric republic to dispense information on production and trade development, and the American Hemispheric Exports Office assured that every Latin American country received commodities at a parity with U.S. civilians. Undeniably, such endeavors aroused Latin American suspicions about the U.S. commitment to hemispheric unity, particularly after the forced departure of Welles from the State Department and Rockefeller's efforts to defuse growing congressional skepticism about U.S. expenditures in Latin America. In December 1943, Senator Hugh Butler (R, Nebraska), who had taken a whirlwind two-month tour of the region, declared that the administration had largely wasted $6 billion in trying to buy the friendship of countries socially backward and with little prospect of developing as democracies. Although Butler denied the charge, some of his colleagues considered his report, a summary of which appeared in the *Reader's Digest*, an indictment of the Good Neighbor policy. In the following months, a report from the Aviation Subcommittee of the House Military Affairs Committee mitigated some of the damage with reassurances about the administration's handling of hemispheric affairs. Latin American readers heartened to some of the passages but just as quickly expressed concerns that its recommendations about continuing U.S. use of air bases after the war would revive anti-Americanism throughout the continent. "If the good feeling that has recently been established is to last," warned an Ecuadorian newspaper, "imperialism must be scrapped once and for all."[16]

For the United States, the most important hemispheric countries were Mexico and Brazil, the most critical region, the circum-Caribbean. Mexico's decision to enter the war on the side of the United States—an unavoidable choice, as Cárdenas had predicted—proved to be one of the most consequential choices in the economic and political history of the nation. By mid-1941, Mexican leaders determined that Germany could not win the war in Europe. Before the end of the year, the Mexican government reached an agreement to compensate the oil barons who had lost out in the 1938 nationalization. In early 1942, Ávila Camacho approved the Mexican-American Joint Defense Commission, named Cárdenas as head of the Pacific Military Region, and called on Mexicans to cooperate fully with the United States. Such a comment befuddled many Mexicans, most of whom retained their instinctive suspicions about North Americans, but Ávila Camacho remembered Carranza's mistake of placating the Germans in World War I. After all, many of the president's political enemies were pro-German, and by acknowledging the U.S. connection he was reminding them of their vulnerability. Besides, Mexico's economic future depended on acceleration of the industrialization program, and that required accommodation with the United States. When a German submarine sank two Mexican tankers in the Gulf of Mexico in May 1942, killing twelve Mexicans, Ávila Camacho demanded a formal apology from the Italian, German, and Japanese governments. When he failed to get a satisfactory response, the president called for a formal declaration of war.[17]

Mexico was a reluctant belligerent, but despite continuing suspicions about alliance with the United States, a determined and organized minority patriotically supported the war, in part because government propaganda portrayed the commitment as a defensive struggle and, frankly, because Cárdenas's assumption of the office of minister of defense offered reassurances that no U.S. troops would occupy Mexican soil. Those Mexicans not organized into any labor union or political party—in other words, the majority of the population— were more ambivalent. Mexicans participated in blackouts and civil defense exercises and, like their North American counterparts, suffered wartime restrictions on consumer goods. As a wartime leader, Ávila Camacho possessed powers that Spanish viceroys would have envied. Congress made the president a virtual dictator of the nation, and he used the wartime emergency to strengthen the government's hold on the country's often factious labor unions. With the timely assistance of the FBI's Special Intelligence Service, the government cracked down on Mexican fifth columnists. It agreed to supply farmworkers (*braceros*) to North American growers, drawing many from the rural areas of west central Mexico, where the *sinarquistas* had been strongest. Other Mexican migrant workers labored on U.S. railroads and in war plants; 250,000 served in the U.S. military, 14,000 of them in a war theater. More significant for the nation's future was the strengthening of economic bonds, symbolically acknowledged in the 1943 meeting between Roosevelt and Ávila Camacho in Monterrey and the creation of the Mexican-American Commission of Economic Cooperation. By 1943, the United States absorbed 90 percent of Mexico's exports. Mexican industrialists expanded old industries and developed new ones. With U.S. assistance, the Mexican government built a modern steel plant at Monclova. National income tripled during the war, creating new wealth and laying a foundation for a modern industrial economy and with it a modern nation. In words that would have perturbed even old Don Porfirio, the Mexican foreign minister described the wartime frontier with the United States as "a line that unites rather than divides us." Had the revolutionary promise of emancipation from the economic grip of the United States been mortgaged in the service of a modern industrial society?[18]

Few asked a similar question in Brazil, which received more Lend-Lease assistance than Mexico because the circumstances of its alliance with the United States were very different. As much as Cordell Hull grumbled about dealing with the Mexican government, he never found reason to call Cárdenas a protofascist. When Getúlio Vargas declared the *Estado Nôvo* in Brazil in 1937, contrastingly, Mussolini and Hitler believed they were now dealing with a New World kindred spirit. In a stroke, Vargas suspended payment on the foreign debt and declared a tax on exchange transactions, thus transferring economic power to the state. But Vargas proved as calculating as his Mexican contemporaries. Before Pearl Harbor he began cracking down on German aliens and closing German social clubs while extending reassurances to Berlin about Brazilian neutrality. In early fall 1941 Vargas signed a Lend-Lease agreement with Washington providing for tanks, planes, trucks, and the development of air defense sites at locations in the vulnerable northeastern bulge. When U.S. negotiators brought up the issue of stationing U.S. troops at the bases, Vargas declined.

The Japanese attack on Pearl Harbor persuaded Vargas that the Brazilian future lay with the United States. At the Rio conference in January 1942, he professed solidarity with the North American cause. Nowhere else in the Americas did fifth columnists receive more ruthless treatment than at the hands of Vargas's police. In August 1942, after the sinking of five Brazilian ships, Brazil became the first South American country to declare war against Germany and Italy and the only Latin American belligerent to send air and ground forces to the European theater. The benefits of the military alliance were considerable: Brazil supplied strategic materials, including chrome, iron ore, manganese, nickel, tungsten, quartz crystals, and industrial diamonds, and in return received financing from the Export-Import Bank to be used in creating a more diverse economy and for constructing the steel refinery at Volta Redonda. With U.S. assistance, the reach of the Brazilian federal state into the economy dramatically escalated, as did the links between the Brazilian military and industry. In the larger countries of Latin America, save for Argentina, government and the private sector formed alliances to carry out a variety of new projects.[19]

Venezuela and Colombia were slower to fall into line. By 1943, it had become obvious to both governments that the consensus achieved at the January 1942 meeting in Rio de Janeiro—severing diplomatic relations with the Axis powers—could withstand neither the exigencies imposed by the war nor the relentless pressure from Washington. Yet the manner by which these two South American nations entered the war indicated a degree of independence and individual choice not often appreciated in traditional accounts. On the eve of Pearl Harbor, the U.S. ambassador compared Venezuela's predicament to that of Spain in the days before a devastating civil war brought the fascists to power and fretted about the pro-German sympathies of President Isaías Medina Angarita. In early 1942, Medina welcomed U.S. troops into the country, explaining to worried Venezuelans that their stay would be short. After the Venezuelan declaration of war, Medina skillfully took advantage of the wartime emergency to chart a modest industrial policy and negotiate an arrangement with U.S. petroleum companies that differed markedly from the Mexican experience; this pleased U.S. officials, yet toward the end of the war Medina steadfastly opposed isolating defiant Argentina from the United Nations. Colombia declared war in late 1943 following the sinking of several national ships by German submarines, although the Liberal president Eduardo Santos began shifting noticeably toward a pro-U.S. stance after Pearl Harbor. These sentiments came at a political price, however, as Colombia's most outspoken Conservative, Laureano Gómez, used the pages of *El Siglo* to denounce U.S. economic penetration of the nation and the "cultural poverty" created by the North American presence. Such denunciations signaled a malaise—the fratricidal character of the nation's political culture—originating in the wars of independence that had devastated Colombia in the early years of the century and would erupt again in *la violencia* after World War II.[20]

Even in the smaller countries of the Caribbean and Central America the war brought sometimes dramatic changes in local politics, economy, and society. The United States stationed 119,000 troops in the region, half of them in the Canal Zone. Although the Axis powers never seriously threatened the canal itself, they did bring the war into the Caribbean. Soon after Pearl Harbor, the German navy unleashed a furious submarine assault, commencing with a daring attack on five tankers at Aruba in February 1942. By the end of the year, German submarines had sunk 336 ships. With the U.S. wartime buildup in the region, particularly in the British West Indies, Panama, and Puerto Rico, the number of losses declined to 35 ships in the following year and only 3 in 1944. But the most dramatic changes occurred in the fragile Caribbean economies, where the wartime economy of the United States spread throughout the region, swallowing resources and mobilizing labor in the name of fighting a global war. In some instances, undeniably, the efforts were truly heroic. To sustain local economies and to ferry military supplies, the United States established a land-sea route connecting Florida, Cuba, Haiti, the Dominican Republic, and Puerto Rico. Food was stockpiled in Cuba and sent at U.S. expense to islands to sustain local populations drawn into the wartime labor force.[21]

Despite these efforts, the distortions in local economies proved severe. Cuba fared better than the other islands because Batista, elected president in 1940, had encouraged the growth of a diverse economy, especially in agriculture. Neighboring Haiti and the Dominican Republic suffered from the limited availability of tires and gasoline for the trucks disseminating food. Elsewhere, the economic situation was even more precarious. In Puerto Rico forty years of U.S. tutelage and the parallel transformation of the countryside by a

voracious sugar plantation economy had produced what Rexford Guy Tugwell, named governor in 1941, called a "stricken land" and a people no longer
able to feed themselves. In the first year of the war, imports of food into the island fell to 20 percent of prewar levels. Factories closed for lack of raw materials; unemployment rose dramatically. Among the West Indian outposts of
European empire, left to fend for themselves, colonial governments frantically
pressured plantation owners to increase the amount of land for growing subsistence crops, but shortages persisted throughout the war.[22]

The war Americanized the hemisphere but not always in a manner that
even the more perceptive observers might have predicted. Virtually everywhere in the circum-Caribbean, the political and economic changes associated with the war and the U.S. cultural presence reached deep into local
economies and societies. Within the British West Indies, social relations between locals and the first wave of U.S. troops dispatched to the islands after the
destroyers-for-bases deal followed predictable racial patterns. In the early
days of this troublesome encounter, U.S. military officers refrained from sending African American troops to the islands lest their presence offend the white
minority. Yet what seemed to matter more to islanders were the racial and cultural bonds forged by politically radical West Indian migrants to Harlem in the
1920s, the ideological appeal of Marcus Garvey's Universal Negro Improvement Association, and the appeal of Ethiopia's cause against Italy among both
West Indians and African Americans.[23]

Roosevelt certainly understood the political implications of such appeals.
He sent his first emissary to the British West Indies, Charles Taussig, with a
letter of recommendation from Walter White, president of the National Association for the Advancement of Colored People (NAACP). The NAACP had
more than a passing interest in the future of the British West Indies. It fun-
neled moneys to Jamaican leader Norman Manley's Peoples' National Party
and actively supported the small but vocal West Indian independence movement. Roosevelt supported the Anglo-American Caribbean Commission, which
had been hastily created to address the persistent problems of health, social
welfare, labor, agriculture, and economic backwardness in the British Caribbean. To the dismay of his British ally, Roosevelt was outspoken in his view
that the war spelled the demise of the British Empire (not, however, of the
United States), though he never went so far as some in Congress in calling for
U.S. annexation of the islands. In any event, the circumstances of the British
West Indies in 1945 or even in 1942 seemed very distinct from those of the prewar years.[24]

   In some countries, the war served to strengthen existing authoritarian governments, yet, paradoxically, it had the same effect on democratic movements. Rafael Leonidas Trujillo of the Dominican Republic emerged from the war with his grip on society unweakened, yet his counterpart in Cuba, Fulgencio Batista, suffered an embarrassing defeat in 1944 to an old nemesis, Ramón Grau San Martín. In Central America, where authoritarian governments dutifully declared war on the Axis powers after Pearl Harbor, the war years witnessed a collective protest against ruling oligarchies, none of which seemed prepared to deal with the multiple social and economic crises of market loss, food shortages, and the sharp rise of rural migration from countryside to city. In 1940, all save Costa Rica labored under strongman regimes—Jorge Ubico in Guatemala, Maximiliano Hernández Martínez in El Salvador, Tiburcio Carías Andino in Honduras, and the redoubtable beneficiary of the 1926 U.S. intervention in Nicaragua, Antonio Somoza García in Nicaragua. Five years later, only Carías and Somoza remained in power, and the beefy Honduran would not survive the decade. The circumstances of their respective downfall varied, but the capacity of ruling elites to resist fundamental changes within the country followed a similar pattern. Martínez, who purposefully refused to use his father's name, was driven from office by a general strike, yet his persecutors enjoyed only a momentary triumph. Like their predecessors in the slaughter (*matanza*) of 1932, most were hunted down and shot, and El Salvador emerged from the war with its oligarchy virtually intact. The revolt that ousted Ubico in Guatemala left a more lasting democratic legacy, as the ultimate victor, Juan José Arévalo, was a returned exile who espoused a reformist socialism and called for the incorporation of the nation's indigenous peoples in a new society.

   Both Ubico and Martínez had dutifully cooperated with the United States in cracking down on German nationals—Ubico proved especially helpful—yet in the course of events their loyalty could not sustain them. In Guatemala and Costa Rica, profoundly different societies and cultures, the promise of the war years provided unheard-of possibilities for a new political culture—urban, reformist, and modern—but in both cases these momentous changes ended in civil war and, in Guatemala's case, the betrayal of democracy. In an expected way, the United States may have inspired these wartime democratic movements. As the ambassador to El Salvador explained, isthmian reformists and revolutionaries during World War II took only too literally the inspirational phrases of the Atlantic Charter and the Four Freedoms. To contend that U.S.

policies sustained or destroyed these movements is to overlook the internal dynamics of isthmian political life in the 1940s—the shift of population from countryside to city, the rise of a more vocal and better organized middle class, a more militant labor force, and the appearance of new political forces to challenge traditional oligarchies—and the reality of their collective impotence against entrenched forces. Civilian reformists led the charge in bringing down Martínez and Ubico, but they could not have succeeded without the acquiescence of the military; in Nicaragua and Honduras, the military remained subservient to the regime. At the end of the war, then, Central American governments retained their authoritarian character. If the United States failed to identify more enthusiastically with the democratic opposition in the five isthmian republics, the reason had as much to do with the opposition's debility as with the failure of U.S. will to champion the cause of democracy.[25]

Elsewhere, the nuances of interwar hemispheric politics persisted for decades after Pearl Harbor. Throughout the southern cone, the lofty rhetoric of the Atlantic Charter had less to do with explaining compliance with the Rio declaration than with political calculation and U.S. pressure. By early 1943, the German military threat in the Caribbean had largely passed, but the political crisis showed few signs of abating. Predictably, Hull attributed the hesitance of South American governments (save Brazil, of course) to break relations with the Axis to Argentine malevolence and fascist sentiment. The reality turned out to be more complicated. Buenos Aires meddled in the politics of its neighbors, certainly, but President Ramón S. Castillo harbored no illusions about a German victory in the war or about a commitment to the Allied cause. Argentine priorities should be those expressed by Roosevelt at the time of the Munich crisis—neutrality—a point of view unacceptable to Washington and equally offensive to the Argentine military. In June 1943, a gaggle of dissident officers seized power on the grounds that the leftist popular front threatened the nation. News of the coup heartened U.S. officials because prominent Argentine liberals urged the leader of the new government, Pedro S. Ramírez, to sever relations with Berlin. Initially, Ramírez indicated his willingness to oblige and naively appealed to the State Department to lift the arms embargo so that Argentina might restore the military balance of power in the Rio de la Plata. Hull adamantly refused, and as pressure on Buenos Aires escalated, liberals abandoned Ramírez's fragile coalition government, leaving in power a coterie of nationalist military officers hostile to the United States and committed to a separatist course in hemispheric affairs. More disturbingly, the nationalist triumph of 1943 went far beyond what the military seizure of power in 1930 had accomplished. It ended the old Argentina—the nation of liberalism, free trade, landed aristocracy, and enlightened oligarchy—by introducing into the nation's convoluted political culture a man whose name and cause largely dictated the course of Argentine politics for two more generations—Juan Domingo Perón.[26]

An early test of the U.S.–Argentine confrontation came in Bolivia, where in late November a coterie of disgruntled military officers led by Gualberto Villaroel overthrew President Enrique Peñaranda in what was described as a "national socialist coup." Peñaranda had accommodated Washington by settling the Standard Oil nationalization in a manner pleasing to Washington. Hull attributed the coup to Argentine meddling; he was similarly persuaded of Buenos Aires's complicity in another rightist conspiracy to overturn the Uruguayan government. Yet what finally broke the hapless Ramírez turned out to be neither the Bolivian nor Uruguayan crises but an embarrassing effort to restore the country's military prestige by secretly purchasing arms from the Germans. Hull learned of the deal from British informants and threatened to make the information public if Ramírez did not break relations with Berlin. In late January 1944, Ramírez complied. Two weeks later, the nationalists in the cabinet forced him into a humiliating resignation.[27]

By the time Hull had compelled the Argentines to relent, Welles had left Washington, driven from power by a secretary of state who resented his access to the president and his alleged coddling of fractious Latin American leaders. The charge was groundless: Welles had ably served Republican and Democratic administrations since World War I. More than anyone, he had preserved a fragile unity at Rio de Janeiro in the troublesome days after the Pearl Harbor attack. In some respects, he could be as unrelenting as Hull in his pressure on wavering Latin American leaders. As the secretary of state busied himself thrashing out issues with Buenos Aires, Welles focused on Chile and President Juan Antonio Ríos, second in a trio of radical Chilean executives elected to power in the Popular Front victory of 1938. In early 1943, in return for a pledge of economic assistance, Chile broke diplomatic relations with Germany. But Ríos resisted pressures to crack down on German business and propagandists. To most Chileans, German settlers were neither Nazis nor like Germans who had migrated to Brazil or Argentina but hardworking, industrious, and anti-Hitler. The nation's immediate concerns, Ríos solemnly declared, were social stability, economic growth, and national unity, a marked departure from the words of his predecessor, (Pedro Aguirre Cerda) and the Front's pledge to lift the Chilean people from their "misery [and] to raise their social, economic, and moral level."[28]

A policy of growth dictated closer economic ties with the United States but not always abject subservience. When six South American governments— Ecuador, Peru, Venezuela, Paraguay, Uruguay, and Chile—declared war on the Axis powers in early 1945, they did so largely because the Russians insisted that only belligerents could participate in the plenary session of the United Nations at San Francisco. The United States successfully parried Argentina's request for a special conference to consider its wartime policies, but Latin American governments (led by the Mexicans) insisted that the Argentine question be made part of the agenda at the March 1945 Mexico City conference on the Problems of War and Peace. The United States entered the sessions dubious about a regional organization because it might understandably conflict with the role of the United Nations in the postwar world. At the gathering, U.S. secretary of the treasury Will Clayton persistently parried Latin American pressures for postwar economic assistance with reminders about the pressing need to reconstruct wartorn Europe. But the United States needed Latin America's cooperation at San Francisco, and to get it Clayton had to relent on the delegates' insistence that Argentina be granted an opportunity to rejoin the hemispheric community. In the end, the U.S. delegation agreed. A few weeks later, Argentina declared war on Germany, but there would be no reconciliation between Washington and Buenos Aires.[29]

The Postwar Crisis

Critics of the U.S. role in the Americas during the war understandably point to Latin America's sacrifice and the parallel distortions the war had on national economies, politics, and even societies. In 1945, they point out, Latin American governments sought a regional association, which the United States reluctantly accepted and the United Nations charter recognized, but they also looked for a new economic relationship with the United States that would sustain their postwar development plans. In the interwar era, Latin America's links to the world lay in its participation in the League of Nations. At the end of World War II, the region's new ties with the United States mediated its role in the postwar order. As Washington shifted its political and economic attention to postwar Europe, these critics argue, Latin America presented the case for its own economic charter. Before the end of the fighting, a Department of

State official had summed up their claim: "We asked for and obtained the help of Latin America in the prosecution of the war—Latin America will ask, and we must give, help in the transition from war to peace."[30]

Just how much the United States could help was not quite clear. The war had affected Latin America in both positive and negative ways. Exports benefited, but there was little to buy with the hard cash generated. The outcome turned out to be overvalued exchange rates and inflation. Generally, the United States increased its influence throughout the hemisphere in missions and foreign advisors, but the U.S. presence also had another consequence: the strengthening of relations between the state and the private sector, the kind of economic ties that inevitably provoked Washington's displeasure in the postwar era. Latin America emerged from the war, then, with conflicting views about economic policy. The structuralists looked toward industrialization with modest state support and financial support from abroad. A second, equally vocal group placed their faith in accommodation with U.S. interests, the free market, and foreign investment. When it became obvious in the following years that the amount of foreign investment once anticipated would not be forthcoming, most Latin American governments made the Hobson's choice of paying higher bills for imported technology and goods and placing their faith in the notion that growth and new opportunities would solve their problems. Sooner or later, a perceptive economic historian has written, they would have to face the consequences.[31]

If the war restored the global reach of the U.S. economy, for much of Latin America the postwar situation confirmed the vulnerability of export economies. When the war began in 1939, several hemispheric countries had begun to experiment with industrial diversification and the development of an internal market. The war accelerated these changes, particularly in Argentina, Brazil, Chile, and Mexico. But it also produced new problems. Although many countries of the region built up enormous dollar reserves ($4.4 billion by 1945) and unsatisfied appetites for consumer goods, whatever benefit that existed at war's end rapidly eroded with postwar inflation and rising costs of imports. Disturbing trends accompanied these changes. Writing in 1945, Arthur P. Whitaker, an astute student of the inter-American condition, noted that the political consequences of the wartime transformation did not readily follow the democratic political promise of the liberal triumph in the war. The grip of authoritarian regimes had lessened, undeniably, and the appeal of internationalism had become stronger, but there were unsettling trends as well. Nationalist sentiments had deepened, not withered. Throughout the Americas, but especially in Latin America, the masses had grown stronger and become more restive.[32]

How political systems would address the demands of their citizenry would be a critical factor in the following years. The rise of the "common man" may have served as metaphor for the age, but the kinds of political regimes emerging in the postwar hemisphere did not always follow traditional patterns. By the end of 1944, dramatic political changes had occurred in Argentina, Bolivia, Guatemala, El Salvador, and Ecuador. In the following year, Getúlio Vargas's fifteen-year dominance of Brazil ended. New political regimes triumphed in Venezuela and Peru. Yet in the nine instances of political transformation of strongman or authoritarian regimes during this period, in only three cases (Peru, Venezuela, and Brazil) were the new governments more democratic than their predecessors. In Brazil, the new government bore an unsettling resemblance to the Vargas regime, without the hints of fascism conveyed by the *Estado Nôvo*. The role of the military in these new governments appeared to increase rather than lessen. As in Europe, governments alert to the power of powerful urban groups, especially labor unions, rarely hesitated to defend traditional values of liberal democracy when confronted with the more compelling agenda of social justice and the demands for a rising standard of living for ordinary people.

Some of the same comments about the disruptive impact of the war on domestic economies applied to the United States and Canada, but the critical issue here lies in the ways the U.S. perception of the hemispheric economy sharply differed from that of its southern neighbors. Most U.S. leaders believed that fundamental political and economic linkages had taken shape during the war and that postwar markets for North American goods and economic ideas would be receptive. The reality turned out to be more complicated. As Washington began its postwar retrenchment, Latin American governments assumed greater, not less, control in confronting the growing demands of a generation for a voice in government and especially for social reforms. At a time when U.S. leaders were persuaded that they had saved the world but could no longer learn much from it, their hemispheric counterparts responded more and more to ideas about development that fell somewhere between the economic strategies espoused by Washington and by Moscow. Economic planning took on a discrete aspect in virtually every Latin American country. The southern hemisphere found its most articulate voice in the Argentine Raúl Prebisch and its most receptive venue in the United Nations Economic Commission for Latin America. Borrowing his economic thought from both John Maynard Keynes and Marx, Prebisch argued that the reasons for Latin America's economic backwardness lay in the region's vulnerability to the North Atlantic nations' domination of world trade. As long as those inequities persisted, Latin America would never catch up. The solution for peripheral economies lay in a policy of import-substitution industrialization, in which governments protected domestic manufacturers with tariff barriers sufficiently high to shield their domestic market from foreign competition and exercised sufficient control over the labor supply to assure an orderly workplace.[33]

These economic discrepancies were one measure of the distinctive postwar experiences of nations in the Americas. Another lay in the variations pursued by hemispheric governments in trying to reconcile domestic political and social agendas with the realities of the postwar world and above all with the powerful, intrusive U.S. economy. The Pan-American system may very well have been the world's oldest example of a viable regional alliance, but the Western Hemisphere of 1945 contained all the disturbing features of that of 1940: twenty-two sovereign nations with disparate political, cultural, and economic positions and governments angry over U.S. domination and the seeming indifference of Washington to Latin America's economic priorities. The United States created further ill will by postponing two important conferences planned at Chapultepec and scheduled to meet in Rio de Janeiro in late 1945 on the grounds that Argentine rightist influence and Perón's political activities made such a meeting inadvisable. But when the Uruguayan government proposed that hemispheric governments safeguard human rights and combat persistent fascism (a veiled reference to Argentina) with a multilateral intervention force, the idea received little support from Washington and other hemispheric leaders. For the first time in history, the United States reigned supreme in the Western Hemisphere, yet in some respects it was more alienated from Latin America than ever. At Chapultepec the United States had acquiesced in hemispheric pressures for a regional alliance; it had stood firm against Latin American "economic heresies," to use a contemporary phrase. In a world of economic heretics, Latin Americans appeared to favor the economic models offered by Great Britain, France, or even the Soviet Union over that of the United States.[34]

Within the U.S. bureaucracy, devoted believers in hemispheric unity and common purpose, for example, Laurence Duggan and Nelson Rockefeller, lost influence, but those who replaced them did not always agree on alternative policies, perhaps because the postwar hemisphere exhibited such a bewildering array of political trajectories. Increasingly, U.S. officials viewed postwar hemispheric problems in simplistic terms. Claude Bowers, U.S. ambassador to Chile in the waning years of the Popular Front, put the matter succinctly in his assessment of a labor strike in U.S.-owned copper mines. In words that would have seemed inappropriate during the war he wrote, "The strike is Communist and revolutionary and . . . will have inevitable effect throughout South America." Anticipating a point of view that common to many of his successors, he warned, "Unless we can and [will] do [more] we may prepare ourselves for a grave Communist triumph in our backyard . . . which will spread to other American nations."[35]

Curiously, Bowers made this observation at a time when the size and especially the influence of communist parties throughout Latin America—many of which had gained legalization during the war—rapidly declined. Governments systematically purged communists from labor unions and the political bureaucracy, yet the fears expressed by Bowers and his contemporaries did not subside. The influence of the Soviet Union was noticeably stronger in the postwar era than in 1940, but the reason had less to do with Soviet diplomatic activities or the militancy of Latin American labor unions than with the impact of anticapitalist ideologies among disheartened Latin American liberals and the belief that the Soviet Union offered a model for social justice.

In some respects, the most volatile political changes occurred not in South America but in the Caribbean and in Central America, where U.S. control had always been greatest. For almost two generations after the war with Spain, the reach of U.S. power into the circum-Caribbean had encountered resistance, and the response to that resistance had oftentimes been severe. What the United States confronted in the region after World War II, however, proved to be less threatening than, say, the Sandino revolt in Nicaragua or even the Cuban troubles of 1933—but it was no less unsettling to Washington. Military intervention had failed to provide security, as Roosevelt had recognized. The Good Neighbor policy had certainly tied the small economies and governments more closely to the United States and its professed purpose in the war, but with the triumph their demands and expectations increased rather than lessened, and the appeal of the U.S. model of political and economic development now seemed inadequate to a generation of reformers. Even in those countries most closely linked to the United States, the prospects for a cordial relationship noticeably diminished when the shooting stopped. Panamanians refused to be reconciled by North American professions of commitment to that nation's economic development and demanded an end to the defense sites agreement of the early war years. In Cuba, the promise of democratic government accompanying the victory of Grau and the Auténticos in the election of 1944 vanished in the reality of graft and corruption. In Haiti, another U.S. surrogate in the Caribbean, a generation of black nationalists challenged the mulatto elite. Elements of the Caribbean Legion, a paramilitary political group dedicated to overturning dictatorships in the region, vowed to topple Trujillo, whose power extended from the era of the U.S. occupation during the Wilson presidency.[36]

As the champion of anticolonialism in the Pacific and in the European Caribbean, the U.S. government faced in Puerto Rico a challenge different from that posed by the nationalists during the 1930s. Luís Muñoz Marín, leader of the Popular Democratic Party, persuaded a generation of Puerto Ricans that economic development, not political warring over the island's status, held the key to the nation's future. In Muñoz's vision, Puerto Rico could become a commonwealth under the protection of U.S. laws and with the benefit of special ties to the U.S. economy but without losing its distinctive cultural identity. The U.S. Congress obliged in 1945 by passing the Aid to Industry Program and later approved an Industrial Incentives Act that laid the basis for reshaping the Puerto Rican economy. Muñoz became the island's first elected governor in 1948 and aggressively campaigned for approval of the commonwealth arrangement two years later on the specious grounds that Puerto Rico would be a "free associated state" (*estado libre asociado*) within the United States. It was a makeshift arrangement that effectively reinforced the island's colonial status, but at a time when the Caribbean Commission detailed the embarrassing economic and political condition of the European Caribbean, Washington's solution to Puerto Rico's development appeared to offer an appealing alternative.[37]

Throughout the Americas in the postwar years, the twin issues of economic development and security remained linked, but their connection took on different meanings in individual countries. The experience of the war years reinforced these distinctions. In the United States, the debate often centered on issues directly related to the cold war. Some U.S. political leaders, among them Secretary of State Edward Stettinius (Hull's successor) and Secretary of Commerce Henry Wallace took positions that either angered Latin American governments or rapidly fell out of favor. Irritated by Latin pressures for a regionalist understanding, Stettinius bluntly declared that the United States "must not be pushed around by a lot of small American republics who are dependent on us in many ways—economically, politically, militarily." Others expressed their doubts about U.S. lecturing of the Soviet Union for trying to create spheres of influence even as it attempted to preserve something similar in the Western

Hemisphere. Wallace lost his job after stating publicly that the United States had no business meddling in Eastern Europe and the Soviet Union none in Latin America. President Harry Truman, alert to the need to build congressional support for his policies, favored the logic of Senator Arthur Vandenberg (R, Michigan), who praised Article 51 of the U.N. Charter—which permitted individual and collective self-defense of member states—on the naive logic that the clause "preserved the Monroe Doctrine and the Inter-American system." Adolf A. Berle, ambassador to Brazil, apprehensive about the introduction of universalist, that is, European, issues into the inter-American forum, favored that approach. Truman clearly sided with the regionalists, as they were known, but the circumstances of the emerging cold war debate dictated that the president link its universalist rhetoric to the particularist agenda of the postwar hemispheric system. His argument in the Truman Doctrine of March 1947—that the United States had an obligation to assist free peoples everywhere to work out their own destinies—thus universalized the Monroe Doctrine in ways politically acceptable to Congress but not to Latin Americans.[38]

In such ambiguous circumstances the postwar inter-American system took root. When the long-awaited hemispheric security conference finally convened at Rio de Janeiro in August 1947, Senator Vandenberg accompanied the U.S. delegation headed by Secretary of State George C. Marshall. President Truman arrived aboard the U.S.S. *Missouri*. The issue at hand was the question of collective assistance. Most of the Latin American delegates applauded the approval of measures condemning war and calling for the peaceful settlement of disputes, but they were noticeably troubled by U.S. insistence on the provision in the Treaty of Reciprocal Assistance that an attack on any American state would be considered an attack on all of them, justifying a response until the U.S. Security Council could act. They approved the entire package because they had expectations of U.S. economic assistance and, quite simply, had no other benefactors. Truman quickly dashed their hopes when he declared that the United States had "to differentiate between the urgent need for rehabilitation of war-shattered areas and the problems of development elsewhere." Not surprisingly, the U.S. Senate quickly approved the Rio treaty by a vote of 72 to 1.[39]

Local circumstances surrounding the Ninth Inter-American Conference at Bogotá, Colombia, in the following spring were very different. Colombia and Brazil may have shared postwar dilemmas over economic development but Colombian politics responded to radically divergent political imperatives. There were no new questions in Colombian political life, only traditional ones in new form. Unlike Brazil, Colombia had been a reluctant belligerent. More important, the concessions of a succession of Liberal leaders to the U.S. presence in the country had roused old Conservative resentments. Hemispheric delegates to the conference had already witnessed the onset of a disturbing civil conflict (the War of National Liberation, led by José Figueres) in Costa Rica, precipitated when a former president committed to social programs, political activism, and closely allied to the communist party tried to prevent the election of a social conservative. They convened in Bogotá as the Costa Rican government began to crumble before the collective pressures exerted by Figueres and the U.S. embassy. Few hemispheric socialists—certainly not Haya de la Torre, the Peruvian Aprista leader—favored the making of "another Czechoslovakia" in Central America. Out of the conflict emerged modern Costa Rica, a middle-class "welfare state" in which the old coffee barons elected to share power with a generation of newcomers in order to prevent a calamitous social revolution from below. Although Figueres remained suspect to U.S. leaders for several more years, principally because of his criticism of anti-German policies during the war and his support of the Caribbean Legion, he knew precisely just how far he could push the Yankee giant. And he was anticommunist.[40]

Colombian political culture after World War II, on the other hand, did not respond to U.S. pressures and agendas any more dramatically than it had early in the twentieth century. President Mariano Ospina, a Conservative, proved to be sufficiently business-minded to appeal to those who wanted an accommodation with the postwar international economy. Emulating an early-twentieth-century Colombian executive, Ospina formed a coalition cabinet of Liberals and Conservatives in a futile effort to placate the nation's divisive political followings. None of these efforts seemed to matter, and by the time delegates began assembling in Bogotá for the Ninth Inter-American Conference, Colombia's postwar civil war—*la violencia*—had already commenced in the eastern departments of the country. The violence hit the capital in spring 1948 just as Bogotá's predominantly Liberal populace had become estranged from the government, and the leadership of the party had fallen under the sway of one of Colombia's most charismatic twentieth-century political figures, Jorge Eliécer Gaitán, former mayor of the capital. Gaitán captivated a generation of Colombians with his social message condemning the country's ruling oligarchy and calling for a government responsive to such popular grievances as inflation, unemployment, and food shortages. He frightened both Conservative and even Liberal politicos by violating one of the nation's oldest political traditions—*convivencia,* literally, a "living with," credo of those who believed in elitist politics—by appealing to the masses in his Plan Gaitán. His assassination on April 9 unleashed a wave of urban riots across the country and virtually doomed all hopes for the restoration of civility to national political life. At the funeral a prominent Liberal and future Colombian president, Carlos Lleras Restrepo, summed up the challenge confronting the nation's political leaders and, by implication, those of other hemispheric nations: "We will solve nothing by distancing ourselves from the masses, and by making them feel different from us."[41]

In the following decade, the violence experienced in 1948 by Colombians appeared to pale by comparison with stark contrasts between left and right, between disorder and order, between communism and liberalism, and, to borrow John F. Kennedy's phrase from 1960, between violent and peaceful revolution in Bolivia in 1952, in Guatemala in 1954, and particularly in Cuba in the late 1950s. Yet what happened in Colombia proved to be a portent of an unsettling hemispheric future. The United States had come to Bogotá persuaded that it could placate other hemispheric nations with vague commitments to development, but the principal concern of U.S. delegates (as at Rio de Janeiro in the preceding year) was security. A gaggle of U.S. delegates, from . Marshall on down the line, reiterated the by-now shopworn argument that hemispheric governments should look to the private, not the public, sector for succor.

Colombia's representatives appealed to Wilsonian precepts about the equality of nations and called for a Marshall Plan for Latin America, but the reality, as far as Marshall was concerned, was a strife-ridden world in which public order must take precedence over other issues. The *bogotazo* confirmed in his mind that communist agitators operated in Colombia as they had in France and Italy in the critical years after World War II. In the end, the United States obtained at Bogotá much of what it had historically sought from other hemispheric nations with a minimum of concessions. The hemisphere had a new political structure—the Organization of American States—with three important subagencies, the Economic and Social Council, the Council of Jurists, and a cultural council. Delegates approved a plan for a general meeting every five years and special meetings of the council of foreign affairs to consider urgent problems. In the Pact of Bogotá, or the American Treaty of Pacific Settlement, they resolved to settle problems by peaceful means, and in the American Declaration of Rights and Duties of States they committed themselves to a human rights agenda more inclusive and encompassing than the U.S. Bill of Rights.[42]

None of these would prevent the revolution they feared.

Part *3*

6

The Cold War

Nineteen forty-eight marked the end of a tumultuous yet undeniably creative decade in the history of the Western Hemisphere. With the signing of the Inter-American defense pact at Rio de Janeiro in the previous year and the creation of the Organization of American States (OAS), the American republics had achieved an understanding that went far beyond what had been fashioned at Lima a decade before or even what James Gillespie Blaine had sought at Washington, D.C., in 1889. For all the grumbling among U.S. leaders about the limitations of regional alliances, the United States had paid a relatively small economic price for Latin American acquiescence in the Rio agreement. There would be no Marshall Plan for Latin America. Although Washington made an obligatory commitment to the Pan-Americanization of the Monroe Doctrine, its willingness to act unilaterally in the hemisphere had not significantly changed despite the fact that no Latin American country after World War II confronted a domestic crisis or the threat of a counterinsurgency similar to that experienced by Greece, Hungary, or Czechoslovakia. The Rio treaty divided the Americas as well as united them. If the Soviet Union constituted the sole extraterritorial threat to the Western Hemisphere, declared Radomiro Tomic of the Chilean congress, then any war would be between the USSR and the United States, not Chile or Argentina or Bolivia; but the Rio treaty obligated

Latin America "to tie its arms and its national destiny to the arms of the North. It is a poor way of beginning to unite America."[1]

Tomic's was not a universal judgment, of course. The National Party of Uruguay praised the Rio treaty as a vital link with the United States, and Chilean president Gabriel González Videla, the last of a trio of Popular Front presidents, acknowledged Washington's cold war priorities by expelling communists from government. The Brazilians followed suit. But the official professions of solidarity and collective will belied a hemisphere still riven by political and economic fissures. Some of these divisions reached back into the age of independence, reminders of an era when U.S. leaders had taken their measure of the new republics to the south and found them wanting. By the late 1940s, these sentiments had lost much of their racist character, certainly, but they had persisted. George Kennan of the Department of State Policy Planning Staff, who penned the famous "X" article on U.S. policy toward the Soviet Union in the prestigious journal *Foreign Affairs,* expressed doubts about the other Americas in phrases as condescending as those of Secretary of State John Quincy Adams in the early 1820s. Though communists stood little chance of gaining power in the hemisphere by popular consent—except, perhaps, in Guatemala—the United States had every right under the Monroe Doctrine to contain communist influence. Failure to do so, Kennan warned, would erode support for the United States in other regions of the world. The United States did not need or want Latin American nations as allies nor did it require military bases in the hemisphere or Latin American troops to augment its military forces. In wartime, the United States depended on Latin America for vital strategic materials, and fanatical communists might disrupt access to these vital supplies. Achieving these goals did not require appeal to Pan-American sentiments, however, as some of Kennan's colleagues advocated. Neither did he believe that Latin American political institutions or political culture, unlike those of the United States, could resist communist influence. The only realistic choice, however unpalatable, lay in tolerating "harsh governmental measures . . . by regimes whose origins and methods would not stand the test of American concepts of democratic procedures."[2]

For understandable political reasons, Secretary of State Dean Acheson gave the report a secret classification, and for thirty years it remained unpublished. Kennan shortly left the State Department for a prestigious position at Princeton. In time, the architect of the "containment" policy repudiated many of his early views about the cold war and how to confront communism. But the beliefs Kennan expressed in 1950 left their mark on U.S. policy and help one understand the ambivalence many Latin Americans of the postwar era felt about the United States. The distinguished Mexican historian Daniel Cosío Villegas perhaps captured those uncertainties when he praised this country's liberal and democratic institutions, yet asked metaphorically, "Is it possible that—not to survive but to aggrandize itself—the United States will find it necessary to create a retrograde, reactionary world made of antiliberal and antidemocratic forces?"[3]

The Korean War

Cosío's is a compelling critique, doubtless, but no hemispheric nation in 1950 could afford to cast its lot with the Soviet Union. Despised by the USSR and taken for granted by the United States, the continent seemed prepared to assert itself after the North Korean invasion of South Korea in June 1950. By a fortuitous circumstance, two Latin American nations—Cuba and Ecuador—served as nonpermanent members of the U.N. Security Council in late June 1950 when that body acted on the U.S. recommendation to respond to North Korea's attack. With Yugoslavia opposed and Egypt and India abstaining, the Latin American votes were critical in the passage of the vote calling for a strong response to the North Korean attack.

In such circumstances, Washington appeared not at all grateful. If anything, U.S. officials were condescending in the face of hemispheric support and critical of any government that wavered. For some governments, the prospect of losing financial aid changed matters. Before the shooting began, Juan Perón had been defiant: "In the event of war," he had declared, "you will defend your part of the hemisphere and we will defend ours"; but when the war commenced he spoke candidly about sending Argentine troops to Korea. His colleagues were aghast. When the fighting approached a stalemate, Perón changed his mind, suggesting that the ABC powers (Argentina, Brazil, and Chile) bond in a neutral bloc. Getúlio Vargas of Brazil, recently returned to power, proved similarly ambivalent. As a candidate in the presidential elections, he spoke enthusiastically about close cooperation with the United States; privately, he grumbled about U.S. pressure. Within the Brazilian congress, resentments of U.S. pressure ran deeper, prompted mostly by fears that the nation would have to sell vital strategic products. In the end, Vargas satisfied both his domestic critics and Washington: no Brazilian troops would be sent to Korea, but Brazil would receive a $300 million Export-Import Bank loan from the United States. Although he had staunchly anticommunist credentials, Chilean president Gabriel González Videla had to deal with increasing resentment over the power of U.S. copper companies. The outbreak of the Korean War revived old charges about North American imperialism. In his run for the Chilean presidency in 1952, Carlos Ibañez cleverly exploited these sentiments. Calling himself the General of Hope, he promised to end inflation and, in a departure from the policies of his predecessor, challenged Washington's cold war prescriptions by calling for the legalization of the communist party and the resumption of diplomatic relations with the Soviet Union. He referred to the proposed military assistance pact with the United States as "a criminal act on the nation's dignity." As president, the General of Hope could not deal with the collapse of the copper boom and the worsening inflation. As the economy spiraled out of control, he reverted to policies he had employed during his first presidency in the late 1920s—repression of labor strikers—and soon began to voice a virulent anticommunism. Slowly but perceptibly, U.S. financial assistance revived.[4]

President Miguel Alemán of Mexico proved similarly evasive. Although U.S.–Mexican relations in the late 1940s were strained by disputes over trade and especially over the treatment of Mexican agricultural laborers in the U.S. Southwest, Alemán was probusiness, noticeably less ideological than Lázaro Cárdenas, and prone to voicing perfunctory anticommunist sentiments, characteristics that pleased U.S. leaders but prompted some Mexicans to state their concerns about social justice and, to employ a phrase still heard in Mexico, "the death of the revolution." In 1947, reciprocating Harry Truman's good will trip to Mexico City, he became the first Mexican president to visit Washington. He received a ticker tape parade down Pennsylvania Avenue, addressed Congress, and visited the U.S. Military Academy at West Point and a Mexican community in Kansas City. On his return to the Mexican capital, 750,000 people thronged the plaza adjacent to the national palace to greet him. When the Korean War began, Alemán stated that Mexico stood on the side of democracy, but when U.S. officials began talking about a security pact with reminders about the interlinking of the two economies, Alemán matter-of-factly announced that Mexican soldiers would defend Mexico, not the United States. Discussion over the security pact soon collapsed. In 1952 Mexico was the single Latin American government refusing to sign the Inter-American Reciprocal Aid Treaty, a military assistance agreement.[5]

Only two hemispheric governments, Canada and Colombia, joined the United States in sending troops to Korea, but neither subscribed fully to Truman's assessment of the international crisis and the stakes involved. Canadian prime minister Mackenzie King had been staunchly anticommunist, as was his successor Louis St. Laurent. Both men shared Washington's innate suspicions of Soviet behavior. And despite the persistence of strong sentiments about the Commonwealth and the monarchical bonds with the mother country, both recognized the political reality underlying the shift of power from London across the Atlantic. Yet from the beginning of the cold war, Canadians qualified their commitment to Washington's anticommunist alliance. During the 1948 Berlin crisis, brought on by the Soviet closing of ground access to the city, King resolutely denied U.S. requests to send Canadian planes to assist in the airlift. True, Canada readily joined the North Atlantic Treaty Organization (NATO) and was presumably one of the "like-minded nations" identified in a famous National Security Council memorandum (NSC 68) as a potential ally in Washington's global anticommunist crusade. Canada dutifully sent troops to Korea, and they acquitted themselves well. But Canadians persisted in believing that U.S. posturing about the Korean War (and similar conflicts in the Third World) only worsened the international situation.[6]

Throughout the Korean War, then, U.S. leaders failed to appreciate the nuances of Canadian foreign policy, and particularly Canadian views about western hemispheric security. Similarly, they may have misread the reasons for Colombia's decision to dispatch a battalion to Korea. In 1949 Colombia still reeled politically and economically from the onset of *la violencia* following Gaitán's assassination, and U.S. officials expressed concerns about the political instability and the danger that would come with guerrilla war. They were pleased when the Conservative leader Laureano Gómez, a devout Catholic and staunch anticommunist, became president in June 1950, and they heartened to the words of the Colombian ambassador to the United Nations, who reminded his Latin American colleagues about Soviet threats to the hemisphere. Such strong ideological support did not mean that Colombians were kindred spirits in Washington's global anticommunist crusade, however. Colombian political culture in these years displayed few similarities to that of the United States. There was no Republican/Democrat consensus about the cold war among Conservatives and Liberals, who made war on one another while the military strived to make social peace. At bottom, Colombians recognized the economic impact of the Korean War on the Western Hemisphere, and they expected an economic payoff for their military commitment. By late 1952 Gómez was threatening to withdraw from the war, a disquieting thought to U.S. officials because it would be politically embarrassing throughout the hemisphere. Yet they were aware of Colombian priorities. In June 1952, the Colombian ambassador to the United States had emphasized to the State Department that domestic security concerns preoccupied the Colombian military more than the war in Korea. Some in the Truman administration, among them Secretary of State Acheson, had few qualms about supplying the Colombian military with arms that might be used for such purposes; others, such as Thomas Mann of the Office of Inter-American Affairs, expressed reservations, though both persisted in the naive belief that U.S. strategic objections in the Western Hemisphere could be distinguished from Colombian domestic problems. As Mann himself noted, the U.S. government should use "good judgment and firmness" in recognizing that Colombians might wish to use military aid from the United States to deal with "insistent internal needs."[7]

Was the Colombian domestic crisis a portent of the hemispheric future? Perhaps, but only from the perspective of the 1990s when most of the 1950s-era cold war calculations about the Latin American condition no longer seemed so compelling. In the views of Department of State soothsayers in the early 1950s, what occurred in Colombia in the aftermath of the *bogotazo* made that country's woes the exception and not the rule. Acheson may have discreetly shelved Kennan's morose description of U.S. priorities, but he had to concede Kennan may have been closer to the mark in sensing the U.S. agenda in the hemisphere than those who spoke so enthusiastically about multilateralism and Pan-Americanism. In any event, in the context of the Korean War there was little likelihood Washington would retreat from its policy of the militarization of the Western Hemisphere. Between 1952 and 1955, the United States signed mutual defense pacts with Colombia, Cuba, the Dominican Republic, Haiti, Honduras, Guatemala, Ecuador, Nicaragua, Peru, Brazil, Chile, and Uruguay. Within a few years, Roosevelt's pledges of nonintervention and noninterference and the parallel commitment to a collective solidarity against external threats weakened before a U.S. determination to revert to its old habits of unilateral action with every expectation that its hemispheric neighbors would acquiesce.[8]

Such a course, critics have generally contended, served less to shield the hemisphere from a threat by the Soviet Union than to lead to a spate of military takeovers and the undermining or co-opting of revolutionary movements. There is a certain logic to this argument. In March 1952 Fulgencio Batista took power in a virtually bloodless military coup in Cuba. A month later, the National Revolutionary Movement (MNR), a militant alliance of tin miners and rural peasants, triumphed in Bolivia. In the same year, General Marcos Pérez Jiménez nullified the election of a civilian when he seized power in Venezuela. General Gustavo Rojas Pinilla followed his example in Colombia in the following year. In the Venezuelan and Colombian cases there was scarcely a murmur of protest from Washington save for predictable regrets that the democratic process had suffered. In 1949 Acheson had matter-of-factly suggested that Soviet espionage in Latin America proved to be a far more critical issue for the United Nations than human rights abuses in Venezuela. In some respects, the United States found working with Rojas Pinilla, who paraded himself as a populist, easier than with his Conservative predecessor. Despite his acknowledged lack of sentimentality about U.S. foreign policy, Acheson stated in April 1950 that conflict within the Western Hemisphere must be settled by "negotiation and reasonable settlement." Achieving that goal, he reminded his audience, had required more than a half century and a recognition that the other American republics rightly distrusted the "Colossus of the North" because of its unilateral actions. Such sentiments, he professed, no longer existed.[9]

What happened in Bolivia troubled Acheson, but the prevailing thinking in the Department of State followed a pattern Woodrow Wilson would have understood: the traditional rightist political parties, the tin barons, and the landlords of the country offered no solution to the country's economic woes. Although U.S. observers spoke warily of the multiclass, multigroup coalition fashioned by Víctor Paz Estenssoro, he was clearly neither a Peronist nor a communist and clearly preferable to his erstwhile political ally and potential rival, Juan Lechín, suspect in Washington because he might be "another Lenin." Better to tolerate Paz than to risk either chaos or communism. When the two Bolivians united to announce the nationalization of the tin mines and land reforms, Paz played a more influential role and, much to Washington's satisfaction, announced that the mine decree would apply solely to the big three mineholders, none of whom was North American, and that the landowners would be compensated. Relations worsened in 1953 when the Eisenhower administration became concerned about communist influence within the Paz government and the MNR party. But the Bolivian revolution did not suffer a CIA-sponsored coup, as did Guatemala in the following year, principally because the Bolivian military, unlike that of Guatemala, offered no alternative had the United States chosen to bring down the Paz government. By fall 1953 the sentiment within the Eisenhower administration generally favored the notion that the best course would be an aid package that would tie the Bolivian revolution to U.S. priorities, and, in the words of an embassy memo, "keep this tinder box, which might set off a chain reaction in Latin America, from striking fire."[10]

The 1950s

But in the euphoria of a rejuvenated economy in the United States there was little likelihood that Truman or even Eisenhower wanted to revert to the practices of the banana war era by reinforcing the Pax Americana with troops. In any event, when Eisenhower took the oath of office most Latin American governments had lined up with the United States on cold war issues, believing that the aid Secretary of State Marshall had said was not available in 1948 because of the pressing needs in Europe and Asia would be forthcoming once Europe recovered. Early on in the new administration, Eisenhower tried to reassure Latin American leaders with a conciliatory speech at the Pan-American Union building announcing that he was sending his brother Milton as personal representative and special ambassador to the region in order to improve relations. With the assistant secretaries of the Departments of Commerce, State, and Treasury in tow, Milton Eisenhower visited ten Latin American republics in summer 1953, the first of three trips to Latin America he would undertake during the Eisenhower presidency.[11]

Eisenhower's soothing words heightened Latin American expectations about Secretary of State Marshall's promise of an economic conference. Before it met, however, the president tended to more immediate concerns in Guatemala. At the Tenth Inter-American Conference in Caracas in March 1954, Secretary of State John Foster Dulles refused to budge on the issue of economic aid until he secured a statement calling for action against those hemispheric governments that served "alien masters." Everyone knew he was referring to the leftist Jacobo Arbenz government in Guatemala. Just as certainly they sensed the United States would act unilaterally despite professions of collective action. The United States effectively discounted that approach on the eve of the Bogotá conference when it failed to follow up on the suggestion of President Eurico Dutra of Brazil for joint action against the supposed menace of communism in the Americas.

Washington preferred the more flexible approach offered by the 1947 Rio treaty. The passing of the Truman administration saw noticeable changes in the rhetoric of U.S. foreign relations, yet early in the Eisenhower administration a National Security Council memo argued the case for hemispheric consultation and refraining from "overt unilateral intervention in the internal political affairs of the other American states," words Truman and Acheson could have supported. But in summer 1953 a select group within the Eisenhower administration authorized to oversee covert operations recommended the toppling of the Arbenz government. The CIA, not the OAS, would be the principal architect of the plan. In part, the choice of the CIA could be justified on the grounds that it had successfully brought down the anti-American government of Iran and that it could operate beyond public scrutiny, but the most fundamental reason had to do with a fear that gnawed at U.S. leaders from the early years of the twentieth century. Former ambassador Willard Beaulac summed it up: "If we intervene overtly [in Guatemala], we are criticized, and if we intervene covertly [and] it is found out, we are criticized not only for intervening but for being sneaky about it. If we do nothing and the country goes communist we are denounced as helpless."[12]

U.S. displeasure with the Guatemalan government commenced during the last years of the Juan José Arévalo administration, then worsened after the controversial election of Arbenz in 1951. Arbenz took the country farther to the left than Arévalo, who had spoken eloquently about "spiritual socialism" and a place for the laborer and especially the nation's indigenous people (a majority of the populace) but lacked a strong political base to carry out his dream. Arbenz was cut from different political cloth. As did contemporary political leaders in 1940s Central America and the Caribbean, he recognized that the shift of population to urban areas, the wartime political coalitions with communist parties, and the growing militancy of labor had weakened the grip of landholders in the countryside. Another isthmian country, Costa Rica, had experienced a similar transformation during World War II, and the clash between rivalrous political factions exploded in the 1948 civil war. Curiously, the ultimate beneficiary of that war, José "Pepe" Figueres, infuriated Washington with his personal war with the Nicaraguan dictator Anastasio Somoza and especially Figueres's notions about state intrusion into the economy. In the eyes of his enemies and to a few in Washington, Figueres the pro-German Nazi sympathizer of the war years became Figueres the communist, yet in the aftermath of the civil war Figueres led the charge against the persecution of the communists. The social democratic tide would transform Costa Rica in ways that overwhelmed the old coffee aristocracy and irritated Washington observers, but there would be no direct confrontation. Besides, in Dulles's eyes, Arbenz was not only more vulnerable but had committed the unpardonable error of defying the United States by calling on Guatemalans to reclaim their sovereignty and by appealing to foreign governments.[13]

The social revolution commenced in the Arévalo years struck some observers as no more dangerous to U.S. interests than that occurring in Costa Rica. Guatemala's military disliked the social and political reforms and twenty times attempted to push Arévalo out, but the president managed to survive, several times by arming urban laborers. Others, including the communists, criticized Arévalo for moving too slowly, and the president cracked down on them. After Arbenz's victory, the political grip of communists within the labor movement and their influence in the government noticeably increased. Arbenz decided to accelerate the revolution in the countryside with a series of agrarian reform laws. By comparison with the Bolivian and Mexican examples, the Guatemalan land expropriation of 1952 was not punitive, as it provided for compensation, but it did unleash forces Arbenz seemed powerless to control. In the Guatemalan countryside, landless peasants dissatisfied with the slow pace of the expropriation began seizing land, a practice that alienated a generation of smaller landowners sympathetic to their plight. Far more serious was the government's confrontation with United Fruit, the country's largest landowner, which forfeited 50 percent of its 470,000 acres under the agrarian reform law. Despised by many Guatemalans for its enormous economic power and control of the country's rail service from the capital to the Caribbean coast, United Fruit decided to fight the decree by retaining a law firm, Sullivan and Cromwell, to defend its cause and hiring an advertising firm to turn out a series of newspaper and magazine articles portraying Guatemala as a "Red menace" in the Americas. A military faction funded by the CIA and styling itself National Liberation under Colonel Carlos Castillo Armas and General Miguel Ydígoras Fuentes began operating on the Honduran border.[14]

Arbenz fought back on several fronts. Unable to obtain arms in the West, he appealed to several East European governments and finally obtained two thousand tons of arms and munitions from Czechoslovakia. He imposed severe restrictions on assembly and gave his approval to the arrest and, it was charged, torture of his political enemies. The government called on the Security Council of the United Nations to investigate the U.S. support of the Guatemalan rebellion, but in the ensuing vote only the Soviet delegate sided with the Guatemalan case. The council did call for a ceasefire, however, and some delegates expressed the belief that the OAS was the appropriate body to mediate the Guatemalan violence. In Guatemala, Castillo lost two of his planes in the fighting. When Eisenhower approved the sending of two P-51 fighter planes via a third country to replace them, the Guatemalans renewed their case within the Security Council. Again, U.S. pressure foiled their efforts. Even in these circumstances, Arbenz might have survived, as Castillo's army consisted of only 150 men and did not seriously threaten the capital. Guatemala's senior military officers, disturbed by the rift between Arbenz and the U.S. government, sent the president an ultimatum calling for his resignation. If he refused, the ultimatum read, they pledged to join the revolt. Desperate, Arbenz ordered the arming of urban workers and government employees but could find no one to deliver the decree. The military conspirators convened with the U.S. ambassador, John Peurifoy, who had been no idle spectator to these

events. Afterward, they gave Arbenz a second ultimatum. This time Arbenz relented, but in a final act of defiance he publicly condemned the "mercenaries"
hired by the United States to overturn his government and recommended his
successor, a colonel who remained loyal to the end. Neither Peurifoy nor Guatemala's conspiring military officers would permit it. Castillo Armas became
Guatemala's new president and began dismantling the revolution, which
earned the plaudits of Dulles and prompted a $6-million grant from the United
States.[15]

National Liberation had triumphed, and for another three decades Guatemala's rural people suffered. Until the triumph of the Cuban revolution in
1959 and the sequence of events leading to the missile crisis of October 1962,
the experience of Guatemala in the decade after the overthrow of Jorge Ubico
in 1944 became a symbol for those who believed that the United States and its
reactionary collaborators were the obstacles to meaningful social and economic reform in Latin America. Regrettably, the story of the social revolution
Arbenz unleashed in the Guatemalan countryside and how the country's rural
people attempted to take control of it proved too complicated to fit neatly into
the conventional accounts of the affair. Guatemala offered numerous "lessons," each confusing. Guatemala's urban middle-class reformers who gen-
uinely sympathized with the plight of the nation's rural dispossessed discovered that the beneficiaries of reforms may not only wish to accelerate the pace
of change but to gain control of their own destiny. Those political leaders who
wished to have influence learned that to prosper or even survive they must accept those demands from below. Those who opposed the revolution and fashioned a coalition to crush it perhaps too readily attributed their victory to the
U.S. connection or to a consensus within the nation's dominant political culture. For others, the Guatemalan experience confirmed the view, often applied generally to Latin America, that reforms, however well intentioned, lead
to more violence rather than prevent it. Too late, the United States learned that
the Guatemalan solution applied only to Guatemala, not to revolutionary
Cuba, where Ernesto "Che" Guevara persuaded Fidel Castro not to make the
mistakes of Arbenz and to prepare for inevitable conflict with the United
States. CIA operatives gloated about the ease of Operation PBSuccess, but the
truth should have sobered them. Arbenz fell because the Guatemalan military
demanded the president resign rather than fight a war it most assuredly could
have won.[16]

Defiance of the United States came from within the U.S. empire as well. Responding to demands from President-dictator José Antonio Remón of Panama,

the United States readily accepted a revised canal treaty that significantly expanded the powers of the Panamanian government over Canal Zone employees
and increased the annuity to almost $2 million annually. Since gaining power
in 1952, Remón had impressed U.S. observers with his economic development
schemes, but his claim of Panamanian sovereign rights over the Canal Zone,
symbolized by the flying of both national flags, jolted North American sensibilities. His outspoken wife, Cecilia, embarrassed Dulles at the OAS meeting
in Caracas by denouncing racism and discrimination against Panamanians in
the Canal Zone. Remón had a keen sense of timing, however: In 1954, Colonel
Gamal Abdel Nasser seized power in Egypt and demanded the British hand
over the Suez Canal, and U.S. pressure on the Arbenz government in Guatemala, as we have seen, aroused widespread hemispheric criticism. In such a
climate, the concessions of the 1955 treaty with Panama seemed acceptable,
though Panamanian nationalists denounced the pact. If anything, the U.S.
presence in the region became more entrenched, as the thirteen U.S. military
installations clustered in the zone contained a jungle warfare school for training Latin American soldiers in counterinsurgency as well as the base for an intelligence operations and an informal inter-American defense network.[17]

In the calculations of some Latin American social democrats, the Guatemalan affair confirmed the belief that meaningful political and social change
required violent revolution. Most were not yet prepared for such a drastic
course, but they were prepared to press the United States about the necessity
for an economic assistance and development program that contrasted sharply
with Washington's recommendations. At the November 1954 meeting of the
Inter-American Economic and Social Council of the OAS at the Hotel Quintandinha, near Rio de Janeiro, the Latin Americans made their case. For Latin
American cooperation in approving the overthrow of the Arbenz government,
Dulles had pledged to carry through with George C. Marshall's 1948 promise
for such a meeting. Secretary of the Treasury George Humphrey, who led the
U.S. delegation, came to this conference reluctantly but determined to take a
stand as a staunch advocate of private enterprise. For the first time at such an
inter-American meeting, the United States confronted what appeared to be a
united front of young, sophisticated Latin American delegates equally committed to fundamental changes in economic policy in their respective countries: Eduardo Frei Montalva, senator and future president of Chile (1965–70),
Carlos Lleras Restrepo, Liberal economic policy maker and future president
of Colombia (1966–70), Felipe Herrera, general manager of the Chilean Central
Bank and future president of the Inter-American Development Bank (created

in 1959), and Roberto de Oliveira Campos, an economist and diplomat, ambassador to the United States during the John F. Kennedy administration, and chief economic policy maker in the military government of Brazil from 1964 to 1967. For the most part, their economic views conformed to the agenda of the U.N. Economic Commission for Latin America (ECLA) and its director, Raúl Prebisch.[18]

Prebisch did not attend the conference, but he had alertly summoned a group of Latin American economists, including Frei and Lleras, to assist in preparing the annual ECLA report and to state Latin America's position on economic policy. The report of the ECLA committee of experts largely agreed with Prebisch's thesis. With the end of the Korean War, the committee's report stated, Latin America's export boom had collapsed just as the spread of knowledge had made its common people aware of the standard of living in more advanced countries and made them more determined to press for such changes throughout Latin America. Without a more satisfactory rate of economic growth to satisfy their demands, the prospect would be "political instability and ever increasing social tensions" that "were frequently transformed into a barren disintegrating struggle to share a communal income which hardly increases at all." Latin America's economic development had fallen behind because of poor domestic savings and dependence on export earnings from primary products like copper, wheat, coffee, and tin. The solution repeated the basic recommendation Prebisch had made in 1949: an aggressive industrialization program that favored domestic manufactures over imports, thus leading to greater diversity in exports; and a guaranteed foreign exchange flow in the transition years to more industrialized economies, which could be achieved by stabilization of prices paid for Latin America's export commodities and long-term low-interest loans.[19]

In fundamental ways, the report of the committee of experts anticipated the recommendations of the Alliance for Progress. For the first time, Latin American representatives had couched their beliefs about assistance in quantitative terms. Viewed from the perspective of the early 1960s, when hemispheric leaders had to deal with a far more radical alternative in the Cuban revolution, what they proposed sounded eminently sensible, but their recommendations grated on Humphrey's orthodox sensibilities. His response sounded ominously like the prevailing neoliberal economic wisdom sweeping the hemisphere in the aftermath of the cold war in the 1990s. Latin Americans did not need an inter-American development bank, he told them in brutally frank terms, nor would the United States support commodity stabilization or national planning.

The route to a healthy economy lay in a commitment to attract foreign investment with realistic exchange rates and control of inflation. Tampering with
market forces and capital movements was an economic sin. Humphrey expressed his regrets for Latin America's economic situation and shortly left for
home, leaving an assistant to soothe the feelings of the expectant delegates.
Most of the Latin Americans came away from the conference with little more
than a U.S. reminder that their economic situation might improve if they kept
spending under control and came up with better ideas. Lleras Restrepo of
Colombia summed up their feelings with a story about a Colombian fish ped-
dlar who put up a sign in the marketplace, "Fresh Fish Sold Here." A succession of three friends told him that he didn't need to use the words "fresh" or
"sold" or "here" because anybody would know that he wouldn't be trying to
sell rotten fish, that he was putting out the fish to sell them, and that he was
selling them in that place. The fourth friend recommended he remove the
word "fish" because the smell made it unnecessary. "And that's the way it is
with United States aid," remarked Lleras Restrepo, "after all the discussions
we have had here, all that is left is the smell."[20]

Few Latin American leaders expressed much surprise, then, when the Economic Conference of the OAS convened in Buenos Aires in August 1957. Little
had changed in Washington's attitudes toward their fundamental economic
proposals. The new U.S. secretary of the treasury, Robert D. Anderson, sounded
more agreeable than his predecessor but reaffirmed the importance of competition and the free play of market forces in hemispheric economic relations.
Since the Quintandinha conference, he noted, Latin American exports to the
United States had increased from $3.4 to $3.6 billion, and U.S. investments in
Latin America had grown by $1.4 billion. His listeners remained unimpressed.
The anticipated development loan fund, designed to make available long-
term, low-interest loans, was stalled in the bureaucracy, and Anderson reiterated shopworn U.S. demurrals to the idea of an inter-American development
bank. Anderson shortly departed, leaving in charge the undersecretary of state
for economic affairs, C. Douglas Dillon, who knew little about Latin American
affairs but had witnessed the European economic recovery and appeared more
receptive to some of the ideas expressed by Latin American delegates.[21]

The conference ended with no perceptible change in the U.S. approach to
hemispheric economic relations, but it was clear that Latin Americans seemed
closer to agreement about economic integration than at any time in history
and looked to the United Nations rather than to the OAS for inspiration. A lame
challenge to U.S. pretensions, perhaps, but a signal to Washington that Latin

Americans no longer believed that their economic problems could be resolved within a hemispheric framework. Pan-Americanism carried with it the burden of U.S. domination and Washington's seemingly instinctive apprehension that the economic integration of Latin America threatened its interests. Pan–Latin Americanism conveyed something far more threatening and begged a fundamental question: What country would articulate a pan-Latin American agenda, particularly if such a course meant defiance of the United States?

The Second Cuban Shock

Cuba would ultimately play this role, although in January 1959, when the guerrilla war led by Fidel Castro finally drove the dictator Fulgencio Batista from power, it had not yet claimed the part. Neither was there compelling evidence that the United States had lost all opportunity to affirm its place among hemispheric nations as a partner rather than a presumptive master of their destinies. Indeed, in 1958, after Vice President Richard Nixon visited several Latin American cities and very nearly lost his life at the hands of a Caracas mob, the Eisenhower administration began to listen to some of the hemisphere's more polite critics, particularly Brazilian president Juscelino Kubitschek. Without a change in U.S. policy, Kubitschek told Assistant Secretary of State for Latin American Affairs Roy Rubottom, the inter-American system would collapse. Kubitschek's reputation ranked high among Latin America's reformist presidents of the late 1950s, and his development program for Brazil, though dependent on U.S. economic investment, symbolized for other South American nations the mix of state intervention and market forces that would transform developing economies. Rubottom and Nixon blamed the Caracas riots on communist conspirators, and Secretary of State Dulles proved just as obstinate until the Brazilian leader refused to appear with him at a press conference.

Only then did Dulles and Eisenhower respond favorably to Kubitschek's call for Operation Pan-America, a general program for long-range economic development funded jointly by the U.S. and Latin American governments to attack misery and injustice throughout the continent. Dulles consented to a special meeting of foreign ministers in Washington, D.C., to consider the proposal. When it met, the United States readily agreed to the creation of a Committee of 21 to assess Latin America's social and economic problems and to the organization of an Inter-American Development Bank. U.S. officials continued to emphasize the primacy of private enterprise and the imperative of anti-inflationary measures, but their actions appeared to signal a departure in

Washington's policies. In November 1958, Eisenhower left on a personal goodwill tour to Argentina, Chile, Brazil, and Uruguay. Aside from a minor incident in Montevideo, the public response to his visit differed sharply from that of the vice president earlier in the year, and the president departed from South America with a sense that his efforts had mitigated Latin suspicions about the U.S. role in the hemisphere. Less than two months later, Castro triumphantly entered Havana.[22]

At first glance, the Cuban revolution seemed typical of political upheavals within the orbit of U.S. power: a despotic leader violates the democratic process and survives because of ties with the United States, the corruption of the political system, and the acquiescence of the middle classes and business and professional sectors. Social justice is a mockery. From the countryside a movement arises to overthrow the tyranny, restore democracy and social justice, and drive the foreign devils from the land. In this sense, Castro's revolution evoked the memory of Martí, who had spoken eloquently about a war of liberation and fought a war of destruction in the countryside; or of Emiliano Zapata in Mexico, who had proclaimed a crusade to restore land and liberty to those who tilled the soil; or of Augusto Sandino in Nicaragua, who raised an army of country people to drive North Americans out of his country and their political lackeys from power in Managua. Certainly, when Castro spoke about the enormous disparities between countryside and city or the lot of those left behind in the postwar economic transformation, he might have been talking about El Salvador or Peru or Mexico or Brazil, each different from the other but sharing those fundamental social problems afflicting much of Latin America at midcentury. "History Will Absolve Me," his statement at his trial for the July 1953 raid on the Moncada barracks in Santiago, described a nation capable of providing for three times as many people and markets overflowing with produce yet suffering from abject poverty. Oriente province in the mountainous east was indisputably the poorest region of the country. Half of its population squatted on land and fought landlords and their lackeys in the rural guard. When Castro and his small band of guerrillas encamped there in 1956, they gained the respect of local people, who readily joined the movement. The appeal of the guerrilla movement among such people indicated that the problems facing the country could not be resolved within the existing political system but were symptomatic of deeper socioeconomic discontents that existed elsewhere in Latin America.[23]

Yet in critical respects Cuba's experience in the 1950s was atypical of Latin America and even of other countries in the Caribbean. The economy of the island was thoroughly integrated into that of the United States, and Cubans had absorbed North American cultural and consumer preferences to a degree greater than Canadians or even Puerto Ricans. Per capita income ranked fourth in the hemisphere behind that of the United States, Canada, and Venezuela. According to the conventional wisdom prevailing in Washington, Cuba's middle classes and professional people should have supported the revolution out of disgust with the political corruption of the Batista regime and not because of the North American presence in the island. But the *fidelista* movement appealed to all sectors of the society, and none more deeply than those with the closest ties to the North American community. Their alienation from Batista and what he stood for stemmed less from political than more fundamental reasons: the Cuban economy could not sustain the expansion necessary to satisfy their expectations.[24]

The role of the United States in Castro's victory should not be underestimated, of course, but it was not critical, and to argue the contrary is to accept a persistent myth that Castro could never have come to power except for the U.S. "betrayal" of Batista. As in 1933, when the displeasure of the Roosevelt administration had helped to bring down the Machado dictatorship, the imposition of an arms embargo and increasing pressure on Batista to resign abetted Castro's movement, undeniably, but the revolution triumphed because Castro's Fourth of July movement had won the military battle and support from all sectors of Cuban society. More important, the revolution had come to power unconditionally, and because of that it could make revolutionary changes. Inevitably, and despite the widespread popularity of Castro throughout the Americas in the early months of 1959, this would mean conflict with the United States, for very rapidly the United States lost its traditional role in Cuban society. The Fourth of July movement had defeated Cuba's U.S.-trained and U.S.-equipped army. Revolutionary tribunals tried and condemned to death the most hated *batistiano* officers and ordered the seizure of property of those who had fled the island. At every level of society, there was a purging of the old, now-discredited order. "That the United States played so prominent a part in this discredited past," writes Louis A. Pérez, Jr., "all but guaranteed a day of reckoning."[25]

Throughout the early days of the revolution, Castro sent mixed messages to other hemispheric countries about the kind of revolution Cubans were going to make. He told a crowd of cheering Venezuelans in Caracas that his revolution would become a model for Latin America; but in a visit to the United States in April 1959, Castro declared that he was not a communist and at a reception at the Cuban embassy made it clear that Cuba did not have diplomatic relations with the Soviet Union. Already, however, the radical course of the revolution had begun to alter the island's relationship with the United States. Cuba supported exile invasions of Haiti, Nicaragua, the Dominican Republic, and Panama, which angered the U.S. government. The agrarian reform law hit directly at North American property owners, reducing the size of their holdings in sugar and cattle. Ambassador Philip Bonsal voiced his objections but stated that the United States would accept the takeovers, provided the Cuban government made fair compensation. Throughout the summer and into the fall, both governments issued statements of conciliation, but neither proved willing to concede very much. In such tense circumstances, few in Washington believed that the Cubans employed socialist means as the most pragmatic way of reviving the faltering sugar economy and not as a direct affront to the United States. Sometime later, Che Guevara recalled the dispute over the agrarian reform law as a critical moment, for failure to push the issue would have meant a reversal of the revolutionary promise: "The more just and the more dangerous course was to press ahead . . . and what we supposed to have been an agrarian reform with a bourgeois character was transformed into a violent struggle."[26]

In May, U.S. officials had their first international encounter with the "new Cuba" at a meeting of the Committee of 21 in Buenos Aires. Castro arrived at the conference wearing his revolutionary fatigues and surrounded by a retinue of security guards and cheered by onlookers. Everywhere he was the center of attention. Sitting at the conference table, he continually distracted everyone in the room by shifting his legs, smoking cigarettes, chewing on his pencil, gesturing toward photographers, or making a comment to the Colombian and Ecuadorian delegates who sat beside him. When he rose to speak, some in the audience perhaps expected a speech similar to those he had delivered in the Plaza de la Revolución in Havana, a montage of denunciations of imperialism and reminders of the revolutionary struggle. His remarks on this occasion, however, sounded conciliatory. In phrases Martí would have approved of, Castro rejected the notion of Latin cultural deficiencies, declaring that Latin America's economic underdevelopment caused rather than resulted from its political instability. Latin America deserved U.S. help, he went on, but economic aid should not depend on the Soviet threat, for "we do not want to be a battlefield of political conflicts." The United States should extend $30 billion over a ten-year period to develop the continent, a commitment that would afford Latin America the ability to create a "humanist democracy." Noticeably irritated, U.S. representative Roy Rubottom pointed to the less ambitious (and less costly) measures already being undertaken—the establishment of an Inter-American Development Bank as well as increased commitments by the World Bank, International Monetary Fund, and Development Loan Fund—and reminded his listeners that what Castro proposed made no mention of the "internal measures which capital importing countries must take in order to make international cooperation effective." The delegates tabled the Cuban proposal, and Castro departed, never again to participate in an inter-American ministers' conference.[27]

In his first month of power, Castro had openly expressed his belief that Cubans had lost confidence in the OAS, but throughout 1959 the Cuban government used the forums of the organization to shield Havana from the growing criticism about the radicalization of the revolution within Cuba and its support of leftist movements elsewhere in Latin America. In August, when hemispheric foreign ministers convened in Santiago, Chile, to deal with unrest in the Caribbean and more generally with problems of human rights and democracy throughout Latin America, the Cuban delegate skillfully thwarted criticism of the regime by focusing on economic issues and reminding his listeners about the efforts of the Rafael Leonidas Trujillo dictatorship to undermine democratic governments in the Caribbean. The meeting ended with a statement (the Declaration of Santiago) reaffirming the principles of democracy and respect for human rights and the granting of temporary power to the Inter-American Peace Committee to investigate cases of invasion by rebels based in another country and attempt to conciliate them. In the deepening rift between Cuba and the United States, the declaration seemed tentative. At the time, however, few within the OAS could have predicted that Cuba and the United States were on a collision course that would plunge the hemisphere into a global crisis, but they were alert to the appeal of the Cuban revolution not only to communists and dissidents but to ordinary people within their own countries. "The Cuban revolution is a national revolution," declared Salvador Allende, the 1958 socialist candidate for the Chilean presidency, "but it is also a revolution for the whole of Latin America."[28]

In early 1960, however, the principal concern of the Cubans was their conflict with the United States, and despite the popularity of the revolution throughout the hemisphere, the prospects of sustaining their cause within U.S.-dominated hemispheric organizations seemed unlikely. Certainly, they could not depend on the OAS to shield them from economic retaliation or a U.S. invasion. Guevara declared that Cuba would not join the Inter-American

Development Bank or participate in any action taken under the 1947 Rio treaty. In February, a Soviet trade delegation arrived to negotiate a major trade agreement obligating the Russians to purchase 425,000 tons of sugar in 1960 and 1 million tons annually for four more years. In addition, Moscow agreed to sell the Cubans crude oil at prices significantly lower than those charged by the oil refineries. The U.S. response and the Cuban counterresponse occurred within rapid succession over the following months In May, the Cuban government ordered the foreign refineries in the country to process the first shipments of crude oil from the Soviet Union. When they refused, the government nationalized them in June. In July, the Eisenhower administration retaliated by imposing drastic cuts (700,000 tons) in the Cuban sugar quota, effectively eliminating it for the remainder of the year. As if on cue, the Cubans followed in August and September by taking over more North American properties—utilities, sugar mills, and Cuban branches of U.S. banks.[29]

By August the clash between the two governments had become sufficiently serious to prompt a meeting of foreign ministers in San José, Costa Rica. The Cuban representative, Raúl Roa, challenged Cuba's accusers. "The revolutionary government of Cuba has not come to San José as defendant," Roa declared, "but as the prosecutor. It is here in order to speak out its relentless *j'accuse* against the richest, most powerful, and most aggressive capitalist power in the world . . . which has failed to intimidate, to force to its knees, or to buy off the revolutionary government." After the indignant Roa had walked out, the delegates unanimously passed a declaration condemning the intervention of an extracontinental power in the affairs of hemispheric republics, prohibiting any hemispheric state from intervening in the affairs of another for the purpose of imposing its "ideologies or its political, economic, or social principles," and concluding that the "inter-American system is incompatible with any form of totalitarianism." Less than a week after the Declaration of San José, Castro issued the Declaration of Havana calling for revolution in the hemisphere, closer ties with the Soviet Union, and military and economic assistance from the People's Republic of China.[30]

Cuba still had considerable support in the hemisphere. If anything, the confrontation with the Yankees had made Castro the David challenging the North American Goliath. At the San José conference, the Mexican delegate attached a reservation that his government's approval of the declaration did not constitute a threat against Cuba, and Venezuela's foreign minister resigned his office rather than sign the condemnatory document. As the Democratic presidential candidate Senator Kennedy increased his attacks on the Eisenhower administration's foreign policy with warnings that the cold war might be lost in Latin America, the Cuban government unleashed an effective hemispheric propaganda war with its own press agency, Prensa Latina. The Cuban government provided financial and moral aid to pro-Cuban movements in every Latin American country and turned its embassies into centers for spreading the revolutionary message. In Mexico, students and workers demonstrated in support of the Cuban revolution, and a pro-Cuba movement coalesced around former president Lázaro Cárdenas and challenged President Adolfo López Mateos to prove his revolutionary mettle. López obliged. Declaring that he stood "on the extreme left inside the Constitution," he professed to emulate the Cuban example with revolutionary measures. The government nationalized several foreign companies and revived the agrarian reform program, distributing in three years almost seventeen million acres to peasants, more than López's two predecessors had confiscated in a decade. The country's financial magnates and business leaders took a more skeptical view of the president's statements in defense of Cuba, however, and urged him to mediate between Washington and Havana. They were fearful of investor confidence in Mexico. But they lacked the political option of throwing their support to an opposition party, and they needed the protected market that the government provided. Even as U.S. pressure on his government increased, López resisted, and over the next two years he tried to placate, first, the left and the right, with criticism of U.S. efforts to overturn Castro and, second, the U.S. government with reminders that Marxism-Leninism and membership in the OAS were incompatible.[31]

In Venezuela, the Cuban example invigorated the opposition to Rómulo Betancourt's reformist, antirevolutionary Acción Democrática government. When Betancourt ordered the expulsion of Castro sympathizers from the party, they formed a rival organization, the Movement of the Revolutionary Left (MIR), which funded terrorist and guerrilla activity in the country. Over the next year, as police clashed with street demonstrators and terrorists, the hapless Betancourt found himself caught between rightists who accused him of being a revolutionary and pro-Castroites who labeled him the lackey of Washington. A similar story unfolded in Brazil, where peasant leagues formed in the impoverished northeast and students, trade union leaders, and even members of the Brazilian parliament declared their support of Cuba, as did the country's new president, Jânio Quadros, who had visited Cuba during his campaign and had publicly chastised anyone who criticized Castro. Quadros would pay a price for such deviance. In 1961 his decoration of Che Guevara and his inability to deal with the country's economic crisis led to his abrupt resignation. The brother of Argentine president Arturo Frondizi formed a pro-Castro "revolutionary left." When leaders of the president's political party, the Radical Civic Union, expressed the belief that the Cuban revolution had prompted Washington to adopt a more favorable Latin American policy, Frondizi defied the Argentine military by taking a neutral position in the conflict between Cuba and the United States. In Chile, the pro-Castro left was sufficiently strong to persuade the rightist Jorge Alessandri government to oppose U.S. policy toward Cuba. Despite the country's dependence on U.S. economic assistance, Bolivia's two houses of parliament resolved in summer 1960 to support the Cuban revolution. Peru's Castroite groups enticed dissident Apristas to defect and formed a Movement of the Revolutionary Left.[32]

The Missile Crisis

Cubans who migrated to the United States, of course, told a different story about the revolution, about food shortages and grumblings from peasants and farm laborers and widespread disaffection. Their tale served to reinforce the determination of the Eisenhower administration to deal with Castro, who seemed capable of meeting every U.S. challenge with even more drastic measures. On October 13, 1960, Eisenhower declared an embargo against the island. Castro responded by nationalizing more property, including the predominantly U.S.-owned hotels, casinos, and food processing plants, effectively eliminating U.S. investments in the island. Within the CIA, arguments for making the "Guatemalan operation" a model for bringing down Castro gained more credence. Castro himself expected an invasion before the end of the year. After the downing of the U-2 spy plane over the Soviet Union and the president's bumbled handling of the aftermath, the agency needed a victory. What better way was there to get one than by using its presumably willing Cuban clients to bring down Castro in more or less the same way the United States had used disaffected Guatemalans and a propaganda campaign to remove Arbenz? On a global scale, the Soviet premier Nikita Khrushchev challenged U.S. resolve. After his narrow victory in the presidential campaign, Kennedy as president-elect received briefings about flash points in the cold war landscape—Berlin, the Middle East, Africa, Southeast Asia, and Cuba, among others. The outgoing president apparently impressed upon Kennedy that he might have to "do something" about Cuba and Laos, both of which might become political battlegrounds of the United States and the Soviet Union. Kennedy presumed that the bureaucracy and the military were better prepared to deal with Cuba, which was closer and more vulnerable. Regrettably, neither Eisenhower nor Kennedy paid sufficient attention to the subtleties of the Cuban–U.S. relation and their unanticipated impact on the concerted efforts of Washington to overthrow Castro. The rapid withering of the U.S. economic presence in fall 1960 devastated the power and influence of those groups that had the wherewithal and willingness to combat the radical course of the revolution. "Not without some irony," Louis A. Pérez, Jr., alertly notes, "the exercise of U.S. authority on such a scale and for so long had stunted the development of independent structures capable of countering from within the appeal of radical change."[33]

And the Cubans who could be counted on were not in Cuba but in Florida and in Washington, D.C. Although they certainly represented more of a cross-section of Cuban society than the first generation of émigrés, they were nonetheless divided save by a common antipathy to the Cuban regime. Some were former Castroites who sincerely believed the revolution had gone astray and, in the historic tradition of Cuban revolutionaries, were eager to return to the island and fight. Others were unrepentant batistianos bent on reviving the old Cuba with its bordellos and gambling, and still others were social democrats who wanted a democratic nation. Their problem ran deeper than lack of consensus about the kind of Cuba they wanted. They were at the beck and call of a young president who had incorporated the general agenda of Operation Pan-America in his call for an Alliance for Progress, a massive joint effort of hemispheric nations to combat Latin America gargantuan socioeconomic dilemmas, but who was in turn dependent on a civilian and military bureaucracy with its own divisions about how to fight Castro. Few among the North Americans placed much credence in the suggestion of former Castroites that the most effective way to defeat the Cuban leader lay in a prolonged guerrilla war using disgruntled Cuban revolutionaries.

In the end, Kennedy acquiesced in a plan that had a fair chance of success (meaning one in four) but no certainty of victory unless the president employed U.S. air and possibly even ground troops. Given the barrage of criticism within the United Nations and the damage to U.S. credibility throughout the hemisphere, he dared not risk that choice. When the exile brigade landed at the Bay of Pigs in mid-April 1961, Castro mobilized Cuban defenses and personally took command of military operations. Declaring a state of emergency, he ordered the arrest of thousands of Cubans expected of complicity in the invasion. Anti-Castro Cubans learned of the invasion only the day before the landing. They could not be expected to risk their lives in a cause of doubtful success and dubious purpose. Throughout the hemisphere, Kennedy's reputation suffered, on the one hand, for trying to bring down a Latin American government that did not directly threaten the United States and, on the other hand, for being indecisive about committing U.S. power to sustain the invasion. Yet in accepting responsibility for the defeat, his resolve to challenge Castro throughout the hemisphere deepened. That determination and Castro's realization that Cuba required an ally to meet the continuing threat from the United States would lead directly to the missile crisis.[34]

But in spring 1961 such a catastrophic outcome to the Cuban–U.S. confrontation appeared remote. Kennedy had already gotten the Alliance for Progress under way, and the initial responses from most Latin American governments were encouraging. The alliance agenda marked an important departure in the U.S. approach to Latin America, an appropriate response to Castro's call for revolutionary change. The task force directing the program reflected not the conservative free-market philosophy of the Eisenhower White House but a liberal developmental attitude. Its leader was Adolf A. Berle, a New Dealer whose participation in international affairs began during the Wilson era and continued during the Roosevelt administration. Berle had impressive Latin American connections. As ambassador to Brazil in 1945, he counseled Brazilian military officers returning from the Italian campaign to overturn the Vargas government. Throughout the 1950s, he met with Dominican exiles plotting to overturn the Trujillo dictatorship and with a new generation of Latin American reformist political leaders, such as Betancourt of Venezuela and Figueres of Costa Rica. Berle was also a close friend of the Puerto Rican governor Luis Muñoz Marín, who had presided over Operation Bootstrap, the U.S. economic program for Puerto Rico in the 1950s. For Berle, the Puerto Rican experience provided the appropriate developmental model for the political and economic transformation of the hemisphere.

Two of the task force members—Teodoro Moscoso, who had headed Operation Bootstrap, and Arturo Morales Carrión—came from Muñoz's inner circle. Lincoln Gordon of the Harvard Business School, another member, had worked on the Marshall Plan and was especially interested in U.S. investments in Brazil's automobile industry. Despite the arguments of some of Kennedy's advisors that the U.S. approach should emphasize economic development, Berle was insisted that the most effective course for the United States in the hemisphere lay in vigorous support of reformist political parties such as Venezuela's Democratic Action party. As befitted his style, Kennedy also called on other Latin American political and economic leaders, among them, ECLA's Raúl Prebisch, who impressed upon the president the importance of a program that captured the imagination of Latin America's common people; but they warned Kennedy that the continent's privileged might resist such fundamental changes. Some of them believed Kennedy raised unrealistic expectations.

In any event, they were persuaded that the U.S. president accepted the Latin American ideology of development. Even to the most naive among them it must have been clear that without the Cuban challenge, Kennedy might not have made the commitment to the alliance. As Kennedy admitted, "If the only alternatives for the people of Latin America are the status quo and communism, then they will inevitably choose communism." The contest between the Soviet Union and the United States for Latin America had gotten under way, and Kennedy mused that the Soviets had an advantage because they could make Cuba a showcase for development while the United States had to worry about the "revolution of rising expectations" throughout the entire continent. His advisors tried to reinforce his will with reassurances about "controlled revolutions" and doomsday warnings about violent upheaval unless Latin America's oligarchies and monied classes moved quickly to address its social inequities—malnutrition, infant mortality, illiteracy, and extreme concentrations of wealth amid widespread poverty.[35]

The problem with this kind of reasoning lay in the fact that it could not be easily reconciled with the political realities confronting Kennedy and virtually every Latin American leader. They could react to situations or propose bold new programs but not really direct the course of events, and the political systems that Kennedy and most hemispheric leaders held up as preferable alternatives to the Cuban regime often frustrated their efforts to move decisively. After the Bay of Pigs, Kennedy recognized that conservative members of the Congress would not support funding for the Alliance for Progress unless development aid and security issues were linked and Latin American recipients joined the United States in isolating and weakening Castro.

Kennedy got an early indication of the problem in trying to manipulate events following the assassination of the Dominican dictator Rafael Leonidas Trujillo, Jr., in late May 1961. Trujillo had long since outlived his usefulness to the Eisenhower administration. In his fury over U.S. and Latin American condemnation of his regime, the Dominican dictator threatened to establish closer relations with communist governments. None showed much interest in his overtures. In August 1960 the OAS imposed sanctions on Trujillo for conspiring to assassinate President Betancourt of Venezuela, and the plan to assassinate Trujillo, remove his family from Dominican politics, and install an interim government became more urgent. As promised, the CIA delivered the arms to the Dominican plotters before the end of the year. After the Bay of Pigs, however, the CIA tried to persuade its putative Dominican clients to postpone the assassination. In May 1961 Castro declared that Cuba was now a socialist republic, and some within the Kennedy administration feared that Dominican communists might gain control in the aftermath of the dictator's killing. On Capitol Hill conservative legislators approvingly contrasted Trujillo with Castro. But the Dominican plotters refused to go along with CIA wishes, and on the last day of May 1961, they waylaid his car on the outskirts of Ciudad Trujillo and killed him. Almost immediately, the plot began to unravel. Trujillo's three sons rounded up most of the conspirators, subjected some of them to the most despicable torture, and for the next six months the Trujillo family threatened to restore the Caribbean's most repressive and vilified dictatorship. They were effectively denied when in November Kennedy dispatched a naval force of eight vessels to anchor off the Dominican capital. Democracy had not triumphed but neither had dictatorship. Mulling over the Dominican situation in these uncertain months, Kennedy assessed U.S. priorities in terms of three possibilities: a democratic government, another dictatorship, or a communist takeover. The first was preferable, but the United States could ill afford to reject the second until it was certain that it could prevent the third.[36]

Cuba remained an obsession with Kennedy, however, and in the months after his humiliation at the Bay of Pigs the administration feverishly tried to regain the initiative. In June, the president dispatched Adlai Stevenson, U.S. ambassador to the United Nations, to South America to repair the political damage and to line up allies for isolating Cuba in the hemispheric system. Attorney General Robert F. Kennedy, commenced a personal vendetta on behalf of his brother by relentlessly pressuring the CIA to do something about the defiant Castro. The agency complied and even enlisted the aid of the Mafia, which despised Castro because he had put an end to its prostitution, drug, and gambling activities in the island. By the end of the year, the White House was coordinating efforts (Operation Mongoose) to remove the Cuban leader by stirring up a revolt and installing a friendly government. The target date for this insurrection was October 1962.

In the meantime, the United States again confronted Cuba at the Inter-American Economic Conference in Punta del Este, Uruguay, in August 1961. The purpose of the meeting was to discuss the Alliance for Progress and Kennedy's pledge of an initial U.S. commitment of $1 billion in assistance during the first year. Kennedy called for broad reforms in education, housing, health, taxation, and landownership. Secretary of the Treasury Dillon electrified the audience with a pledge of $20 billion from external sources, most of it from public funding from the United States. It was a daring offer, for Dillon lacked specific figures and Congress had yet to authorize alliance monies. Che Guevara, who led the Cuban delegation, sensed Dillon's predicament and challenged him to be more precise about the U.S. economic commitment. In the beginning of the sessions, Guevara had proved conciliatory and even held out a tentative peace offering to the United States. By the end of the conference, however, his mood had dramatically changed. Without U.S. assistance, he said, Cuba would prove more successful in achieving the goals of the alliance. When it became clear that the charter creating the alliance would pass, Guevara denounced it as yet another form of U.S. imperialism and mockingly asked if Cuba could expect to receive any benefits from it. Dillon's response made clear that there would be neither reconciliation between Washington and Havana nor a recognition of the Cuban government: "This we do not do and never will do, because to do so would betray the thousands of patriotic Cubans who are still waiting and struggling for the freedom of their country."[37]

The Dillon-Guevara exchange at Punta del Este I made clear there could be no reconciliation between Washington and Havana and that Kennedy intended to make his vendetta against Castro a hemispheric cause by pushing for Cuba's expulsion from the OAS. Some governments sensed U.S. priorities and began cutting their ties with the Cubans. In November President Betancourt of Venezuela, angered over Castro's encouragement of the Venezuelan left, announced the closing of Venezuela's embassy in Havana. A few weeks later, in one of his marathon speeches in the Plaza de la Revolución, Castro declared his conversion to Marxism-Leninism. The announcement triggered yet another meeting at Punta del Este in January 1962, at which OAS foreign ministers unanimously condemned the Cuban government for its alliance with the Sino-Soviet bloc; despite considerable U.S. pressure however, they only narrowly agreed to expel Cuba from the organization, as the ministers from Argentina, Bolivia, Brazil, Chile, Ecuador and Mexico declined to support the resolution on the grounds that such an act required changing the OAS charter. (In the end, there was a bit of legal hairsplitting—the resolution stipulated that the Cuban government but not Cuba had been voted out.) In the shuffling about both to placate the U.S. government and to reaffirm his nation's commitment to self-determination and nonintervention, the Mexican foreign minister, Manuel Tello, denounced Castro's profession of Marxism-Leninism as incompatible with OAS principles (the Tello thesis), then just as determinedly refused to go along with the resolution. Later, Tello appeared on U.S. television to explain his vote and reassure his listeners that "Mexico is not communist . . . [and] could never be a communist country." The Cuban foreign minister stormed out of the conference defiantly shouting that Cuba could be kicked out of the OAS but not out of the Western Hemisphere.[38]

Cuba was now a flash point in the cold war, as both Kennedy and Khrushchev knew. Kennedy had elected to contest Castro's revolution; Khrushchev, to defend it. The fundamental question for the Russian leader lay in the risk in challenging the United States over Cuba and in calculating how his North American counterpart might react. Had Kennedy done nothing about Castro, pundits later speculated, Khrushchev would have interpreted U.S. indifference to confidence rather than weakness. Conversely, if Kennedy had moved to crush his Cuban adversary, Khrushchev could have responded to his detractors that defending a communist regime in the U.S. backyard was not worth it. But Kennedy had chosen neither of these courses: The first would have been out of character and politically unacceptable; the second, a denial of the president's belief that bringing down Castro with an invasion might remove one problem but create a host of others. In summer 1962, when Raúl Castro visited Moscow with a renewed plea for defending the revolution from a U.S. invasion, Khrushchev sensed an opportunity to dislodge U.S. troops from West Berlin and compel Kennedy to remove fifteen Jupiter missiles he had deployed in neighboring Turkey in fall 1961. Sending short-range missiles to Cuba offered Khrushchev a means of shielding a communist government and gaining the initiative in the cold war. As he explained to his defense minister, "Let us launch a hedgehog into the pants of those next door."[39]

A risky move, certainly, but not altogether unexpected, given Khrushchev's political dilemmas and U.S. amphibious exercises off Vieques Island in Puerto Rico (Operation Ortsac) simulating the overthrow of a Caribbean tyrant. Khrushchev complicated matters somewhat by denying Castro's wishes for a formal defense alliance and a public deployment of the missiles. Perhaps he believed the Russians would be able to conceal the missiles until fully operational, and then Kennedy would not dare risk a military assault and North Americans would be compelled to live uneasily with Soviet missiles only ninety miles away. When photos from a U-2 reconnaissance flight over the island revealed their existence, some in the military called for an invasion or an air strike. Kennedy chose to impose a blockade around the island. His language conveyed something far more menacing. In a nationwide television address on October 22, Kennedy warned that the U.S. government would regard missiles launched from Cuba against any hemispheric nation "as an attack by the Soviet Union on the United States, requiring a full retaliatory response upon the Soviet Union."[40]

Twice during the following week the confrontation brought the two super-powers to the nuclear brink: on October 22 when a Russian submarine surfaced to accompany two Russian cargo ships headed for Havana; and five days later when a Soviet SAM missile downed a U-2, killing its pilot, and Cuban antiaircraft fire damaged but did not fell a reconnaissance plane. The first crisis eased when the Soviet vessels stopped dead in the water, but the second prompted Kennedy to consider an air strike and possibly an invasion. In that event, we now know, the Russian commander in Cuba was authorized to use tactical nuclear weapons. At this point, Khrushchev began to vacillate, knowing that U.S. missiles could destroy the Soviet Union and correctly sensing that Kennedy wanted to avoid a war. In the frantic negotiations that followed over the next month, Kennedy informally agreed not to invade Cuba once he had assurances that the Soviets had removed their missiles. Castro showed his displeasure at being treated like a spectator rather than a participant in these exchanges by refusing to permit a U.N. inspection of the island. Soviet troops and conventional weapons remained on the island after the removal of the missiles, and the U.S. covert war on the Cuban government and Castro continued.[41]

The missile crisis of October 1962 produced no clear-cut winners, as Castro's grip on power within Cuba deepened. Thirteen months later, Lee Harvey Oswald, an ex-Marine active in the Fair Play for Cuba movement, shot and killed Kennedy. Some conspiracy theorists have suggested that Kennedy was the victim of plotting by anti-Castro Cubans outraged over his betrayal of their cause or by Castro himself in retaliation for assassination attempts by the CIA. In 1964 the Central Committee of the Communist Party stripped Khrushchev of his powers, citing, among other reasons, his adventurism in foreign policy. During and immediately after the crisis, undeniably, Castro's reputation suffered throughout Latin America. The day following Kennedy's missile crisis address, the OAS unanimously resolved that member governments would "take all measures, individually and collectively, including the use of armed force," to bring about the removal of offensive weapons from Cuba. The post-crisis efforts by the United States to isolate Cuba in the hemisphere politically and economically appeared to be working when in July 1964 OAS foreign ministers resolved that Cuba had violated the Rio treaty by committing acts of aggression and intervention in the internal affairs of Venezuela and recommended that member governments break diplomatic relations and suspend trade (except in medicines and foodstuffs) with the island. There was grumbling about U.S. pressure, but all save Mexico eventually complied. Castro, not yet "tamed" by his Soviet benefactors, responded to the OAS decision by declaring that "the people of Cuba consider themselves to have equal right to help . . . the revolutionary movements in all countries that engage in such intervention in the internal affairs of our country."[42]

7

The Critical Decade

The missile crisis not only marked the high tide of the cold war in the Americas; it reaffirmed U.S. determination to prevent another Cuba in the hemisphere. Khrushchev had made the Soviet Union the benefactor of a socialist state ninety miles from U.S. soil. He had dispatched missiles to Cuba for myriad reasons, among them to show Washington how unsettling it was for Russians to worry about U.S. nuclear arms in the hands of the Germans. In this gamble, Khrushchev had been thwarted and Castro had failed to mobilize a continent on behalf of the revolution, but the survival of the Cuban revolution meant that no U.S. president could afford to tolerate "another Cuba" in the Caribbean. It meant as well that the left in every hemispheric country now had an example of an alternative route to development than that envisaged in the Alliance for Progress. One can be relatively certain that the Bay of Pigs led directly to the missile crisis. One cannot be so confident in stating that had these crises not occurred the Alliance for Progress might have proved a success, only that Cuba and the U.S. response to the Cuban revolution figured in the equation.[1]

Both the Cuban revolution and the alliance spoke to the social impact of economic change throughout the Americas and the political choices governments made to address the problems associated with that change, the results

of their choices, and the sometimes unexpected consequences of their actions. In the early months of the Kennedy administration, the president's
advisors on Latin America warned about the likelihood of violence if the continent's ruling elites did not respond to the "revolution of rising expectations"
(a favorite phrase of social scientists of those days) among Latin America's poor
with measures that alleviated the region's overwhelming social injustices—
malnourishment, illiteracy, subsistence plots of land in the midst of vast estates in the countryside, miserable hovels in the shadow of mansions in the
cities. Just as confidently they called for "controlled revolution" carried out not
by generals or dictators but tough, democratically elected leaders who recognized such a course as the only way to prevent the kind of revolution Cuba had
experienced. Adolf A. Berle, who headed President Kennedy's Task Force on
Latin America, articulated the U.S. purpose in a memo titled "Psychological
Offensive in Latin America." In a telling passage, Berle noted that "the chief
task is to set up an organization and a method of canalizing the vast, powerful,
disparate American intellectual effort so that it reaches Latin America and
Latin Americans at all levels, giving effective support to the United States so-
cial-economic-political system." The welfare of the United States required not
only military security but the political stability and economic well-being of its
southern neighbors.[2]

The Alliance for Progress

In 1961 the prospects for success in this endeavor appeared to be good. Virtually all the Latin American economies experienced an economic growth during
the fifties that rivaled the boom years of the late nineteenth and early twentieth centuries and exceeded that of China, the rest of Asia, and Africa. Average
per capita income doubled between 1940 and 1960. Although the old middle
class had declined in the smaller provincial towns, a new generation of professionals, managers, and office workers had mushroomed in the larger cities,
where easier access to education increased social mobility. Import substitution industrialization (ISI), which Prebisch and his colleagues at ECLA had
identified as the most effective means of enabling Latin America to catch up
with the advanced industrial economies, had achieved modest success, as the
gross domestic product for Latin America rose more than 5 percent annually
during the 1950s. All of the republics had entered the first stage of industrialization, and a few, notably Mexico and Brazil, had surpassed expectations.
Central America's growth rate—5 percent per annum despite a population increase of 3 percent annually—was even more impressive, and in 1960 the five

republics created the Central American Common Market, which ushered in the "golden age" of the isthmian economy. In the same year, eleven South American governments founded the Latin American Free Trade Association, designed as the foundation for a much more ambitious common market.[3]

The political scene brightened as well, as the cycle of authoritarian governments that had appeared in the late forties and early fifties gave way to democratic regimes. Military governments and dictatorships succumbed to civilian rule in Venezuela, where Rómulo Betancourt of the left-of-center National Revolutionary Movement became president in 1958, in Peru, and in Colombia. In an effort to end the decade-old strife that had taken two hundred thousand lives, Colombian Liberal and Conservative leaders created a National Front and agreed to alternate the presidency for sixteen years. The Argentine generals who had thrown out Juan Perón in 1955 finally accepted a civilian government three years later. In Brazil, Juscelino Kubitschek fashioned a coalition of the nation's disparate political sectors by promising "fifty years of progress in five" and placated a restive military with large arms purchases. At his urging, the government built a new capital in the interior, Brasília, which the French critic André Malraux called the "hope of the world." Costa Rica emerged from the turmoil of civil war in 1948 as a model of isthmian democracy. With the acquiescence of the military, Hondurans elected a Liberal civilian president in 1956 who managed to survive until 1962. In 1958 and 1959, when Castro came to power in Cuba, eight countries that had suffered authoritarian or military governments returned to democratic rule. In *The Twilight of the Tyrants,* the journalist Tad Szulc, a close student of Latin American affairs, confidently forecasted a democratic future for the hemisphere.[4]

Within a few years, that prediction seemed premature. Not only had Castro's triumph brought to power a socialist government in the shadow of the world's mightiest capitalist nation, but the revolution he had led now challenged the capability of these democratic regimes to bring about social and economic change and at the same time improve their rankings in the global economy. As the fifties came to a close, Prebisch gloomily concluded that the industrialization scheme crafted at ECLA may have improved Latin American economies but, paradoxically, had actually *increased* foreign dependence because of the need for foreign investment and capital goods. In the course of a decade, Latin America's share of total world export trade fell by a third. Such admissions served to strengthen the arguments of such radical intellectuals as André Gunder Frank (who penned the phrase, the "development of underdevelopment"), Sergio Bagú, and the Mexican sociologist Pablo González

Casanova, who contributed the equally compelling phrase, "internal colonialism," which referred to the Mexican countryside but had powerful implications for other countries in Latin America. In a stimulating book, Bagú concluded that the real enemies of social and economic change in Latin America
were not the foreign imperialists but local bourgeoisie. Contrary to what
ECLA's economists had been saying, Frank wrote, the only way to liberate the
continent from its dependence and lessen the gap between developed and
underdeveloped nations lay in revolution. By the time Kennedy became president and the Alliance for Progress got under way, guerrilla movements had
either emerged or gained strength in a number of Latin American countries.
Almost coincidentally, of course, apprehension about the Cuban revolution
had strengthened reformist movements, and the proponents of the Alliance for
Progress, particularly in the United States, looked to a generation of tough-
minded, anticommunist Latin American reformers—Betancourt in Venezuela, Alberto Lleras Camargo and Carlos Lleras Restrepo of Colombia, Fernando Belaúnde of Peru, and Eduardo Frei of Chile, among others—to lead
the controlled revolution that would deny a Marxist victory. A Kennedy advisor, Arthur M. Schlesinger, Jr., remembered that for those who crafted the alliance, the choices seemed clear: "The future of Latin America . . . lay between
the Castro road and the Betancourt road."[5]

North American liberals instinctively subscribed to such either/or calculations, believing that the first involved unacceptable levels of violence and massive social changes that could not be controlled while the second provided an
alternative model of development to address the "revolution of rising expectations" but reassured the middle classes and those with an instinctive fear of
the masses. In the late forties, Betancourt's leftist politics would have made
him a poor choice in the eyes of U.S. officials, but in the early 1960s the
Venezuelan president looked the perfect candidate to carry out a controlled
revolution because he possessed the necessary intellectual capability and political skills to guide Venezuela along the tortuous path toward a modern, liberal, democratic, and capitalist society. But danger lay in the "Betancourt
road," as the noted economist Albert O. Hirschman pointed out in a seminal
article appearing in the alliance's first year. Applauding the Kennedy administration's alignment with those Latin Americans committed to social progress,
Hirschman sounded a cautionary note: "If we care for the attainment of what
we are after, we ought to recognize that with this new policy we are entering
uncharted territory. Unlike the Russians, we do not have much experience in
promoting social change abroad." Actually, Kennedy's advisors, notably Walt

Whitman Rostow and Adolf A. Berle, had considered the perils of the course they were advocating for Latin America. The United States did not have a monopoly on the formula for transforming traditional cultures and societies into replicas of the modern industrial world. Through aid, trade, and encouragement of guerrilla war, the Soviet Union might be capable of demonstrating to the presumably malleable minds of Latin Americans that the Cuban model offered the quickest route to that goal. The only way to wean them from such delusions lay in channeling rather than containing the revolutionary currents sweeping the continent.[6]

The charter of the Alliance for Progress drawn up at Punta del Este in August 1961 appeared to conform not only to what those on Kennedy's task force were saying but to the social agenda Prebisch and his coterie of ECLA advisors had been advocating since Castro's triumph. In sweeping phrases, the charter called for bold new measures in public health, housing, and education that would increase life expectancy at birth by five years, cut infant mortality in half, provide potable water and sewage facilities to 70 percent of urban and 50 percent of rural inhabitants, build affordable houses for low-income families, wipe out adult illiteracy, and provide every child with at least six years of primary education. Even more ambitious was the charter's mandate for agrarian reform to address the desperate condition of the masses of small farmers, landless peasants, and farmworkers who eked out a subsistence living on small plots of less than twenty-five acres (*minifundia*) in countries in which a fraction of the landowning population occupied estates of almost twenty-five hundred acres (*latifundia*) and at the same time improve agricultural production. The architects of the alliance resolved to address the thorny political issue of tax reforms with the purpose of not only raising revenue but creating a more equitable tax system. Governments applying for external assistance would be required to draw up a national development plan identifying target goals in agriculture, industry, and improvements in rural and urban life, the means to achieve those goals and the priorities assigned to each, and estimates of the costs in achieving them. Because such a major undertaking would drain already financially strapped governments of resources and reduce the standard of living for millions of people, the United States pledged to fund over ten years the major portion of the $20 billion in external assistance that participating countries required.[7]

In a stroke, the diplomats gathered at Punta del Este had achieved something novel and daring in the inter-American system: a program for development that linked social and political objectives with an economic agenda that the Brazilian minister of finance described as an "economic revolution . . . carried forward with equally needed social reforms." They had been able to accomplish this task only by framing the charter in ambiguous terms and relying on individual governments to carry out the alliance's goals. As head of the U.S. delegation, Douglas Dillon spoke forcefully and eloquently about the U.S. commitment, but he had no authority to make any special trade concessions, a major concern of most Latin American governments, or to give details about the funding of projects. Dillon focused on achieving agreement, and to that end individual governments retained considerable latitude in interpreting how specific mandates should be carried out.

The clauses in the charter relating to agrarian reform were modified with intentionally ambiguous phrases to placate those governments that had already undertaken major agrarian reform, such as Mexico, or did not give them high priority, such as Argentina, or would be able to satisfy alliance standards with token measures. Both Dillon and Guevara voted for the agrarian reform proposal. Some leaders, notably Frondizi of Argentina and Quadros of Brazil, considered themselves as progressives but thought Kennedy's preoccupation with social reform was misplaced. Their political mandates called for an acceleration of economic development, particularly in heavy industry. Several representatives from smaller governments complained to Dillon that they required emergency aid and threatened to denounce the alliance if they did not get it. Others grumbled that some on Kennedy's task force, notably Lincoln Gordon, had "swallowed the ECLA line" and believed that too much emphasis on private investment would provoke a harsh reaction in Latin America. A dozen bankers and businessmen with experience in Latin America attended the Punta del Este conference and expressed their willingness to work with the Inter-American Development Bank on alliance projects, but the task force did not follow up on their ideas.[8]

Despite these early doubts and the limitations on funding imposed by Congress, the alliance got under way with fanfare and publicity. Kennedy tapped the Puerto Rican Teodoro Moscoso to serve as coordinator. Moscoso had headed up Operation Bootstrap, the U.S. development program for the island, and brought to his new post an infectious dedication that won plaudits from Latin Americans and respect for those who labored with him on what everyone agreed was a gargantuan task. The Soviets and Cubans derided the program as yet another tool of U.S. imperialism in the Americas, but through television the United States Information Agency disseminated the alliance message, and Latin Americans could see what was being accomplished at the grassroots level. By ordinary measures the early statistics on the alliance seemed impressive: in three years, the program constructed 8,130 schools, 139,800 houses, and 900 hospitals, and Latin American governments had received $4.5 billion in direct aid and $1 billion in institutional financing. Recipient governments had contributed more than $22 billion in funding. By mid-decade, more than a year after Moscoso had departed as coordinator, alliance projects had constructed 7,000 miles of roads, developed irrigation systems for 136,000 acres of farmland, provided more than 500,000 kilowatts of electricity, built new classrooms for a million students, and erected 450 health facilities. Five thousand industrial firms received $200 million in financing; 450,000 farmers got $250 million in credit.[9]

The Fragmenting of the Alliance for Progress

From the beginning there were problems, ranging from inevitable delays because of congressional balking at appropriating funds to recipients' frustrations about projects left uncompleted. Curiously, the charter of the alliance had not stated whether the amount of external assistance Latin America actually received—more than $18 billion by 1969—would be gross or net. More than half of these monies went to servicing the continent's long-term debt. Congress imposed other debilitating requirements. In response to appeals from Harold Geneen, president of International Telephone and Telegraph, who was fearful about leftist pressures on the Brazilian government to expropriate foreign-owned utilities, Senator Bourke Hickenlooper (R, Neb.) secured passage of legislation requiring the suspension of economic assistance to any government that expropriated U.S. property without adequate compensation.

But the principal financial difficulty affecting alliance funding related to the position of the United States in the global economy. Although the alliance occupied a special status in funding, in the early 1960s the United States no longer enjoyed the strong balance of payments and competitive advantage it had held twenty years before when the Marshall Plan got under way. Marshall Plan funds were "untied," enabling recipients to purchase goods and services anywhere, though most of the funds were spent in the United States because of the comparative strength of the U.S. economy in the late 1940s. By the early 1960s, Japan and several West European countries had gained an advantage in world markets in several key industrial areas, and the U.S. balance of payments now showed a chronic deficit. Not surprisingly, Congress reacted by stipulating that purchases under the Foreign Assistance Act must be made in the United States unless the president determined by special finding that such a requirement would be detrimental to national interests. In addition, the act required that at least 50 percent of commodities financed under the appropriation be transported on U.S. vessels and, where practicable to do so, that small U.S. businesses should "participate equitably" in supplying those commodities. To carry out the provisions of this act, the Agency for International Development created an office of material resources, consisting of two bureaucracies, field operators, including technicians, loan officers, and economists, and staff officers in Washington. Those in the field dealt with Latin Americans and represented the development constituency; those in Washington worked with other government agencies, Congress, and lobbyists. "The pressures of all these groups," wrote Jerome Levinson and Juan de Onís in their study of the alliance, "had ramifications of harrowing complexity for the actual work of the Alliance."[10]

As the early enthusiasm waned, some members of Congress traveled to various hemispheric countries and returned to Washington echoing Latin American complaints about the snail's pace of alliance projects. The former CIA official Richard Bissell made a strong case for shifting responsibility and control of the alliance to Latin Americans, a view independently seconded in a report by two former Latin American presidents, Juscelino Kubitschek of Brazil and Alberto Lleras Camargo of Colombia. Skeptics in the Department of State finally relented, and in November 1963 the OAS Economic and Social Council created the Inter-American Committee for the Alliance for Progress (CIAP), whose board would run alliance programs and control its funds. The new body was not everything Moscoso had hoped for, and the fact that Latin Americans dominated the board did not silence the grumbling or cynical remarks that the name *Alianza para el Progreso* could also be read facetiously to mean "Alliance stops progress."

Moscoso believed that the fundamental problem of the alliance had been the failure to make the agency a truly multilateral organization at its creation. In the early days of the Kennedy administration, however, politics and ideology, not organization, dominated U.S. thinking about the program. Not surprisingly, the initial tests of the alliance came in the political arena. By the end of the alliance's first year, a succession of political calamities in Brazil, Argentina, and Peru shook the optimism that had prevailed at Punta del Este I and prompted Kennedy to express doubts about Latin America's commitment to democracy. In July 1962, when the Peruvian military ousted Manuel Prado, Kennedy publicly denounced the action as a serious blow to the alliance and to the democratic goals of the inter-American system, a reaction that contrasted sharply with his muted disapproval of the Argentine military's removal of Arturo Frondizi four months earlier. The president recalled the U.S. ambassador to Peru and announced that a pending economic and military aid package amounting to more than $80 million would be held up. Doubtless influenced by Kennedy's strong stand, nine Latin American governments joined the United States in breaking diplomatic relations with the military junta. Some in the Department of State had urged Kennedy to publicly disavow the Argentine generals despite their strong disapproval of Frondizi's efforts to create bonds of friendship with Brazil and especially his efforts to conciliate the conflict between Havana and Washington. But the U.S. ambassador to the OAS, DeLesseps Morrison, forestalled the effort by arguing that Frondizi was a troublemaker.[11]

For both Kennedy and Morrison what really mattered was Frondizi's and Prado's respective views about communism and their willingness to conform to U.S. directives on development. The fact that Frondizi's commitment to the alliance and to its reformist agenda was probably stronger than Prado's made little difference. His notions about development—invite foreign investment into the country but control it—did not follow Washington's prescription. In the Peruvian case, there were other complications. The military had acted to prevent their old adversary, Haya de la Torre and the Aprista party, from sharing power with Prado's probable successor, former president Manuel Odría. Curiously, both the Peruvian generals and U.S. leaders favored a reformist candidate for president, Fernando Belaúnde Terry. What Kennedy really feared was the Peruvian military's heightened sense of its role as "nation builders," a sense of purpose nourished in part by their experience at the U.S. Army Command School at Fort Leavenworth and their growing concern about the Peruvian countryside and particularly the role of the International Petroleum Company in the nation's political and economic life. As things turned out, the local U.S. business community, apprehensive that the severing of diplomatic relations between Lima and Washington would lead to economic reprisal, urged Kennedy to reconsider his action. The military junta obtained recognition within a month by agreeing to new elections (in which Belaúnde emerged victorious) and reassuring the OAS that constitutional rights would be respected. But the junta expected the new president to deal with International Petroleum.[12]

In their estimation of the national condition and their impatience with civilian government, the Peruvian generals displayed a determination matched only by Kennedy's obsession with Castro. Perhaps they instinctively understood that Kennedy's distaste for military government paled in comparison to his hatred of the Cuban leader. Not even the most cynical of analysts of the Latin American condition in the early 1960s would have predicted that in the first eight years of the alliance sixteen civilian governments would succumb to military coups. Occasionally, the threat of force appeared to serve the cause of democracy, as Kennedy demonstrated in summer 1962 when he dispatched U.S. warships to the Dominican Republic as a warning to the Trujillo family not to interfere in the presidential elections. Clearly, there were limits to Kennedy's antimilitary resolve, as he demonstrated when the Guatemalan military seized power in order to prevent the election of Juan José Arévalo, whose prospective return to power troubled the president. Similarly, the president was sufficiently concerned about the Marxist Guianan leader Cheddi Jagan to pressure the British to delay Guianan independence until London (read Washington) identified a less controversial candidate. Critical turning points came with military takeovers in Ecuador in July 1963, in the Dominican Republic in September, and in Honduras in October. The Ecuadoran officers removed a drunkard, Carlos Julio Arosemena, who as vice president had succeeded to the presidency, but the Hondurans ousted a Liberal reformer, Ramón Villeda Morales, a supporter of the alliance.

In the Dominican coup, which ended the seven-month presidency of the mercurial Juan Bosch and closed the National Assembly, the leader of the takeover, the air force general Elías Wessin y Wessin, justified the ouster of Bosch on the grounds that he had "plunged the country into chaos" and been soft on communism. Two days later, the generals named a civilian junta to run the country, but the military retained power. The Kennedy administration suspended economic aid and withheld diplomatic recognition, but over the following months the junta expanded its political base sufficiently to appease Washington, and in mid-December, the new Lyndon B. Johnson administration recognized the junta and restored economic aid early in the new year. The much-heralded Dominican experiment in democracy, cobbled out of a fleeting political alliance between the United States and the OAS and a Dominican poet and reformer, had failed. Bosch had placed too much faith in Kennedy, in the alliance, and in the U.S. ambassador, John Bartlow Martin, whose admiration for Dominican elites instinctively aroused in him a virulent hatred for Bosch, their most persistent critic.[15]

A year before, the military takeovers might have resulted in severe U.S. condemnation. Instead, they prompted a formal reappraisal of U.S. policy, accompanied with the obligatory expressions of commitment to civilian regimes.

Assistant Secretary of State for Latin American Affairs Edwin A. Martin, in a statement approved by Kennedy, summed up Washington's continuing faith in the hemispheric middle class as the strongest support for democracy; he lamented that military takeovers "thwart the will of the people, destroy political stability and the growth of the tradition of respect for democratic constitutions, and nurture communist opposition to their tyranny." But it was no longer possible to deny the critical importance of Latin America's military in the political culture. When the military seized power by unconstitutional means, he continued, "we must use our leverage to keep these regimes as liberal and considerate of the welfare of the people as possible" and "support and strengthen the civilian components against military influences and press for new elections as soon as possible so that these countries once again may experience the benefits of democratic legitimacy."[14]

Six weeks later, Kennedy was assassinated in Dallas, and in the minds of his admirers, the alliance lost its most articulate advocate, however questionable some of his decisions about the resurgence of military governments in the hemisphere and his obsessive hatred of Fidel Castro. Kennedy had championed reform, spoken for the downtrodden, and condemned the poverty that ravaged a continent. In four Latin American countries he had personally launched alliance programs. Peace Corps workers in Colombia testified to his appeal when they observed his photo displayed alongside images of Jesus Christ in rural hovels. Before his death he had grown more cynical about the enormity of the task confronting the alliance, conceding that the reconstruction of Europe after World War II through the Marshall Plan succeeded because Europeans possessed political institutions, technology, and (save perhaps Germany) a democratic tradition that most Latin American countries appeared to lack. His spirited advocacy of the larger purpose of the alliance did not wane, however, Kennedy's defenders continue to insist. They are less attentive to another commitment illustrating his resolve: "Every resource at our command," the president declared a few days before his death, would be used "to prevent the establishment of another Cuba in the hemisphere."[15]

With the Texan Lyndon B. Johnson in the White House and another Texan, Thomas Mann, replacing Moscoso as coordinator of the alliance, the "business approach" to Latin America gained favor. Unlike most of Kennedy's "point men," Mann had experience in Latin American affairs dating back to World War II. He was anticommunist, though he had opposed the Bay of Pigs invasion, and probusiness. An early supporter of the alliance, he began to change his mind about Moscoso's priorities during his tenure as ambassador to Mexico. Meaningful social reform, he declared in a 1962 speech, required economic growth. By the time he became coordinator as well as assistant secretary of state for Latin American affairs in December 1963, he had become even more outspoken in his belief that Kennedy's priorities in Latin America had been misplaced. Martin had only reluctantly acknowledged the role of the military in politics; Mann embraced the generals. In mid-March 1963, only a few months after taking over from Moscoso, he outlined the principles of U.S. policy in a confidential talk to chiefs of mission in Latin America. The Mann Doctrine emphasized economic growth, protection of U.S. direct investments (estimated at $9 billion), nonintervention in the internal affairs of hemispheric countries, and anticommunism. Several who heard him said later that he never mentioned the alliance, and when his remarks were leaked to the *New York Times,* Szulc incorporated them in a front-page story titled "U.S. May Abandon Efforts to Deter Latin Dictators." Two weeks after Mann spoke, the Brazilian military removed President João Goulart, who fled with his family to Uruguay. Johnson waited only twelve hours after the provisional government took office to express his "warmest wishes" to Brazil's new rulers. Secretary of State Dean Rusk followed shortly with his own congratulations. "It would be hard to figure out from the public and official pronouncements," a *Times* editorialist wrote, "who got more satisfaction in the overthrow of President Goulart, the Brazilians or the United States State Department."[16]

The connection between the Brazilian coup and the obvious U.S. approval of the ouster of Goulart was undeniable. For several years, U.S. officials had expressed unconcealed dissatisfaction with Goulart, particularly his failure to follow through with an economic stabilization plan. Frustrated with the Brazilian leader's populist leanings and his inability to contain communist influence in the labor unions, they began channeling aid monies to what were called "islands of sanity," state governments whose political leaders shared their concerns about the Brazilian president's policies. Opponents in São Paulo and Belo Horizonte organized civic marches for "God, nation, and family," funded in part by the CIA. The military did not wait for the public clamor over Goulart to reach the point of insurrection, however. When the president failed to deal severely with a mutiny by Brazilian marines over inadequate food and in response appeared to be sympathetic with their plight, the generals made their move. From the state of Minas Gerais, General Olympio Mourão Filho joined the governor in a radio address denouncing Goulart and ended their address with the statement that the war against communism had begun. Goulart had few friends to defend him. He learned that the United States had already pledged to recognize a new government, and businessmen in São Paulo, a center of anti-Goulart sentiment, revealed that Ambassador Lincoln Gordon knew about the plot and welcomed it. Washington had a contingency plan (Brother Sam) to assist the conspirators with supplies and arms, but the Brazilian generals required neither U.S. arms nor inspiration to act and certainly did not need U.S. advice on how to wage their anticommunist revolution. Within a few days of taking power, the military junta, operating under an institutional act, arrested thousands of Brazilians without formal charges. Four hundred government officials lost their political rights, among them the former presidents Goulart, Quadros, and Kubitschek, six state governors, fifty-five congressmen, and prominent labor leaders. Gordon, who had approved the coup, was so shaken by these flagrant violations of political rights that he offered his resignation, but his superiors in Washington persuaded him to remain with the admonition that he should use his influence to moderate Brazil's new military rulers and the country's new president, General Humberto Castello Branco.[17]

Such a prospect seemed unlikely, given the Brazilian military's confidence about running the country and Castello Branco's adeptness in winning support of anticommunist political parties. In Bolivia, however, the U.S. ability to influence the government seemed stronger. Since the 1952 revolution, the victorious MNR party had become more dependent on the United States. When Paz Estenssoro returned to the presidency in 1960, he had no wish to repeat the economic policies of the 1952–56 period, which had failed to address the problems of the Bolivian countryside. The Cuban revolution and the Alliance for Progress, which raised expectations among Bolivia's rural people, complicated Paz's problems. Increasingly, he relied on the military to contain rural dissidents, and in the early 1960s the Bolivian military slowly but effectively began to reassert its authority in the countryside. The army used U.S. financial aid to operate rural programs, build new schools and houses, and construct roads. Under U.S. pressure, Paz acquiesced in voting to expel the Cuban government from the OAS. As the 1964 election approached, Paz again weakened under Washington's directives to deal more severely with increasingly militant tin miners and to deny the pro-Cuban vice president, Juan Lechín, an opportunity to succeed him. In the bitter infighting within the Bolivian regime, Lechín broke ranks and formed his own political party.

As the spirit and promise of the revolution dissipated, Paz increasingly relied on the military to sustain the government. He agreed to accept General René Barrientos as his vice presidential running mate in the 1964 elections.

The concession came too late. In 1952, the MNR had mobilized tin miners and rural peasants in a revolution that had transformed Bolivian society and politics and raised expectations among these historically abused groups. The civilian victors had survived only because they had found a benefactor—the United States—but by 1964 the combination of diminished U.S. interest in the reformist agenda of the Alliance for Progress and the Bolivian military's weariness in defending a weak regime had taken a toll. In early November Barrientos seized power in a military coup. The 1952 revolution had failed, a victim of both domestic political choices and U.S. demands, a succession of concessions made by Bolivian leaders intended to preserve the revolution but which undermined it. "One concession led to the next in a sequence that made it impossible to tell the seriousness of each new step," wrote a Bolivian critic. "The revolution did not crumble from a single blow, it fell bit by bit, piece by piece."[18]

Empire Reaffirmed

The Brazilian coup was Lyndon Johnson's second hemispheric crisis. His first came in Panama in January 1964, when a confrontation between Panamanian and U.S. students at Balboa High School in the Panama Canal Zone escalated into riots that took twenty-two Panamanian and three U.S. lives and resulted in a suspension of diplomatic relations between Panama and the United States and the declaration of what amounted to a state of siege in the zone. The president handled the crisis in much the same way he dealt with domestic political problems.

The immediate origins of the confrontation lay in the decision of Balboa High students to fly the U.S. flag at their school in defiance of Governor Robert Fleming's 1963 order that both the U.S. and Panamanian banners be flown at designated civilian sites and the U.S. flag taken down elsewhere, including in front of Balboa High. When Panamanian students heard about the flag raising, they marched into the zone with the intention of raising their own flag at the same site. The roots of the crisis went much deeper, of course, and were infinitely more complex, involving everything from day-to-day resentments of Panamanians over the markedly different standard of living of North Americans in the "red, white, and blue paradise" and the Panamanians and West Indians living next door in Panama City and Colón to the persistent efforts of successive generations of Panamanian leaders to affirm the nation's sovereign rights over the zone, rights wrongly surrendered in the November 1903 Hay-Bunau-Varilla Treaty and persistently misinterpreted by North Americans.

With every Panamanian assertion of its claims and every concession granted by modification of that treaty—the last occurred in 1955 during the Eisenhower administration—Washington just as determinedly reaffirmed that such agreements in no way seriously diminished U.S. authority. Zonians saw these concessions as signs of weakness, granted only because Panamanian leaders had the ability to mobilize an angry populace and threaten to invade the zone or sabotage the canal. Uncommon in many ways, Zonians and Panamanians shared a frustration in dealing with governments and with leaders who appealed to their patriotism and raised their expectations only to dash their hopes with decisions that resolved little.

Panamanian leaders had more reason to fear their own people. In 1959 there were three insurrections, two of them indirectly inspired by the Cuban example and one involving Cuban support. In the same year, the unemployed of Colón, the country's second largest city, staged a hunger strike, and angry student protestors twice marched into the zone to affirm Panamanian sovereignty by raising the flag. Anti-American violence reached new heights. The outgoing Eisenhower administration tried to placate the Panamanian government with a nine-point program, including an $11-million grant, recommendations for a sea-level canal, and provisions for a joint display of both flags at the entrance to the zone. For Panamanian dissidents, such concessions meant little, and in the 1960 national presidential campaign Robert Chiari called for broad social and economic reforms to prevent a revolution. Victorious, Chiari secured sufficient Alliance for Progress funds for the Panamanian government to embark on an ambitious construction program—roads, housing, hospitals, and a bridge across the Pacific terminus of the canal—but pressures on him to secure even more concessions from the United States came from every sector of Panamanian society. Above all, he must resolve the issue that had plagued every Panamanian leader since 1903—affirmation of Panama's sovereignty over the canal. Flying to Washington for personal discussions with President Kennedy, Chiari returned to Panama with a variety of concessions, including an agreement to permit the flying of both the U.S. and Panamanian flags at selected sites in the zone. Kennedy could go only so far in dealing with Panamanian claims on the canal. In U.S. calculations, that issue was linked to a sea-level canal, a prospect made more uncertain by the signing of the Nuclear Test Ban Treaty—most plans for a sea-level canal assumed that the excavation would be carried out by a series of nuclear blasts.[19]

On a per capita basis, Panama was the largest single recipient of aid under the Alliance for Progress, but those figures counted for little to either Panama-

nians or Zonians in the 1964 crisis. Panamanians felt deceived by Chiari's failure to wrangle a U.S. concession on the critical issue of the canal, and Zonians
had friends in Congress ready to condemn every gesture of accommodation to
Panamanians. The most outspoken was Representative Daniel Flood (D, Penn),
who had described the decision to permit the flying of the Panamanian flag in
the zone as "another Munich." Johnson refused to budge during the early
stages of the crisis until Chiari proved that he could restore order and was not
using the riots to obtain further concessions, though he did agree to accept an
OAS investigation. When the Panamanian National Guard finally restored
order, the situation noticeably improved. In December, following his landslide
victory in the presidential election over Barry Goldwater, Johnson appeared
on national television to announce that the United States intended to build a
sea-level canal (hinting that it *might* be in Panama) and with its construction
would agree to end the 1903 Panama Canal treaty. This was a concession fundamentally linked to U.S. security concerns. Despite political obstacles in both
countries and doubts among the U.S. military about giving up the canal, both
Johnson and his Panamanian counterpart, Marco Robles, were able to agree
on a series of three treaties covering transfer of the canal to Panama, a new
sea-level canal, and the security of the canal. Regrettably, the explosive political climate in Panama prevented approval of the treaties, as the Panamanian
National Assembly impeached Robles because of his negotiation of the treaties.
Without prior Panamanian approval, Johnson chose not to submit the treaties
to the U.S. Senate.[20]

It was not so obvious at the time, but the "flag riots" in Panama proved to
be more than a turning point in U.S.–Panamanian relations. Johnson's victory
was a Pyrrhic one. In linking the construction of a sea-level canal to the abro-
gation of the 1903 treaty, Johnson had, indirectly but inevitably, committed the
United States to the transfer of the canal to Panama and the end of the Canal
Zone. That in turn would mean profound changes for the zone's distinct society of proud but now embittered civilians, some of them the children and
grandchildren of the first generation of zone workers, and the small number
of North Americans who lived in the republic. For both U.S. and Panamanian
leaders, what was most troubling about the crisis was not the delays it imposed
on two governments in ending the 1903 treaty, a process which required more
than another decade of negotiation to accomplish, but the often unexpected
violence of local people in an urban area and the threat it meant for political
leaders, including those who have raised popular expectations and encouraged social protest. In such circumstances, often, the choice is to contain the

violence and placate the disaffected, which can be risky, or to crush the uprising with such overwhelming power that the alienated dare not try again.

In the Dominican civil war of April 1965, Johnson chose the latter, and the decision would have far more serious implications for hemispheric relations than the crisis in Panama, where the civilian government effectively used the National Guard to restore order. In the Dominican case, the civilian junta led by Donald Reid Cabral failed to curb its own military. Reid had assumed power with every intention of reforming the Dominican military. He cut the military budget and promoted civic action, which Bosch had done, and adopted counterinsurgency tactics in the Dominican countryside, which his predecessor had disdained. With military support, he might have been able to build a broad political base in Dominican society. But the old guard military wanted to bring back Joaquín Balaguer, Trujillo's vice president, elevated to the presidency by the dictator to "democratize" the government. After the assassination of Trujillo, Balaguer stayed on as president because of the justifiable fears among Dominicans that the Trujillo family might try to seize power. When they left, however, Dominicans pushed Balaguer out. Younger military officers wanted to restore the exiled Bosch as president on the grounds he had been unconstitutionally removed from office by the September 1963 military coup. For Bosch personally, the revolt of April 1965 constituted a distinct phase in the Dominican revolutionary tradition, frustrated in the nineteenth century by the poor material conditions and lack of unity plaguing the country but accelerated in the twentieth by the U.S. military occupation of 1916–24.[21]

The officers' determination to return Bosch to power plunged the country into civil war in late April 1965, a conflict dividing Dominicans along political, social, and economic lines. Constitutionalists drew their support from students, urban workers, small farmers, and leftist political parties; their Loyalist adversaries, from the majority of military officers, large farmers, and most of the middle class. The warring factions divided not only on the critical issue of Bosch's return to the presidency but on the equally controversial matter of U.S. intervention. Constitutionalists viewed U.S. intervention as detrimental to their revolution; Loyalists, as an essential short-term necessity. In the uncertain days immediately following the coup, the military junta representing the Loyalists appealed to U.S. ambassador W. Tapley Bennett, Jr., to intervene to prevent a communist takeover. Bennett demurred. The leaders of the Constitutionalists asked him to mediate. He refused. As the Loyalists renewed their appeals to Bennett, the Constitutionalists seized the national palace, and armed civilian supporters of the Constitutionalists roamed the streets, killing and beating officers of the despised national police. Planes from San Isidro air base strafed the palace. Throughout the city, factions of the two sides warred, plunging the Dominican capital into chaos. As the Constitutionalists seemed on the verge of winning, Johnson decided to intervene, justifying the initial landing of four hundred marines on April 28 (four days after the Constitutionalist coup) on the plausible grounds that U.S. citizens in Santo Domingo were in danger. Two days later the president dispatched the first contingents of U.S. Army Airborne troops under General Bruce Palmer. Their numbers would soon reach twenty-three thousand. Clearly, such a massive force far exceeded what would have been necessary to protect U.S. citizens. In an address to the country, Johnson stated that "Communist conspirators" had subverted a genuine democratic movement. In his memoir of the intervention, General Palmer offered another explanation: "My stated mission was to protect American lives and property; my unstated mission was to prevent another Cuba and, at the same time, another Vietnam."[22]

Most North Americans and a sizable majority in Congress approved of the intervention. On the eve of a massive military buildup in Southeast Asia, Johnson could ill afford to appear too restrained in dealing with a crisis so much closer to home. Academic specialists, some journalists, and several prominent international lawyers found the president's reasoning about the Dominican crisis not only violative of international law but a marked departure from the Good Neighbor policy and the Alliance for Progress. The Johnson Doctrine, they noted, alienated our democratic friends in Latin America and violated the OAS charter by sanctioning the unilateral use of force. When the OAS Organ of Consultation convened to discuss the matter, however, the United States not only prevented any condemnation of its actions but pushed through a resolution creating an Inter-American Peace Force (IAPF) under a unified OAS military command in the Dominican Republic. The political price for this diplomatic victory was high, as the Venezuelan, Mexican, Uruguayan, and Chilean delegations severely criticized the intervention. A special Inter-American Conference scheduled to meet in Rio de Janeiro in June had to be postponed because of anticipated criticism over the U.S. military presence in Santo Domingo. In the end, Latin America's contribution turned out to be token. Save for Costa Rica, which dispatched twenty police to the IAPF, troops came from either military governments (Brazil and Honduras) or dictatorships (Nicaragua and Paraguay).[23]

Without U.S. intervention, undeniably, the human, economic, and political costs of the civil war (approximately six thousand Dominican casualties) would have mounted, particularly if the vengeful Loyalists had won the civil war. Yet the intervention also deepened anti-Americanism in the republic, certainly among the constitutionalists and urban masses but also among moderates. As things turned out, the Johnson administration refused to be rushed into a quick solution. To the delight of some Constitutionalists, Hector García Godoy, liberal, progressive, and independent, became provisional president, and Bosch got another opportunity to regain the presidency in a contest with Balaguer in the June 1966 elections. Not surprisingly, the former president won overwhelmingly in Santo Domingo but lost badly to Balaguer in the interior. The "Godoy formula" effectively assured a Balaguer victory because his transitional presidency provided Bosch's opponents in the military time to organize. Three months later, the last IAPF troops departed. True to his electoral promise to unite the republic, Balaguer appointed Dominicans representing divergent political and social philosophies (excepting communists, of course) to his cabinet, named women as provincial governors, and sent several prominent military officers to diplomatic and consular posts abroad. Among the last were General Elías Wessin y Wessin, Loyalist commander in the civil war, and Colonel Francisco Caameño Deñó, the Constitutionalist commander.

By the end of his first term, however, Balaguer reverted to his old style of rewarding his friends and punishing his enemies. Bosch went into exile in Spain, wrote a bitter account of the intervention, and in 1968, to the dismay of true believers in his Dominican Revolutionary Party, declared that he was abandoning social democracy in favor of popular dictatorship. In 1970 he returned to the republic, disdaining any efforts to unite the leftist parties against Balaguer. In an election riddled with fraud and intimidation, Balaguer easily won reelection. The president readily dealt with other pretenders. In 1971, General Wessin y Wessin attempted to depose Balaguer in a coup, failed miserably, and was deported. Two years later, Colonel Caameño Deñó landed with a small guerrilla force, but Balaguer quickly mobilized his army and crushed the invasion. In the fighting, Caameño was killed.[24]

The Dominican intervention appeared to be an unqualified success for Washington's counterrevolutionary strategy. Having failed to crush Castro, the U.S. government had proved to the hemisphere that it would stamp out revolution within a region it still considered within its sphere of influence. Ironically, Castro's failure to abet the Constitutionalist cause in a neighboring country prompted some on the left throughout Latin America to criticize the Cuban leader for his passivity throughout the crisis. But the Cubans were not going to risk U.S. retaliation to aid a revolution that bore little similarity to the

Cuban struggle. And where the guerrilla insurrection did closely model the Cuban experience, as in Mexico, the Cubans refused to help out, valuing more Mexico's refusal to break diplomatic relations. At mid-decade, Castro's rhetoric retained its familiar revolutionary fire, and in 1966 Cuba hosted the Tricontinental Conference, the gathering of third world leaders. When Guevara returned from his disastrous African sojourn, Castro sent him to Bolivia to incite the first of "many Vietnams" in the Americas. Guerrilla movements had sprung up in numerous Latin American countries (including Cuba) in the first half of the decade, but in every case the counterguerrilla military forces, some of them trained under U.S. supervision, overcame them, an indication that the Cuban example might inspire hemispheric revolutionary followings but they could not replicate the Cuban experience, certainly not in Bolivia, where U.S.-trained Bolivian soldiers tracked down Guevara and killed him in 1967.

Guevara's defeat seemed to confirm Washington's policy of urging reforms while strengthening the role of a Latin American military as agents of regional and national security. Yet in Bolivia, as elsewhere in Latin America, reliance on the military could be risky, for General Barrientos and his successors proved unwilling to follow Washington's script about waging counterguerrilla war and about developing the country. Each situation had its own peculiarities, of course. In the Bolivian case, military officers divided sharply over the country's future. Barrientos turned out to be much weaker, in large part because of his dependence on Washington. After the death of Guevara, Castro obtained a copy of Guevara's diary, obtained from a Bolivian official angry about the president's ties with the CIA. To counter the inevitable backfire, Barrientos abruptly altered his policies, improving relations with the Soviet Union and supporting the return of the Cuban government to the OAS. As Barrientos distanced himself from Washington, his influence within the country diminished and with his death in 1969, U.S. control of the Bolivian revolution declined.[25]

In death Guevara's appeal increased, especially among those who had lost faith in reformist politics and liberal development programs to bring about fundamental social change. They became "Che's guerrillas," young men and women who starved in northern Argentina, drowned in their own excrement in Brazil's notorious torture chambers, and endured unspeakable hardships in Guatemala's civil war. In revolutionary mythology Guevara replaced Castro as the figure who united a continent's revolutionaries, portrayed by one sensitive writer as the century's first Latin American, a man who could not abide the ambivalence of the modern world and found his response in struggle. "There is no experience more profound for a revolutionary than warfare," he had written an Argentine friend to describe why revolution in Latin America was necessary. "It was not the isolated act of killing or carrying a weapon or waging a particular kind of combat but the entire experience of being a warrior and knowing that an armed man is a combatant equal to any other armed man and does not fear his armed opponents." Latin America required such a revolutionary voice, perhaps, but Che's legions of admirers too often forget that in life he demanded the impossible and exacted the same from his followers. In an untidy world, the perfect cause does not exist.[26]

The Frustrations of Development

The Cuban revolution may not have been the perfect cause, but it had at least offered to a generation the belief that revolution throughout Latin America was possible even though the Cubans failed to make their revolution happen anywhere else. Without it, there probably would have been no Alliance for Progress. At the end of the decade, Guevara's 1961 challenge at Punta del Este that Cuba would come closer to achieving the broad socioeconomic goals of the Alliance for Progress than any Latin American country appeared to be validated: Cuban educational, literacy, and health standards easily outperformed any of the major Latin American countries, and the living standards of Cuba's country people had improved dramatically. Within a decade, the revolution had transformed not only an economy but its culture as well. The image of Cuba within the African Caribbean improved as well, a change attributed less to the appeal of the Cuban economic model than to the revolution's commitment to ending racism and reminders of Cuban's African heritage. The price for these dramatic changes had been high: the virtual ending of the capitalist system and private property, the wiping away of the old political parties, severe restrictions on individual liberty, and undeniable dependence on the Soviet Union, whose leaders used the familiar carrot and stick method to tame him. In 1968, when the Russians crushed the progressive government of Czechoslovakia, Castro uttered no protest. He could always argue, of course, that the U.S. economic embargo and the presence of a militant exile community in Miami necessitated Cuba's alignment with the Soviet Union. At the end of the first revolutionary decade, sugar was still the island's principal export, but little of the Old Cuba remained. Cuba may not have achieved the goals of the alliance, as Guevara in 1961 had confidently predicted it would, but the revolution had survived, and in the course of a decade it had transformed the island and its people. In a curious but understandable way the United States abetted this transformation, directly by giving Castro a powerful propaganda tool with its opposition to the revolution and indirectly by encouraging the immigration of Cubans and potential counterrevolutionaries to the United States. Such were the ties of "singular intimacy" of which President William McKinley had spoken at the turn of the century.[27]

Defenders of the alliance could claim nothing so dramatic. By a strictly economic measure, the alliance had failed to live up to expectations, as Kennedy had feared. Even its most stalwart defender, Harvey Perloff, conceded that from 1961 to 1967 Latin America's economic performance fell short of the original goal of an annual growth rate of 2.5 percent per capita. Five of the seven countries exceeding that rate were Central American, beneficiaries of a dramatic boom in prices for their exports in the early years of the decade. Mexico, Bolivia, and Panama, each a recipient of major alliance funding, also surpassed the 2.5 percent mark. But Brazil, Chile, and Colombia also received generous financial support from the alliance yet attained only modest economic growth. Two of the slowest-growth South American economies in the decade were Argentina and Uruguay, both of which had per capita incomes exceeded only by oil-rich Venezuela. In 1969, a special staff report of the U.S. Senate Foreign Relations Committee singled out Colombia for falling embarrassingly short of attaining alliance goals despite having received 11 percent of alliance funding for all Latin America.[28]

By the end of the century, North American and European observers would be tempted to explain these disappointments by citing cultural differences, but contemporary analysts pointed to the enormous barriers to development confronted by Latin American and Caribbean peoples: too few skilled workers, weak social and political institutions, insufficient export earnings to meet foreign exchange needs, and the want of a strong institutional and political base for charting long-range developmental strategies. The developmental model heretofore used—carrying out large-scale programs through national governments and within national barriers—ill-served a continent in which most countries lacked a sufficient domestic market or human resources to develop a modern industrial economy. A common market provided benefits, of course, as the Central Americans had learned, but the unfortunate economic reality was the coexistence of pockets of wealth and progress—cities such as São Paulo, Rio de Janeiro, Caracas, Mexico City, Buenos Aires, and Lima, together with advanced farming and mining areas—with a hinterland of backward zones scarcely affected by modern ways. These "pockets of progress," Perloff wrote, must become the dynamic centers of development.[29]

Such was the conventional wisdom inherited from the Kennedy years necessarily modified by unsettling lessons of the Latin American and Caribbean
condition in the late 1960s. Other contemporary assessments were more critical, occasionally bordering on the extreme. The North American journalist
and respected Latin Americanist Tad Szulc suggested that the alliance failed
to create a political mystique and thus became vulnerable to opposition from
both left and right. Víctor Alba argued that the United States should cease all
assistance to Latin American governments and their militaries on the grounds
that they sustained oligarchs and instead grant support directly to universities,
unions, cooperatives, and related grassroots developmental programs. (In the
closing years of the decade, several amendments to foreign assistance bills in
the U.S. Congress stipulated that the amount of aid for a particular country
would be reduced proportionately to the amount that country spent on unnecessary military equipment.) In this way the United States would identify with
hemispheric revolutionary movements and deprive Castro of a psychological
advantage. At the other extreme stood the economist Simon Hansen, editor of
Inter-American Economic Affairs, who measured Kennedy's 1961 prediction
that the day of the strongman had passed in Latin America and the Caribbean
against a 1968 U.S. House of Representatives Armed Services Committee report
that gloomily noted the fall of nine countries to military rule, which meant that
the number of Latin American and Caribbean peoples living under military
dictatorship (123 million) surpassed by 20 million those enjoying democratic
regimes of varying degrees. The quality of life appeared to have deteriorated,
sometimes in Latin America's more advanced societies. In Colombia, considered a showcase model of the alliance, the U.S. comptroller-general reported
that the caloric intake of the country's poor may actually have gone down during the decade. In Brazil, another heavy beneficiary of alliance funding, the
percentage of income going to low-income groups declined during the sixties.
In Brazil and elsewhere in Latin America, housing construction fell woefully
short of expectation and needs and unemployment worsened.[30]

Central America may be considered a test case of the alliance as well as of
U.S. economic and political influence. In 1960 the isthmus entered what some
Central Americans refer to as a golden age, years of a dynamic agro-export
economy. Though all save Costa Rica suffered strongman or military regimes,
economic prospects for the region were high despite an unparalleled growth
in population. (From 1950 until the overthrow of the Somoza dynasty in Nicaragua in 1979, Central America's population tripled.) In 1960 Central American leaders created the Central American Common Market (CACM), and isth-

mian governments proved to be eager participants in the Alliance for Progress. Except for El Salvador, each took advantage of the agrarian reform initiatives of the alliance to distribute expropriated acreage to landless country people. At mid-decade, the CIA confidently assured President Johnson that Central America was pro–United States, committed to alliance goals, and had militaries quite capable of meeting any threat from guerrilla activity.

By the end of the decade, however, Central America had imploded politically. The most tragic violence occurred in Guatemala. In 1960, a group of junior officers, frustrated by their failure to oust the country's conservative president, launched a guerrilla war following the same strategy employed by Castro and Guevara in Cuba. With U.S. acquiescence, the military seized power in 1962 in order to keep former president Juan José Arévalo from regaining the presidency. Although a moderate, Mario Méndez Montenegro, became president four years later, the guerrilla war not only continued but spread to urban areas. President Johnson favored a military solution and authorized the dispatch of U.S. Green Berets to Guatemala. The country's conservatives had their own solution to the social crisis: death squads (Mano Blanco) whose members killed not only guerrillas but anyone suspected of being their sympathizers. Guerrillas carried out kidnappings and assassinations. They killed the chief of the U.S. military mission, his aide, and U.S. ambassador John G. Mein.[31]

A decade that had begun with such ambitious economic and political prospects for isthmian peoples collapsed in 1969 in the Soccer War between Honduras and El Salvador, a hundred-hour conflict whose origins lay in the dramatic expansion of the agro-export economy and its often tragic consequences for poor Salvadoran migrants in Honduras and, indirectly, for isthmian country people. In 1960, as we have seen, the Central American governments had fashioned an ambitious regional trade agreement. For a few years, the arrangement worked reasonably well. Intraregional trade grew dramatically—more than 700 percent over the course of the decade—new industries in chemicals, fertilizers, tire manufacturing, and food processing, among others were founded, and the region's agro-export economy expanded rapidly. Rather than shift dramatically to an industrial economy by placing greater demands for financing on the region's agro-exporters, however, isthmian political leaders created a hybrid economy, favoring agro-exporters while increasingly relying on foreign investment for industrial development. From 1959 to 1969, foreign direct investment grew from $14.6 to $233 million. Reformist, urban-oriented political movements such as Christian Democracy gained strength.[32]

Distortions and perceived inequities between the different states were inevitable. Hondurans felt particularly aggrieved because of trade imbalances and blamed their troubles on neighboring El Salvador. Honduras could not compete economically with its neighbor, but it did enjoy a comparatively large amount of underused land. Ever since the 1920s, as Salvadoran coffee growers began consolidating their holdings, displaced Salvadoran workers had migrated to Honduran banana fields as workers or settled on Honduran land. As Honduras's economic situation worsened, the militant Honduran peasant association demanded enforcement of the country's 1962 agrarian reform law. The law conformed to the spirit of the alliance charter—replacement of latifundias and minifundias with a fair system of land distribution—but recipients had to be Honduran citizens. Elsewhere in Central America, the U.S.-sponsored counterinsurgency program often frustrated agrarian reforms and grassroots development inspired by the alliance, occasionally with tragic human consequences. In the Honduran case, however, the military government bowed to pent-up national resentments and hatreds of the three hundred thousand Salvadorans who lived in Honduras. Thousands of displaced Salvadorans, sometimes forcibly evicted from their Honduran plots, returned to El Salvador at a time of severe economic decline in the coffee industry. Unwilling to deal with their plight, the Salvadoran government elected to invade Honduran soil. Outmatched, the Honduran military nevertheless held its own, and the OAS mediated an end to the fighting. But the war left elites in both countries visibly shaken by the experience and determined to consolidate their respective positions to prevent a recurrence of movements in the countryside. In such a crisis, they would have to depend on their militaries to contain such potential threats to the social order.[33]

Central America's crisis of 1969 proved to be an omen of the social and political convulsions that would wrack the isthmus in the decade following the overthrow of the Somoza dynasty in Nicaragua in 1979. The immediate cause of the Soccer War lay in the unwillingness of two governments to confront the social problem in the countryside, but the crisis pointed as well to the inadequacies of the alliance approach, which had been founded on the twin principles of anticommunism (or anti-Castroism) and broad social and economic reforms within a democratic political framework. By the end of the decade, however, the initial enthusiasm for the reformist approach had largely dissipated before the power of an entrenched society determined to preserve its place and the shift of political emphasis away from the quality of life for Latin America's marginal to shielding those at society's core.

At the 1966 OAS Economic and Social Council meeting in Panama, representatives from Chile and Mexico (both heavy recipients of alliance aid) pointed to the U.S. emphasis on security concerns as the principal reason for disappointments in the alliance's social and economic program. In both cases, however, the explanation was far more complicated. (The Mexican case is discussed below.) With $3 million in support from Washington and the acquiescence of Chilean conservatives, the Christian Democrat Eduardo Frei became president of Chile in 1964. Frei had won not so much because the United States had helped to finance his campaign as because Chile's powerful conservatives preferred his reformist approach to address the nation's social and economic problems to the draconian solutions of the Socialist Salvador Allende. Aware of Chilean resentments over the role of U.S. copper companies in the country and Washington's anticommunist crusade in the hemisphere, Frei, known among his U.S. benefactors as the "last, best hope" for Chile, promised a dignified relationship with the United States and an independent foreign policy. He embarked on an ambitious program—reduce inflation, build 360,000 homes, construct new schools, stimulate the nation's sagging industrial plant, undertake a massive agrarian reform in the country to address the social condition of Chile's landless rural people (*inquilinos*), and wrest more benefits from the copper companies to help finance his social programs—all within the framework of liberal democracy and social justice.

For a few years, Frei's approach appeared to be working. With Chileanization (partial ownership) of the copper companies, the government expropriated 6 million acres and resettled 26,000 families at a cost of $10,000 per family. But this fell far short of his campaign pledge. Worse, nationalists and leftists criticized his payout to the copper companies, particularly to Kennecott. The left assailed him for doing too little for the landless; the right, for expropriating their property. Within a few years, his 1964 promise to be the "first president of the first really democratic, popular, national and revolutionary government in the history of Chile" had collapsed before the reality of a failing economy and a political culture more deeply divided than ever. Throughout the decade, Chile's political leaders had determined to achieve growth but avoid inflation and foreign indebtedness. The result was frustrated development, a condition attributable mostly to choices made by Chileans and not to the U.S. obsession with security over social and economic issues, as Frei himself recognized in 1970. "From a technical point of view the procedures for containing inflation are well known," he wrote. "But what happens here is that the patient calls the doctor and then he doesn't want to take the medicine. The problem is mainly political."[34]

Cubans had dealt with this issue by adopting socialism along the Soviet rather than the West European pattern, which had resulted in an economic disaster but had indeed transformed Cuban society at every level. But for the rest of Latin America and the Caribbean in the 1960s the Cuban solution would be unacceptable. One alternative was the Brazilian model, which rested on economic growth favoring the core society—industrial and financial elites, large rural landowners, and substantial portions of the growing middle sectors—managed by technocrats and the military. Technicians ran the bureaucracies while the military controlled populist politicians, students, labor, and other dissidents through repression. Such an approach had tremendous human costs, despite the apparent support of the regime by the proliferation of "Brazil—Love It or Leave It" bumper stickers and the enthusiasm of the nation's middle class for the military regime. In a repressive political climate, activists increasingly resorted to extrainstitutional means to voice their protests, and the military government responded with even more repression. Contrastingly, the Peruvian military solution lay in carrying out a social program by making new and more favorable arrangements with foreign businesses in the country and by placing severe restrictions on the press and judiciary. Like their Brazilian counterparts, the Peruvian officers who seized power in October 1968 condemned traditional political parties, but unlike them launched what may properly be described as a populist military government—nationalization of International Petroleum Company (a festering issue for several decades), fisheries, minerals, hydrocarbons, electricity, and transportation, and the passage of South America's most sweeping agrarian reform program in the decade. Their inspiration came from below. As the leader of the military junta, General Juan Velasco Alvarado explained, "The masses in Latin America are starting to stampede. We in the military are the only ones who are capable of leading them—and us—into safe ground."[35]

A month following the Peruvian military takeover, the Panamanian National Guard removed recently elected President Arnulfo Arias, a champion of Panama City's poor and twice before the victim of a military coup. Arias's ouster was a slap in the face of the United States and its policy of justifying military assistance to Latin American governments on the grounds that the program helped to sustain constitutional regimes. Later in the year, Washington received another setback when Marshal Artur da Costa e Silva, who had succeeded President Castello Branco in 1967, assumed dictatorial power and closed the Brazilian congress. Since the military takeover in 1964, the U.S. ambassadors Lincoln Gordon and his successor, Covey Oliver, had defended the $1.6 billion in bilateral assistance to Brazil as crucial to the nation's return to constitutional government. Under the Fifth Institutional Act, the Brazilian political climate rapidly worsened, though the economic condition of the country improved. Costa e Silva had worried lest the act anger the United States government, but his economic advisors assured him that "the Americans would go along with anything" if Brazil continued to stay the course with the economic stabilization program. That prediction was inaccurate, as U.S. officials expressed their concern about Brazil's precipitous slide into political authoritarianism. Prominent congressmen warned President Richard M. Nixon of their opposition to increased financial assistance to Brazil.[36]

Their demurral was a reminder to the president of the moral dimensions of U.S. foreign policy and of the special importance of Latin America to the country. Nixon had failed to mention the other American republics in his inaugural, but one of his first decisions was to dispatch New York governor Nelson Rockefeller on a special fact-finding missions to Latin America in May and June 1969. Rockefeller's mission proved to be as troubled as that of Vice President Nixon a decade before. In Honduras and Ecuador his presence occasioned riots. The Venezuelan, Chilean, and Peruvian governments canceled his visit. Ironically, Rockefeller's self-described role in Venezuela from the mid-1930s to the mid-1950s had been as social reformer as well as businessman. In Brazil, the military government, fearful of adverse publicity, prohibited the press from publishing any criticism of his mission and arrested or detained thousands of students, politicians, and other suspected troublemakers until Rockefeller and his staff departed. The governor's visit provoked other outbursts in Argentina and Uruguay. In his 1958 visit, Nixon had blamed communist agitators for the explosive riots accompanying his visit. Rockefeller attributed the outbursts of 1969 to the failure of the United States to maintain its "special relationship" with Latin America, but he was quick to warn that communism remained a menace as long as the "forces of anarchy, terror, and subversion are loose in the Americas."[37]

In some respects, the Rockefeller report echoed those assessments of the early 1960s that had warned about the challenge to democracy and the prospects of revolutionary change if major social and political issues were not addressed. As did Kennedy's advisors, Rockefeller affirmed traditional U.S. strategies in Latin America even as he condemned the paternalism implicit in

Washington's approach. But in fundamental ways Rockefeller departed from the conventional wisdom in his recommendations. For too many people in Latin America, he conceded, the quality of life had deteriorated in the decade. He recognized that the resurgence of military governments throughout the hemisphere came at the expense of democratic processes, yet he remained alert to the fact that in several countries the military and the Roman Catholic Church, historically identified with the preservation of the social order, had adopted progressive, reformist approaches that the United States should applaud. The military appeared to offer the poor Latin American male an opportunity for social advancement unavailable in the private sector. Certainly, there were perils in tolerating military regimes, given their "ideological unreliability" and "vulnerability to extreme nationalism," but "exposure to the fundamental achievements of the U.S. way of life" through military training programs countered those influences.[38]

Nineteenth-century political economists would have heartened to Rockefeller's call for expanding the division of labor in the Americas, but his contemporaries might have been taken aback by his remarks that what the nation needed was skilled labor immigrants to meet the demands of the U.S. workplace and to permit the country to import those goods it was producing inefficiently. In the process, both the United States and the less-developed countries of the hemisphere would gain. In a departure from the Kennedy and Johnson approaches, Rockefeller recommended the naming of a secretary of Western Hemisphere affairs to coordinate on behalf of the president and secretary of state all U.S. government activities and a Western Hemisphere policy staff director on the National Security Council to assist key agencies or departments in the shaping of hemispheric policy. To address the bureaucratic entanglement of diplomatic and financial/technical operations in the State Department, Rockefeller called for the creation of two new administrative units—an Economic and Social Development Agency in the Executive Office to take over responsibilities carried out by the Agency for International Development and an Institute of Western Hemisphere Affairs within this agency to oversee social and economic programs in the hemisphere.[39]

Rockefeller frankly sought to alarm the Congress and particularly the president, yet in the political climate of the late 1960s his warning of the coming storm in Latin America and his recommendations on how to meet it struck some as a mandate for a failed approach. Striving to divert attention from the Vietnam War, where the U.S.-sponsored enterprise of nation building had foundered, Rockefeller unintentionally reminded his audience of similar failures in the hemisphere. As prominent national political figures abandoned the Vietnam commitment in the late 1960s, they became similarly disenchanted with an activist policy in Latin America. Some, notably Senator Frank Church (D, Idaho), chair of the Latin American subcommittee of the Senate Foreign Relations Committee, and Senator J. William Fulbright (D, Arkansas), author of a critique of U.S. foreign policy, became early critics of U.S. policy after the Dominican intervention. Others, Moscoso among them, assailed the assistance programs funded by the Agency for International Development.

As Latin American politicos began to reassess the role of the military in addressing the monumental task of social integration, their U.S. counterparts began to question the capability of the United States to serve as a model for a continent tested not by foreign war but by social convulsions from below and a parallel fear in the middle class of the consequences of rapid, uncertain political and social change. For Rockefeller, there was only one choice: "Either we meet this challenge or the prospect is for revolutionary changes leading we know not where." Then, as a postscript to a decade of political and social upheaval, he added, "Unless we are wholly to fail of our purpose as a nation, we must therefore meet the hopes of our own people for a decent and dignified life. Only if we do this can we lead, can we inspire, can we add to the quality of life for free men throughout the hemisphere." His comment was an oblique reference to the dramatic and sometimes violent changes within the United States during the decade, accompanied by reminders that the gulf between the advantaged and disadvantaged in Latin America and the Caribbean had widened and by the admission that the way the nation responded to change both at home and within the hemisphere would be critical for the future.[40]

The Seedtime of Greater North America

Such was the common predicament of hemispheric governments. It was especially relevant for Greater North America—Canada, the United States, and Mexico—three distinctive cultures and political systems with differing but interlocking histories in the decade. For the United States, the domestic experience of the 1960s acquired its contemporary relevance in the civil rights movement and the legislation it inspired, the violence devastating such major cities as New York, Los Angeles, Detroit, Newark, and Washington, D.C., the war on poverty and the completion of the social agenda set down in the 1930s in Johnson's Great Society program, the Vietnam antiwar movement, and the assassination of three public figures: John and Robert Kennedy and Dr. Martin Luther King, Jr.

Canadian memories of the decade reveal similarities but also subtle divergences. Outwardly, Canadians appeared to mimic their southern counterparts, above all in the movement for civil rights and in antiwar demonstrations. Canadians proved to be deeply anticommunist, but they did not wage an ideological anticommunist crusade and prided themselves that in the 1960s Canada created a welfare state in the Canada Assistance Plan while the United States molded a warfare state at the expense of the war on poverty. In the course of the decade, Canada appeared to escape the racial tension and violence that devastated U.S. cities. Increasingly, immigrants preferred Canada over the United States for quality of life and tolerance. Whereas the United States addressed the issue of discrimination in laws that prohibited discrimination in access to public accommodation and denial of the right to vote, Canada adopted the principle of "equal partnership" between the nation's two founding "races" of French and English. The U.S. immigration law of 1965, the Hart-Cellar Act, abandoned the national origins quotas of the acts of the 1920s in favor of family reunification and needed job skills; Canada's 1967 immigration law rejected the de facto preferences given to whites in favor of a points system based on education, language skills, and occupational demand. As the social and cultural fabric of the United States fragmented in the wake of urban riots and protests against the Vietnam War, Expo 67 in Montreal gave Canadians an unparalleled opportunity to display their cultural maturing and material progress despite the continuing tensions between Anglos and Quebecers.[41]

The following year Mexican leaders exulted in the hosting of the Olympic Games, a celebration of the dramatic economic and social changes wrought by the postwar "Mexican miracle" and the commitment of one of the hemisphere's most authoritarian governments to economic development and the well-being of the middle class while retaining the revolutionary promise to ordinary Mexicans. From the early years of the decade, when the two governments had collided over the issue of Cuba, Mexico–U.S. relations had followed a pattern of conflict even as their economies became more intertwined. To assert the nation's independence in the global arena, Mexican president Adolfo López Mateos (1958–64) traveled to India, Indonesia, France, Poland, and Yugoslavia. Both López and his successor, Gustavo Díaz Ordaz, criticized U.S. interventionism in the hemisphere and chafed at Washington's decision to end the *bracero* labor program in 1964.

For Mexican leaders, both decisions seemed at odds with a commonsensical approach, but, then, Mexicans knew the realities of living next door to a country determined to dominate in the name of national security and in need of Mexican labor. Mexico benefited not only politically but economically from the U.S. embargo against Cuba, and terminating the bracero program, Mexicans knew, would not end the migration of Mexicans northward. After World War II, U.S. southwestern agribusiness had begun hiring undocumented Mexican workers because they could be more easily controlled. Mexico had protested, going so far as to recommend that the U.S. government prohibit the hiring of undocumented workers! But patterns of migration from small Mexican towns were too well established to be easily changed with an alteration in the bracero law. And in the mid-1960s the Mexican government had ambitious plans for the northern frontier, the Border Industrialization Program, designed to transform the northern cities from drinking and whoring towns for gringos into modern cities employing the exploding youth population of Mexico. Mexico's leaders knew the middle-class beneficiaries of the "economic miracle" complained about the arbitrariness of their rule and the social travesty committed against the nation's forgotten poor, the "other Mexico," in their failure to fulfill the revolutionary promise, but they were equally convinced their hold on power was inviolable.[42]

In August 1968 whatever feelings of security Mexico's ruling political elite possessed were dramatically shattered by the most serious political crisis since the *cristero* revolt of the late 1920s. The uprising that shook the foundations of one of the hemisphere's most secure political regimes began as a street confrontation between rival high schools and a protest by university students that millions of Mexicans could see the magnificent sports edifices being constructed for the Olympics but could not afford to attend the games. Students in the United States denounced authority and presumed to speak and march on behalf of those who lacked a voice to protest social injustices, but they never seriously threatened to bring down a government at any level. What happened in Mexico City during these months proved to be far more ominous for Mexico's political leaders. In successive incidents of escalating protest, the government refused to concede, regarding every demand as a challenge to its authority and the economic program it had followed since World War II. The culminating battle occurred at the Plaza de las Tres Culturas in Tlatelolco, near the Foreign Relations building and a neighborhood of apartments occupied by middle-class Mexicans. Four thousand Mexicans, many of them women and children, gathered to hear incendiary speakers call upon them to "unite and take the city." When they refused to disperse, the police moved in with clubs, but the crowd fought back, driving the police from the area. At that moment, the government sent in a battalion of paratroopers, who fired randomly at fleeing civilians as snipers from nearby buildings fired on the troops. For nine hours, the historic area of Tlatelolco became a bloody spectacle of a government making war against its own people in a confrontation both sides had wanted.[43]

No other Western government challenged by a student rebellion had responded so severely as Mexico's in fall 1968, certainly not the U.S. government, whose legitimacy may have been questioned by a generation but whose authority remained intact. In the United States, protest movements remained fragmented, and as middle-class disillusion with the Vietnam War escalated, the burden of fighting it was shifted to the working class. But there was no event in U.S. or Canadian history in the 1960s—not even the bloody confrontation between police and protestors at the 1968 Democratic National Convention in Chicago or the Canadian government's response to Québécois terrorists—that compared with the tragedy of Tlatelolco and its impact on national history. What U.S. viewers remembered about "Mexico '68" was the embarrassment to Olympic officials when two African American athletes received their medals with their fist raised defiantly in the Black Power salute. Pierre Trudeau, a Québécois, became prime minister of Canada in 1968 believing that the way to defuse the nationalism fueling separatism lay in the Canadian tradition of tolerance and respect for the democratic process. Réné Levesque of the Parti Québécois, who advocated separation, agreed with the latter sentiment, but he also held strongly to the belief that Quebec constituted a nation suffocating from federal domination and deserved either independence or, at the least, associated state status. Such words grated on Trudeau's liberal sensibilities, but when he took the reins of government in 1968 he confronted not only more determined spirits in the Parti Québécois but a willingness on the part of some Conservatives and New Democrats in English Canada to acquiesce in the idea of "two Canadas." Trudeau effectively countered them when he declared in a speech in Winnipeg, "If you start talking of two nations you start talking of two states and that's not the way we want to go."[44]

Those remarks from a French Canadian effectively diminished the appeal of "two nations" in English Canada, at least for a few years, but it did little to placate Levesque and the Parti Québécois. Yet in the volatile political climate of the late 1960s in Canada, Trudeau, like Nixon, astutely recognized that governments may not be able to resolve some issues or even mitigate them, but there are situations in which a government must draw the line. Extremists in Quebec formed a Liberation Front (its French acronym was FLQ) and commenced a wave of strikes, protest marches, and bank robberies on behalf of the separatist cause. In summer and fall 1970, the FLQ unleashed a terrorist campaign and kidnapped Richard Cross, head of the United Kingdom trade commission, and Pierre LaPorte, Quebec's minister of labor and immigration. Quebec's provincial government appealed to Ottawa for support. Confronted with a list of demands from the separatists, Trudeau's government responded with the War Measures Act, which declared the FLQ an unlawful association and stated that anyone who belonged to it or any organization that advocated the use of force would be liable to a jail sentence of up to five years. In the aftermath, the FLQ fell into disfavor, as Trudeau capitalized by acting swiftly in the face of a threat, then demonstrating leniency. The entire affair left many in Quebec with apprehensions about the decline of francophone culture.[45]

The differing histories of these three nations in the 1960s have largely obscured some subtle commonalities: a demographic revolution in which the numbers of those under twenty-five grew dramatically, impressive economic growth, an unparalleled increase in the numbers attending colleges and universities, and, except for Mexico, sweeping social legislation. In each case, the impact of these changes was not to bring about unity but to deepen the divisions within the three societies. Separatist movements gained strength. Economic inequities rose. Political systems dedicated to modernizing their respective economies while addressing a host of social problems were badly shaken by a succession of crises. Each repulsed the threat, but the experience demonstrated that the middle classes, the acknowledged beneficiaries of economic growth, now seriously doubted the ability of their political leaders to resolve the social problems that accompanied economic expansion.

By decade's end, both Mexico and Canada witnessed a revival of anti-Americanism and resurgence of economic nationalism, yet in 1970 the economic linkages between these two countries and the United States were tighter than ever. Mexico's efforts to bind its northern frontier cities more closely to the center with the Border Industrialization Program and with the maquiladoras ("in-bond" assembly plants that employed Mexicans but exported without tariff charges to the United States) in effect bound the northern frontier more closely to the United States. At mid-decade, the U.S. Congress reinforced the bonds of Greater North America with the passage of a sweeping new immigration law that discarded the old racial and ethnic quotas of the laws of the 1920s in favor of a plan emphasizing family reunification and job skills. Each country was assigned a numerical allotment of 20,000. For the Western Hemisphere, Congress imposed a ceiling of 120,000, with no country limit, which meant Mexico and Canada would be the principal beneficiaries. In 1965, Mexico and Canada sent almost equal numbers to the United States. A decade later, legal Mexican immigration surpassed that of Canada by ten times, and undocumented entry from Mexico increased dramatically.[46]

These and related issues would bring sometimes bitter discord between the three governments and conflicts reaching all the way to local communities; but such ties helped to create as well the symbiotic union that found tangible expression in the creation of the North American Free Trade Agreement in the early 1990s. Viewed in a hemispheric perspective, they point to some of the unexpected and unintended consequences of the sixties in the Americas, a decade that began in the ideological blood feud between the United States and Cuba and ended with the Cuban revolution intact, the Alliance for Progress in disarray, and the problematic though peaceful election of a socialist president in Chile. Subsequent generations instinctively associate the decade with reformist efforts that fell short, racism, an increase in economic inequities, a revival of U.S. gunboat diplomacy, the resurgence of military governments, and the disappointments if not failure of the economic model for modernization crafted by a generation of social scientists. Undeniably, the sixties were years of uncertainty and chaos, but what is often forgotten in this equation is the creativity and opportunity that uncertainty and chaos can provide to a generation whose language spoke in terms of possibilities and not limits.

8

Order and Progress

In his report on the hemisphere, Rockefeller had attributed Latin American dismay over the Alliance for Progress to the paternalistic attitude of the United States. For many Latin American leaders, his recommendation that Washington should bear the principal responsibility for maintaining order in the hemisphere understandably detracted from some novel and progressive features of the report. In any event, President Nixon evinced little interest in embarking on a bold new course within the hemisphere, in part because he believed that Latin American and Caribbean countries wanted "trade, not aid," and because he subscribed to an east–west perspective, a way of thinking about the world favored by those who considered themselves realists about the nation's fundamental interests. Within this framework, Latin America and the Caribbean became a peripheral region—except, of course, where cold war issues were at stake.

Nixon followed up on few of Rockefeller's recommendations, but he did outline his plan for a "new partnership" with Latin America in "Action for Progress in the Americas," an address before the Inter-American Press Association in October 1969. Nixon shared Rockefeller's belief that trade, not aid, should be central to inter-American relations, but in place of the recommendation for unilateral tariff preferences for Latin America, the president substituted a plan for providing developing nations with general tariff preferences. He abolished the "additionality" requirements on "tied loans," which allowed governments to use aid moneys to purchase goods anywhere in the Americas. Like Rockefeller, Nixon believed that the private, not the public, sector should take the lead in economic development, though he conceded to each hemispheric country (except Cuba) the right to consider the role of private investment in such endeavors. In contrast to Rockefeller's unambiguous declaration that the United States must take the lead in confronting the hemispheric security threat posed by communism, Nixon expressed a more guarded view: "We must deal realistically with governments in the inter-American system as they are. We have of course a preference for democratic procedures and we hope that each government will help its people to move forward to a better, fuller, and freer life."[1]

The contrast between Nixon's rhetoric and that of John F. Kennedy in the early 1960s was striking, intentionally so. To encourage "peaceful revolution" throughout Latin America, Nixon believed, was to risk another Cuba and to saddle an increasingly strapped U.S. treasury with aid programs that by Rockefeller's admission had not dramatically altered the condition of Latin America's impoverished peoples. After all, the Cuban revolution had been contained, and the largest countries of the hemisphere were now safely under military rule or at least staunchly anticommunist governments. Rockefeller had warned Nixon that the failure to lead in containing the hemispheric security risk would be costly. What both had failed to gauge was the diminishing strength of U.S. political and especially economic influence in the hemisphere. The Cuban revolution had been contained, certainly, but it had survived the U.S. assault. West European nations had not rushed to the aid of Cuba, but neither had they abandoned it. Most, in fact, deeply resented the dangers of nuclear war occasioned by the missile crisis in October 1962, and in the following years they took advantage of the economic embargo by expanding their trade with the island. By the early 1970s, West European governments, Canada, and Japan were challenging U.S. economic predominance in Latin America. Their combined economic might compelled Nixon to abandon the gold standard in international trade to prevent a U.S. financial crisis. As the European and Japanese economic presence in Latin America increased, the governments of the hemisphere became more independent of U.S. influence in their foreign and economic policies.

The Chilean Tragedy

The actions of the Nixon administration soon belied the president's profes-sions about creating a new partnership with hemispheric governments. Nixon did not adopt the Rockefeller report's recommendation for a new office of hemispheric affairs to deal with security issues, yet he was as preoccupied as Rockefeller with the threat to U.S. interests from communist and guerrilla movements in the region. Nixon preferred to wage a largely covert war. The results were usually ineffective and the consequences sometimes tragic. Nixon was the first U.S. president to link drug trafficking in the Americas with the na-tional security agenda, a not unreasonable strategy, but one lamentable out-come of the tactics the administration employed to carry out this mission was to enmesh U.S. agencies, particularly the CIA, ever more deeply in the inter-nal affairs of Latin American and Caribbean governments. In return for the as-sistance of high-ranking foreign officials and military officers in gathering in-formation on guerrillas, communists, and anti-American public figures, these agencies not only gave a subsidy to their "foreign operatives" but tolerated their drug trafficking, money laundering, and other illegal activities. Occa-sionally, U.S. agencies worked at cross-purposes, one striving to combat a drug trafficker and the other trying to keep the perpetrator out of harm's way on the grounds of national security interests. Manuel Noriega of Panama was but one of these strategically placed foreign military officers favored by the U.S. government.[2]

A related and similarly controversial program during these years was the Agency for International Development's Office of Public Safety (OPS), an out-growth of U.S. efforts during World War II to provide security assistance to hemispheric governments confronted with domestic Nazi threats. In the post-war era, OPS programs expanded to include assistance, including military and police training, to regimes desiring "protection" from Communists. By justify-ing their role as essential to safeguarding the recipient country from "internal menaces" to its security, OPS agents operated virtually independently as "po-litical police," although their acquiescence in human rights violations by client governments made them accomplices to the crime. The Nixon adminis-tration found OPS more useful than the CIA in carrying out paramilitary oper-ations on behalf of the Department of State or the National Security Council or even the president himself. In the early years of the Nixon presidency, the OPS program in Brazil fell under increased scrutiny and criticism from human rights organizations, academic professional organizations, the press, and ulti-mately Congress. Early in 1970, Senator Frank Church (D, Idaho) chaired a subcommittee of the U.S. Senate Committee on Foreign Relations investigating U.S. programs in Brazil. When discussions shifted to the notorious reputation of the Brazilian government for torturing political prisoners, Theodore Brown, OPS police advisor in Brazil, lamely commented that he could not rightfully judge Brazil's police or military. Collaboration with that country's public security officials, he believed, should continue, "barring development of a political disorientation of the [Brazilian] Government . . . from a pro-West, pro-U.S. stance."[3]

Congress's study of OPS activities soon widened to other countries in the hemisphere. The Senate dispatched an investigative team to Guatemala and to the Dominican Republic, both beneficiaries of OPS's international police training program. Guatemala's police had received fourteen years of instruction, the report stated, yet had absorbed little from it and operated beyond the control of their U.S. advisors. The political costs far outweighed any tangible improvements in police efficiency. When Senator James Abourezk (D, N.D.) commenced yet another inquiry, CIA director William Colby aggressively defended OPS, arguing that it had trained one million police from foreign countries and parceled out the equivalent of $200 million in arms and equipment to paramilitary and police units. The economic benefits of such aid, Colby declared, would extend years after OPS departed the country. Abourezk held another opinion: such assistance made "repressive regimes more oppressive."[4]

Inevitably, Congress's scrutiny of U.S. covert activity in the hemisphere extended to Chile. When the Socialist candidate Salvador Allende emerged with a plurality of the vote in the 1970 Chilean presidential contest, former president Jorge Alessandri concocted a bizarre scheme to forestall Allende's selection by the National Assembly. If the assembly chose Alessandri, he agreed to resign his office, enabling Frei, who was constitutionally prohibited from succeeding himself, to run in a new election. With the support of the nation's powerful conservatives and his own Christian Democrats, Frei appeared a certain victor. But Allende stood firm, threatening to plunge the country into a civil war if the assembly refused to follow through with its constitutional obligation and name him the winner. As Chileans wrangled, the Nixon administration unnecessarily insinuated U.S. influence into the process. Henry Kissinger believed Allende intended to create the hemisphere's second Marxist dictatorship, with indirect consequences for U.S. policy in Western Europe, where Washington had concerns about Eurocommunism. The CIA worried that an Allende victory would jeopardize U.S. efforts in fashioning an anticommunist hemispheric coalition, and the agency's Forty Committee recommended U.S.

encouragement of a coup to prevent Allende from taking power. Nixon and Kissinger were enthusiastic about the plan, but Ambassador Edward Korry astutely informed them that no coup could succeed without support from Chile's military. When Chile's senior military officer, General René Schneider, made clear his opposition to the plot, the CIA began funneling arms to a gaggle of conspirators who planned to capture Schneider and create a military junta. They twice failed, although a renegade faction within the group attempted a third time. In the ensuing melee, Schneider was killed. The outcome of the entire sordid affair deepened Chilean suspicions about the United States and created a solidarity for Allende and the constitutional process. He took the oath of office in November 1970.[5]

Nixon and Kissinger were in no mood to make their peace with Allende, and the new Chilean president had no intention of placating them. To do so would have required a virtual sea change in his bipolar view of the world—the developed capitalist countries versus the Soviet Union, Eastern Europe, the People's Republic of China, and most of the Third World—and abandonment of his belief that Chile's economic stagnation had resulted largely because of the presence of foreign companies and their domestic lackeys. Outsiders and their Chilean accomplices had despoiled the country's resources. He set about to fashion a new foreign policy, establishing diplomatic relations with Cuba, North Vietnam, North Korea, the German Democratic Republic, Albania, the People's Republic of China, and the Viet Cong. Allende brought Chile into the nonaligned movement and used international forums (among them, the United Nations Commission on Trade and Development) to indict foreign capital for the harm it had done to developing nations.

Although Allende could be relatively assured that the United States would not intervene militarily in Chile, he had good reason to be worried about Chile's South American neighbors acting at Washington's behest. Argentina and Brazil had anti-Marxist military governments. Peru's ruling military junta shared some of his progressive views, but they retained bitter memories of the country's humiliation in the War of the Pacific. With each, however, Allende obtained an understanding by espousing the notion of "ideological pluralism" and by reaffirming the principles of nonintervention and self-determination. To the distress of Washington, Allende became the advocate of Latin American hemispheric solidarity, reminding other governments that the United States used the OAS to dominate its southern neighbors. He spearheaded the diplomatic insurrection within the OAS that by 1973 had effectively split the organization into a Washington–Brasilia group composed of Brazil, Paraguay, Bolivia, Central America, and the United States and the Havana–Lima bloc, which Chile influenced. Nixon had good reason to be worried. Within the space of a few years, Allende appeared to be nearing his longtime goal of building a socialist "bridgehead in the southern part of the continent" and leading a hemispheric coalition against the world's most powerful capitalist nation.[6]

Allende continued his assault on U.S. economic interests by fulfilling his pledge to nationalize the copper companies, a move supported by the left and, surprisingly, by the Chilean right. To oppose the measure would have appeared unpatriotic. The nation's political conservatives, most of whom reflected the views of Chile's large landowners, held lingering resentments against the United States for its support of Frei's agrarian reform program, which had resulted in the breakup of numerous large estates. In this instance, Allende not only angered the Nixon administration but found himself at loggerheads with prominent Chilean political leaders and jurists when he invoked a rarely used provision that permitted him as president to reduce the amount of compensation to the copper companies if they had earned "excess profits." The U.S. Treasury stood to lose because of guarantees to the companies by the Overseas Private Investors Corporation. For a brief time, it appeared a compromise might be possible and that Washington would settle for a token payment. "Pay just a dollar, but pay something," Kissinger allegedly told Orlando Letelier, Chile's ambassador to the United States. But Allende had to placate the hard-liners in his government. Any concession might jeopardize his fragile political coalition.[7]

By then, of course, the U.S.–Chilean confrontation had become a cause célèbre not only in the Western Hemisphere but in Europe as well. Emboldened, Allende pushed ahead with his program to transform the Chilean economy with state takeovers of critical elements of industry, insurance companies, and banks. He was careful to avoid going after foreign companies from those countries from which Chile sought credit but rarely spared U.S. companies. Yet Nixon refrained from invoking the Hickenlooper amendment, lest such a move afford Allende an excuse to repudiate Chile's foreign debt of $1 billion. Instead, Nixon urged U.S. banks to scale down their loans to Chile, and he vetoed Chilean applications for loans from the International Monetary Fund, the World Bank, and the Inter-American Development Bank. The president found other ways to punish Chile. Under a congressional amendment to an appropriations bill, he could direct U.S. representatives to international lending agencies to oppose loans to any country nationalizing U.S. property without proper compensation. The CIA had authorization to spend up to $8 million to destabilize the Chilean economy and support any effort to overthrow Allende.[8]

When Allende's government fell in a bloody military coup in September 1973, the role of the Nixon administration in its collapse seemed critical. In actuality, the president's responsibility proved to be of less importance in explaining the Chilean tragedy than other factors. Allende failed because he could not maintain the tenuous political coalition that had made his victory possible in 1970. Committed to restructuring Chilean society to benefit the nation's poor and laboring class, his government had raised taxes, frozen prices, and increased wages, which effectively augmented the workers' share of national wealth by 50 percent. These measures won Allende plaudits as the "second Fidel." Unlike Castro's Cuba, however, Allende's Chile had no reliable benefactor. As the country began to show the strain brought on by a domestic economy unable to keep up with rising demand from a new generation of consumers, the government resorted to increasing imports, including food. The economic downturn worsened Chile's standing among international lending agencies. Within the country, the political consensus of the first year rapidly withered. Protest marches over rising prices and the falling value of the Chilean *escudo* became common. In the midst of the economic crisis, the Christian Democrats, so vital to Allende's victory in 1970, abandoned their coalition with the left. Allende was outraged. He responded by declaring a state of national emergency, banning public meetings, and authorizing the police to arrest persons without a warrant. In Bolivia or Peru, the government might have been able to get away with such practices, but in Chile they provoked a new wave of protests from storekeepers, professional groups, and truckers. At this critical moment in his presidency, Allende may have reflected on the agreement to respect civil liberties (Statute of Democratic Guarantees) he had signed in 1970 in order to get Christian Democratic support for ratification of his presidential victory. The belief that the president-elect had to guarantee to respect the constitution demonstrated the serious erosion of trust in the political system.[9]

As Allende lost ground with the center and right, he came to depend more and more on his political base among the nation's poor, who turned out in large numbers to assure Popular Unity a significant victory in March 1973 elections. Allende interpreted the outcome as validation of the socialist experiment. In doing so, he erred. Senior military officers became increasingly wary of Allende's ability to maintain public order. His control over workers was not secure, as local unions, inspired by their newfound powers, began to act more independently. In some instances, they seized control of plants and began to arm themselves. The political crisis culminated in August 1973 when the Chamber of Deputies declared the president's policies illegal and invited the military to defend the constitution by searching buildings and factories for caches of arms. For a brief time, the commander-in-chief of the armed forces, General Carlos Prat, tried to mediate between hostile political groups and to rein in the officer corps, but then abruptly resigned, declaring he had failed.

In these circumstances, a peaceful solution to the economic and political stalemate was virtually impossible to achieve. Fear of revolution and three years of chaos had exacted their toll. When a group of military officers under General Augusto Pinochet decided to overturn the government, they did not require U.S. urging to act. Nixon and Kissinger, of course, welcomed the coup and exhibited little remorse at Allende's death, allegedly by his own hand, during the fighting. But neither they nor most Chileans could have found any comfort in the repression and deaths that followed the coup, estimated at between three and thirty thousand, nor justified the barbarities committed in the name of national security and the relentless manner in which the military government tried to eliminate social and political movements. "Allende tried to have a revolution without blood," Castro is said to have remarked on hearing of the Chilean's death, "but instead he got blood without a revolution."[10]

Myths and Realities of the North–South Axis

In the aftermath of the Chilean tragedy the United States tried to ameliorate decades of ill will with new endeavors both public and private, such as the North–South Dialogue, negotiation of a new canal treaty with Panama, and the invigoration of human rights policy in the Jimmy Carter administration. Although each offered persuasive evidence of a more benign approach in Washington's dealings with other hemispheric nations, none effectively reversed the widespread perceptions of weakening U.S. influence. In the Caribbean, governments that had previously identified with U.S. policies in the 1960s, such as Jamaica, Guyana, and Trinidad and Tobago, adopted economic strategies at variance with Washington's prescriptions.

The defections of Forbes Burnham of Guyana and Eric Williams of Trinidad and Tobago from the U.S. developmental model were less threatening to U.S. leadership than that of Michael Manley of Jamaica. Manley admired Castro, opened up new links with Cuba, and in 1974 announced that Jamaica would be transformed into a "democratic socialist" state. Private enterprise would survive, he pledged, but not the evils of the capitalist system. Analysts and commentators spoke of the "end of American hegemony," a phrase virtually unthinkable in the mid-1960s but common at the end of the 1970s. Within the OAS Economic and Social Council, the diminished effectiveness of the United States prompted a Kennedy-era official, William D. Rogers, to call for U.S. withdrawal from the organization. Kissinger did not go so far, but he expressed his doubts about the character of hemispheric affairs when he declared in a speech before a Venezuelan audience that "the Americas—North and South—recognize that they require a global as well as a regional vision if they are to resolve their problems."[11]

One disturbing reality for Washington was the twenty-five-member Economic System of Latin America (SELA), which excluded the United States but included Cuba. Its principal organizers were Luis Echeverría and Carlos Andrés Pérez, presidents of Mexico and Venezuela, respectively. Their alienation from the United States had less to do with security issues than with the place of each country in the new international economic order and widespread apprehensions about the materialism identified with U.S. culture and its perceived threat to traditional culture. Echeverría, who had directed the harsh repression of dissidents in the Tlatelolco uprising of 1968, wanted to placate Mexicans disturbed over U.S. economic penetration of the country. Pérez's defection proved to be more complicated. In the early 1960s, Venezuela had been a showcase of the Alliance for Progress and dutifully hostile toward the Cuban revolution. Venezuela was also a founding member of the Organization of Petroleum Exporting Countries (OPEC), and though its government did not join the oil embargo of the early 1970s, Congress withdrew the General System of Preferences for the country in the 1974 Trade Act. After Kissinger hinted that security concerns might require seizing Venezuela's oil fields, the rhetoric on both sides rapidly escalated. President Gerald R. Ford denounced the power of petroleum exporters in a speech in the United Nations General Assembly. Before the same audience Foreign Minister Efraín Schacht Aristeguieta of Venezuela condemned the United States, with its 6 percent of the world's population, for devouring half the globe's mineral resources. Pérez was more strident. Nationalist, populist, and committed to the "south–south" connection, he warned other Latin American leaders that "either we must achieve the economic integration of Latin America, or the transnational companies will do it for us."[12]

Such was the political condition of the hemisphere when Jimmy Carter became president. Carter faced a hemisphere of states often defiant and hostile toward any presumption of U.S. tutelage, however benign or well intentioned. Carter at least enjoyed a brief opportunity to push for human rights, which acquired unprecedented emphasis during his presidency. Unfortunately for Carter, human rights violations in much of Latin America could no longer be explained as arbitrary excesses by individual leaders and sadistic minor officials. In Argentina, Brazil, Uruguay, and Chile, harsh dictatorships had replaced pluralistic governments, but the historic strongman, or *caudillo*, had been supplanted by what the Argentine political scientist Guillermo O'Donnell called bureaucratic-authoritarian rule, which appeared in Brazil in the mid-1960s, in Argentina in 1966 and again in 1976, in Uruguay in 1972–73, and in Chile in 1973. Bureaucratic-authoritarian regimes, unlike their military counterparts, acquired power not to end fighting between political factions or to seek permanent power but to destroy any challenge to the traditional society of privilege, namely, the military, the church hierarchy, landowners, and exporters, from popular groups and new political participants, including urban workers, the salaried middle sectors, industrialists, and occasionally the peasants, and those who had presumed to speak for them: Vargas, Quadros, and Goulart in Brazil, Perón in Argentina, Allende in Chile.[13]

The appeal of these leaders depended largely on popularity; their survival rested on an ability to placate a new generation of supplicants with material benefits. In the United States and Canada, expectations of material improvement could usually be met with an expanding economy, but in much of Latin America and the Caribbean in the 1960s the rate of economic growth proved inadequate to fund the growing demands of new pressure groups. Agrarian reform constituted a direct challenge to the society of privilege and was thus too risky for popular governments, which turned increasingly to printing money to meet the growing demands on government payrolls, to pay for social programs, and to maintain low prices on basic commodities. The middle sectors more than others suffered from the inflationary pressures of these policies because they could neither shield themselves against rising costs nor benefit directly from these programs. Indirectly, popular regimes challenged the old order by their support of labor relations boards by which agricultural laborers could protect themselves from the arbitrary actions of landowners and by granting legal rights to domestic servants. Probably the most damaging threat to privileged sectors was the erosion of working-class deference toward them. In these circumstances, popular governments are doubly vulnerable: they are unable to maintain control of economic policy in the face of demands from their supporters and the orthodox requirements of international lending agencies and, more important, they find it difficult to maintain a pluralist political system in societies in which the opponents of popular governments control the wealth.[14]

The bureaucratic-authoritarian regimes appearing in Latin America in the 1960s and 1970s had their flaws, obviously, but they enjoyed advantages popular governments did not possess. In the economic sphere, they could implement policies that favored growth, accumulation, and limited government intervention in the market. They were able to limit political pressure groups by abolishing labor unions, cracking down on the media, and even disbanding political parties. In some instances, these governments could argue that draconian measures were necessary to combat guerrilla insurgencies that had taken root years before they assumed power; in Uruguay, for example, the Tupumaros constituted a threat to the government. But in almost every case the leaders of bureaucratic-authoritarian regimes in Chile, Brazil, Uruguay, and Argentina exceeded any defensible strategy of counterguerrilla activities by their sadistic brutality and determination to wipe out those institutions— unions, university faculties, political parties, peasant cooperatives—that nourished political dissent. More traditional forms of human rights violations occurred in Guatemala, Bolivia, El Salvador, Haiti, Nicaragua, and Paraguay.[15]

Chile after the September 1973 military coup was indisputably the most egregious example of the brutal thoroughness of these governments in the political and social cleansing of the nation. In the first month after the overthrow of Allende, the military junta dissolved congress; imposed martial law, a curfew, and strict press censorship; declared illegal all Marxist parties and all non-Marxist parties in recess; abolished the eight-thousand-member Central Workers' Federation; suspended university autonomy, replaced university rectors with government appointees, and closed technical schools as wells as schools of sociology, journalism, and education in Chilean universities; and arrested seven thousand persons. The Chilean government reported three hundred deaths in the September 1973 violence; CIA director William Colby put the figure between two and three thousand. According to an Amnesty International investigation, in its first year in power the Pinochet regime killed at least five thousand and possibly as many as thirty thousand Chilean dissidents, a "death toll . . . unprecedented in Latin American history." The Inter-American Commission on Human Rights shortly followed with a 175-page report condemning the Chilean government of "extremely serious violations" of ten basic human rights.[16]

The U.S. government was initially tentative in its response to these developments, but as the evidence of human rights violations accumulated, no responsible official could ignore what was happening or continue to cite security concerns as sufficient reason for looking the other way. Further, human rights activists in the United States, incensed over official support to a repressive South Vietnamese government, began looking more closely at U.S. indifference to human rights violations by repressive regimes in Latin America. The collapse of the Nixon administration following the Watergate affair culminated in the election of a Democratic Congress that compelled the Ford administration to follow a more proactive policy toward human rights. In November 1974 the U.N. General Assembly passed two resolutions on human rights violations in Chile. The U.S. representative abstained on both, citing their vagueness, but did endorse the General Assembly's denunciation of the Chilean government for its practice of torture, a sign that the Ford administration intended to distance itself from Pinochet. In an address to OAS foreign ministers in June 1976, Kissinger noted continuing violations of human rights by the Chilean government. His audience expected the orthodox criticism of the Cuban government for its communist heresies but heard instead the most severe formal criticism to date by any member of the OAS against another member government.

On assuming office, Carter continued these policies, giving them a moral emphasis noticeably absent in the approach of his predecessor. In mid-June 1977, at the seventh general assembly of the OAS on the island of Grenada, Secretary of State Cyrus Vance directly addressed the persistent question of human rights violations as a necessary tool in the antiterrorist campaigns of hemispheric governments by stating that "there are no circumstances which justify torture, summary executions or prolonged detention without trial contrary to law." In private meetings with OAS foreign ministers, Vance reaffirmed his public statements linking economic assistance to respect for human rights. The meeting proved to be the high point of U.S. efforts to use the Inter-American Commission on Human Rights, as Latin American governments were almost uniformly suspicious of Washington's motives. It was clear that Latin America's repressive governments had little to fear from the multilateral sanctions of the OAS. Carter elected to focus on bilateral efforts to advance the cause of human rights in the hemisphere.[17]

Argentina soon became the test case. The origins of the Argentine–U.S. confrontation during the Carter administration had their roots in the ouster in 1966 of President Arturo Illia by military officers led by General Juan Carlos Onganía. For four years Argentina's military rulers sought to restore order at home and carve out a special place for the nation in the international community. Emulating Francisco Franco of Spain, they stifled dissent and controlled labor. In foreign affairs, they looked to improve relations with Brazil, in part out of need for Brazil's aid in developing hydroelectric energy and in part to woo the Brazilians from their accord with the United States. For a short time, the Argentines talked seriously of an Argentina–Brazilian–South African anticommunist alliance, but in 1970 the project of a new Argentine order collapsed when Onganía's colleagues removed him. Their solution lay in restoring the exiled Juan Perón to power. With their blessing he returned with his third wife (Isabel) to a deeply divided and fragmented society, and after a political campaign riddled with disorder and inflammatory charges the Peróns (Juan as president, Isabel as vice president) took power in October 1973. Nine months later, Juan lay dead, and over the next two years the hapless Isabel tried and failed to stem the disorder and chaos in Argentine society. In March 1976, the military returned to power, and the junta's leader, General Jorge Videla, vowed it would remain long enough to carry out the restructuring of society. Argentina's dissidents soon learned what he meant. As the governor of Buenos Aires, General Ibérico St. Jean, allegedly stated, "First we will kill all the subversives, then their collaborators, then their sympathizers, then those who are indifferent, and finally, the timid."[18]

Not even the thugs of Pinochet's Chile sounded so brutally determined, although in practice they probably killed just as many. The dirty war carried out by security forces in the name of order and progress ravaged a generation of largely though not exclusively middle-class Argentines, who were indiscriminately arrested, tortured, killed, and dismembered, their legs and arms and heads sometimes being buried with other persons' torsos so as confuse future forensic investigators. Some of the sordid details did not become widely known until years later, but the dismal record of the Argentine government in human rights violations was sufficiently publicized by early 1977, when Pat Derian became director of the new office of Human Rights in the U.S. Department of State, to rouse Washington's official disapproval. Curiously, neither Carter nor Vance appeared unduly preoccupied with Argentina, but Derian proved unrelenting in her verbal assaults on Buenos Aires. Videla defended the dirty war both inside Argentina and before the world as necessary to preserve "order and civilization." The U.S. pressure had only limited impact. For one thing, the bureaucracy within the Carter administration divided in often fundamental ways over human rights as an instrument of foreign policy. More important, Washington's critique gave Videla a degree of legitimacy as defender of the nation before the North American colossus, and it indirectly served the interests of the Argentine opposition, where anti-Americanism also ran strong. Through informal negotiations, Canadian officials accomplished much more than their U.S. counterparts in promoting human rights in Argentina.[19]

Five years later, the Argentine generals determined to restore their image as savior of the nation by resolving an issue that had festered since the early years of Argentine independence: reclaiming the Malvinas, or Falkland Islands, from British control. Their nemesis Carter had ignominiously left Washington, and they were convinced that his successor, Ronald Reagan, would respond to Buenos Aires's support for U.S. policy in Central America by acquiescing in their seizure of the islands. Argentina's South American neighbors would be supportive of military action to regain what they considered legitimate Argentine territory. Great Britain would not undertake a costly and unpopular military campaign to retake the Malvinas, and if they threatened a counterattack, the United States would keep them from overreacting. None of these calculations worked out. There was internal bickering in the Reagan administration about the Argentine claim between U.N. ambassador Jeane Kirkpatrick and Secretary of State Alexander Haig, but as the crisis unfolded it became clear that the United States failed to play a neutral role. In a furious round of shuttle diplomacy, Haig tried to persuade Argentine leaders that theirs was a hopeless cause. After the British decided to retake the islands, Washington supplied them with critical intelligence information about the movement of Argentine vessels. In the aftermath, Argentine leaders complained about the U.S. betrayal of their cause, but they suffered the final ignominy, for the brief war in the Falklands exposed the military's weakness and stripped the regime of any lasting claim to legitimacy. When the generals turned over political power to civilians in 1982, they did so voluntarily. Their legacy was a nation fragmented and purposeless, ill prepared for the demanding tasks of building a democratic political culture.[20]

The Central American Crisis

The Malvinas war may have tested hemispheric loyalties but not U.S. willingness to employ its political and military power in the traditional fashion of an imperial nation. That challenge came not from the hemisphere's most powerful or largest states but from some of its smallest and least threatening. These were countries that had suffered U.S. intervention in the twentieth century and whose peoples harbored deep anti-American feelings yet who had absorbed North American cultural values.

The initial challenge in the early 1970s came from Omar Torrijos of Panama, the principal beneficiary of the 1968 military coup that had ousted Arnulfo Arias. Torrijos brought a novel dimension to Panamanian politics, to the debate over the canal, and above all to Panama's relationship with the United States. He infuriated Panama's anti-American elites with his populist rhetoric, inspired Panamanians of all social levels with his nationalistic bluster, and jarred a succession of U.S. presidents with his seemingly iron-willed determination to crack the alliance forged by the 1903 canal treaty. He vigorously expanded Panama's international banking industry by ensuring secrecy of accounts and transactions, which pleased a generation of financiers. He supported import industrialization substitution, a new labor code favoring unions, income redistribution, rural development, agrarian reform, public health, and housing, which earned him the title of populist. Castro praised him. So did John Wayne. When Richard Nixon suggested that he was unwilling to go as far as his predecessor and negotiate a new canal treaty, Torrijos hinted that Panamanians were prepared to seize the canal. Cleverly, he chose instead to use the forum of the U.N. Security Council meeting in Panama City in March 1973 to approve a resolution—13–1–1, the U.S. representative casting the single nay vote and Great Britain abstaining—criticizing the United States for its failure to conclude a new canal treaty. The veto effectively killed the resolution, as Torrijos anticipated, but the Panamanians had managed to bring the canal debate before an international forum. Juan Tack, Panama's foreign minister, summed up Nixon's dilemma when he declared, "The United States has vetoed Panama, but the world has vetoed the United States."[21]

At this point, Nixon realized that he really could not avoid meaningful negotiation with Panama, and Kissinger, now elevated to secretary of state, belatedly revived the moribund discussions about the future of the canal. Predictably, as the talks became more serious, domestic political rhetoric about U.S. de facto sovereignty over the Canal Zone sharply escalated. Panama had few friends within the U.S. Congress; the Canal Zone and the Panama Canal, a sizable number. The House of Representatives registered its displeasure by approving a rider denying funds to the Department of State for negotiating any agreement surrendering the canal to Panama. In the 1976 Republican presidential primaries, Governor Reagan revived his failing campaign against President Ford by championing retention of the canal with now-familiar comments that Theodore Roosevelt had bought the canal and the ten-mile swath of territory it traversed. As the rhetoric against concessions to Panama became more strident, Torrijos became more defiant, angering Washington further by restoring Panamanian diplomatic relations with Cuba.[22]

Relations with Panama became Jimmy Carter's first meaningful test in hemispheric affairs. In the interim between his election and inauguration, he received a report from the Commission on United States–Latin American Relations, chaired by Sol Linowitz, which urged a speedy resolution of the Panama Canal issue before the isthmus exploded in another round of anti-American violence. Carter concurred, giving top priority to rectifying what he considered a lingering injustice from the nation's imperial past and a major obstacle to his goal of fashioning a new relation with Latin America. By the end of summer 1977, Panamanian and U.S. negotiators had finally thrashed out their major differences and signed two treaties, one providing for transfer of the canal to Panama at the end of 1999 with governance by a joint U.S.–Panamanian commission in the interim period, and the other, a neutrality treaty, addressing the still volatile matter of canal security.

Both prompted a bitter political debate in the country and in the U.S. Senate, where a number of senators wanted to retain the right of intervention to protect the canal; and in Panama, where legislators demanded assurances that Panamanian sovereignty would be respected. In October, Carter summoned Torrijos to Washington, D.C., where they issued a Statement of Understanding designed to placate critics in both countries. Torrijos returned home to conduct a national plebiscite on the treaties in which he assured Panamanians that there would be no unilateral intervention under the terms of the projected treaties. Despite opposition from several notable intellectuals and political figures (some of them in exile), Panamanians approved the treaties by a two-thirds majority. The U.S. Senate finally ratified the treaties by a narrow margin in March and April 1978 and only then with the attachment of a controversial amendment sponsored by Senator Dennis DeConcini (D, Ariz.) granting the United States the right to intervene in Panama to ensure the security of the canal. Panamanians denounced the proviso as an unwarranted violation of national sovereignty. Two senators, Robert Byrd (D, W.V.) and Howard Baker (R, Tenn.), tried to placate them with yet another amendment forswearing any U.S. intervention in Panama's internal affairs.[23]

Panamanians were jubilant. Had the treaties failed, Torrijos was prepared to invade the Canal Zone. Instead, under OAS pressure he turned over direct governance of the country to a civilian, Aristides Royo, resumed his command of the National Guard, and waited expectantly for treaty implementation in October 1979. Some groups, of course, failed to benefit from the transition. Most long-time Zonians had anticipated approval of a new agreement in the sixties and continued to depart for the states. Descendants of West Indians who lived in the Canal Zone, particularly those employees of the Panama Railroad and Zone port facilities, also stood to lose because their lodgings and jobs would soon fall under Panamanian jurisdiction. Meanwhile, treaty implementation in the Congress ran afoul of resentments within the House of Representatives, whose members played no legal role in the debate over ratification in the Senate but did have authority in the funding of the Panama Canal Commission and the disposal of U.S. government property. An early version of the Panama Canal Act sponsored by a longtime treaty foe, John Murphy (D, N.Y.) made the commission dependent on the Department of Defense and required annual congressional approval for its budget and activities. The intent was to embarrass Carter for "giving away our canal" and punish Torrijos for his support of the revolution against Anastasio Somoza in Nicaragua. Somoza's fall in July 1979 made the latter tactic meaningless, and the House and Senate finally approved the implementing legislation less than a week before the October 1 deadline, two decades after Panamanians had rioted to claim the Canal Zone and the Panama Canal as their own.[24]

The revolution often anticipated by the Latin American left and widely feared by the right occurred not in Panama but in Nicaragua with the overthrow of the Somoza dynasty in July 1979 and the military coup and subsequent guerrilla uprising in El Salvador three months later. Over the years, Anastasio Somoza DeBayle—son of the founder of the country's familial dynasty following U.S. intervention in 1926–33—had secured a virtual stranglehold over Nicaragua by his domination of the Liberal party, intimidation of the political opposition, bribery, and, most important, his control of the National Guard. Most of the democratic leaders of Latin America abominated Somoza and looked forward to his fall from power, if necessary by violence. Somoza had few friends within the U.S. Department of State, but he did have his defenders in Congress, and he managed to preserve his U.S. connections despite his brazen pocketing of aid dispatched after the destruction of downtown Managua by an earthquake in 1972.

Somoza alienated many of Nicaragua's prominent families by his greed and aroused the political opposition with his crackdown on the press and labor. By 1977, even the church had turned against him. Leaders of the dictator's principal adversary, the Sandinista Liberation Front, explained the revolutionary ferment as the inevitable consequence of decades of U.S. exploitation and its legacy of poverty and misery. The reality proved more complicated. From the 1950s Nicaragua's economic and social progress had been impressive, and its reliance on the United States as an export market had actually declined, an indicator of the country's lessening dependence. Health and education had improved. In the process, however, the inequities that often accompany rapid economic growth had actually widened the gap between rich and poor and city and countryside. The most visible economic fissure lay between the Somoza family and the rest of the country.[25]

These conditions were not unique to Nicaragua. In Honduras, Panama, and even in relatively more prosperous Costa Rica, political leaders responded fitfully to the growing popular militancy over economic inequities and declining standards of living with sufficient reforms to prevent widespread violence. In Nicaragua, El Salvador, and Guatemala, however, elites fiercely resisted any challenge to the prevailing social structure. Repression of dissidents intensified. In Guatemala and El Salvador, militaries had become more confident with U.S. arms and training and proved uncharacteristically defiant when Carter abruptly cut off military, though not economic, aid. After the fraudulent election of General Carlos Humberto Romero in El Salvador in 1977, the terror escalated. Death squads under the control of ORDEN, the notorious right wing spy agency created with U.S. assistance in the 1960s, executed dissidents. The futility of peaceful political change served to increase the ranks of the guerrilla movements and make civil war a virtual certainty.

Conflict in Guatemala followed a similar pattern, the guerrillas benefiting from the popular protests and mobilizations of students, political dissidents, labor leaders, and radical Catholic clergy against the government. In the countryside, the government confronted an increasingly militant indigenous population that responded to the recruiting efforts of guerrillas and popular organizations. The ensuing conflict was in many respects a continuation of the violence erupting after the overthrow of Arbenz in 1954, but its intensity and death toll increased noticeably between 1977 and 1983. As the government and military grew more frustrated in trying to maintain control over the countryside, and at times over the capital itself, the ability of the United States to exercise meaningful control over its behavior noticeably weakened, as Carter discovered.[26]

When Carter became president, the civil conflict in Nicaragua was rapidly deteriorating into a war of an entire society against the Somoza dictatorship, less brutal perhaps than the regimes in El Salvador and Guatemala but no less despised and certainly no less arrogant. In dealing with the Nicaraguan crisis Carter proved well intentioned but limited in what he could achieve. He singled out the Somoza regime for its violations of human rights and cut back U.S. military assistance to Nicaragua. Somoza remained undeterred, though he suffered embarrassment with the assassination in January 1978 of one of his most outspoken critics, Pedro Joaquín Chamorro. In the following months Nicaragua collapsed into civil war. Moderates called on Somoza to resign or, that failing, for the United States to remove him.

As the political crisis unfolded in late 1978 and early 1979 the president desperately sought a political solution that would rid Nicaragua of Somoza by peaceful means yet preserve the National Guard and prevent the Sandinistas from dominating the new government. The OAS tried and failed to mediate the crisis. In his final weeks of power, the desperate Somoza unleashed a savage attack against Nicaragua's urban population. Most North Americans remembered these days not for the losses of Nicaraguan lives but for the shooting of an American Broadcasting Corporation network television reporter, a killing captured on film and broadcast on nightly news across the United States. When Somoza resigned and left the country in mid-July 1979, his flight signaled not only the end of a familial dynasty intimately linked to U.S. power but the military and political victory of a broad coalition of Nicaraguans led by seasoned guerrillas with a program for reconstructing Nicaraguan society.[27]

The fall of Somoza surprised few, but the suddenness of the collapse of one of the hemisphere's most durable dictatorships left Nicaragua with a battered economy and a fragile political coalition. Of all the anti-Somocista groups, the Sandinistas had emerged from the conflict in the strongest position. They had control of the military force that had defeated Central America's best-equipped military. They were not formally bound by the agreement drawn up by anti-Somocista political leaders in Costa Rica calling for political pluralism, a mixed economy, a nonaligned foreign policy, the creation of a nonpartisan army, and minority participation by the Sandinista National Liberation Front (FSLN) on the Council of State. Sandinistas effectively controlled the five-member junta that governed the country and from the beginning set out to create a "new Nicaragua." Both the newly formed standing army and police force were highly partisan, their training and political education being in the hands of East Europeans and Cubans.

Skeptics, including some notable anti-Somocistas within Nicaragua, were persuaded that Nicaragua intended to follow the Cuban economic model, although such a choice was not initially apparent. True, the national directorate of the FSLN remained committed to a socialist economy, but representatives of the private sector dominated the economic portfolios in the government. They readily accepted the creation of a vigorous state sector and nationalization of Somocista properties, financial institutions, foreign trade, and national resources. Indeed, the most vocal critics of the new regime lay among Nicaragua's extreme left; they incited demonstrations and strikes and prompted the Sandinistas to crack down with harsh countermeasures. These early clashes were symptomatic of a deeper problem confronting the Sandinistas. To reconstruct an economy devastated by years of conflict meant sharing power with people the *comandantes* did not really trust (and who did not trust them) as well as depending on economic advice and moneys from foreign governments and private organizations. To create the new Nicaragua and save the revolution required building a new army and state security apparatus strong enough to deal with internal dissidents and to deter the United States from launching an invasion to install a friendly government. In the crunch, the Sandinistas chose the latter course, and for that alternative their only reliable advisors were the Cubans.[28]

Critics argued that Carter should have anticipated this eventuality and taken measures to prevent it. But removal of Somoza and prevention of Sandinista control of a successor government would have required military intervention—the choice in 1912 and again in 1926—and would have been a political disaster for the president. Ironically, Carter's frustrations in dealing with Nicaragua may have prompted him to change course in El Salvador, where a military coup in October 1979 forced out General Romero. Senior members of the new junta wanted to avoid another Nicaragua by invigorating the campaign against the country's disparate guerrilla forces, but they lost out in a political struggle with their junior colleagues, who contended that the only way to prevent a revolution in El Salvador lay in bringing civilians into the government, undertaking broad social and political reforms, and dissolving ORDEN. For the remainder of the year, the junta tried to govern amidst rising demands, protests, and human rights abuses. Alarmed by the agitation and the prospect of a guerrilla victory, Carter elected to support those in the Salvadoran military who wanted to pacify the countryside, a less risky approach, he believed, than providing political and economic sustenance to the reformers in the government. In early 1980, civilians from the governing junta and cabinet abruptly resigned, declaring that continuing human rights abuses by the military prevented "a peaceful and democratic solution" to El Salvador's social problems.[29]

In this instance, the president's choice had unanticipated and tragic consequences. El Salvador's rightists were encouraged. Without U.S. support, the Salvadoran military stood little chance of containing the four thousand well-organized, highly motivated fighters of the Farabundo Martí National Liberation Front (FMLN). In the twelve months between the collapse of the government in January 1980 and the guerrilla offensive of early 1981, a succession of military juntas combined reform with repression. They struck at the power of the coffee elite by nationalizing the banking system and the coffee export sector. In March 1980, they commenced an agrarian reform that if fully carried out would have stripped the coffee proprietors of much of their holdings and followed it up with a declaration of a state of siege. In Nicaragua, the Sandinistas had pursued a similar course, but their land seizures had come largely at the expense of Somoza and his cronies. Nicaragua (and Costa Rica) also had historic traditions of state direction of the economy, but in Guatemala and especially in El Salvador, the coffee barons customarily expected governments, whether military or civilian, to do their bidding. In their outrage at the Carter administration, the Christian Democrats, and radical military officers, they looked to their military allies to undo these reforms and restore their place in Salvadoran society by crushing their enemies. Their friends in uniform launched a campaign of violence in the countryside and in the cities in which perhaps thirty thousand people died, among them the outspoken archbishop of San Salvador, Oscar Romero, who had condemned the atrocities and implored Salvadoran soldiers not to fire on their own people.[30]

As El Salvador sank into bloody social conflict, the U.S. presidential campaign between Carter and the Republican nominee Ronald Reagan entered its most contentious phases. From the beginning Carter found himself on the defensive for his alienation of once-friendly governments such as Argentina and Guatemala, which were angered by his human rights advocacy and the loss of Nicaragua to a Marxist regime. The setbacks in the hemisphere did not explain his loss of the presidency to Reagan. His fresh approach to the region struck many in Latin America and the Caribbean as not only humane but realistic, a recognition that national security depended less on sustaining anti-communist governments, which are often inherently unstable, than on encouraging progressive democratic regimes. The major drawback to this approach lay in the perceptions of weakness and indecisiveness of a government trying to manipulate the internal politics of another country wrestling with revolutionary change after the overthrow of a dictator, as was the case in Nicaragua, or sustaining a corrupt military on the grounds that U.S. security interests were at stake, the issue in El Salvador, and to do so by relying on economic co-ercion to induce reforms and professions of good intentions.

In El Salvador, Carter confronted the contradictions of that policy. Without revolutionary change, reforms alienated the wealth that was required to bring about the reforms in the first place. El Salvador's oligarchs reacted by selling their land at inflated prices and moving the money into U.S. and Swiss bank accounts and, tragically, by unleashing the death squads against the country's peasantry. As the death toll of civilians rose, the opposition movements coa-lesced, forming a united political Revolutionary Democratic Front (FDR) and guerrilla front (FMLN), the first controlled by moderates and the second by Marxists. Fearful that radicals within the movement would ultimately domi-nate, as he believed they had in Nicaragua, Carter committed the country even more deeply to the Salvadoran military.[31]

If Carter appeared unfocused and vacillating, he could nonetheless re-mind his critics of the complexity of isthmian society and politics and the anti-Americanism that was the legacy of U.S. meddling and intervention in the region and of the necessity of reform to prevent revolution. Reagan, too, ap-pealed to the historical record, but his referents were those grand successes of the nation's imperial past. Whereas Carter brought his notable analytical skills to bear on a problem, Reagan appealed to his instinctive understanding of public frustrations about the nation's weakening stature in the hemisphere. Like Carter, he chose to support the Salvadoran military on strategic grounds, but he would go much further than his predecessor in addressing the chal-lenge to U.S. power in Central America by supporting the anti-Sandinista forces in Nicaragua—the contras, or, as they preferred to be called, the Resistance—transforming Honduras into a virtual military outpost, and compromising the fragile neutrality of Costa Rica with persistent and increasingly resented diplo-matic pressures.

In an effort to deal with the bureaucratic dissension over Latin American policy in the Carter administration, the Reagan team conducted a thorough purging of the State Department's Latin Americanists, a housecleaning that reminded some longtime Washington observers of Wisconsin Senator Joseph McCarthy's defamation of the "China hands" following the "loss of China" to communists in 1949. What Reagan soon discovered, however, was that the cleansing of the bureaucracy of dissenters to a more aggressive approach to hemispheric affairs did little to restrain those grassroots organizers across the country whose vocal members may have liked the president personally but questioned the militarization of Central American policy and particularly the administration's support of the Salvadoran military. As the Washington spokes-person of the American Baptist Churches testified before Congress in 1981, "The United States and the right-wing junta are aiding the elimination of the center as a political reality in El Salvador. Just at the time we should be mid-wifing the birth of a new center, we are instead arming the terrorist right more thoroughly." Such comments revealed the intensity of sentiments held by a re-markably diverse number of North American religious and civil groups about the direction of U.S. policy in Central America.[32]

Reagan had come to the presidency believing that the conflict in the isth-mus conformed to traditional cold war scenarios of a Cuban–Soviet conspir-acy to take over indigenous revolutionary movements and subvert them. In an effort to bolster its case, the administration issued in 1981 a white paper enti-tled "Communist Interference in El Salvador," a hastily crafted document cit-ing Cuba as the surrogate agent of Soviet conspiracy in Central America. Harsh public reaction to the document proved so compelling that the State Depart-ment created an Office of Public Diplomacy for Latin America to publicize of-ficial goals in the hemisphere. When Congress refused to go along with the president's request for more support for El Salvador's military, Reagan used his executive power to dispatch fifty-six military advisors and $25 million in aid to the country, with the provision that the governing junta schedule elec-tions for a national assembly. But even here the United States suffered further embarrassment when the right wing National Republic Alliance (the ARENA party) emerged victorious.

In the aftermath, the civil war intensified, government troops losing ground despite the U.S. training of Salvadoran officers and the infusion of aid. Terror-ism sharply escalated, not only in El Salvador but in neighboring Guatemala, where a brutal military counterinsurgency in 1982 and 1983 resulted in the deaths of 75,000 peasants, the destruction of 440 villages, and the displace-ment of 100,000 to 500,000 of the country's indigenous population, many of whom fled into neighboring Mexico. Critics of administration policy attributed the killings in El Salvador to death squads controlled by security forces; the ad-ministration itself said the violence was caused by extremists from the left and right. Congress, apparently agreeing with the critics, increased its pressure on the White House to do something. In December 1983 the president relented by sending Vice President George Bush with an ultimatum to thirty-one Salvado-ran military commanders to curb the death squads or risk losing U.S. aid. In the following year, the killings dropped dramatically.[33]

There was no immediate resolution of El Salvador's civil war or of the crisis between the United States and the government of Nicaragua over covert aid to the contras, which until late 1983 had included the use of CIA agents to mine Nicaraguan harbors, the carrying out of military exercises from bases in Honduras, and high-level discussion of direct U.S. military intervention. In the first two years of the administration, the hard-liners in the administration clearly held the ascendancy. Diplomatic and policy personnel who suggested following up on Sandinista offers to negotiate outstanding security issues lost their jobs. The administration suspended the economic aid to Nicaragua commenced by Carter, reduced Nicaragua's sugar quota by 90 percent, and pressured West European governments and international lending institutions to decrease or reject financial aid to Managua. In March and April 1983, the president gave major addresses on El Salvador and Central America, the latter delivered to a joint session of Congress. Invoking President Harry Truman's warnings to Congress in 1947 about Soviet expansion in the world, Reagan declared that the "security of all the Americas is at stake in Central America." He followed with a request for almost $300 million in aid for the isthmus, half of it earmarked for El Salvador. Democrats on Capitol Hill remained suspicious of Reagan's motives in Central America and persisted in questioning more military assistance to El Salvador. To end the bickering, in July 1983 the president announced the creation of the National Bipartisan Commission on Central America, chaired by Kissinger and generally referred to as the Kissinger Commission, to conduct a study of the Central American crisis and make recommendations for U.S. policy toward the isthmus. Washington insiders took the commission as a signal that the moderates might be winning out in the bureaucratic battles for control of Central American policy.[34]

The militarization of administration policy in the hemisphere continued in October 1983 with the invasion of the tiny eastern Caribbean island of Grenada, ostensibly to rescue U.S. medical students placed in danger by the takeover of government by Marxists but in actuality to prevent Cuban soldiers and engineers from completing an airfield and perhaps to send a warning to the Sandinistas that they might be next. In his television address on the crisis, Reagan spoke for only ten minutes and mentioned the Soviet Union and Cuba fourteen times in his efforts to prove they intended to use Grenada to export terror and undermine democracy. Critics were angered or befuddled by the seeming contradictions between the president's appeals for military assistance and rejection of negotiations on the one hand and the invocation of a democratic purpose on the other. As a shrewd political "communicator," Reagan remained untroubled by the disparity between his deeds and his rhetoric. As he declared in his March speech, "Despite all I and others have said, some people still seem to think our concern for security assistance means that all we care about is a military solution. . . . Bullets are no answer to economic inequities, social tensions or political disagreements. Democracy is what we want."³⁵

In the Name of Democracy

The Kissinger Commission report on the Central American crisis, released in early 1984, appeared to confirm this judgment, although with qualifications Reagan must have found disturbing. In an apparent repudiation of earlier cold war judgments as well as of some of the convictions of the Reagan team, it denied that dictatorships or authoritarian governments were required to prevent anarchy or communism and confirmed what some administration critics were stating about the urgency of political reform and social justice in the isthmus. In an obvious reference to Nicaragua, the report conceded that "there is room in the hemisphere for differing forms of government and different forms of government," including those gaining power through revolution. Self-determination constituted the gravamen of the issue. "The United States can have no quarrel with democratic decisions," the report continued, "as long as they are not the result of foreign pressure and external machinations." Nowhere did the report suggest that the United States may have been one of the pernicious foreign influences in isthmian affairs. In a reversion to traditional cold war rhetoric, it condemned Cuban and Soviet efforts to use Central American revolution as part of a geostrategic challenge to the United States. It called upon the governments of the inter-American system to support political pluralism, human rights, free elections, and freedom of expression; to promote economic and social development for the benefit of all; and to modernize the hemispheric security system to meet the threat. "Just as there can be no real security without economic growth and social justice," the report warned, "so there can be no prosperity without security."³⁶

And it was imperative that the United States respond to the challenge in Central America. Not to do so would be as consequential as acting hastily. Nothing in the report expressed doubts about the ability of the United States to make a difference in Central America. This was the kind of reasoning—optimism tinged with arrogance—that mandated support for the Christian Democrat José Napoleon Duarte in El Salvador. Duarte enjoyed a reputation as a reformer and a democrat. The Reagan administration considered his election critical to its efforts to persuade Congress to increase military and economic aid to El Salvador. War-weary Salvadorans heartened to his promises to curb military excesses, which pleased U.S. leaders, and to open discussions with guerrilla leaders, which irritated Reagan. For a year or so, the strategy appeared to be working. It then faded when it became apparent that Duarte was too beholden to Washington to shackle the military or to deal with the country's escalating economic problems. He left office in 1989 with the civil war still raging; seventy thousand Salvadoran lives were lost over the decade. Yet, in a small but significant way, his appearance on the political scene had given Salvadorans an unprecedented opportunity to criticize the government and to participate in a historically elitist political culture. Salvadoran politics did not revert to its pre-1979 form. North American pressures had produced unanticipated effects.[37]

When the Sandinistas won an overwhelming electoral victory in Nicaragua in summer 1984, in circumstances as trying as those confronting the United States during the civil war, the Reagan administration discounted the results by pointing out that the armed opposition had refused to participate and that the limited degree of political participation made Nicaragua undemocratic. Liberals made similar charges about the "demonstration elections"—a term used to describe elections whose principal purpose was to persuade the United States to continue its economic assistance—in El Salvador and Guatemala. What followed over the remainder of the decade is a tale of tragedy, political intrigue, and deception: devastating civil wars in El Salvador and Nicaragua that threatened the well-being of their neighbors, and in Washington an administration so driven to sustain one government and overturn the other that it defied the U.S. Congress, scoffed at Latin American efforts to negotiate a peaceful settlement, and even violated the law. The most embarrassing revelation occurred in the second Reagan administration. As Central American leaders tried fitfully to reconcile their differences through negotiation, hardliners in the administration ran the contra war from the White House basement, using a U.S. marine colonel, Oliver North, to raise moneys for the effort. Reagan himself came under scrutiny when the press reported that with the president's implicit approval North had arranged to sell arms to Iran, officially declared a supporter of terrorism, in return for the release of U.S. hostages taken by terrorists. The intent was to raise funds to prosecute the contra war, in a manner circumventing the express prohibitions of Congress against any expenditures aimed at bringing down the Nicaraguan government. Even the stalwarts of the Reagan team were taken aback by the damage.[38]

Fortuitously, the failure of the president to bring down the Sandinista government and the chaotic nature of Central American policy in the Reagan administration provided Central Americans themselves with an opportunity to revive peace efforts that had seemingly collapsed in the wake of Reagan's overwhelming 1984 reelection victory and the U.S. House approval of contra aid in summer 1986. Earlier peace proposals from the Contadora group of Latin American governments (originally made up of Mexico, Panama, Venezuela, and Colombia and later expanded to include Argentina, Brazil, Peru, and Uruguay) had faltered because of U.S. opposition and the insistence on respecting the sovereignty of individual Central American countries and their right to settle internal affairs without foreign involvement. President Oscar Arias of Costa Rica, the architect of a new peace proposal, argued that assurances of a common standard of democracy were critical to achieving isthmian peace. Although not explicitly singling out any Central American country, the Arias plan was clearly aimed at Nicaragua. His isthmian colleagues were at first wary, as was the White House, but as the Iran-contra hearings got under way, the Congress became more responsive. In March 1987 the Senate overwhelmingly endorsed the Arias plan in a nonbinding resolution. As criticism of Central American policy grew more intense in Congress, White House Chief of Staff Howard Baker thrashed out an isthmian peace proposal with House Majority Leader Jim Wright. The plan called for a ceasefire, the end of military aid to all belligerents, and respect for the civil and political rights of Nicaraguans. Critics surmised that Reagan made the offer in the belief that the Sandinistas would reject it and that in frustration Congress would renew contra aid.[39]

Like several of his predecessors in the White House, Reagan had underestimated the determination of Central Americans to chart their own affairs. In a succession of meetings, isthmian presidents set aside the peace plan from Washington and with the support of other Latin American governments devised their own. By the time Reagan's vice president, George H. W. Bush, was inaugurated as president Central American leaders were well on their way to resolving the isthmian crisis. In August 1978, at a meeting in Tela, Honduras, in a former United Fruit Company compound, Sandinista leaders formally agreed to respect the political rights of their opponents, to liberalize the national electoral law, to release three thousand political prisoners, to hold national elections in February 1990, and in the economic sphere to reverse their nationalization policies. In El Salvador, President-elect Alfredo Cristiani agreed to negotiate with the FMLN to end the civil war. Central American foreign ministers and military officers obtained the approval of the OAS and United Nations to commence policing their borders to ensure that the contras would be disbanded. The last stipulation particularly irritated those in Washington (Bush among them) who insisted that the most reliable assurance for isthmian peace lay in maintaining the Nicaraguan armed opposition.[40]

But pursuing a military solution in Nicaragua was a losing cause, as Bush soon realized, for it was bound to reopen old political wounds with Congress and cause further discord with Latin American governments. Carlos Andrés Pérez, inaugurated as Venezuelan president a few weeks after Bush took the oath of office, reminded his North American counterpart of the need to redirect U.S. hemispheric policy toward more fundamental issues. Venezuela had played a leading role in efforts to mediate the Central American crisis through the Contadora group. Often critical of U.S. policy, Venezuelan leaders nonetheless candidly recognized that an isthmian peace settlement acceptable to the United States was unlikely, however difficult it became to persuade the Reagan administration of the futility of seeking a military solution. Such an outcome appeared unlikely at mid-decade, but not after Reagan left office.[41]

In his remarks Pérez was alluding to the political changes that had taken place throughout much of Latin America during the eighties and the parallel problems accompanying them. Beginning with the embarrassing collapse of the Argentine military government in 1982 after its defeat in the Falklands war and culminating with the demise of the Pinochet dictatorship in Chile at the end of the decade, military regimes gave way to democratic rule. U.S. leaders would proudly claim to have encouraged these changes, but in reality the early policies of the Reagan administration aimed at strengthening ties with military governments in Brazil, Argentina, Chile, and other countries did little to reassure democratic elements. (Bolivia constituted an exception to U.S. support of military regimes because of the complicity of the government in drug trafficking.) Once it became obvious that the United States had little to gain by continuing to maintain strong ties with rightist governments, the Reagan administration abruptly altered course and expressed its support for these changes. But the apparent reversal of U.S. policy toward military governments, though genuine, was of less importance than domestic considerations in explaining Latin America's democratic resurgence. The failure of military regimes to deal with the economic crisis that ravaged much of Latin America in the decade, the decline of leftist and guerrilla movements either through repression or incorporation into the political culture, greater political participation from middle and even lower social and economic sectors, and growing disillusion with military and authoritarian governments, among other factors, largely dictated the hemispheric democratic turnaround.[42]

Regrettably, these political changes rested on an uncertain economic foundation. Latin America's experience in the 1980s did not conform to the prescription that economic growth led to an improved standard of living. Twenty years of rampant and uneven development in the 1960s and 1970s had produced economies that in many ways were as distorted and exhibited the same social inequities as those of the 1950s. While there had been progress in many areas, by 1990 much of the continent had fallen behind North America and Western Europe. A mounting external and internal debt brought on by heavy borrowing in the 1970s precipitated a hemispheric financial crisis in the following decade. The first calamity occurred in mid-August 1982, when the Mexican government declared that it could no longer service its foreign debt. U.S. officials cobbled together a makeshift bailout. The Mexican debt crisis, however, led to a succession of declarations by other Latin American governments of a similar predicament. For a year or so, there were signs that the indebted would ban together to pressure for resolution of their problem. In January 1984 a consortium of governments called upon creditor nations to address the precipitous fall in living standards throughout Latin America. Later in the year, President Belisario Betancur of Colombia declared that the debt crisis threatened the precarious democracies that had emerged during the decade. Initially, neither the U.S. government nor the International Monetary Fund appeared responsive. Their solution called for draconian cuts in public expenditures. And Mexico and Brazil, which carried the largest debt burdens, were disinclined to join a common front.

A glimmer of hope appeared in 1985 when the newly appointed secretary of the treasury, James Baker, proposed a debt readjustment scheme calling for a $20-billion loan from private banks over three years followed in the third year by a $9-billion loan from the World Bank and Inter-American Development Bank. The Baker plan produced limited results, principally because many of the regional lending banks in the United States commenced to write off their Latin American debt, which in turn put greater pressure on the "money center" banks in New York and California. When prospects for the success of his plan faded, Baker put forth new financial mechanisms for reducing Latin American debt, among them a controversial debt-equity conversion scheme whereby an indebted government used national resources to obtain loans from foreign investors. By the end of the Reagan administration international creditors had become disillusioned with most Latin American governments, which they regarded as well intentioned but unwilling to conform to global economic realities. New loans depended on restructuring; economic growth, on the willingness of elites to stem capital flight by investing in their own countries.[43]

Democracy had survived but at a frightful cost. At the onset of the eighties, 120 million Latin Americans (40 percent of the population) lived in poverty. By 1985, their numbers had risen to 170 million, and by the end of the decade to a staggering 240 million. In the absence of the informal economy, earnings from drug trafficking, and immigration, their situation would have been much worse. In an earlier era, doubtless, a populist leader—another Perón or Vargas or Cárdenas—would have emerged to reclaim the national patrimony and restore confidence by demonizing the foreigner and the *vendepatria* who sold out the country to him. But in the economic circumstances of the eighties, such a recourse did not seem probable. Domestic investors could send their moneys to Geneva, New York, and Miami instead of using it to prop up their national economies, a recourse their fathers and grandfathers did not usually enjoy.

As the international financiers imposed even more draconian solutions, Latin American leaders gloomily recognized not only that they lacked a collective debt strategy but that the state itself had lost the authoritative presence in the rapidly changing society. As the soldier-ruler returned to the barracks, the civilian who assumed his place now confronted new predicaments that went beyond the wrangling with legislatures and inefficient bureaucracies. Civilian institutions historically positioned to play a central role in the political culture, such as organized labor, business associations, and popular organizations, proved too weak or too fragmented to exercise a controlling authority over individual members. In the uncertainty of the times, perhaps the most inept in making the adjustment to the dramatic social changes of the eighties were leftist organizations, which had played a marginal role in the political battle against authoritarian and military governments. In an era of neoliberal solutions, with their espousal of privatization and market economies, the left's demand for a return to state developmentalism and its ability to mobilize the urban poor, peasants, and workers against entrenched elites turned out to be a losing cause.[44]

In the early 1960s, such hemispheric issues as security, development, democracy, and even ideology acquired their meaning within the context of the cold war and the bitter and sometimes violent conflicts in the name of reform and revolution. Thirty years later, with the collapse of the Soviet Union and the apparent triumph of liberal capitalism everywhere in the Americas except Cuba, those issues remained as compelling and relevant as ever. The context had changed, sometimes dramatically so. Guerrilla movements survived, driven not by a desire to gain power in order to transform the political culture or to create a socialist utopia but to show their alienation from society or, as in Peru, to destroy the indigenous society they presumed to defend. Their persistence coupled with the explosive growth of drug trafficking fundamentally altered the meaning of security.

The developmental model extolled by the United States as the alternative to that created in Cuba acquired new adherents, although in 1990 its success depended less on the choices of political leaders than on the vagaries of the market and the migration of labor and peoples. Democratic leaders replaced dictators, but by the early 1990s the corruption and inefficiency and arbitrariness once ascribed to those who had gained power unconstitutionally too often became the trademark of those who had won office by the vote or, as turned out to be the case in Panama and in Haiti, by U.S. military intervention. In 1960 and 1970 hemispheric leaders spoke of the benefits of hemispheric trade. Few of them could have anticipated the dramatic and daring proposals of their successors for the economic integration of the Americas or the more substantive regional trade agreements. The Alliance for Progress had advanced the cause of democracy and social justice; the Summits of the Americas in the 1990s would not only reaffirm but enhance those principles and add to them a concern for the environment.

The legacy of these and other changes—some of them more than a century in the making and others largely explained by cold war exigencies—would be a new hemisphere, united and fragmented, the creation of governments and of people.

Epilogue

In Europe, it is sometimes said, the tearing down of the Berlin Wall and the dissolution of the Soviet Union ended not only the cold war but the short twentieth century that had commenced in 1914 with the onset of World War I. For the Western Hemisphere, however, the seminal contemporary event was a display of U.S. military power in the Greater Caribbean. Five days before Christmas 1989, President George H. W. Bush ordered a military intervention in Panama, Operation Just Cause. The purpose of the invasion was the removal of the Panamanian strongman General Manuel Noriega, a onetime political ally and CIA confidant. In the 1970s and early 1980s, Noriega had proved useful to U.S. officials in their efforts to bring down the Sandinista government in Nicaragua, and his position as commander of the Panama Defense Force (PDF) reassured high-ranking U.S. officials about the security of the Panama Canal in a politically volatile and strategically vital region of the hemisphere. By mid-decade, however, Noriega was coming under criticism in the U.S. press and in the Congress for his drug trafficking, money laundering, smuggling, and gun running. His diminishing utility and his interference in Panamanian domestic politics prompted the Reagan administration to force him out by a succession of moves: indictments in federal courts for drug trafficking, decertification for international borrowing, suspension of Panama Canal payments

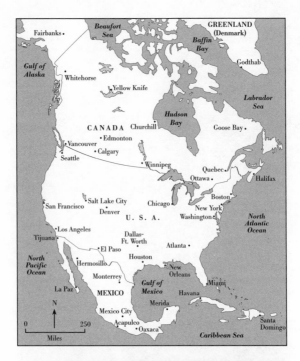

3. The Americas at 2000

and trade preferences, and the halting of shipments of U.S. dollars (Panama's currency) to the country. These efforts failed, embarrassingly so, and Noriega became increasingly defiant. Matters eased somewhat before the U.S. presidential elections of 1988, when the Reagan administration obtained a pledge from Noriega to leave Panama if the indictments were dropped. Noriega violated this commitment and further infuriated Washington by using PDF troops and his political goons to overturn the May 1989 Panamanian presidential election and prevent what most observers agreed would be a victory for his opponents. The OAS tried to mediate by urging Noriega to call new elections but did not recommend his removal if he refused. By October 1989 Bush concluded that Noriega had to be ousted by force.

The military phase of Operation Just Cause turned out to be briefer than comparable operations in Nicaragua in 1912 and 1926 and in the Dominican Republic in 1965. For four tumultuous, chaotic days, U.S. forces, whose numbers ultimately reached twenty-four thousand, clashed with Noriega's so-called Dignity Battalions and PDF soldiers in Panama City. Entire blocks of some of the poorest neighborhoods in the city were set ablaze in the fighting. The victors of the May election assumed power over a Panamanian government that was, like that of November 1903, a creation of the United States. Less than a week of fighting had resulted in more than a thousand Panamanian deaths and a few hundred U.S. casualties. Pentagon officials called Operation Just Cause a success in every respect, a notable contrast with the foul-ups of the Grenada invasion of 1983. Noriega was not captured. During the fighting he eluded his U.S. pursuers and took refuge in the papal nunciature, remaining there for nine days until the papal nuncio, himself under intense pressure from U.S. officials, persuaded him to surrender. The Panamanian government could guarantee neither his safety nor his prosecution in Panama, and despite the lack of an agreement on extradition with the United States, Noriega was whisked off to Miami to stand trial.[1]

In marked contrast to Reagan's spirited addresses on the Central American crises a few years earlier, Bush made no mention of Cuba or the Soviet Union in explaining why he had ordered military action in Panama. In some respects, the Panama affair of December 1989 mirrored that of November 1903, when Theodore Roosevelt had used the U.S. navy to create the forced alliance with the new republic of Panama. An undeniable beneficiary of the intervention, the Panamanian president Guillermo Endara voiced Panamanian ambivalence about the country's relation with the United States when he declared that the Christmas invasion of 1989 was "like a kick in the head. . . . I would have been happier without an intervention."[2]

Hemispheric Dreams

Endara's remarks conveyed a cynicism about the U.S. role in the hemisphere and revived old worries that the Panama invasion signaled a reversion to the unilateralism of earlier years and the rejection of cooperation with other hemispheric governments. Something different occurred, for reasons only marginally related to the rapid decline and collapse of the Soviet Union and the parallel weakening of the anticommunist dynamic within the inter-American system. The institutional character of the hemispheric system changed rapidly in the last decade of the twentieth century and with it the relations among the countries of the Americas and the challenges and problems they confronted. Governments persisted in identifying and debating these issues according to domestic political priorities, but hemispheric political leaders acknowledged that their resolution would require a collective approach. Unilateral action might have the advantage of movement without the restrictions imposed by multilateral organizations but suffered from an undeniable liability. Without the cooperation of other hemispheric governments, the United States could not effectively protect its interests or ensure stability.

In some areas, such as efforts to promote hemispheric trade, there were ambitious undertakings. Six months after dispatching U.S. military forces against Panama, Bush announced a new hemispheric economic regime, the Enterprise of the Americas Initiative (EAI), which echoed sentiments expressed by Woodrow Wilson, Franklin D. Roosevelt, and John F. Kennedy, but went beyond earlier endeavors by connecting free trade with debt relief, promotion of investment, and environmental concerns. Bush linked the EAI to the Uruguay round of the General Agreement on Tariffs and Trade and particularly to completion of the North American Free Trade Agreement (NAFTA) between Mexico, the United States, and Canada. The inspiration for NAFTA came not from Washington but from President Carlos Salinas de Gortari of Mexico. The project was born in the hope and desperation of the dominant Partido Revolucionario Institucional (PRI) party to revitalize an economy devastated by debt and high unemployment and to restore its withering political fortunes in the dynamic north, where the opposition National Action Party had fared well. By the late 1980s, when the Harvard-educated Salinas became president, the north had become the country's most impressive economic and its most volatile political region. The solution to the country's economic woes, Salinas argued, lay in cultivating northern business and political elites by reducing industrial subsidies, privatizing many of the state-owned properties, and promoting free trade, especially with the United States, Mexico's and Canada's largest trading partner. At a time when European and Pacific Rim nations were fashioning economic blocs and absorbing investment dollars, the logic of a North American variant—the union of 360 million people in a $7-trillion economy—proved compelling.[3]

For two or three years in the early 1990s, the rhetoric emanating from Washington indicated that multilateral cooperation had replaced the strategic globalism central to U.S. policy during the previous decade. North American leaders did not go so far as to endorse the One America concept of security, but they increasingly defined issues and problems as the common concerns of hemispheric governments. As Secretary of State James Baker said, "Democracy; development; drugs; debt; trade; migration; the environment; [and] nuclear proliferation . . . are neither North American nor Latin American responsibilities. They are the common challenges that we are going to have to confront together to shape successfully our shared destiny." Leaders of the largest Latin American nations and Canada, which assumed full membership in the OAS in 1990, subscribed to these priorities. Yet Baker was quick to remind his hemispheric audience (as had Wilson, Franklin D. Roosevelt, and Kennedy) of the primacy of the U.S. model in this presumably collective endeavor: "The United States enjoys political stability, peacetime succession of power, *unquestioned civilian authority,* and the steady expansion of human rights. . . . We are committed to helping Latin America wage that successful democratic struggle as well."[4]

When a Democratic administration under President Bill Clinton took office in January 1993, descriptions of the hemispheric relationship emanating from Washington reached new rhetorical heights. Five months before the December Summit of the Americas in Miami (already referred to as "the capital of Latin America" and "Havana, USA"), Vice President Al Gore hosted a dinner at the U.S. Naval Observatory for a newly formed hemispheric Encounter Group of playwrights, academics, political leaders, and social commentators representing a broad range of social and political views. The occasion for the gathering was a frank discussion of the rapid political and economic changes taking place in the hemisphere and what they portended as well as a reconsideration of the Uruguayan José Enrique Rodó's comparison in his essay *Ariel* (1900) of the pragmatic and material North American with his spiritual and presumably ineffectual Latin neighbor to the south. A few expressed some apprehension that the atmosphere in the sessions would be contentious, but the discussions turned out to be civil, even cordial. Such words as "Pan-Americanism" and "inter-Americanism" failed to elicit angry responses from Latin American and

Caribbean delegates about North American domination. As James Lemoyne, formerly the Central American bureau chief for the *New York Times,* remarked, "Nobody talked about 'imperialism', [or] about anti-Americanism, about 'the revolution', about coup d'etats and armies. That was not possible five, even three years ago."[5]

Other participants expressed some doubts about the hemispheric future. By the mid-1990s, Latin American governments had either dismantled or at least reduced the cumbersome and inefficient bureaucratic and mercantile states in their adoption of market economic philosophies. They had also incorporated sizable numbers of their populations into the political culture. Whether these changes would lead ultimately to middle-class societies and address the poverty continuing to afflict much of Latin America remained an uncertainty. While Orlando Patterson applauded the creation of an "ecumenical America" linking the U.S. East with the Caribbean, the Southwest with Mexico, and southern California with Asia, his less optimistic colleagues, among them, the distinguished sociologist Seymour Martin Lipset, deplored the decline of political participation and other forms of civic engagement in the United States at a critical moment in the Americas. Perhaps the most telling demurral came from the writer Richard Rodríguez at the November plenary session. Responding to a comment that hemispheric unity rested on a willingness to abandon the ways of one's country of birth for those of the new country of residence. Rodríguez solemnly observed that Puerto Ricans and Mexicans and, by implication, most Latin American and Caribbean peoples who migrate to the United States rarely discarded their culture in the process. They migrated to the United States not to absorb its storied political freedoms or traditions but to work.[6]

Representatives of those governments participating in the Summit of the Americas in Miami expressed few doubts about the prospects of hemispheric unity. In sweeping language, they resolved to strengthen democracy throughout Latin America and the Caribbean and reinforced their pledge to create a free trade area for the Americas by 2005 as well as eradicate poverty and discrimination and provide access to those seeking a quality education. At the summit's closing session, Clinton extolled the willingness of negotiators to create a new framework for hemispheric initiatives. Four years later, when delegates convened in Santiago, Chile, at the decade's second Summit of the Americas, their enthusiasm for lofty projects of hemispheric integration had diminished very little, despite persuasive evidence that the neoliberal capitalist model had probably exacerbated old social and economic inequities, even in the United States and Canada. Except perhaps for hemispheric economic integration, the solution for most of the summit's goals lay not with the United States but with Latin American and Caribbean governments. Several Latin American nations led by Brazil created a southern economic bloc (Mercosur) and in 1999 commenced trade negotiations with the European Union. Their intent was to counter what they perceived as a North American ploy to use the Free Trade Area of the Americas as an economic vehicle for hemispheric political domination.[7] In late 2002, the Mercosur nations (Argentina, Brazil, Paraguay, and Uruguay) and two affiliates (Bolivia and Chile) took an important step toward regional integration by approving a plan that permits their 250 million people to work and live in any member country and enjoy the same rights as citizens of the country in which they reside. No NAFTA government has suggested anything so far-reaching.

Despite the flowering of such subregional associations as NAFTA and Mercosur, the enthusiasm for a united hemisphere has persisted. At the 2001 summit in Quebec City, promotion of democracy, respect for human rights, and economic development remained central concerns, though in the final declaration hemispheric leaders voiced some apprehension about the dangers to civilian rule and social stability by organized crime, paramilitary forces, and corruption. In sweeping phrases, they dedicated themselves to compliance with the International Labor Organization's Declaration on Fundamental Principles and Rights of Work, affirmed their belief that economic and social development and democracy were essential to combating poverty, and dutifully acknowledged the dissonant voices of those attending the Indigenous Conclave of the Americas and the Indigenous Peoples Summit of the Americas, at which participants had questioned the political and economic wisdom expressed at summits one and two. Contrary to the pessimism about development and its costs that circulated at these countersummits, those gathering at summit three in Quebec City summed up their labors with a resounding commitment: "We do not fear globalization nor are we blinded by its allure," they declared. "We are united in our determination to leave to future generations a Hemisphere that is democratic and prosperous, more just and generous, a Hemisphere where no one is left behind. We are committed to making this the century of the Americas."[8]

Hemispheric Realities

The achievement of such a lofty aspiration will depend on much more than the resolution or, frankly, the mitigation of continuing nagging issues ranging from drug trafficking and immigration to the fragility of democratic political institutions and the limits of liberal market mechanisms to address unemployment, underemployment, and social inequities. Fundamental differences persist between the governments of the Americas and within individual countries over the most expedient and humane way to deal with these problems. Few would disagree that narcotics trafficking threatens not only the political and judicial system but the social well-being of several Latin American countries. Too many North Americans are loath to admit their involvement and the U.S. government's complicity in the dramatic development of this odious trade during the cold war or persist in believing that its resolution depends on the use of force. Modern debates over immigration and the viability of hemispheric community resonate with comments and homilies from the early twentieth century about cultural differences as explanation for Latin America's alleged backwardness or how the West and particularly the United States may be perilously close to cultural death because of unassimilable immigrants.

Throughout Latin America and the Caribbean in the post–cold war years—with the notable exception of Cuba—democracy, capitalism, the free market, and privatization presumably triumphed over authoritarian governments and the statist economic models of the past. In Mexico, for example, the numbers of nationalized industries shrank from two thousand to a small number in the power, petroleum, and petrochemicals industries, and in 2000 the candidate of the major opposition party (National Action), Vicente Fox, won a stupendous victory in the presidential election over the reigning Institutional Revolutionary Party (PRI), which had held power since the late 1920s. But levels of economic growth were uneven, and income inequality and unemployment remained distressingly high. From Mexico to Argentina, the World Bank reported in early 2002, one-third of 502 million people lived in poverty. Alarmingly, income inequities ranged highest in Mexico and Brazil—where more than 50 percent of the population of Latin America and the Caribbean reside—countries enjoying some of the most impressive growth rates since World War II. A few months later, the Latin Barometer, a survey of more than eighteen thousand people in seventeen Latin American countries, noted widespread public dissatisfaction with economic policy, corruption, unemployment, and poverty.

Neither was the much-touted democratic consolidation of the post–cold war hemisphere an unqualified success story. Certainly, military regimes had relinquished power and elections became the norm, but the political "distress list" of Latin America and the Caribbean early in the twenty-first century included countries once deemed safely within the democratic orbit. Colombia remains a deeply fragmented nation, devastated by a thirty-year guerrilla war in which three armies—representing the government, the guerrillas, and the paramilitaries—share power and influence with narcotraffickers and their legions of hired killers. The parallels of this conflict with the Thousand-Day War of the early twentieth century are unsettling. Colombians in 1902 feared U.S. intervention if the war persisted. Liberal rebel leaders became apprehensive about their diminished control over their followers and the lessening enthusiasm for their cause as the war continued. Colombians in 2002 are also deeply apprehensive about U.S. military aid to a Colombian government determined to suppress a guerrilla insurgency that has lost much of its credibility with the public. Admittedly, U.S. aid may be critical, but it might also revive the nationalist credibility of the insurgents.

In neighboring Venezuela, an electorate that overwhelmingly chose the populist Lieutenant-Colonel Hugo Chávez president in 1998 had within two years become disillusioned with his political arbitrariness and his failure to rejuvenate a stagnant economy. Chávez irritated Washington with his overtures to Fidel Castro and his opposition to wider U.S. involvement in Colombia. In April 2002 the Venezuelan military, alert to the growing domestic opposition to Chávez, removed him, but massive demonstrations on the deposed president's behalf resulted in his restoration a few days later. Six months earlier, the United States had supported the Inter-American Democratic Charter, which provided for OAS deliberation in the event of the unconstitutional removal of a member government. Although President George Walker Bush did not immediately condemn the coup, as had most hemispheric leaders, the obligatory criticism of Chávez's ouster by the United States in the OAS appeared at best halfhearted and revived lingering doubts about U.S. commitment to democratic processes. The beleaguered Venezuelan president held on to power, but the nation continued its downward spiral into a social and political crisis that the OAS seemed incapable of resolving.[9]

Political problems also befell the Brazilian government, which had ambitious plans to replace the United States as the major economic power player in South America but suffered a financial crisis in 1998 similar to that experienced by Mexico in 1994. Both cases led to billion-dollar bailout packages. In fall 2002, disgruntled Brazilians repudiated a decade of austerity policy by electing Luiz Inácio Lula da Silva, a former labor leader, as president. The election of Alejandro Toledo in Peru in July 2001, it was generally acknowledged, formally ended ten years of authoritarian rule under Alberto Fujimori, who had fled into exile in Japan to avoid prosecution for corruption; but Toledo did not bring about the fundamental institutional reforms vital to the creation of a modern democratic society. Equally alarming was the financial calamity afflicting Argentina, whose government had adopted U.S.-sponsored financial prescriptions—among them, establishing the Argentine peso at par with the dollar—in the early 1990s but a decade later suffered a massive economic collapse and a dramatic loss of public faith in the nation's political and financial institutions. In the 1980s, Central America had been devastated by guerrilla war in Nicaragua and El Salvador and had attained a fragile peace in the following decade. The contemporary dilemma for Central America, wrote an investigative journalist in late 2001, lay in preventing seven small, vulnerable countries traumatized by corruption, narcotics trafficking, gang wars, urban poverty, and overpopulation from becoming "Colombianized," a phrase conjuring up the most distressing images of political and social collapse and in some minds justifying a military solution. In March 2002, the Washington Office on Latin America gloomily noted that a decade of U.S. assistance to Colombia had not only failed to stem the flow of illicit drugs northward or strengthen human rights or democracy but exacerbated human rights conditions in that country.[10]

But the often virulent anti-Americanism typically associated with such shifts of public opinion did not occur. In a survey of the Americas in the early twenty-first century, Peter Hakim, president of the Inter-American Dialogue, noted that the majority of Latin American and Caribbean peoples did not indict the United States for their political and economic setbacks in the 1990s. Most governments of the continent looked to Washington as a critical player in their efforts to deal with pressing national problems. Yet fundamental suspicions remained. Reforms deemed essential by the United States often carried unpopular and familiar consequences such as double-digit unemployments rates and financial austerity. Few governments in the Americas continued to voice much support for Washington's security agenda and the interventionist logic accompanying it. By the end of the cold war, membership in the OAS included thirty-five states and forty-one nonhemispheric observers; and the Inter-American Development Bank, twenty-eight hemispheric and sixteen nonhemispheric participants. But only twenty-one governments subscribed to the Inter-American Treaty of Reciprocal Assistance (the Rio treaty), the cornerstone of the hemispheric security system erected after World War II. (In the early 1960s the OAS General Assembly dropped the requirement that governments wishing to join the OAS must also subscribe to the Rio treaty.)

Clinton's failure to obtain fast-track authority for the Free Trade Area of the Americas revived doubts throughout the hemisphere about Washington's commitment to free trade. President Bush succeeded in winning that authority, but concerns on Capitol Hill about environmental and labor standards south of the Rio Grande soon aroused Latin resentments about pressures from the north. Fears about a deepening quagmire in the Andes, Washington's antipathy toward Venezuelan President Chávez, the troubling economic and social conditions in Nicaragua and Haiti, and the worsening of U.S.–Cuban relations, among other developments, prompted doubts over predictions about a new era in the Americas. Even where relations had dramatically improved in the 1990s, as with Mexico and Canada in the creation of NAFTA, the intrusion of "intermestic" issues—trade disputes, narcotics trafficking, immigration, environmental damage identified with transnational companies, and U.S. border security in the aftermath of the September 2001 bombings of the Pentagon and the World Trade Center—called into question the belief that the twenty-first century belonged to the Americas.[11]

The hemispheric condition was as troubled in the early years of the new century as in the age of José Martí, who died believing in the liberating power of revolution and fearing the power of the United States, and of Theodore Roosevelt, who feared the consequences of not using that power to quell what he perceived as disorder and chaos in a turbulent Caribbean. Martí invoked the example of Simón Bolívar in his apprehension of the U.S. menace to the other America; Roosevelt transformed the sentiments expressed in the famous paragraph of President James Monroe's December 1823 message to Congress into a mandate for the exercise of police power in the Americas. In such an international atmosphere of suspicion and fear, those calling for a hemisphere of common purpose and aspiration encountered disbelief and sometimes ridicule.

The creation of NAFTA and its proposed expansion in a hemispheric free trade area is perhaps the most oft-cited example of the prospects for uniting the Americas in a common economic if not political and cultural union. In the mid-1990s, a trio of social scientists looking at the impact of NAFTA concluded that the peoples of each country clung to their distinctive cultures yet shared a diminished confidence in governmental institutions, the media, schools, legal systems, the military, and churches. A significant minority of Canadian and one-fourth of Mexican respondents seriously questioned what purpose their respective border with the United States served. A prominent Canadian historian commented on the death of anti-Americanism among Canadians despite their persistent affirmation that a Canadian is "not American." In the aftermath of the Helms-Burton Act of 1996, which permitted U.S. citizens to bring suit against foreign nationals "trafficking" in property confiscated in Cuba after 1959, Canadians and Mexicans quickly discovered they enjoyed no special relationship with the United States. But the myth persisted. A short time after his inauguration, President Bush expressed his satisfaction with the prospects of North American integration: "With Canada, our partner in NATO and NAFTA, we share not just a border but a bond of goodwill. Our ties of history and heritage with Mexico are just as deep."[12]

Ties That Bind

In such platitudes and contradictions we have a metaphor for the modern Western Hemisphere and especially for Greater North America and the smaller countries and European and U.S. dependencies in the Caribbean and Central America. Although there are undeniable similarities, what is happening in the Americas does not easily conform to globalization or Europeanization, as some observers contend. The increasing dollarization in the Western Hemisphere is something different from the use of the Euro. Americanization and Europeanization are dissimilar cultural dynamics. Throughout Western Europe the issues of transnational labor migration and immigration often appear to be as volatile and controversial as in the United States (and, increasingly, in Canada), and on both sides of the Atlantic remittances of immigrants to their home countries play an increasingly important role in the income of sending countries. But the dynamics of these and parallel factors in the cultures and economies of the Western Hemisphere and particularly of Greater North America have followed a pattern distinct from that experienced by Europeans. Remittances from the 15 million Latin Americans and Caribbeans who have migrated to the United States since 1980 to their home countries reached $20 billion in 2000, an amount more significant for several receiving nations in the Western Hemisphere than moneys sent by foreign laborers in Western Europe to their homelands in southeastern Europe, North Africa, and the eastern Mediterranean. At the current rate of growth, remittances from the United States to Latin American and the Caribbean will reach $300 billion in the first decade of the twenty-first century.[13]

In several countries in the Americas, these moneys have become vital to the national economy. According to official calculations by the Mexican government, Mexicans received $9 billion from relatives in the United States in 2001, a 35 percent increase from the preceding year. Informal estimates of remittances from Mexicans in the United States reached $10 billion in 2002, an amount equal to national earnings from tourism and two-thirds of that gained from oil exports. Remittances of the 2 million Dominicans in the United States to their homeland were twelve times what the country received in official developmental aid and three times the value of Dominican exports. Remittances of the 1 million Haitians in this country in 1999 were estimated at $720 million, 17 percent of Haiti's gross domestic product, twice the value of the country's exports, and four times that of official development assistance. Remittances of Jamaicans amounted to 12 percent of gross domestic product and more than thirty-five times official development assistance. Hondurans sent back $400 million to their homeland in 2000, a sum more than twice Honduras's earnings from tourism and equal to the amount received in official development assistance. Remittances from Nicaraguans in the United States in 1999 amounted to $345 million—informal estimates place the amount at $700 million—exceeding foreign direct investment, twice that earned in coffee, and three times the amount earned from shrimp and lobster sales. Since 1959, 1 million Cubans have migrated to the United States. By 2000, their remittances, limited by U.S. law to $100 per month per family, reached an astonishing $1 billion annually. Because most of these migrants came from whiter and wealthier Cuban families, the moneys returned to the island are restoring the old, socially stratified Cuba the revolution had presumably demolished.

For most South American countries, the U.S. connection is less critical, of course, but four stand out in the official estimates of foreign remittances: Colombia, Brazil, Ecuador, and Peru. Remittances from the 2 million Colombians in the United States in 2000 were calculated at 50 percent of the earnings from coffee exports. Some 700,000 Brazilians lived in the United States at the end of the twentieth century. Together with the 350,000 Brazilians in Paraguay and another 250,000 Brazilians of Japanese ancestry in Japan, they remitted almost $2 billion annually to the home country, an amount nearly two thousand times greater than official development assistance. In 2001, Ecuador had one of the most rapidly growing rates of remittances in South America. The 500,000 Ecuadorans living outside the country, 250,000 of them in the United States, sent back more than $1.2 billion in remittances, second only to oil exports as a source of foreign currency, five times the amount earned by banana exports, three times larger than tourism moneys, and twice what Ecuador gains in foreign direct investment. The 250,000 Peruvians living in the United States in 2000 along with other Peruvians living outside their home country, most in Chile and Bolivia, sent back more than $800 million to the home country in 1999, twice the amount received by Peru in developmental assistance and greater than the moneys received from agricultural and fish exports.[14]

In one sense, the role these rapidly increasing sums play in the local economies confirms the benefits of Americanization, or what is sometimes described as soft imperialism, a term occasionally used by those who believe cultural influence is a preferable and certainly less violent means of achieving U.S. goals than military power. In the early decades of the twentieth century, North Americans often extolled the moral uplift accompanying the spread of material goods and the incorporation of ever larger number of peoples into a market economy. The fostering of a consumer culture in the United States, they believed, had not only played a vital role in the dramatic economic expansion of the age but also helped to bring more stability to the industrial workplace by the presumably unassailable logic that a laborer who is also a consumer will subscribe to the credos of material self-improvement. In the 1990s, two familiar structures of the U.S. consumer culture—the shopping mall and the supermarket—began to dot the Latin American urban landscape.

But there have been unanticipated, even revolutionary, consequences of the Americanization of the hemisphere, particularly in the circum-Caribbean, where U.S. military and economic power has been so pervasive. Critics often attribute the rise of anti-Americanism in these places to the resentments of U.S. intervention and Washington's support of antidemocratic governments in the name of stability and progress. What was obscured in the Americanization of vulnerable but proud cultures, especially in Cuba, was the legacy of what most North Americans presumed to be a success story: the inability of these economies to fulfill the ever-increasing demands of a consumer culture. In the 1950s, Castro's revolutionary message resonated among those middle-class Cubans who had absorbed North American cultural values (or had converted to Protestantism) but who had become disillusioned with the political system and frustrated with the cost of living. In a story too well known to be detailed here, the triumphant Cuban revolution exported the counterrevolution in the migration of disaffected Cubans to the United States and undertook the task of removing not only the U.S. political and economic grip on the island but also the appeal of North American cultural preferences among Cubans. The first has largely succeeded, but the second has not, a reminder of the bonds between the hemisphere's cold war adversaries. Ironically, considering the animosity between the U.S. and Cuban governments, the Americanization of Cubans has been more distinctive than that of Puerto Ricans, who have lived under U.S. tutelage for more than a century.[15]

The remittances reinforce human as well as economic linkages, yet they do not sufficiently explain the distinctive bonds among diverse nations of the

Americas with the United States any more than the expressions about "special relationships" between nations or presumed convergence of values between their peoples. Too often what is missing from these calculations is an intangible as relevant in the America of Martí and Roosevelt as it is today: fear, particularly fear of the consequences of doing nothing or doing too little. Fear has played an underappreciated role in uniting as well as dividing the nations of the Americas, and fear is as powerful a dynamic in explaining U.S. policy as the proverbial arrogance often rightly attributed to Washington in its dealings with other hemispheric countries and especially its relations with its North American neighbors and the smaller countries of the Caribbean and Central America. Fear as much as purpose drove Martí and Roosevelt, Castro and Kennedy, and in the post–cold war hemisphere it continues to befuddle those who have power and must act or react to crises. In its relations with former adversaries such as Vietnam and the People's Republic of China the United States may practice what is euphemistically described as engagement; but in dealing with Cuba, the U.S. government follows a different agenda and not only because Congress has set many of the rules for this nation's policy toward the island but because fear dictates that policy. Theodore Roosevelt's generation feared a Cuban revolution that menaced U.S. property and defied Washington. More than a century later, those fears remain, but nowadays they are explained less by any perceived Cuban threat to U.S. interests than by other uncertainties, among them the belief that openings toward Cuba would be politically risky or that an easing of relations might produce further waves of emigrants from the island or, more ominously, that the fall of Castro and the collapse of Cuban socialism will be followed by chaos.

In such an atmosphere of uncertainty, those who govern sometimes act as much from apprehension or desperation as from purpose or conviction. When Salinas proposed the free trade pact with the United States, he did so out of fears that Mexico's economic future depended on foreign, principally U.S., investment. Brian Mulroney brought Canada into the agreement out of fears that Mexico would eventually supplant Canada as the number one trading partner of the United States. Both the U.S. Congress and the president, often at loggerheads over U.S. policy in the hemisphere, are wary over the deteriorating political and social climate in Colombia, fearing that the entire Andean region will be convulsed. In September 1994, President Clinton threatened to use force to remove the Haitian military and reinstall the deposed Haitian leader Jean-Bertrand Aristide only when he became convinced that failure to act would result in yet another wave of Haitian refugees fleeing the island. In the end, the Haitian generals stepped down and U.S. troops moved onto the island without a military confrontation, but the entire affair, called Operation Uphold Democracy, demonstrated that fear as much as purpose or resolve can be a powerful incentive to act. Washington's economic assistance to Puerto Rico proved critical in the raising of per capita income from $121 in 1940 to more than $6,800 a half century later, but at the close of the twentieth century the residents of eleven other Caribbean countries and dependencies enjoyed higher per capita incomes. Most Puerto Ricans and an increasing number of influential U.S. political leaders express dissatisfaction with the current rela-tionship, yet the prospects of changing it—either the "perfecting" of the commonwealth, independence, or statehood, each of which is technically permissible—generally founder out of fear and uncertainty over the conse-quences.[16]

In *The Promise of American Life* (1909), Herbert Croly described a hemi-sphere in which the uncertainties and discord in several Latin American and Caribbean states (and Canada's relation with Great Britain) presented formi-dable obstacles to the building of a peaceful "American international system" inspired by the U.S. commitment to "order and good government" in the Americas. Almost a century later, the convictions he expressed about Wash-ington's mission in the hemisphere and the dilemmas confronting the United States have been muted somewhat by sobering reminders of the limits of U.S. power. Croly's observations and recommendations and the doubts his con-temporaries expressed about them are still relevant to understanding the modern hemisphere, however much the Americas have changed in the twen-tieth century. Canada is now a full member in the inter-American system, market economies and civilian governments prevail almost everywhere, and the institutional and human bonds between hemispheric governments and peoples have surpassed even the most optimistic predictions of the early twen-tieth century. But in the euphoric prognostications that this will be the century of the Americas, it is well to remember that for all their differences Martí and Roosevelt shared the apprehension that their class, whether out of indiffer-ence or economic self-interest, would abandon the responsibility of leader-ship. Without their critical role in maintaining unity, institutions counted for less. That common fear, more than any of the formal bonds between hemi-spheric governments, may very well be the most critical for the future of the Western Hemisphere.

And that is why I believe that the Americas of Roosevelt and Martí may pro-vide more insights into the hemispheric future and especially that of Greater

North America than the cold war years. For the United States at 2000, immigration has become a determining factor in population growth, even more so than in the first decade of the twentieth century. In the 2000 census, peoples from Latin America and the Caribbean accounted for more than 50 percent of the foreign-born population of the United States. Their participation in the U.S. labor force, as it was in the early twentieth century, is a reminder of the continuing dependence of certain sectors of the U.S. economy on foreign workers. Their visibility in the population and, increasingly, in small towns has revived anti-immigration and nativist movements. In the early years of the twentieth century, a fundamental challenge confronting some hemispheric governments—Brazil, Argentina, Canada, and the United States—was the place of the newcomer in society and that person's relationship with governments at all levels. For Canada and especially the United States, which in the early twenty-first century is undertaking the enormous social experiment of assimilating 31 million immigrants into society, that question remains as vexing now as it was in the early twentieth century.[17]

Admittedly, the hemisphere of our times no longer suffers the sharp, sometimes violent conflicts between capital and labor of the pre–World War I years, and the United States does not exercise a policing role in the Caribbean with the same arrogance and moral self-righteousness Roosevelt extolled and Martí condemned. But the relevance of those years to the modern hemisphere cannot be dismissed. The fundamental question of our times is not the confrontation between industrial laborer and magnate or country baron and hapless rural worker, and the harshness of industrial and rural life for ordinary people of the early twentieth century may no longer be so commonplace. Roosevelt grew frustrated over what he perceived as "race suicide" among whites; Martí feared that Afro-Cubans and by implication other people of color would subordinate nation to racial identity. Some modern social commentators are viewing ethnicity and race and especially the declining birthrate among whites with a pessimism unsettlingly similar to that displayed in early-twentieth-century tracts.

Modern economic development in the hemisphere, especially in the United States, Canada, and Mexico, is strikingly different from that of the early decades of the twentieth century. Yet throughout the modern hemisphere, including the United States, disparities in income and wealth are reviving concerns about the politics of rich and poor and wealth versus commonwealth. Even NAFTA contains provisions pitting local and state governments against transnational companies in disputes that are resolved not in courts but by arbitral boards. A transnational hemispheric economy based on the expansion of NAFTA may create unprecedented opportunities for development and trade, but it also reinforces the power of transnational companies and, inevitably, tests the loyalties of political leaders and the constituencies they are elected to serve. The freedom to buy may flourish in a market economy, but democracy may wither in a market society.

Perhaps the most deceptive beliefs in the Americas of Roosevelt and Martí— and the most relevant to our times—held that economic development and the parallel encouragement of material consumption will bring forth more prosperous, more peaceful, and more progressive societies and that unity and integration are more or less the same thing. The experience of the hemisphere in the twentieth century has neither validated nor disproved those beliefs. If the twenty-first is to be the century of the Americas, it may be prudent for us to remember that experience, its promise and its costs. And however much Canadians and North Americans and Mexicans and Cubans and Puerto Ricans and other nationalities of the Americas continue to claim an identity distinctive from that of their hemispheric neighbors, we should recall the remarks of the Mexican diplomat Luís Quintanilla during World War II: "We are all in the same boat." His observation is a reminder that countries and cultures do not always have to profess common values and political beliefs in order to be linked by ties that bind.

Notes

Full citations are provided only for those works not listed in the bibliography.

Introduction

1. The American Assembly, Columbia University, *U.S. National Interests and the Western Hemisphere,* ed. Albert Fishlow and James R. Jones (New York, 1998), 3.
2. Mark Peceny, "The Inter-American System as a Liberal 'Pacific Union'," *Latin American Research Review* 29:3 (1994): 188–201, reviews some of the literature on the Americas in the post–cold war economic order.
3. Quoted in Langley, *The Americas in the Age of Revolution, 1750–1850,* 240.
4. O'Brien, *The Revolutionary Mission: American Enterprise in Latin America, 1900–1945,* 329–30.
5. On comparisons between the United States and Latin America in the era of the Latin American wars of independence, see John J. Johnson, *A Hemisphere Apart: The Foundations of United States Policy Toward Latin America* (Baltimore, 1990).
6. Zea, "Identidad continental multiracial y multicultural," *Cuadernos Americanos* [Mexico] 80 (March-April 2000): 15.

1 Theodore Roosevelt's America

1. Quoted in Henry May, *The End of American Innocence: A Study of the First Years of Our Own Time, 1912–1917* (New York, 1917), 8.
2. *Theodore Roosevelt: An Autobiography* (1913; repr. New York, 1926), 362–65.
3. "Buffalo Bill's Wild West and Congress of Rough Riders of the World" (Chicago, 1893), 22; see also White, "Frederick Jackson Turner and Buffalo Bill," in James R. Grossman, ed., *The Frontier in American Cultutre* (Berkeley and Los Angeles, 1994), 9–11; Turner, "The Significance of the Frontier in American History," in Allan G. Bogue, Thomas D. Phillips, and James E. Wright, eds., *The West of the American People* (Itasca, Ill., 1970), 10.

4. Rowland Berthoff, *The Republic of the Dispossessed: The Exceptional Old-European Consensus in America* (Columbia, Mo., 1997), 21; Richard Maxwell Brown, "Violence," in Clyde Milner II, Carol A. O'Connor, Martha A. Sandweiss, eds., *Oxford History of the American West* (New York, 1994), 399, 415–18.

5. Alan Trachtenberg, *The Incorporation of America: Culture and Society in the Gilded Age* (New York, 1982), 28; Limerick, *Legacy of Conquest*, 260–61.

6. Slotkin, *Fatal Environment*, 420.

7. Quoted in Alan Dawley, *Struggles for Justice: Social Responsibility and the Liberal State* (Cambridge, 1991), 29. For Teller's comments, see Frederick Pike, *The United States and Latin America: Myths and Stereotypes of Civilization and Nature* (Austin, 1992), 174.

8. Dawes is quoted in Limerick, *Legacy of Conquest*, 198; see also Larry McMurtry, "Broken Promises," in *New York Review of Books* (October 23, 1997), 14.

9. Carlos G. Vélez-Ibañez, *Border Visions: Mexican Cultures of the Southwest United States* (Tucson, 1996), 78–81, 94–95; Limerick, *Legacy of Conquest*, 242–43; Richard Griswold del Castillo, *The Treaty of Guadalupe Hidalgo: A Legacy of Conflict* (Norman, Okla., 1990), 108–11, 118–21, 128–30.

10. Paul J. Vanderwood, *Disorder and Progress: Bandits, Police, and Mexican Development* (1981; repr. Wilmington, Del., 1992), 50–51.

11. W. Dirk Raat, *Mexico and the United States: Ambivalent Vistas* (Athens, Ga., 1992), 86–87; Leopoldo Zea, *El positivismo y la circunstancia mexicana* (Mexico City, 1943), 179.

12. Mira Wilkins, *The Emergence of Multinational Enterprise: American Business Abroad from the Colonial Era to 1914* (Cambridge, 1970), 115.

13. Stephen H. Haber, *Industry and Underdevelopment: The Industrialization of Mexico, 1890–1940* (Stanford, 1989), 60–61, 190–93. See also John H. Coatsworth, *Growth Against Development: The Economic Impact of Railroads in Porfirian Mexico* (DeKalb, Ill., 1981), 4–6, 10–15.

14. Quoted in Richard Salvucci, "Texas, Tyrants, and Trade with Mexico," in Richard Salvucci, ed., *Latin America and the World Economy: Dependency and Beyond* (Lexington, Mass., 1996), 68. See also David Pletcher, *Rails, Mines, and Progress: Seven American Promoters in Mexico, 1867–1911* (Ithaca, N.Y., 1958), 2–3, 24–25, 308–09; and William Beezley, *Judas at the Jockey Club* (Lincoln, Neb., 1987), 8–11.

15. Vanderwood, *Disorder and Progress*, 63–67, 70–71, 102; Charles A. Hale, *The Transformation of Liberalism in Late-Nineteenth Century Mexico* (Princeton, 1989), 232–33, 237. For a different perspective on the Mexican countryside during the Porfiriato, see Beezley, *Judas at the Jockey Club*, 67–68, 78–85, 128–29. On the nature of Díaz's control over regional elites, see John Tutino, *From Intervention to Revolution in Mexico: Social Bases of Agrarian Violence, 1750–1940* (Princeton, 1986), 280–83.

16. The cultural historian Robert Kelley cautions against facile comparisons of the violent U.S. solution to the question of sectionalism (i.e., the U.S. Civil War); the Canadian accommodationist approach to Quebec; and the troublesome "Irish question" for the British. The United States was the only one of the three countries to resolve the issue—Quebec remains defiant at the end of the twentieth century, and the British eventually lost Ireland. See Kelley, *The Transatlantic Persuasion: The Liberal-Democratic Mind in the Age of Gladstone* (New York, 1969), 28–29. W. Thomas Easterbrook, *North American Patterns of Growth and Development: The Continental Context* (Toronto, 1990), 200, notes that Canadian development reflected the "pattern of dominant centres and weak margins" but that of the United States encouraged "new centres of initiative that took on a life of their own. . . . U.S. western expansion was one of power widely dispersed, and investment strategies in banking and finance, land policies, and transportation underline a frontier expansion that was free, at least in comparative terms, of central direction and control."

17. Kenneth McNaught, *The Penguin History of Canada* (London, 1988), 179. For a favorable assessment of Macdonald's national policy, see Donald Creighton, *Sir John A. Macdonald: The Old Chieftain* (Toronto, 1955).

18. As Goldwin Smith, one of those late-nineteenth-century Canadians calling for a union between the United States and English Canada similar to that between England and Scotland, commented, "Who will there be to take his place?" Quoted in McNaught, *The Penguin History of Canada*, 183.

19. Smith's bitter analysis of the reasons for Canadian backwardness in *Canada and the Canadian Question* (1891) appeared during economic hard times, which gave his arguments some credibility. Within a few years, however, the depression lifted and the appeal of continentalism sharply declined.

20. Robin Weeks, *The Relevance of Canadian History: U.S. and Imperial Perspectives* (Lanham, MD, 1988), 20–23; McNaught, *Penguin History of Canada*, 156–59, 166–67, 172–73.

21. The contemporary sociologist Max Weber described the character of modernity in the late nineteenth century when he wrote, "The Puritan wanted to work in a calling; we are forced to do so. . . . This [modern] order is now bound to the technical and economic conditons of machine production which today determine the lives of all the individuals who are born into the mechanism, not only those directly concerned with economic acquisition, with irresistible force" (quoted in Takaki, *Iron Cages*, 254).

22. Quoted in Neil Irvin Painter, *Standing at Armageddon: The United States, 1877–1919* (New York, 1987), xvii–xviii. See also Eric Hobsbawm, *The Age of Empire, 1875–1914* (New York, 1987), 44, 50–55.

23. Quoted in Thomas C. Cochran and William Miller, *The Age of Enterprise: A Social History of Industrial America* (New York, 1942), 145; see also 124–25, 129–31, 136, 139–40, 144–45, 152–53, 354–55; Martin Sklar, *The United States as a Developing Country: Studies in U.S. History in the Progressive Era and the 1920s* (New York, 1992), 32.

24. Quoted in Cochran and Miller, *Age of Enterprise*, 157. For a contrasting view, see Leonard White, *The Republican Era, 1869–1901: A Study in Administrative History* (New York, 1958), 395.

25. Veblen, *The Theory of the Leisure Class* (1899; repr. New York, 1994), 1–3; Wiebe, *The Search for Order*, 112–13.

26. Quoted in Gillis J. Harp, *Positivist Republic: Auguste Comte and the Reconstruction of American Liberalism, 1865–1920* (University Park, Pa. 1995), 9; see also Robert Wiebe, *Self-Rule: A Cultural History of American Democracy* (Chicago, 1995), 6–7.

27. Quoted in Trachtenberg, *The Incorporation of America*, 84–85.

28. Quoted in Wiebe, *The Search for Order*, 9.

29. Quoted in Edwin C. Rozwenc and Thomas Lyons, eds., *Reconstruction and the Race Problem* (Lexington, Mass., 1968), 57. For a different perspective on black-white labor relations in the South, see Gavin Wright, *Old South, New South: Revolutions in the Southern Economy Since the Civil War* (New York, 1986), 48–49, 68, 84–85.

30. Quoted in Trachtenberg, *Incorporation of America*, 77.

31. For a synopsis of the labor movement in these years, see Philip S. Foner, *History of the Labor Movement in the United States*, vol. 2, *From the Founding of the American Federation of Labor to the Emergence of American Imperialism*, 2d ed. (New York, 1975).

32. Slotkin, *Fatal Environment*, 497, 438–44, 478–87, 492–93, 496.

33. "It is clear to every thoughtful workingman, skilled or unskilled, organized or unorganized," wrote a labor editorialist, "that the time has arrived for a more perfect system of labor organization. . . . Those now styled 'unskilled laborers' must be organized in one great union so that they may not be used against each other" (quoted in Robert R. Montgomery, "'To Fight This Thing Till I Die': The Career of George Edwin McNeill," in Ronald C. Kent, Sara Markham, David R. Roediger, and Herbert Shapiro, eds., *Culture, Gender, Race, and U.S. Labor History* [Westport, Conn., 1993], 15–16).

34. One of the prosecutors reminded his listeners that the public had to confront social disorder in the city and the anarchists' sinister role in fomenting urban violence. Those on trial recognized that they had achieved a notoriety long denied them. One of them blurted out, "I despise your order; your laws, your force-propped authority. HANG ME FOR IT!" Quoted in Carl Smith, *Urban Disorder and the Shape of Belief: The Great Chicago Fire, the Haymarket Bomb, and the Model Town of Pullman* (Chicago, 1995), 129; also 6–9.

35. Perhaps the most strikingly different assessments of U.S. populism were those of Richard Hofstadter in *The Age of Reform* and Lawrence Goodwyn, *Democratic Promise: The Populist Movement in America*, published in the mid-1950s and mid-1970s, respectively. Hofstadter portrayed the populists as backward, intolerant people incapable of adapting to a modern society; Goodwyn, as a cooperative movement expressing democratic goals. Two studies focusing on the cultural and religious dynamics (as contrasted with political and economic issues) of the age are Paul Kleppner, *The Cross of Culture: A Social Analysis of Midwestern Politics, 1851–1900* (New York, 1970); and Richard Jensen, *The Winning of the Midwest: Social and Political Conflict, 1888–1896* (Chicago, 1971). For comparisons with Latin American populism, see Ferenc Szasz, "United States Populism," in Michael L. Conniff, ed., *Latin American Populism in Comparative Perspective* (Albuquerque, 1982), 191–215.

36. Michael S. Kimmel, "'Disheveled Improvisation': Agrarian Resistance to Industrialization in Late 19th Century," in Francisco O. Ramírez, ed., *Rethinking the Nineteenth Century: Contradictions and Movements* (Westport, Conn., 1988), 127. On the "money question," see Irwin Unger, *The Greenback Era: A Social and Political History of American Finance, 1865–1879* (Princeton, 1974).

37. Norman Pollack, ed., *The Populist Mind* (Indianapolis, 1967), 110–11, 156–63. See also Robert McMath, *American Populism: A Social History* (New York, 1993), 110–13, 122–23.

38. Wiebe, *Self-Rule*, 114–15; Goodwyn, "The Irony of Populism," in William F. Holmes, *American Populism* (Lexington, Mass.), 179.

39. Adams, *The Education of Henry Adams: An Autobiography* (Boston, 1927), 344.

40. Both quotations are in C. Vann Woodward, *Origins of the New South, 1877–1913* (1951; repr. Baton Rouge, 1971), 369.

41. Theodore Roosevelt gleefully left his post as assistant secretary of the navy to join a unit of volunteers, the Rough Riders, for the Cuban invasion. Roosevelt recapitulated the popular motivation for U.S. intervention when he wrote in a postwar edition of his popular multivolume work, *The Winning of the West*, that "our people as a whole went into the war, primarily, it is true, to drive out the Spaniard once for all from America; but with the fixed determination to replace his rule by a government of justice and orderly liberty." For him, more so than for his contemporaries, the war against Spain was the culminating chapter "in the expansion of the nation across the North American continent" (Roosevelt, "Foreword," *The Winning of the West*, vol. 1, *From the Alleghenies to the Mississippi, 1769–1776* (1889; repr. Lincoln, Neb., 1995), xxxiv–xxxv.

42. Henry Adams opposed annexation of the Philippines but not of Puerto Rico. He wrote, "Porto Rico [*sic*] must be taken . . .; whatever the American people might think or say about it, they would sooner or later have to police those [West Indian] islands not against Europe, but for Europe, and America too" (*The Education of Henry Adams*, 363–64).

43. Quoted in Anders Stephanson, *Manifest Destiny: American Expansionism and the Empire of Right* (New York, 1995), 99. On Hoar and the anti-imperialists, see the authoritative study by Robert Beisner, *Twelve Against Empire* (New York, 1968).

44. Quoted in Walter LaFeber, *The American Search for Opportunity, 1865–1913* (New

York, 1993), 58. See also Brooks Adams, *The Law of Civilization and Decay: An Essay on History* (New York, 1943), 334–35; Pike, *United States and Latin America*, 174–77.

45. Thomas G. Dyer, *Theodore Roosevelt and the Idea of Race* (Baton Rouge, 1980), 143–45, 168–69.

46. Frank Ninkovich, *Modernity and Power: A History of the Domino Theory in the Twentieth Century* (Chicago, 1994), xii–xiii; Carnegie to McKinley, July 27, 1898, in LaFeber, *American Search for Opportunity*, 47; Jack Eblen, *The First and Second United States Empires: Governors and Territorial Government, 1784–1912* (Pittsburgh, 1968), 8.

47. Robert Rydell, *All the World's a Fair: Visions of Empire at International Expositions, 1876–1916* (Chicago, 1984), 39–41, 127–29.

48. Root, "Porto Rico, Cuba, and the Philippines," in Robert Brown Scott, ed., *The Military and Colonial Policy of the United States: Addresses and Reports by Elihu Root* (Cambridge, 1916), 161.

49. Quoted in Walter A. McDougall, *Promised Land, Crusader State: The American Encounter with the World Since 1776)* (Boston, 1997), 105. See also John Milton Cooper, Jr., *The Warrior and the Priest: Woodrow Wilson and Theodore Roosevelt* (Cambridge, 1983), 36.

2 José Martí's America

1. Edward P. Crapol, *James G. Blaine: Architect of Empire* (Wilmington, 2000), 70–74, 118–19; David M. Pletcher, *The Diplomacy of Trade and Investment: American Expansion in the Hemisphere, 1865–1900* (Columbia, Mo., 1998), 212–13.

2. Quoted in Enrico Mario Santí, "'Our America'," the Gilded Age, and the Crisis of Latinamericanism," in Jeffrey Belnap and Raúl Fernández, eds., *José Martí's 'Our America': From National to Hemispheric Cultural Studies* (Durham, 1998), 179.

3. Ibid., 188–89; Mary Louise Pratt, *Imperial Eyes: Travel Writing and Transculturation* (London, 1992), 189; Louis A. Pérez, Jr., *On Becoming Cuban: Identity, Nationality, and Culture* (Chapel Hill, 1999), 46.

4. Whitaker, *Western Hemisphere Idea*, 63–65, 70–75; Whitaker's account of Pan-Americanism in the late nineteenth century is based on Leopoldo Zea, *Dos etapas del pensamiento en Hispanoamérica* (Mexico City, 1949). See also Stanley J. Stein and Barbara H. Stein, *The Colonial Heritage of Latin America: Essays on Economic Dependence in Perspective* (New York, 1970), 170–71, 174–83. On Latin America's appropriation of foreign political and economic models, Susan and Peter Calvert caution, "It was not the decision to adopt Western political models in Latin America which proved problematic—they were the only models available and were in any case adapted—but rather the way such models functioned in states where national social and economic systems did not at that stage exist" (*Argentina: Political Culture and Instability* [Pittsburgh, 1989], 48).

5. Jesús María Henao and Gerardo Arrubla (J. Fred Rippy, trans. and ed.), *History of Colombia* (1910; repr. Chapel Hill, 1938), 485. See also Frank Safford, "Politics, Ideology, and Society in Post-Independence Spanish America," in Leslie Bethell, ed., *The Cambridge History of Latin America*, vol. 3, *From Independence to c. 1870* (New York, 1985), 409–10; and for the parallel "Federalist Wars" in Venezuela, Catalina Banko, *Las luchas federalistas en Venezuela* (Caracas, 1996).

6. Stephen Randall, *Colombia and the United States: Hegemony and Interdependence* (Athens, Ga., 1992), 60.

7. Malcolm Deas, "Venezuela, Colombia, and Ecuador: The First Half-Century of Independence," in Bethell, *The Cambridge History of Latin America* 3:534. On the Liberal revolts in Panama, see Michael Conniff, *Panama and the United States: The Forced Alliance* (Athens, Ga., 1992), 41–53.

8. David Bushnell, *Reform and Reaction in the Platine Provinces, 1810–1852* (Gainesville, Fla., 1985), 102–03.

9. On the convolutions of nineteenth-century Argentine liberalism, see the definitive statement by Tulio Halperín-Donghi, "Liberalism in Argentina," in Joseph L. Love and Nils Jacobsen, eds., *Guiding the Invisible Hand: Economic Liberalism and the State in Latin American History* (New York, 1988), 100–03, 104–05, 109–10.

10. *Vida de Juan Facundo Quiroga,* quoted in Eduardo Galeano (Cedric Belfrage, trans.), *Memory of Fire* (New York, 1985–87), vol. 2, *Faces and Masks,* 169. For a summary of the political and economic changes of these years, see David Rock, *Argentina, 1516–1982* (Berkeley, 1985), 120–52; and J. Valerie Fifer, *United States Perceptions of Latin America, 1850–1930: A 'New West' South of Capricorn?* (Manchester, 1991), 2–3.

11. John Lynch, "The River Plate Republics from Independence to the Paraguayan War," *Cambridge History of Latin America* 3:657–58.

12. Quoted in Maurice Zeitlein, *The Civil Wars in Chile, or The Bourgeois Revolutions That Never Were* (Princeton, 1984), 36.

13. On Paraguay's nineteenth century history, see John Hoyt Williams, *The Rise and Fall of the Paraguayan Republic, 1800–1870* (Austin, 1979). Richard Alan White, *Paraguay's Autonomous Revolution, 1810–1840* (Albuquerque, 1978), makes the case for a genuine social revolution in Francia's Paraguay, while Thomas Whigham, *The Politics of River Trade: Tradition and Development in the Upper Plata, 1780–1870* (Albuquerque, 1991), esp. 22–29, skillfully places "El Supremo" in the tradition of Spanish patrimonial elites.

14. Aureliano Cândido Tavares Bastos, *Cartas do Solitário,* quoted in Richard Graham, *Britain and the Onset of Modernization in Brazil, 1850–1914* (Cambridge, 1968), 35; see also 23–27, 208–11, 319. For a more pessimistic assessment of the benefits of Brazil's absorption into the North Atlantic economy in the nineteenth century, see Emilia Viotta da Costa, *The Brazilian Empire: Myths and Histories* (Chicago, 1985), 90–93, 172–73, 200–01, 247–48.

15. On the Paraguayan war, see Charles Kolinski, *Independence or Death: The Story of the Paraguayan War* (Gainesville, Fla., 1965), and Thomas Whigham, *The Paraguayan War,* vol. 1, *Causes and Early Conduct* (Lincoln, Neb., 2002); and two works by Efraím Cardozo, *Vísperas de la guerra del Paraguay* (Buenos Aires, 1954), and *El Imperio del Brasil y el Río de la Plata* (Buenos Aires, 1962). See also Anyda Marchant, *Viscount Mauá and the Empire of Brazil* (Berkeley, 1965).

16. Lynch, "The River Plate Republics," 3:673.

17. Quoted in Charles A. Hale, "Political and Social Ideas in Latin America, 1870–1930," in *Cambridge History of Latin America* 3:372; Richard Graham, "Brazil from Independence to the Paraguayan War," in *Cambridge History of Latin America* 3:786–94. For the perspective of an economic historian, see Nathaniel Leff, "Economic Development in Brazil, 1822–1913," in Stephen Haber, ed., *How Latin America Fell Behind: Essays on the Economic Histories of Brazil and Mexico, 1800–1914* (Stanford, 1997), 34–64.

18. Viotta da Costa, *The Brazilian Empire,* 202–85; Ada Ferrer, *Insurgent Cuba: Race, Nation, and Revolution, 1868–1898* (Chapel Hill, 1999), 2–5.

19. Peter F. Klarén, *Peru: Society and Nationhood in the Andes* (New York, 2000), 172–82; Lawrence A. Clayton, *Peru and the United States: The Condor and the Eagle* (Athens, Ga., 1999), 74–75; Kenneth D. Lehman, *Bolivia and the United States: A Limited Partnership* (Athens, Ga., 1999), 47–50.

20. Philip D. Curtin, *Two Jamaicas* (Cambridge, 1955), 101–03, 176–77, 194–95; Thomas Holt, *The Problem of Freedom: Race, Labor, and Politics in Jamaica and Britain, 1832–1938* (Baltimore, 1991), 298–301, 306–09.

21. Francisco A. Scarano, "Labor and Society in the Nineteenth Century," in Franklin W.

Knight and Colin A. Palmer, eds., *The Modern Caribbean* (Chapel Hill, 1989), 51–73; Jay R. Mandle, "British Caribbean Economic History," in ibid., 234–37.

22. Quoted in Charles C. Tansill, *The United States and Santo Domingo, 1798–1873 : A Chapter in Caribbean Diplomacy* (1938; repr. Gloucester, Mass., 1967), 452; see also Pletcher, *Diplomacy of Trade and Investment*, 162–63; and Luís Martínez Fernández, *Economy, Society, and Patterns of Political Thought in the Hispanic Caribbean, 1840–1878* (Athens, Ga., 1994), 221.

23. Harry Hoetink, "The Dominican Republic, 1870–1930," in Leslie Bethell, ed., *The Cambridge History of Latin America*, vol. 5, *c. 1870 to 1930* (New York, 1986), 287–306; Hoetink (Stephen Ault, trans.), *The Dominican People, 1850–1900: Notes for a Historical Sociology* (Baltimore, 1982), 4–11, 30–31, 42–45.

24. Gérard Pierre-Charles, *L'Economie haïtienne et sa voie de développement* (Paris, 1967), 45, cited in Brenda Gayle Plummer, *Haiti and the Great Powers, 1902–1915* (Baton Rouge, 1988), 36.

25. McCreery, *Rural Guatemala, 1760–1940* (Stanford, 1994), 3–4, 12–15, 186–88, 192–95, 262–64, 293; Robert G. Williams, *States and Social Evolution: Coffee and the Rise of National Government in Central America* (Chapel Hill, 1994), 15–17, 102–03, 144–45, 147, 230–33, 248–49.

26. José Reina Valenzuela and Mario Argueta, *Marco Aurelio Soto, Reforma liberal de 1876* (Tegucigalpa, 1978); Arturo Taracena Arriola, "Liberalismo y poder político en Centroamérica (1870–1929)," in Víctor Hugo Acuña Ortega, ed., *Las repúblicas agroexportadoras (1870–1945)*, vol. 4 of *Historia general de Centroamérica* (Madrid, 1993), 179–83.

27. Quoted in Thomas Schoonover, *The United States in Central America, 1860–1911: Episodes of Social Imperialism and Imperial Rivalry in the World System* (Durham, 1991), 43.

28. For a summary of Nicaragua's "delayed" Liberal revolution, see Charles Stansifer, "José Santos Zelaya: A New Look at Nicaragua's Liberal Dictatorship," *Revista Interamericana* 7 (Fall 1977): 468–85.

29. See Schoonover, *The United States in Central America, 1860–1911*, 1–11; and Lester D. Langley and Thomas Schoonover, *The Banana Men: American Mercenaries and Entrepreneurs in Central America, 1880–1930* (Lexington, Ky., 1995), 6–32.

30. Conniff, *Panama and the United States*, 39. See also Alfredo Figueroa Navarro, *Dominio y sociedad en el Panamá colombiano: 1821–1903* (Panama, 1978).

31. A Panamanian wrote, "Isthmian sacrifices were for the benefit of two *foreign* nations—Colombia and the United States" (quoted in Alex Pérez-Venero, *Before the Five Frontiers: Panama from 1821–1903* [New York, 1978], 91).

32. As President Rutherford B. Hayes declared in 1880, "The policy of this country is a canal under American control. The United States cannot consent to the surrender of this control to any European power or to any combination of European powers" (quoted in Pletcher, *Diplomacy of Trade and Investment*, 130). Joseph Bucklin Bishop, "The French at Panama," *Scribner's Magazine* 53 (January–June 1913), 25–45; Conniff, *Panama and the United States*, 49.

33. David McCullough, *The Path Between the Seas: The Creation of the Panama Canal, 1870–1914* (New York, 1977), 169–81.

34. Edelberto Torres-Rivas (Douglas Sullivan-González, trans.) *History and Society in Central America* (Austin, 1993), 23–25; McCreery, *Rural Guatemala*, 11, 336; see also Mario Semper K., "Café, trabajo, y sociedad en Centroamérica (1870–1930)," in Ortega, ed., *Las repúblicas agroexportadoras*, vol. 4, *Historia general de Centroamérica*, 104–05; and Arturo Taracena Arriola, "Liberalismo y poder político en Centroamérica (1870–1929)," ibid., 168.

35. "There are laws of political as well as physical gravitation," Adams noted in 1823,

"and if an apple, severed by a tempest from its native tree, cannot choose but fall to the ground, Cuba, forcibly disjoined from its own unnatural connection with Spain, and incapable of self-support, can gravitate only towards the North American Union, which, by the same law of nature, cannot cast her off from its bosom" (quoted in Louis A Pérez, Jr., *Cuba and the United States: Ties of Singular Intimacy* [Athens, Ga., 1990], 38).

36. On nineteenth-century Cuban revolutionary thought, see Sheldon Liss, *Roots of Revolution: Radical Thought in Cuba* (Lincoln, Neb., 1987), 4–5, 13–18, 26–29.

37. Quoted in Philip S. Foner, *A History of Cuba and Its Relations with the United States*, vol. 2, *From the Era of Annexation to the Outbreak of the Second War of Independence* (New York, 1963), 2:339.

38. Louis A. Pérez, Jr., *Cuba Between Empires, 1878–1902* (Pittsburgh, 1983), 14; see also Martí, *Inside the Monster: Writings on the United States and American Imperialism*, ed. Philip S. Foner (New York, 1975).

39. Pérez, Jr., *Cuba Between Empires*, 10–11; Teresita Martínez Vergne, "Politics and Society in the Spanish Caribbean During the Nineteenth Century," in Franklin Knight and Colin Palmer, eds., *The Modern Caribbean* (Chapel Hill, 1989), 188–91; Francisco A. Scarano, "Labor and Society in the Nineteenth Century," ibid., 80–81.

40. Martí, "A Vindication of Cuba," letter to the editor of the Philadelphia *Evening Post*, March 25, 1889, in Martí, *Our America*, 234–35; see also Carlos Márquez Sterling, *Síntesis de una vida extraordinaria* (Mexico City, 1982), 116–17, 132, 134, 143–44, for suggestions about Martí's views on Cuban autonomy, racism, imperialism, and socialism.

41. Louis A. Pérez, Jr., *Lords of the Mountain: Social Banditry and Peasant Protest in Cuba, 1878–1918* (Pittsburgh, 1989), 12–13. For a contrasting view of social banditry, see Rosalie Schwartz, *Lawless Liberators: Political Banditry and Cuban Independence* (Durham, 1989).

42. Quoted in Pérez, Jr., *Cuba and the United States*, 52; see also 65–72. On the "subversive" character of North American materialism among Cubans see Pérez, *On Becoming Cuban*, 66, 80.

43. Michael Hunt, *Ideology and U.S. Foreign Policy* (New Haven, 1987), 60–61, 80–81. On the divisiveness engendered by the debate over Philippine annexation, see Richard E. Welch, Jr., *Response to Revolution: The United States and the Philippine-American War, 1899–1902* (Chapel Hill, 1979), 6–9, 158–59.

44. Quoted in Willard Gatewood, *Black Americans and the White Man's Burden, 1898–1903* (Urbana, Ill., 1975), 159; see also 10–12, 20–21, 40. See also Kevin Gaines, "Black Americans, Racial Uplift Ideology as Civilizing Mission: Pauline E. Hopkins on Race and Imperialism," in Kaplan and Pease, eds., *Cultures of United States Imperialism*, 434–35, 442. On the image of Cuban rebels in the United States, see Gerald F. Linderman, *The Mirror of War: American Society and the Spanish-American War* (Ann Arbor, 1974), 130–33.

45. Pérez, *Cuba Between Empires*, 376–81.

46. Lester D. Langley, *The Banana Wars: U.S. Military Intervention in the Caribbean, 1898–1934* (Lexington, Ky., 1983), 14–15; Military Government of Cuba, *Civil Report of Major-General John R. Brooke, 1899* (Washington, D.C., 1900), 6–7; J. H. Hitchman, *Leonard Wood and Cuban Independence, 1898–1902* (The Hague, 1971), 17–18.

47. Root, "The American Solder," Address by the Secretary of War at the Marquette Club in Chicaco, October 7, 1899, in response to the toast, "The American Soldier," in Robert Brown Scott, ed. *The Military and Colonial Policy of the United States: Addresses and Reports by Elihu Root* (Cambridge, 1916), 11. See also Pérez, *Cuba Between Empires*, 275–76.

48. For contrasting assessments of the Cuban occupation, see David Healy, *The United*

States in Cuba, 1898–1902: Generals, Politicians, and the Search for Policy (Madison, 1963), 179–99; Philip S. Foner, *The Spanish-Cuban-American War and the Birth of American Imperialism, 1895–1902*, 2 vols. (New York, 1972), 2:339–465; and Pérez, *Cuba Between Empires*, 270–365.

49. Quoted in Louis A. Pérez, Jr., *The War of 1898: The United States and Cuba in History and Historiography* (Chapel Hill, 1998), 35.

50. On Puerto Rico's Afro-Mestizo culture, see José Luís González (Gerald Guinness, trans.), *Puerto Rico: The Four-Storeyed Country* (1980; repr. Princeton, 1993).

51. On the divisions among the *autonomistas* in the critical years before the U.S. invasion, see Pilar Barbos de Rosario, *La Comisión Autonomista de 1896* (San Juan, 1957).

52. Luís Muñoz Rivera, "La situación en 1896," in *Diario de Puerto Rico*, July and August 1900, in *Campañas políticas: Seleccionadas y recopiladas por Luís Muñoz Marín*, 3 vols. (Madrid, 1925), 1:1.

53. Quoted in José Trías Monge, *Puerto Rico: The Trials of the Oldest Colony in the World* (New Haven, 1997), 30. U.S. military officers read similar proclamations in Cuba and the Philippines, but nowhere among those places "liberated" by the United States is there more bitterness about "betrayal" of a solemn promise. See Nancy Morris, *Puerto Rico: Culture, Politics, and Identity* (Westport, Conn., 1995), 23.

54. On the "war after the war," see Fernando Picó, *La guerra después de la guerra* (Río Piedras, P.R., 1987), 202–04; and Mariano Negrón Portillo, *Cuadrillas anexionistas y revueltas campesinas en Puerto Rico, 1898–1899* (Río Piedras, P.R., 1987), 2–5, 8–10, 13–15, 45–46, 51–53.

55. Quoted in Raymond Carr, *Puerto Rico: A Colonial Experiment* (New York, 1984), 33.

56. Trías Monge, *Puerto Rico*, 32–33, 42–43. The Supreme Court largely confirmed Congress's assertion that the Constitution did not follow the flag in a series of decisions known as the Insular Cases. Justice John Marshall Harlan vigorously dissented: "This nation is under the control of a written constitution, the supreme law of the land and the only source of the powers which our government . . . may exert at any time or at any place" (quoted in ibid., 49–51).

3 The End of the Long Century

1. See Berger, *Under Northern Eyes: Latin American Studies and U.S. Hegemony in the Americas, 1898–1990*.

2. On the urban transformation in Latin America, see James R. Scobie, "The Growth of Latin American Cities, 1870–1930," in Leslie Bethell, ed., *Cambridge History of Latin America*, vol. 4, c. *1870 to 1930* (New York, 1986), 233–65. For North America, see James T. Lemon, *Liberal Dreams and Nature's Limits: Great Cities of North America Since 1600* (Toronto, 1996). On the hemispheric cultural dynamics of the early twentieth century, see Pike, *The United States and Latin America*, 182, 196–205.

3. Of the forty-two million people who migrated to the Americas from 1871 until 1915, twenty-nine million went to the United States; the largest portion of the others went to Argentina, Brazil, and Canada. For contrasting developmental patterns in the hemisphere, see the essays in Bernecker and Tobler, *Development and Underdevelopment in America*. See also Bulmer-Thomas, *The Economic History of Latin America Since Independence*, 49–55, 66–69; and Colin M. Lewis, "Industry in Latin America," in Bernecker and Tobler, *Development and Underdevelopment in America*, 265–67; and Bernecker, "Latin America and Europe in the Nineteenth Century," ibid., 148–55.

4. Glade, "Economy and Society, 1870–1914," in Bethell, *Cambridge History of Latin American*, 4:48–51, 54–56; Bulmer-Thomas, *Economic History of Latin America*, 92–95, 102; Diana Balmori, Stuart Voss, and Miles Wortman, *Notable Family Networks in Latin America* (Chicago, 1984), 42–51; Kenneth Duncan and Ian Rutledge, "Patterns of Agrarian Capitalism," in Duncan and Rutledge, eds., *Land and Labour in Latin*

America: Essays on the Development of Agrarian Capitalism in the 19th and 20th Centuries (London, 1977), 14–17. On the British West Indies, see Gad Heuman, "The British West Indies," in Andrew Porter, ed., *Oxford History of the British Empire*, vol. 3, *The Nineteenth Century,* ed. Wm. Roger Louis (New York, 1999), 490–92.

5. Charles Bergquist, *Labor and the Course of American Democracy: U.S. History in Latin American Perspective* (London, 1996), 65–67; Philip S. Foner, *Militarism and Organized Labor, 1900–1914* (Minneapolis, 1987), 9–13. The classic statement about the social impact of economic expansion in the nineteenth century is Karl Polanyi, *The Great Transformation* (1944; repr. Boston, 1957).

6. Emily J. Rosenberg, *Spreading the American Dream: American Economic and Cultural Expansion, 1890–1945* (New York, 1982), 7; see also 23, 42–43. On the international character of Progressive social politics, see the seminal study by Daniel T. Rodgers, *Atlantic Crossings: Social Politics in a Progressive Age* (Cambridge, 1998).

7. Quoted in Elihu Root, *Speeches Incident to the Visit of Secretary Root to South America, July 4 to September 30, 1906* (Washington, 1906), 292.

8. David Healy, *Drive to Hegemony: The United States in the Caribbean, 1898–1917* (Madison, 1988), 136–37. On Root's place in the evolution of U.S. foreign relations in the early twentieth century, see Walter LaFeber, "Technology and U.S. Foreign Relations," *Diplomatic History* 24 (Winter 2000): 7–12.

9. Robert Craig Brown and Ramsey Cook, *Canada, 1896–1921: A Nation Transformed* (Toronto, 1974), 1–5, 186–87; Kenneth McNaught, *The Penguin History of Canada* (1969; repr. London, 1988), 190–95.

10. Tulio Halperín Donghi, "Argentines Ponder the Burden of the Past," in Jeremy Adelman, ed., *Colonial Legacies: The Problem of Persistence in Latin American History* (New York, 1999), 157; Charles A. Hale, "Political and Social Ideas in Latin America, 1870–1930," in Bethell, *Cambridge History of Latin America*, 4:380–82.

11. On the North Americanization of Peru and Bolivia, see Clayton, *Peru and the United States,* 74–103; and Lehman, *Bolivia and the United States,* 38–55.

12. Mira Wilkins, *The Emergence of Multinational Enterprise: American Business Abroad from the Colonial Era to 1914,* 124–25, 130–31, 168–71, 194–95; O'Brien, *The Century of U.S. Capitalism in Latin America,* 28–31; idem, *The Revolutionary Mission: American Enterprise in Latin America, 1900–1945.*

13. Franscisco García Calderón, *Latin America: Its Rise and Progress* (London, 1913), 306. See also Joseph Love, "Structural Change and Conceptual Response in Latin America and Romania," in Love and Nils Jacobsen, ed., *Guiding the Invisible Hand: Economic Liberalism and the State in Latin American History* (New York, 1988), 10–11.

14. On the creation of "banana empires," see Charles David Kepner, Jr., and Jay Henry Soothill, *The Banana Empire: A Case Study in Economic Imperialism* (1935; repr. New York, 1967).

15. Lester D. Langley and Thomas Schoonover, *The Banana Men: American Mercenaries and Entrepreneurs in Central America, 1880–1930* (Lexington, Ky., 1995), 33–57; O'Brien, *The Revolutionary Mission,* 64–65, 82–83.

16. Edelberto Torres-Rivas (Douglass Sullivan-González, trans.), *History and Society in Central America* (Austin, 1993), 38–41.

17. Germán Arciniegas (Joan MacLean, trans.), *Latin America: A Cultural History* (New York, 1967), 488; Pike, *United States and Latin America,* 194–203. See also William R. Stead, *The Americanization of the World or The Trend of the Twentieth Century* (1902; repr. New York, 1972).

18. Hale, "Political and Social Ideas in Latin America," in Bethell, *Cambridge History of Latin America* 4:400–11; Gilberto Freyre (Rod W. Horton, trans.), *Order and Progress: Brazil from Monarchy to Republic* (New York, 1970), 255–57.

19. Healy, *Drive to Hegemony*, 176–79; Ninkovich, *Modernity and Power*, 14–15.
20. The Roosevelt quotation is taken from Healy, *Drive to Hegemony*, 2. See also Richard Challener, *Admirals, Generals, and American Foreign Policy, 1898–1914* (Princeton, 1974), 15. Langley, *The Banana Wars*, 20; Robert Freeman Smith, "Latin America, the United States, and the European Powers," in Bethell, ed., *Cambridge History of Latin America* 4:98–99.
21. Whitaker, *The Western Hemisphere Idea*, 87–88.
22. Quoted in Healy, *Drive to Hegemony*, 13.
23. Quoted in Walter A. McDougall, *Promised Land, Crusader State: The American Encounter with the World Since 1776* (Boston, 1997), 115. For the corollary's impact on the "western hemisphere idea," see Whitaker, *Western Hemisphere Idea*, 100–01.
24. Quoted in Stuart and Tigner, *Latin America and the United States*, 55; Davis, Finan, and Peck, *Latin American Diplomatic History: An Introduction*, 171–72. See also Langley, *Banana Wars*, 31–33.
25. Emily S. Rosenberg, *Financial Missionaries to the World: The Politics and Culture of Dollar Diplomacy, 1900–1930* (Cambridge, 1999), 38–39.
26. Sáenz's comments are quoted in Whitaker, *Western Hemisphere Idea*, 84. See also Joseph S. Tulchin, *Argentina and the United States: A Conflicted Relationship* (Boston, 1990), 22–27.
27. E. Bradford Burns, *The Unwritten Alliance: Rio-Branco and Brazilian American Relations* (New York, 1966), 153, 200–01, 208–09; Fredrick B. Pike, *Chile and the United States, 1880–1962: The Emergence of Chile's Social Crisis and the Challenge to U.S. Diplomacy* (Notre Dame, 1963), 130–33.
28. Conniff, *Panama and the United States*, 64–65. See also Charles Bergquist, *Coffee and Conflict in Colombia, 1886–1910* (Durham, 1978), 163, 167–69.
29. Alex Perez-Venero, *Before the Five Frontiers: Panama from 1821 to 1903* (New York, 1978), 121, quoted in Conniff, *Panama and the United States*, 60. On the Thousand Day War in Panama, see Humberto E. Ricord, *Panamá en la Guerra de los Mil Dias* (Panama City, 1989), 234–35, 312–13.
30. David Bushnell, *The Making of Modern Colombia: A Nation in Spite of Itself* (Berkeley, 1993), 153.
31. Leonard, *Central America and the United States*, 58.
32. On the Hay–Bunau-Varilla Treaty, see John Major, "Who Wrote the Hay–Bunau-Varilla Convention?" *Diplomatic History* 8 (Spring 1984): 115–23; Charles D. Ameringer, "Philippe Bunau-Varilla: New Light on the Panama Canal Treaty," *Hispanic American Historical Review* 46 (Feb. 1966): 28–52; and Charles D. Ameringer, "The Panama Canal Lobby of Philippe Bunau-Varilla and William Nelson Cromwell," *American Historical Review* 68 (April 1963): 346–63.
33. The controversial clause is in Conniff, *Panama and the United States*, 69. Roosevelt offered the lame argument that had an advanced nation like Argentina, Chile, or Brazil been in possession of the isthmus, any one of them might have built the canal, and he would not have interfered. "But in the actual fact," he concluded, "the canal would not have been built at all save for the action I took" (Theodore Roosevelt, *Autobiography* [New York, 1914], 540–41).
34. By then, Roosevelt had unnecessarily insinuated himself into a public debate over his role in the Panama affair, which began with an ill-advised suit by his attorney-general against the New York *World* for a series of stories on the "taking of Panama" that Roosevelt deemed libelous, continued with an even more embarrassing investigation by a special committee in the House of Representatives in 1912, and ended in 1921 (two years after Roosevelt's death) with an apologetic treaty the outgoing Woodrow Wilson administration signed with the Colombian government. In none of the unfa-

vorable accounts of the Panama affair would the Panamanians be portrayed as anything other than willing accomplices or, along with the Colombians, as victims. Reyes's comments are cited in Randall, *Colombia and the United States,* 90.

35. Pérez, Jr., *Cuba and the United States,* 114–17; idem., *On Becoming Cuban: Identity, National, and Culture* (Chapel Hill, 1999), 95, 116–17. For a revisionist Cuban version of the war and the U.S.-Cuban connection, see the works of Emilio Roig de Leuchsenring, especially *Cuba no debe su independencia a los Estados Unidos,* 3d ed. (Havana, 1960), and *Los Estados Unidos contra Cuba Libre* (Havana, 1960).

36. Pérez, Jr., *Cuba and the United States,* 147.

37. Ibid., 152–55.

38. Langley, *The United States and the Caribbean in the Twentieth Century,* 38–39; Langley, *Banana Wars,* 36–37, 41–42.

39. A standard account is David Lockmiller, *Magoon in Cuba: A History of the Second Intervention, 1906–1909* (Chapel Hill, 1938); see also Allan Reed Millett, *The Politics of Intervention of Cuba, 1906–1909* (Columbus, 1968).

40. Quoted in Hugh Thomas, *Cuba: The Pursuit of Freedom* (New York, 1971), 504. Magoon's style distracted observers from the accomplishments of the occupation. In less than three years the provisional government built more than 600 kilometers of road (and 120 bridges), twice that constructed by Estrada and more than ten times what had been built under Wood's tutelage. Part of Magoon's problem was timing: his tenure in Cuba coincided with an economic downturn that culminated in the banking crisis of 1907. The debt incurred for public works projects (some of them unfinished by the time Magoon left) rose to an alarming $16.5 million.

41. Aline Helg, *Our Rightful Share: The Afro-Cuban Struggle for Equality, 1886–1912* (Chapel Hill, 1995), 2, 4–7.

42. Herbert Croly, *The Promise of American Life* (1909; repr. New Brunswick, 1996), 302.

43. Norman Angell, *The Great Illusion: A Study of the Relation of Military Power in Nations to Their Economic and Social Advantage* (New York, 1911), 50–52.

44. Tulio Halperín Donghi, "Argentina: Liberalism in a Country Born Liberal," in Love and Jacobsen, *Guiding the Invisible Hand,* 114–16; Jeffrey D. Needell, "Optimism and Melancholy: Elite Response to the *fin de siècle bonaenrise,*" *Journal of Latin American Studies* 31 (July 1999): 551–88.

45. Quoted in E. Bradford Burns, *A History of Brazil,* 3d ed. (New York, 1993), 252. See also Jeffrey Needell, "The Domestic Civilizing Mission: The Cultural Role of the State in Brazil, 1808–1930," *Luso-Brazilian Review* 36 (Summer 1999): 1–18.

46. Richard Graham, *Patronage and Politics in Nineteenth-Century Brazil* (Stanford, 1990), 269. For an expression of the political disillusionment in the first republic in Brazil, see F. J. de Oliveira Vianna, "Ideal and Real: Constitutional Provisions and Political Practice," in Richard Graham, ed., *A Century of Brazilian History Since 1865: Issues and Problems* (New York, 1969), 105–13.

47. Joseph Schull, *Laurier, the First Canadian* (Toronto, 1965), 521–30; Thompson and Randall, *Canada and the United States,* 79–92.

48. Langley, *Banana Wars,* 63–76.

49. For two often very different interpretations of the origins of the Mexican revolution see John Mason Hart, *Revolutionary Mexico: The Coming and the Process of the Mexican Revolution* (Berkeley, 1987), esp. 348–63; and Alan Knight, *The Mexican Revolution,* vol. 1, *Porfirians, Liberals, and Peasants* (1986; repr. Lincoln, 1990).

4 The Fractured Continent

1. Robert Freeman Smith, "Latin America, the United States, and the European Powers, 1830–1930," in Leslie Bethell, ed., *Cambridge History of Latin America,* vol. 4, c.

1870–1930 (Cambridge, 1986), 106; Rosenberg, *Financial Missionaries to the World,*
   80–81.

2. Healy, *Drive to Hegemony,* 166.

3. Frank Ninkovich, *The Wilsonian Century: U.S. Foreign Policy Since 1900* (Chicago,
   1999), 12–14.

4. Quoted in Gilderhus, *Pan American Visions,* 17.

5. Wilson's remarks are quoted in Gilderhus, *Pan American Visions,* 18. For those Latin
   American critics of U.S. policy in the hemisphere since the turn of the century the
   most meaningful way for Wilson to demonstrate his "good intentions" lay in respecting the right of self-determination of Cubans, Nicaraguans, and Mexicans. "We [Latin
   Americans] love and respect the United States," Manuel Ugarte had written in a public letter to Wilson on the day of the president's inaugural, but "we do not want the
   Monroe Doctrine to transform us into beneficiaries of the United States or anybody."
   Manuel Ugarte, "Letter to Thomas Woodrow Wilson," March 4, 1933, in Ugarte (Nor-
   berto Galasso, comp.), *La nación latinoamericana* (Caracas, 1978), 83.

6. Quoted in Langley, *The Banana Wars,* 87.

7. For a North American perspective on the Veracruz intervention, see Robert Quirk, *An
   Affair of Honor: Woodrow Wilson and the Occupation of Veracruz* (Lexington, Ky.,
   1961); and for a Mexican, Berta Ulloa, *La revolución intervenida: Relaciones
   diplomáticas entre México y los Estados Unidos, 1910–1914* (Mexico City, 1971).

8. Gilderhus, *Pan American Visions,* 32–33; Alan Knight, *The Mexican Revolution,* vol. 2,
   Counterrevolution and Reconstruction (New York, 1986), 153–55. Huerta went to
   Long Island, New York, and in the following year tried to reenter Mexico via El Paso,
   where he was arrested and incarcerated for violation of U.S. neutrality laws. He died
   in January 1916 of cirrhosis of the liver.

9. James Sandos, *Rebellion in the Borderlands: Anarchism and the Plan of San Diego,
   1904–1923* (Norman, 1992), xvi, 79–83, 172–75. The Plan of San Diego (6 January
   1915) is reprinted in Oscar J. Martínez, Jr., *Fragments of the Mexican Revolution: Personal Accounts from the Border* (Albuquerque, 1983), 145–48.

10. Quoted in Mark T. Gilderhus, "Wilson, Carranza, and the Monroe Doctrine: A Ques-
    tion in Regional Organization," *Diplomatic History* 7 (Spring 1983): 111; see also,
    Scott Nearing and Joseph Freeman, *Dollar Diplomacy: A Study in American Imperial-
    ism* (New York, 1925), 111–13, and Esperanza Durán, *Guerra y revolución: Las
    grandes potencias y México, 1914–1918* (Mexico City, 1985), 146–47.

11. Linda B. Hall and Don M. Coerver, *Revolution on the Border: The United States and
    Mexico, 1910–1920* (Albuquerque, 1988), 22–23; Friedrich Katz, *The Secret War in
    Mexico: Europe, the United States and the Mexican Revolution* (Chicago, 1981),
    552–53, 560–61, 564–65, 576–77; Mark Gilderhus, *Diplomacy and Revolution: U.S.-
    Mexican Relations under Wilson and Carranza* (Tucson, 1977), 46–47; Smith, *United
    States and Revolutionary Nationalism in Mexico,* 62–63.

12. Victor Bulmer-Thomas, *The Economic History of Latin America Since Independence*
    (New York, 1994), 157.

13. For the congressional report on the Haitian and Dominican occupations, see U.S.
    Congress, *Inquiry into the Occupation and Administration of Haiti and Santo
    Domingo: Hearings,* 67th Cong., 1st and 2d sess. (Washington, D.C., 1922).

14. In such a context, anti-Americanism sometimes means something other than what
    the term presumably means. As Manuel Ugarte (Martí's successor as literary advo-
    cate of pan–Latin American solidarity) wrote, "To hate the United States is a senti-
    ment of inferiority which leads nowhere. . . . What it is urgent to consider is not what
    our adversary has done to harm us, but what we ourselves have failed to do to
    counteract his aggression, and what we shall have to achieve tomorrow if we do not

wish to be annihilated" (Ugarte [J. Fred Rippy, trans.], *The Destiny of a Continent* [New York, 1925], 126).

15. Gilderhus, *Diplomacy and Revolution,* 114–16; Gilderhus, *Pan American Visions,* 125–27. Smith, *United States and Revolutionary Nationalism in Mexico,* 80; Emily Rosenberg, *World War I and the Growth of United States Predominance in Latin America* (New York, 1987), 2–7, 12–13, 26–29. The closest official expression of the Carranza doctrine was Hermila Galindo, *La Doctrina Carranza y el acercamiento indolatino* (Mexico City, 1919).

16. Gilderhus, *Pan American Visions,* 135–37, 152–53. On the debate over the U.S. role in "determining" the course of the Mexican revolution, see Alan Knight, *U.S.-Mexican Relations, 1910–1940: An Interpretation* (San Diego, 1987), 26–27,108–9, 112–115; John Mason Hart, *Revolutionary Mexico: The Coming and the Process of the Mexican Revolution* (Berkeley, 1987), 16–17, 370–71; Friedrich Katz, *The Life and Times of Pancho Villa* (Stanford, 1998), 816–18.

17. One sentence in the "manifesto" read, "Above all things the Pan-American Federation of Labor should stand as a guard on watch to protect the Western Hemisphere from being overrun by military domination from any quarter" (quoted in Philip S. Foner, *U.S. Labor Movement and Latin America: A History of Workers' Responses to Intervention* [Boston, 1988], 174); Sinclair Snow, *The Pan-American Federation of Labor* (Durham, 1964), 28–30, 104–07, 148–50.

18. Josefina Vázquez and Lorenzo Meyer, *The United States and Mexico,* (Chicago, 1985), 124–25; Raat, *Mexico and the United States,* 132–33.

19. Quoted in Stuart and Tigner, *Latin America and the United States,* 132. Delegates to the 1923 conference also approved a treaty for the conciliation of disputes between American states, known as the Gondra convention after the president of Paraguay, Manuel Gondra. For Brum's views about Pan Americanism, see Frederick Pike, *Hispanismo, 1898–1936: Spanish Conservatives and Liberals and Their Relations With Spanish America* (Notre Dame, 1971), 321–22.

20. Quoted in Barry Eichengreen, "House Calls of the Money Doctor: The Kemmerer Missions to Latin America, 1917–1931," in Paul W. Drake, ed., *Money Doctors, Foreign Debts, and Economic Reforms in Latin America from the 1890s to the Present* (Wilmington, Del., 1994), 111. See also O'Brien, *The Century of U.S. Capitalism in Latin America,* 46–49, 50–53, and O'Brien, *The Revolutionary Mission: American Enterprise in Latin America, 1900–1945,* 313–16.

21. On the place of Haya de la Torre and Aprismo in Latin American thought and politics, see Fredrick Pike, *The Politics of the Miraculous in Peru: Haya de la Torre and the Spiritualist Tradition* (Lincoln, 1986).

22. Quotations are from Thompson and Randall, *Canada and the United States,* 98, 125, 113, respectively. Though no public figure in either country would have admitted it, the United States and Canada were alike in one important respect: Both were nations of immigrants, yet in both countries significant numbers of their peoples (including immigrants) came to fear the immigrant and oppose immigration.

23. Quoted in Emily Rosenberg, "Revisiting Dollar Diplomacy: Narratives of Money and Manliness," *Diplomatic History* 22 (Spring 1998): 164. A rebuttal came from Sumner Welles of the Department of State in the September 1924 issue of *Atlantic Monthly.*

24. Paul W. Drake, "Introduction," in Drake, ed., *Money Doctors, Foreign Debts, and Economic Reforms,* xiv–xv, xxvi–xxix. On the parallel admiration of Spanish Americans for North American materialist culture and fear of its social consequences, see Pike, *Hispanismo, 1898–1936,* 7–9.

25. Robert N. Seidel, "American Reformers Abroad: The Kemmerer Missions in South America, 1923–1931," in Pike, *Hispanismo, 1898–1936,* 100–03; Lester D. Langley, *Mexico and the United States: The Fragile Relationship* (Boston, 1991), 17–19.

26. Quoted in Smith, "Latin America, the United States, and the European Powers, 1830–1930," in Bethell, ed., *Cambridge History of Latin America* 4:117.

27. Jean Meyer, "Mexico: Revolution and Reconstruction in the 1920s," in Bethell, *Cambridge History of Latin America*, vol. 4, c. *1870 to 1930*, 192–94. See also Raat, *Mexico and the United States*, 138; and Jean Meyer, *El sinarquismo: ¿Un fascismo mexicano?, 1937–1947* (Mexico City, 1979), 19–22.

28. Quoted in Langley, *Banana Wars*, 184.

29. Quoted in ibid., 191.

30. The classic account of the Sandino rebellion is Neill Macaulay, *The Sandino Affair* (Chicago, 1967). For Stimson's account, see Stimson, *American Policy in Nicaragua* (New York, 1927).

31. Quoted in Langley, *Banana Wars*, 205. On Sandino's style of warfare see Xavier Campos Ponce, *Los yanquis y Sandino* (Mexico City, 1962), 66, 71.

32. Richard Millett, *Guardians of the Dynasty: A History of the U.S.-Created Guardia Nacional de Nicaragua and the Somoza Family* (Maryknoll, N.Y., 1977), 132–34.

33. Quoted in Robert Whitney, "The Architect of the Cuban State: Fulgencio Batista and Populism in Cuba, 1937–1940," *Journal of Latin American Studies* 32 (May 2000): 440. On the Cuban revolution of 1933, see Leonel Soto, *La revolución del 33*, 3 vols. (Havana, 1977); and Luís Aguilar, *Cuba 1933: Prologue to Revolution* (Ithaca, 1972).

34. Quoted in Morton Keller, *Regulating a New Economy: Public Policy and Economic Change in America, 1900–1933* (Cambridge, 1991), 17.

35. Ellis Hawley, *The Great War and the Search for a Modern Order* (New York, 1979), 226–29; Arthur A. Ekirch, Jr., *The Decline of American Liberalism* (New York, 1969), 278–79. On Canada in the thirties, see H. B. Neatby, *The Politics of Chaos* (Toronto, 1972); and A. E. Safarian, *The Canadian Economy in the Great Depression* (Toronto, 1959).

36. Thomas C. Cochran and William Miller, *The Age of Enterprise: A Social History of Industrial America* (New York, 1942), 354–57.

37. Carlos Marichal, *A Century of Debt Crisis in Latin America from Independence to the Great Depression, 1820–1930* (Princeton, 1987), 201–13; Rosemary Thorp, "Introduction," in Thorp, ed., *Latin America in the 1930s: The Role of the Periphery in the World Crisis* (New York, 1984), 2.

38. Dick Steward, *Trade and Hemisphere: The Good Neighbor Policy and Reciprocal Trade* (Columbia, 1975), 89–122, 210–13. See also Paul Varg, "The Economic Side of the Good Neighbor Policy: The Reciprocal Trade Program and South America," *Pacific Historical Review* 45 (February 1976): 47–71.

39. Jesús Silva Herzog, "Imperialismo y buena vecindad," (Mesa Rodante) in *Cuadernos Americanos*, Mexico (Sept.-Oct., 1947): 67. On Puerto Rico in the thirties, see Thomas Mathews, *Puerto Rican Politics and the New Deal* (Gainesville, 1960). In some instances, the appeal of Good Neighbor rhetoric prompted small merchants in Central America to importune Roosevelt to use his power to break the monopoly of United Fruit in the banana industry. Though small growers and merchants had benefited from the banana industry, they increasingly resented the control UFCo exercised. For country people, writes Thomas O'Brien, "the encounter was even more traumatic . . . [because] work disciplines . . . disrupted existing family and work relations" (*Revolutionary Mission*, 105).

40. Roberto Querejazu Calvo, *Historia de la Guerra del Chaco* (La Paz, 1990), 26–27; Lehman, *Bolivia and the United States*, 70–75.

41. Lawrence A. Clayton, *Peru and the United States: The Condor and the Eagle* (Athens, Ga., 1999), 142–49.

42. Carlos Ibarguren, *La historia que he vivido* (Buenos Aires, 1955), 380.

43. Joseph H. Love, *Rio Grande do Sul and Brazilian Regionalism, 1882–1930* (Stanford, 1971), 242–43.

44. Laurence Whitehead, "State Organization in Latin America Since 1930," in Bethell, *Cambridge History of Latin America*, vol. 6, pt. 2, *Politics and Society*, 22, 66.

45. Franklin D. Roosevelt, *Franklin D. Roosevelt: His Personal Letters, 1928–1945*, vol. 3, ed. Elliott Roosevelt (New York, 1947), 634; Cordell Hull, *The Memoirs of Cordell Hull*, vol. 1 (New York, 1948), 349.

46. Raat, *Mexico and the United States*, 140–42.

47. Friedrich E. Schuler, *Mexico Between Hitler and Roosevelt: Mexican Relations in the Age of Lázaro Cárdenas, 1934–1940* (Albuquerque, 1998), 1–5, 15, 18–19, 57, 67. See also José Antonio Matesanz, *Las raices del exilio: México ante la Guerra Civil Española, 1936–1939* (Mexico City, 1999); and Fernando Serrano Migallón, "La política internacional de Cárdenas," in Teresa Jarquín Ortega, coordinator, *Isidro Fabela: Pensador, Política y Humanista (1882–1964)* (Zinacentepec, Mexico, 1966), 199–227.

48. Jonathan C. Brown, *Oil and Revolution in Mexico* (Berkeley, 1992), 372–74; Meyer, *El sinarquismo*, 19–22, 200–01.

49. Quoted in Lorenzo Meyer, *Mexico and the United States in the Oil Controversy, 1917–1942* (Austin, 1977), 167–68. As things worked out, the oil workers did not get their wage increase. And with the creation of PEMEX (the Mexican national oil company), they fell under even greater control of the state.

5 The Decade of Global War

1. David Haglund, *Latin America and the Transformation of U.S. Strategic Thought, 1936–1940* (Albuquerque, 1984), 39–40.

2. On this point, see David Green, *The Containment of Latin America: A History of the Myths and Realities of the Good Neighbor Policy* (Chicago, 1971).

3. Irwin Gellman, *Secret Affairs: Franklin Roosevelt, Cordell Hull, and Sumner Welles* (Baltimore, 1995), 168–69.

4. Dick Steward, *Trade and Hemisphere: The Good Neighbor Policy and Reciprocal Trade* (Columbia, Mo., 1975), 273–75; Green, *Containment of Latin America*, 60–74.

5. Stetson Conn, Rose C. Engelman, and Byron Fairchild, *The Western Hemisphere: Guarding the United States and Its Outposts* (Washington, D.C., 1964), 328; Lester D. Langley, *The United States and the Caribbean in the Twentieth Century*, rev. ed., (Athens, Ga., 1985), 163–76.

6. Nicholas Spykman, *America's Strategy in World Politics: The United States and the Balance of Power* (New York, 1942), 457; see also 194–95. The response, though oblique, came from Samuel Flagg Bemis, who believed that the "security of the United States has become identified with the security and welfare of the whole New World defending itself under the leadership of the Continental Republic" (Bemis, *The Latin American Policy of the United States: An Historical Interpretation* [New York, 1943], x).

7. Haglund, *Latin America and the Transformation of U.S. Strategic Thought, 1936–1940*, 2–3, 5, 218.

8. Conniff, *Panama and the United States*, 92–93; Conn, Engelman, Fairchild, *The Western Hemisphere: Guarding the United States and Its Outposts*, 321.

9. Haglund, *Latin America and the Transformation of U.S. Strategic Thought, 1936–1940*, 165–71.

10. Had this occurred, wrote a Brazilian historian a quarter century later, the effect on U.S. relations with Brazil would have been devastating. Paulo de Queiroz Duarte, *O Nordeste na II Guerra Mundial: Antecedentes e Ocupaçao* (Rio de Janeiro, 1971), 36; Haglund, *Latin America and the Transformation of U.S. Strategic Thought, 1936–1940*, 215.

11. Thompson and Randall, *Canada and the United States*, 147–48.

12. Samuel Guy Inman, *Latin America: Its Place in World Life* (Chicago, 1937), 3–5.

13. Eric Sevareid, "Where Do We Go From Here?" *Saturday Evening Post* (March 28,

1942), quoted in Arthur P. Whitaker, "Politics and Diplomacy," in Whitaker, ed., *Inter-American Affairs: An Annual Survey, 1942* (New York, 1943), 13. Irwin Gellman, *Secret Affairs: Franklin Roosevelt, Cordell Hull, and Sumner Welles* (Baltimore, 1995), 276–77.

14. John A. Humphrey, "Canada," in Whitaker, ed, *Inter-American Affairs, 1943*, 44–45.

15. Quoted in Office of Inter-American Affairs, *History of the Office of the Coordinator of Inter-American Affairs* (Washington, D.C., 1947), 168–69. See also Elizabeth A. Cobbs, *The Rich Neighbor Policy: Rockefeller and Kaiser in Brazil* (New Haven, 1992), 40–41; and Gerald K. Haines, "Under the Eagle's Wings: The Franklin D. Roosevelt Administration Forges an American Hemisphere," *Diplomatic History* 1 (Fall 1977): 373–88.

16. *El Día* (December 9, 1943), quoted in Whitaker, "Politics and Diplomacy," in Whitaker, *Inter-American Affairs, 1943*, 43.

17. Blanca Torres Ramírez, *Historia de la revolución mexicana, periodo 1940–1952: México en la segunda guerra mundial* (Mexico City, 1979), 66–67.

18. Quoted in Rosemary Thorp, "The Latin American Economies in the 1940s," in Rock, *Latin America in the 1940s*, 45; see also Luis G. Zorrilla, *Historia de relaciones entre México y los Estados Unidos de América, 1800–1958*, 2 vols. (Mexico City, 1966), 2:502–03; and Torres, *México en la segunda guerra mundial*, 85–86.

19. Hélio Vianna, *História diplomática do Brasil* (Río de Janeiro, 1958), 195–202; Laurence Whitehead, "State Organization in Latin America Since 1930," in Leslie Bethell, ed., *Cambridge History of Latin America*, vol. 6, *Latin America Since 1930: Economy, Society, and Politics*, pt. 2, *Politics and Society* (New York, 1994), 66.

20. Ewell, *Venezuela and the United States*, 147–48; Randall, *Colombia and the United States*, 164–76.

21. C. Moran, "The Evolution of Caribbean Strategy," United States Naval Institute *Proceedings* 68 (1942): 365–73.

22. Rexford Guy Tugwell, *The Stricken Land: The Story of Puerto Rico* (New York, 1947), 212–15; H. N. Stark, "War Poses Problems for British West Indies," *Foreign Commerce Weekly* 9, no. 12 (1942): 8–12, 34–36.

23. Winston James, *Holding Aloft the Banner of Ethiopia: Caribbean Radicalism in America* (New York, 1996).

24. Wm. Roger Louis, *Imperialism at Bay: The United States and the Decolonization of the British Empire, 1941–1945* (New York, 1975), 8–9; see also Gary Fraser, *The United States and the Genesis of West Indian Independence, 1940–1964* (Westport, Conn., 1994).

25. Victor Bulmer-Thomas, "La crísis de la economía de agroexportación, 1930–1945," in Víctor Hugo Acuña Ortega, *Las repúblicas agroexportadoras, 1870–1945* (Madrid, 1993), 385; see also 386–95; and Edelberto Tomás Rivas, "Central America Since 1930: An Overview," in Bethell, *Cambridge History of Latin America*, vol. 7, *Latin America Since 1930: Mexico, Central America and the Caribbean* (New York, 1990), 172–75.

26. Robert A. Potash, ed., *Perón y el G.O.U.: Los documentos de una logia secreta* (Buenos Aires, 1984), 101–03; Ysabel Rennie, *The Argentine Republic* (New York, 1945), 344.

27. Lehman, *Bolivia and the United States*, 77–83; David Rock, "Argentina, 1930–1946," in *Cambridge History of Latin America*, vol. 8, *Latin America Since 1930: Spanish South America*, 60–61.

28. Quoted in Arturo Olaverría, *Chile entre los dos Alessandri*, 4 vols. (Santiago, 1962, 1965), 1:455.

29. Tulchin, *Argentina and the United States*, 90–91.

30. Quoted in Samuel Baily, *The United States and the Development of South America, 1945–1975* (New York, 1976), 44; Arthur Whitaker, "Summary and Prospect," in Whitaker, *Inter-American Affairs: An Annual Survey, 1941* (New York, 1942), 175.

31. Rosemary Thorp, "The Latin American Economies, 1939–c. 1950," in Leslie Bethell, ed., *Cambridge History of Latin America*, vol. 6, pt. 1, *Spanish America, c. 1930 to the Present* (New York, 1994), 154–58.

32. 238–56; Whitaker, "Summary and Prospect," in Whitaker, *Inter-American Affairs, 1945*, 232–43.

33. Joseph Love, "Furtado, Social Science, and History," in Jeremy Adelman, ed., *Colonial Legacies: The Problem of Persistence in Latin American History* (New York, 1999), 183–205.

34. Whitaker, "Summary and Prospects," in Whitaker, *Inter-American Affairs, 1945*, 238.

35. Quoted in Samuel Baily, *The United States and the Development of South America, 1945–1975* (New York, 1976), 44.

36. Charles D. Ameringer, *The Caribbean Legion: Patriots, Politicians, Soldiers of Fortune* (University Park, Pa., 1996).

37. Juan Angel Silen, *Historia de la nación puertorriqueña* (Río Piedras, P.R., 1973), 326–28; the most damning indictment of U.S. rule in Puerto Rico is Gordon Lewis, *Puerto Rico: Freedom and Power in the Caribbean* (New York, 1968), 113–33.

38. The quotations are from Gilderhus, *The Second Century*, 117 and 120.

39. Quoted in Roger R. Trask, "The Impact of the Cold War on United States-Latin American Relations, 1945–1949," *Diplomatic History* 1 (Summer 1977): 277–78.

40. Kyle Longley, *The Sparrow and the Hawk: Costa Rica and the United States During the Rise of José Figueres* (Tuscaloosa, Ala., 1997), 22–23, 26–29, 64–65, 92–93, 164–67.

41. Quoted in Herbert Braun, *The Assassination of Gaitán: Public Life and Urban Violence in Colombia* (Madison, 1985), 190; see also Christopher Abel and Marcos Palacios, "Colombia, 1930–1958," in Leslie Bethell, *Cambridge History of Latin America: Latin America Since 1930*, vol. 8, *Spanish South America* (New York, 1996), 610–12.

42. Randall, *Colombia and the United States*, 188–96.

6 The Cold War

1. Quoted in Alejandro Magnet, *Nuestros vecinos justicialistas* (Santiago, 1955), 155.

2. Quoted in Gaddis Smith, *The Last Years of the Monroe Doctrine, 1945–1993* (New York, 1994), 70. See also Roger R. Trask, "George F. Kennan's Report on Latin America," in *Diplomatic History* 2 (Summer 1978): 307–11.

3. Cosío Villegas (Américo Paredes, trans.), *American Extremes* (Austin, 1964), 52.

4. Perón's comments are quoted in F. Parkinson, *Latin America, the Cold War, and the World Powers, 1945–1973: A Study in Diplomatic History* (Beverly Hills, 1974), 22; Ibañez's, in Boris Yopo, *Los partidos radical y socialista y Estados Unidos: 1947–1958* (Santiago, 1985), 36.

5. Raat, *Mexico and the United States*, 158; Mario Ojeda, *Política exterior de México* (Mexico City, 1976), 50–51, 57.

6. Thompson and Randall, *Canada and the United States*, 181–214.

7. Quoted in Randall, *Colombia and the United States*, 204. Maintaining the Colombian battalion in Korea cost the United States $7.6 million.

8. On this point see Bryce Wood, *The Dismantling of the Good Neighbor Policy* (Austin, 1985).

9. Quoted in ibid., 202.

10. Quoted in Lehman, *Bolivia and the United States*, 45.

11. For an account of these trips, see Milton Eisenhower, *The Wine Is Bitter: The United States and Latin America* (Garden City, N.Y., 1963).

12. Letter to Bryce Wood, 26 January 1980, in Wood, *Dismantling of the Good Neighbor Policy*, 205–06; see also 200–04.

13. Coatsworth, *Central America and the United States*, 88.

14. On UFCO's public relations campaign against Arbenz, see Leonard, *Central America and the United States*, 137–38.

15. Among the numerous English-language accounts of U.S. involvement in the Guatemalan affair, two merit special notice: Richard Immerman, *The CIA in*

Guatemala: The Foreign Policy of Intervention (Austin, 1982); and Stephen
Schlesinger and Stephen Kinzer, *Bitter Fruit: The Untold Story of the American Coup
in Guatemala* (Garden City, N.Y., 1982).

16. When Eisenhower heard about their decision, his response was, "Incredible." See
Nick Cullather, *Secret History: The CIA's Classified Account of Its Operations in
Guatemala, 1952–1954* (Stanford, 1999), 109.

17. Conniff, *Panama and the United States*, 107–11.

18. Levinson and de Onís, *The Alliance That Lost Its Way*, 38–39.

19. "Report of the Preparatory Group Appointed by the Secretariat of the United Nations
Economic Commission for Latin America," in U.N. document E/CN 12/359, quoted in
ibid., 39- 40.

20. Quoted in Levinson and de Onís, *The Alliance That Lost Its Way*, 42.

21. Ibid., 42–43; Miguel S. Wionczek, "Latin American Free Trade Association," *International Conciliation*, no. 551 (January 1965): 24–25.

22. Levinson and de Onís, *The Alliance That Lost Its Way*, 44–46.

23. Louis A. Pérez, Jr., *Cuba: Between Reform and Revolution* (New York, 1988), 293–95.

24. Pérez, Jr., *Cuba and the United States*, 235.

25. Ibid., 239.

26. Quoted in ibid., 241.

27. Quoted in Levinson and de Onís, *The Alliance That Lost Its Way*, 47.

28. Allende, Preface to J. Tabares del Real, *La revolución cubana* (Havana, 1960), quoted
in Boris Goldenberg, *The Cuban Revolution and Latin America* (New York, 1966), 311.

29. Pérez, Jr., *Cuba and the United States*, 242–43.

30. Roa is quoted in Alonso Aguilar (Asa Zatz, trans.), *Pan Americanism: From Monroe to
the Present* (New York, 1968), 112. The quotations from the resolutions are in Jorge I.
Domínguez, *To Make a World Safe for Revolution: Cuba's Foreign Policy* (Cambridge,
1989), 27.

31. Mario Ojeda, *Alcances y límites de la política exterior de México* (Mexico City,
1976), 80–81.

32. Goldenberg, *The Cuban Revolution and Latin America*, 312–15.

33. Pérez, Jr., *Cuba and the United States*, 245.

34. Contemporary appraisals of the Bay of Pigs may be found in Karl Meyer and Tad
Szulc, *The Cuban Invasion: The Chronicle of a Disaster* (New York, 1962); and on the
Cuban side in *Playa Girón, derrota del imperialismo* (Havana, 1961). For an official
analysis of the Cuban invasion, made in 1961 but not published until 1981, see Luis
Aguilar, ed., *Operation Zapata: The "Ultrasensitive" Report and Testimomy of the
Board of Inquiry on the Bay of Pigs* (Frederick, Md., 1981), which concluded (p. 43)
that "preparations and execution of paramilitary operations such as Zapata are a
form of Cold War action in which the country must be prepared to engage. If it does it
must engage in it with a maximum chance of success."

35. Quoted in Levinson and de Onís, *The Alliance That Lost Its Way*, 56.

36. Atkins and Wilson, *The Dominican Republic and the United States*, 116–26.

37. Quoted in Levinson and de Onís, *The Alliance That Lost Its Way*, 67.

38. Quoted in Arthur K. Smith, "Mexico and the Cuban Revolution: Foreign Policy making in Mexico Under President Adolfo López Mateos, 1958–1964" (Ph.D. diss., Cornell
University, 1970), 127–28.

39. Quotation attributed to the historian Dmitri Volkogonov, in Yuri Pavlov, *Soviet-Cuban
Alliance, 1959–1991* (Miami, 1994), 32.

40. Quoted in David Reynolds, *One World Divisible: A Global History* (New York, 2000), 178.

41. Aleksandr Fursenko and Timothy Naftali, *"One Hell of a Gamble": Khrushchev, Castro, and Kennedy, 1958–1964* (New York, 1997), 240–43.

42. Quoted in Domínguez, *To Make a World Safe for Revolution*, 29. Canada, though not

a member of the OAS, also refused to break diplomatic relations with Cuba. Though he agreed with Kennedy about Cuba, Canadian prime minister John Diefenbaker was justifiably angered because his government learned about Kennedy's decision to impose a blockade only at the "eleventh hour." As a member of NATO and NORAD, Diefenbaker believed, Canada was entitled to consultation, and only after considerable pressure from Washington and from within his own cabinet did he grant permission to the United States to station its nuclear-armed aircraft in Canada. See Robert W. Reford, *Canada and Three Crises* (Lindsay, Ont., 1968), as cited in Halperin, *Rise and Decline of Fidel Castro*, 178; and Thompson and Randall, *Canada and the United States*, 218–19, 223–24.

7 The Critical Decade

1. For a brief but compelling discussion of the difficulties of explaining the missile crisis, see Bruce Kuklick, "Reconsidering the Missile Crisis and Its Interpretation," *Diplomatic History* 25 (Summer 2001): 517–23.
2. Quoted in Jules Benjamin, "The Framework of U.S. Relations with Latin America in the Twentieth Century: An Interpretive Essay," *Diplomatic History* 11 (Spring, 1987): 107–08.
3. Ricardo Ffrench-Davis, "The Latin American Economies, 1950–1990," in Leslie Bethell, ed., *Cambridge History of Latin America*, vol. 6, *Latin America Since 1930: Economy, Society, and Politics*, pt. 1, *Economy and Society* (New York, 1994), 159–69.
4. The British Caribbean experienced a transformation as well, though the political process did not follow the course London had crafted. In the late 1940s, in the interests of efficiency and centralization of the colonial bureaucracy, the Crown had pushed the idea of modified self-government, but a generation of West Indians led by Norman Manley and Alexander Bustamante of Jamaica and Eric Williams of Trinidad pushed for independence. What emerged in 1958 was the West Indian Federation, composed of ten territories (British Guiana and British Honduras were excluded), cobbled together from weak and strong constituents. Lacking any meaningful support of Jamaica and Trinidad—Williams, Bustamante, and Manley refused to participate in the federal elections—the federation collapsed after three years, and Jamaica and Trinidad declared their independence.
5. Quoted in Tony Smith, "The Alliance for Progress: The 1960s," in Abraham Lowenthal, ed., *Exporting Democracy: The United States and Latin America* (Baltimore, 1991), 87. See also Joseph Love, "Economic Ideas and Ideologies in Latin America Since 1930," in Bethell, *Cambridge History of Latin America*, vol. 6, pt. 1, 427–28, 430, 442–45.
6. Hirschman, *The Reporter* (25 May 1961), 20–23, quoted in Hirschman, *A Bias for Hope: Essays on Development and Latin America* (New Haven, 1971), 176; Michael E. Latham, "Ideology, Social Scientist, and Destiny: Modernization and the Kennedy-Era Alliance for Progress," *Diplomatic History* 22 (September 1998): 199–229.
7. Harvey S. Perloff, *Alliance for Progress: A Social Invention in the Making* (Baltimore, 1969), 26–29.
8. Jerome Levinson and Juan de Onís, *The Alliance That Lost Its Way: A Critical Report on the Alliance for Progress* (Chicago, 1970), 68–69, 82–83; the quotation of the Brazilian minister of finance is on p. 73.
9. A. W. Maldonado, *Teodoro Moscoso and Puerto Rico: Operation Bootstrap* (Gainesville, 1997), 180–84.
10. Levinson and de Onís, *The Alliance That Lost Its Way*, 116–17.
11. Tulchin, *Argentina and the United States*, 120–22.
12. Daniel Masterson, *Militarism and Politics in Latin America: Peru from Sánchez Cerro to Sendero Luminoso* (New York, 1991), 157–84.

13. Quoted in Atkins and Wilson, *The Dominican Republic and the United States,* 130. On Bosch's failure as leader, see the memoir of the U.S. ambassador, John Bartlow Martin, *Overtaken by Events* (Garden City, N.Y., 1966). Bosch described Martin (and his associate) as similar to "two Dominicans as anxious as the best of Dominicans to accomplish the impossible for us. They were not functionaries with cold souls, attentive only to the interests of their country and their government" (in Bosch, *Crisis de la democracia de América en la República Dominicana* [Mexico City, 1964], 155).

14. Quoted in Levinson and de Onís, *The Alliance That Lost Its Way,* 86–87.

15. Quoted in Rabe, *Most Dangerous Area in the World,* 98.

16. April 7, 1964, edition; quoted in Levinson and de Onís, *The Alliance That Lost Its Way,* 90.

17. Levinson and de Onís, *The Alliance That Lost Its Way,* 88–91; Michael Weis, *Cold Warriors and Coups d'Etat: Brazilian-American Relations, 1945–1964* (Albuquerque, 1993), 134–67.

18. Sergio Almaraz Paz, *Réquiem para una república,* quoted in Kenneth D. Lehman, *Bolivia and the United States: A Limited Partnership* (Athens, Ga., 1999), 144.

19. Conniff, *Panama and the United States,* 116–18.

20. William J. Jordan, *Panama Odyssey* (Austin, 1984), chap. 4.

21. Juan Bosch, "La revolución de abril," in Bosch, *La guerra de la restauración de abril* (Santo Domingo, 1982), 213–15.

22. Bruce Palmer, Jr., *Intervention in the Caribbean: The Dominican Crisis of 1965* (Lexington, 1989), 5. For another military perspective on the intervention, see Lawrence Yates, *Power Pack: U.S. Intervention in the Dominican Republic, 1965–1966* (Ft. Leavenworth, Kan., 1989).

23. Julio C. Estrella, *La revolución dominicana y la crisis de la OEA* (Santo Domingo, 1965).

24. Atkins and Wilson, *The Dominican Republic and the United States,* 133–49, 153–56; Piero Gleijesis (Lawrence Lipson, trans.), *The Dominican Crisis: The 1965 Constitutionalist Revolt and American Intervention* (Baltimore, 1978), 299–300.

25. Lehman, *Bolivia and the United States,* 155–57.

26. Guevara, "Latinoamérica: La revolución necesaria," in *Cuadernos de Cultura Latinamérica,* no. 60 (September 1979): 7; Alma Guilleroprieto, "The Harsh Angel," *New Yorker* (Oct. 6, 1997), 104–11.

27. Jorge Castañeda, *Utopia Unarmed: The Latin American Left After the Cold War* (New York, 1993), 89; Pérez, *Cuba and the United States,* 252–54.

28. Perloff, *Alliance for Progress,* 65–69; Stephen J. Randall, *Colombia and the United States: Hegemony and Interdependence* (Athens, Ga., 1992), 240.

29. Perloff, *Alliance for Progress,* 106–07, 165.

30. Szulc, *The Winds of Revolution,* cited in Perloff, *Alliance for Progress,* 88; Alba, *Alliance Without Allies,* 208–15; Simon Hanson, *Dollar Diplomacy, Modern Style: Chapters in the Alliance for Progress* (Washington, D.C., 1970), 4–16.

31. Leonard, *Central America and the United States,* 154–65.

32. Victor Bulmer-Thomas, *The Political Economy of Central America Since 1920* (Cambridge, 1987), 189–97. Bulmer-Thomas astutely notes that in 1970 Central Americans dominated 70 percent of industrial production.

33. James Rowles, *El conflicto Honduras-El Salvador (1969)* (San José, C.R., 1980), 50 passim, cited in Manuel Rojas Bolaños, "La política," in Héctor Pérez Brignoli, *De la posguerra a la crisis (1945–1979),* vol. 5 of *Historia general de Centroamérica* (Madrid, 1993), 126.

34. Frei's remarks are quoted in Alan Angell, "Chile since 1958," in Leslie Bethell, ed., *Cambridge History of Latin America,* 8:336, 316, respectively; see also Sater, *Chile and the United States,* 141–58. The assessment of "frustrated development" is a theme in Aníbal Pinto, *Chile, un caso de desarrollo frustrado* (Santiago, 1962).

35. Quoted in Levinson and de Onís, *The Alliance That Lost Its Way,* 310. See also Abraham Lowenthal, "Peruvian Experiment Reconsidered," in Cynthia McClintock and Abraham Lowenthal, eds., *The Peruvian Experiment Reconsidered* (Princeton, 1983), 416–21.

36. Quoted in Levinson and de Onís, *The Alliance That Lost Its Way,* 103.

37. *The Rockefeller Report on the Americas: The Official Report of a United States Presidential Mission for the Western Hemisphere* (Chicago, 1969), 60; see also 21, 35.

38. Ibid., 33. For a different perspective on the putative benefits of U.S. military training of Latin American officers, see Jan Knippers Black, *Sentinels of Empire: The United States and Latin American Militarism* (New York, 1986), 41.

39. *Rockefeller Report on the Americas,* 44–47, 63, 102.

40. Ibid., 142–43; see also 24; Levinson and de Onís, *The Alliance That Lost Its Way,* 318–19.

41. Eric Foner, *The Story of American Freedom,* 280–87; Randall and Thompson, *Canada and the United States,* 230–52.

42. Lester D. Langley, *Mexico and the United States: The Fragile Relationship* (Boston, 1991), 58–65.

43. Manuel Moreno Sánchez, *Crisis política de México* (Mexico City, 1970), 11–17. In 1967 a CIA report noted, "Mexico's general record is one of progress and political stability, but unrest . . . points up two basic problems. One is the failure to fulfill a fundamental aspiration of the Revolution of 1910—improving the lot of the peasants. . . . The second problem stems from the success of Mexico's educational system, which has brought to the expanding middle class of the general prosperous areas to a level of sophistication that will bring it into conflict with Mexico's paternalistic system of government" (quoted in Langley, *Mexico and the United States,* 121–22).

44. James Laxer and Robert Laxer, *The Liberal Idea of Canada: Pierre Trudeau and the Question of Canada's Survival* (Toronto, 1977), 177.

45. Kenneth McNaught, *The Penguin History of Canada* (New York, 1988), 316–22. The terrorists murdered LaPorte.

46. David Reimers, *Still the Golden Door: The Third World Comes to America* (New York, 1985), *passim.*

8 Order and Progress

1. White House Press Release, October 1969, quoted in Jerome Levinson and Juan de Onís, *The Alliance That Lost Its Way: A Critical Report on the Alliance for Progress* (Chicago, 1970), 318.

2. See, among others, Bruce M. Bagley, *Myths of Militarization: The Role of the Military in the War on Drugs in the Americas* (Coral Gables, Fla., 1991); Jonathan Marshall, *Drug Wars: Corruption, Counterinsurgency, and Covert Operations in the Third World* (Forestville, Calif., 1991); and John Dinges, *Our Man in Panama: How General Noriega Used the U.S.—and Made Millions in Drugs and Arms* (New York, 1990).

3. Quoted in Martha Knisely Huggins, *Political Policing: The United States and Latin America* (Durham, 1998), 188.

4. Quoted in ibid., 193; see also 194–95. These inquiries were the beginning of the end for OPS. As the congressional scrutiny broadened to OPS's global operations, public awareness of the political damage and human suffering attributed to international police training heightened. Revelations of OPS's complicity in the building of South Vietnam's infamous "tiger cages" and an OPS–CIA bomb-making school in Texas were especially damaging. President Gerald R. Ford closed the OPS rather than risk another inevitably damaging inquiry.

5. Paul Sigmund, *The Overthrow of Allende and the Politics of Chile, 1964–1976* (Pittsburgh, 1977), 111–13; Sater, *Chile and the United States,* 162–64.

6. Joaquín Fermandois Huerta, *Chile y el mundo, 1970–1973* (Santiago, 1985), 44; see also 57.

7. Quoted in Sater, *Chile and the United States*, 172; see also 169–71.

8. U.S. Congress, Senate Select Committee to Study Government Operations with Respect to Intelligence Activities, *Covert Action in Chile, 1963–1973*, 94th Cong., 1st Sess., 1975, 20; Sater, *Chile and the United States*, 172–73.

9. Arturo Valenzuela, *The Breakdown of Democratic Regimes: Chile* (Baltimore, 1978), 49.

10. Allende's foreign minister later commented on the U.S. role in Allende's fall. "If the armed forces had not been predisposed to oppose the government," he wrote, "the Pentagon's call for a military uprising would have gone unheeded" (quoted in Sater, *Chile and the United States*, 186–87). See also Alan Angell, "Chile Since 1958," in Leslie Bethell, ed., *Cambridge History of Latin America*, vol. 8, *Latin America Since 1930: Spanish South America* (Cambridge, 1991), 345–61.

11. Speech at the U.S.–Venezuelan Symposium II, Macuto, Venezuela, printed in Henry Kissinger, *The Americas in a Changing World* (Washington, D.C., 1976), 4; Gerard Pierre Charles, *El Caribe contemporáneo* (Mexico City, 1981), 292–332.

12. Pérez, "La integración de Latinoamérica la hacemos nosotros o la harán por nosotros las compañías transnacionales," in *La política internacional de Carlos Andrés Pérez*, 2 vols. (Caracas, 1980), 1:169–70; see also Ewell, *Venezuela and the United States*, 195–97, 204–07.

13. Guillermo O'Donnell, *Modernization and Bureacratic Authoritarianism: Studies in South American Politics* (Berkeley, 1973), 89–95.

14. Lars Schoultz, *Human Rights and United States Policy Toward Latin America* (Princeton, 1981), 8–10.

15. Ibid., 13–14.

16. Quoted in ibid., 12.

17. Quoted in ibid., 132–33.

18. Quoted in Tulchin, *Argentina and the United States*, 144.

19. Ibid., 144–48.

20. Ibid., 154–58.

21. Quoted in Rómulo Escobar Bethancourt, *Torrijos: Colonia americana no!* (Bogotá, 1981), 207.

22. Hayakawa's remarks are quoted in William Jorden, *Panama Odyssey* (Austin, 1984), 612; see also chap. 11; and Walter LaFeber, *The Panama Canal: The Crisis in Historical Perspective* (New York, 1978), 186–87.

23. Conniff, *Panama and the United States*, 135–36.

24. In the last analysis the United States got the better of the deal, though public opinion in the country ran strong against both treaties. Half of those senators who voted favorably and were standing for reelection in 1980 lost, as did "one President," Carter noted in his memoirs. Jimmy Carter, *Keeping Faith: Memoirs of a President* (New York, 1982), 184. See also Conniff, *Panama and the United States*, 137–38.

25. Nicaragua's example conforms with Samuel Huntington's observation that revolution "is most likely to occur in societies which have experienced some social and economic development and where the processes of political modernization and political development have lagged behind the processes of social and economic change" (*Political Order in Changing Societies* [New Haven, 1968], 265. On the role of the United States as a factor in Nicaragua's economic development, see Jaime Wheelock Román, *Imperialismo y dictadura: Crisis de una formación social*, 6th ed. (1975; repr. Mexico City, 1982).

26. James Dunkerley, "Guatemala Since 1930," in Leslie Bethell, ed., *Cambridge History of Latin America*, vol. 7, *Latin America Since 1930: Mexico, Central America, and the Caribbean* (Cambridge, 1990), 240–43.

27. Edelberto Torres Rivas, "Central America Since 1930: An Overview," in Bethell, *Cambridge History of Latin America*, 7:203–04. Somoza fled to Florida, where he irritated the Carter administration by acting as if he intended to try and regain power. Rightfully fearful of assassination, he fled to Paraguay, where he was killed by Argentine terrorists in September 1980. Circumstantial evidence indicated involvement of the Sandinista National Liberation Front.

28. Castañeda, *Utopia Unarmed: The Latin American Left After the Cold War*, 110–12; Michael D. Gambone, *Capturing the Revolution: The United States, Central America, and Nicaragua, 1961–1972* (Westport, Conn.: Praeger Publishers, 2001), 50–62.

29. Quoted in Coatsworth, *Central America and the United States*, 152.

30. Jeffrey M. Paige, *Coffee and Power: Revolution and the Rise of Democracy in Central America* (Cambridge, 1997), 34.

31. LaFeber, *Inevitable Revolutions*, 255.

32. Quoted in Lars Schoultz, *National Security and United States Policy toward Latin America* (Princeton, 1987), 4–5.

33. Coatsworth, *Central America and the United States*, 191–92; Cynthia Brown, *With Friends Like These: The Americas Watch on Human Rights and U.S. Policy in Latin America* (New York, 1985), 235–36. For a critique of the distortions of the Salvadoran white paper by administration critics, see Mark Falcoff, *Small Countries, Large Issues: Studies in U.S.–Latin American Asymmetries* (Washington, D.C., 1984), 40–43.

34. Quoted in Carothers, *In the Name of Democracy: U.S. Policy Toward Latin America in the Reagan Years*, 28. The members of the Kissinger Commission were Nicholas Brady (managing director, Dillon, Read, and Co.), Mayor Henry G. Cisneros (San Antonio), Governor William P. Clements (former governor of Texas), Dr. Carlos Díaz Alejandro (professor of economics, Yale University), Wilson S. Johnson (president, National Federation of Independent Business), Lane Kirkland (president, AFL-CIO), Richard Scammon (political scientist), Dr. John Silber (president, Boston University), Justice Potter Stewart (associate justice of the Supreme Court, retired), Ambassador Robert Strauss (attorney-at-law), and Dr. William B. Walsh (president, Project Hope).

35. Quoted in Carothers, *In the Name of Democracy*, 28.

36. *The Report of the President's National Bipartisan Commission on Central America* (New York, 1984), 14, 16.

37. Terry Karl, "Exporting Democracy: The Unanticipated Effects of U.S. Electoral Policy in El Salvador," in Nora Hamilton, ed., *Crisis in El Salvador: Regional Dynamics and U.S. Policy in the 1980s* (Boulder, 1988), 174–88.

38. George P. Schultz, *Turmoil and Triumph: My Years as Secretary of State* (New York, 1993), 810–11. "People on the N[ational] S[ecurity] C[ouncil] were so obsessed with the issues of Central America that their judgment had become flawed and their actions counterproductive" (ibid., 321).

39. Coatsworth, *Central America and the United States*, 198–203.

40. Leonard, *Central America and the United States*, 189–91.

41. As the Venezuelan foreign minister commented in 1986 after a meeting of Latin American foreign ministers with Secretary of State George Schultz, "Without Washington there was no way to progress in the search for peace in the region, and with Washington it didn't seem probable" (quoted in Ewell, *Venezuela and the United States*, 223).

42. Carothers, *In the Name of Democracy*, 253–55.

43. Riordan Roett, "The Debt Crisis and Economic Development in Latin America," in Hartlyn, Schoultz, and Varas, *The United States and Latin America in the 1990s: Beyond the Cold War*, 131–51.

44. Marcelo Cavarozzi, "The Left in Latin America: The Decline of Socialism and the Rise of Political Democracy," in ibid., 116–18; Castañeda, *Utopia Unarmed*, 5–6, 18–21.

Epilogue

1. Noriega was found guilty of drug trafficking and money laundering and sentenced to forty years in a Miami prison. In a 1997 memoir, *America's Prisoner*, he accused prominent U.S. officials of high crimes but provided little evidence to support his claims. Others, among them former Attorney General Clark Clifford, charged that the Pentagon had underestimated the numbers of Panamanian casualties in the assault, a viewpoint dramatized in a documentary, *Panama Deception*, but a congressional inquiry largely confirmed the Pentagon's estimates.

2. Quoted in Conniff, *Panama and the United States*, 167; see also 160–66.

3. Raat, *Mexico and the United States*, 190–95; Augusto Varias, "From Coercion to Partnership: A New Paradigm for Security Cooperation in the Western Hemisphere?" in Hartlyn, Schoultz, and Varas, *The United States and Latin America in the 1990s*, 51.

4. James A. Baker, "Latin America and the United States: A New Partnership," *Current Policy*, no. 1160 (March 30, 1989): 6. See also Alberto van Klaveren, "Las relaciones de los paises latinoamericanos con Estados Unidos: Un ejercicio comparativo," in Mónica Hirst, ed., *Continuidad y cambio en las relaciones América Latina y los Estados Unidos* (Buenos Aires, 1987).

5. Quoted in Robert S. Leiken, "Introduction," in Leiken, *A New Moment in the Americas* (Miami, 1994), x.

6. Richard Rodríguez, "Pocho Power," in ibid., 121–30.

7. Albert Fishlow, "The Foreign Policy Challenges for the United States," in Fishlow and Jones, *The United States and the Americas: A Twenty-First Century View*, 197–205; *New York Times*, 24 November 2002.

8. Summit of the Americas, 2001, Final Declarations, April 22, 2001.

9. Charles Bergquist, "Waging War and Negotiating Peace: The Contemporary Crisis in Historical Perspective," in Charles Bergquist, Ricardo Peñaranda, and Gonzalo Sánchez, eds., *Violence in Colombia, 1990–2000: Waging War and Negotiating Peace* (Wilmington, Del., 2001), 201–03; *New York Times*, 3 January 2003.

10. Ana Arana, "The New Battle for Central America," *Foreign Affairs* (November/December 2001): 88–101; Washington Office on Latin America, "Taking Stock: Plan Colombia's First Year," *Colombia Monitor* (March 2002): 1.

11. Peter Hakim, "The Uneasy Americas," *Foreign Affairs* (March/April 2001): 46–61. For a suggestive commentary on the economic and even cultural integration of Mexico, Canada, and the United States, see Anthony DePalma, *Here: A Biography of the New American Continent*. Under Chapter 11 of the NAFTA agreement, corporations which believe they have suffered because of the actions of a state no longer have to obtain permission of a government to sue for damages but may take their case directly to an arbitral commission. A PBS Report ("Now with Bill Moyers") detailed the case of a Canadian chemical company, Methanex, that brought suit against the state of California over the decision of the state government to halt the use of MTBE (a chemical additive in gasoline designed to improve air quality) on the grounds that MTBE threatened California's underground water. In its suit, Methanex argued that the California decision was tantamount to confiscation and sought almost a billion dollars in damages if the state persisted in its decision to stop the use of MTBE.

12. Quoted in DePalma, *Here*, 349; see also John Thompson and Stephen Randall, *Canada and the United States: Ambivalent Allies*, 3d ed. (Athens, Ga., 2002), 313.

13. Estimates of remittances are drawn from a May 2001 background report to "Remittances as a Development Tool," a May 2001 conference in Washington, D.C., sponsored by the Inter-American Development and the Inter-American Dialogue. For a discussion of the "new realities" of modern Latin American and Caribbean migration to the United States see the series of essays in "Focus on Immigration," *LASA Forum* 29 (Summer 1998): 17–25.

14. See "Remittances as a Development Tool." For a brief discussion of the positive and negative consequences of remittances, see Deborah Waller Meyers, "Migrant Remittances to Latin America: Reviewing the Literature," Tomás Rivera Policy Institute and Inter-American Dialogue (Fall 1997).

15. Louis A. Pérez, Jr., *On Becoming Cuban: Identity, Nationality, and Culture* (Chapel Hill, 1999), 452–91.

16. For the consequences of the economic transformation and Americanization of Puerto Rico, see José Trías Monge, *Puerto Rico: The Trials of the Oldest Colony in the World* (New Haven, 1992).

17. Reimers, *Unwelcome Strangers*, is essential reading.

Select Bibliography

The Americas in the Modern Age relies exclusively on secondary sources in English and Spanish, as the endnote citations attest. A detailed bibliography for the history of the Americas and inter-American relations since the mid–nineteenth century would require a separate volume. The following list of sources is limited to titles in English and is designed principally for the general reader and undergraduate student. It is organized according to the major themes and periods I have covered in this book. Those books with extensive bibliographies are noted with an asterisk.

For the contemporary Americas, an excellent information source is the internet, which may be accessed by name or title, such as OAS, NAFTA, or Free Trade Area of the Americas, or by topic, such as trade, immigration, or remittances.

History of the Americas

Bannon, John F. *History of the Americas*. 2d ed. 2 vols. 1952. Reprint, New York: McGraw-Hill, 1963.

*Berger, Mark T. *Under Northern Eyes: Latin American Studies and U.S. Hegemony in the Americas, 1898–1990*. Bloomington: Indiana University Press, 1995.

*Bethel, Leslie, ed. *The Cambridge History of Latin America*. 11 vols. New York: Cambridge University Press, 1984–. Volume 11 (1995) is *Bibliographical Essays*.

Conniff, Michael L., and Thomas J. Davis. *Africans in the Americas: A History of the Black Diaspora*. New York: St. Martin's Press, 1994.

Dealy, Glen Caudill. *The Latin Americans: Spirit and Ethos*. Boulder, Colo.: Westview Press, 1992.

Hanke, Lewis, ed. *Do the Americas Have a Common History? A Critique of the Bolton Theory*. New York: A. A. Knopf, 1964.

Holmes, Vera Brown. *A History of the Americas*. Vol. 2, *From Nationhood to World States*. New York: Ronald Press, 1964.

Jones, Peter d'A. *Since Columbus: Poverty and Pluralism in the History of the Americas.* London: Heinemann, 1975.

Joseph, Gilbert M., Catherine C. LeGrand, and Ricardo D. Salvatore, eds. *Close Encounters of Empire: Writing the Cultural History of U.S.–Latin American Relations.* Durham: Duke University Press, 1998.

Knight, Franklin W. *The Caribbean: Genesis of a Fragmented Nationalism.* 2d ed. 1978. Reprint, New York: Oxford University Press, 1990.

Langley, Lester D. *The Americas in the Age of Revolution, 1750–1850.* New Haven: Yale University Press, 1996.

Marley, David. *Wars of the Americas: A Chronology of Armed Conflict in the New World: 1492 to the Present.* Santa Barbara: ABC-Clio Press, 1998.

*Magnaghi, Russell M. *Herbert E. Bolton and the Historiography of the Americas.* Westport, Conn.: Greenwood Publishers, 1998.

Morse, Richard. *New World Soundings: Cultural Ideology in the Americas.* Baltimore: Johns Hopkins University Press, 1989.

Pérez Firmat, Gustavo, ed. *Do the Americas Have a Common Literature?* Durham: Duke University Press, 1990.

Pike, Frederick. *The United States and Latin America: Myths and Stereotypes of Civilization and Nature.* Austin: University of Texas Press, 1992.

Rángel, Carlos *The Latin Americans: Their Love-Hate Relationship With the United States.* 1977. Reprint, New Brunswick, N.J.: Transaction Publishers, 1987.

Ribeiro, Darcy. *The Americas and Civilization.* Translated by Linton Lomar Barrett and Marie McDavid Barrett. New York: Dutton, 1971.

Slatta, Richard W. *Comparing Cowboys and Frontiers.* Norman: University of Oklahoma Press, 1997.

Trigger, Bruce, et al., eds. *The Cambridge History of the Native Peoples of the Americas.* 3 vols. New York: Cambridge University Press, 1996.

Wiebe, Robert. *Self-Rule: A Cultural History of American Democracy.* Chicago: University of Chicago Press, 1995.

Whitaker, Arthur. *The Western Hemisphere Idea: Its Rise and Decline.* Ithaca: Cornell University Press, 1954.

Woodward, C. Vann, ed. *A Comparative Approach to American History.* 1968. Reprint, New York: Oxford University Press, 1997.

Woodward, Ralph Lee, Jr. *Central America: A Nation Divided.* 2d ed. New York: Oxford University Press, 1985.

Inter-American Relations

Aguilar, Alonso. *Pan Americanism from Monroe to the Present: A View from the Other Side.* Translated by Asa Zatz. New York: Monthly Review Press, 1966.

*Atkins, G. Pope. *Handbook of Research on the International Relations of Latin America and the Caribbean.* Boulder, Colo.: Westview Press, 2001.

Bergquist, Charles. *Labor and the Course of American Democracy: U.S. History in Latin American Perspectives.* London: Verso, 1996.

Blasier, Cole. *The Hovering Giant: U.S. Responses to Revolutionary Change in Latin America.* Rev. ed. 1976. Reprint, Pittsburgh: University of Pittsburgh Press, 1985.

Callcott, Wilfred H. *The Western Hemisphere: Its Influence on United States Policies to the End of World War II.* Austin: University of Texas Press, 1968.

Connell-Smith, Gordon. *The United States and Latin America: An Historical Analysis of Inter-American Relations.* New York: Halsted, 1974.

Davis, Harold Eugene, John J. Finan, and F. Taylor Peck. *Latin American Diplomatic History: An Introduction.* Baton Rouge: Louisiana State University Press, 1977.

Gilderhus, Mark. *The Second Century: U.S.–Latin American Relations Since 1889.* Wilmington, Del.: Scholarly Resources, 1999.

Kenworthy, Eldon. *America/América: Myth in the Making of U.S. Policy Toward Latin America.* University Park: Pennsylvania State University Press, 1995.

Langley, Lester D. *America and the Americas: The United States in the Western Hemisphere.* The United States and the Americas Series. Athens: University of Georgia Press, 1989.

———. *The United States and the Caribbean in the Twentieth Century.* 4th ed. 1980. Reprint, Athens: University of Georgia Press, 1989.

Longley, Kyle. *In the Eagle's Shadow: The United States and Latin America.* Wheeling, Ill.: Harlan Davidson, Inc., 2002.

Pastor, Robert. *Whirlpool: U.S. Foreign Policy Toward Latin America and the Caribbean.* Princeton: Princeton University Press, 1992.

Randall, Stephen J., and Graeme S. Mount. *The Caribbean Basin: An International History.* New York: Routledge, 1998.

Schoultz, Lars. *Beneath the United States: A History of U.S. Policy Toward Latin America.* Cambridge: Harvard University Press, 1998.

Slater, Jerome. *The OAS and United States Foreign Policy.* Columbus: Ohio State University Press, 1967.

Smith, Peter H. *Talons of the Eagle: Dynamics of U.S.-Latin American Relations.* 2d ed. 1996. Reprint, New York: Oxford University Press, 2000.

Stoetzer, O. Carlos. *The Organization of American States.* 2d ed. 1965. Reprint, Westport, Conn.: Praeger, 1983.

Stuart, Graham H., and James L. Tigner, eds. *Latin America and the United States.* 6th ed. Englewood Cliffs, N.J.: Prentice-Hall, 1975.

Vaky, Viron P., and Heraldo Muñoz. *The Future of the Organization of American States.* New York: Twentieth Century Fund Press, 1993.

Walker, William O. *Drug Control in the Americas.* Albuquerque: University of New Mexico, 1989.

Weinberg, Albert K. *Manifest Destiny: A Study of Nationalist Expansionism in American History.* Baltimore: Johns Hopkins University Press, 1935.

Bilateral Relations

Atkins, G. Pope, and Larman C. Wilson. *The Dominican Republic and the United States: From Imperialism to Transnationalism.* The United States and the Americas Series. Athens: University of Georgia Press, 1998.

Coatsworth, John H. *Central America and the United States: The Clients and the Colossus.* New York: Twayne Publishers, 1994.

Clayton, Lawrence A. *Peru and the United States: The Condor and the Eagle.* The United States and the Americas Series. Athens: University of Georgia Press, 1999.

Conniff, Michael L. *Panama and the United States: The Forced Alliance.* 2d ed. The United States and the Americas Series. 1992. Reprint, Athens: University of Georgia Press, 2001.

Ewell, Judith. *Venezuela and the United States: From Monroe's Hemisphere to Petroleum's Empire.* The United States and the Americas Series. Athens: University of Georgia Press, 1996.

LaFeber, Walter. *Inevitable Revolutions: The United States in Central America.* 2d ed. New York: Norton, 1993.

Leonard, Thomas M. *Central America and the United States: The Search for Stability.* The United States and the Americas Series. Athens: University of Georgia Press, 1991.

Lehman, Kenneth D. *Bolivia and the United States: A Limited Partnership.* The United States and the Americas Series. Athens: University of Georgia Press, 1999.

Pérez, Louis A., Jr. *Cuba and the United States: Ties of Singular Intimacy.* The United States and the Americas Series. 2d ed. Athens: University of Georgia Press, 1997.

Plummer, Brenda Gayle. *Haiti and the United States: The Psychological Moment.* The United States and the Americas Series. Athens: University of Georgia Press, 1992.

Raat, W. Dirk. *Mexico and the United States: Ambivalent Vistas.* 2d ed. The United States and the Americas Series. 1992. Reprint, Athens: University of Georgia Press, 1996.

Randall, Stephen J. *Colombia and the United States: Hegemony and Interdependence.* The United States and the Americas Series. Athens: University of Georgia Press, 1992.

Sater, William F. *Chile and the United States: Empires in Conflict.* The United States and the Americas Series. Athens: University of Georgia Press, 1990.

Thompson, John Herd, and Stephen J. Randall. *Canada and the United States: Ambivalent Allies.* The United States and the Americas Series. 1994. 3d ed., Athens: University of Georgia Press, 2002.

Tulchin, Joseph S. *Argentina and the United States: A Conflicted Relationship.* Boston: Twayne Publishers, 1990.

Political Economy

Alba, Victor. *Alliance Without Allies: The Mythology of Progress in Latin America.* New York: Frederick A. Praeger, 1965.

Bulmer-Thomas, Victor. *The Economic History of Latin America Since Independence.* New York: Cambridge University Press, 1994.

Bernecker, Walther L., and Hans Werner Tobler, eds. *Development and Underdevelopment in America: Contrasts of Economic Growth in North and Latin America in Historical Perspective.* Berlin: Walter de Gruyter, 1993.

Chilcote, Ronald H., and Joel C. Edelstein. *Latin America: Capitalist and Socialist Perspectives on Development and Underdevelopment.* Boulder, Colo.: Westview Press, 1986.

Dietz, James H., and James H. Street, eds. *Latin America's Economic Development: Institutionalist and Structuralist Perspectives.* Boulder, Colo.: Lynne Rienner, 1987.

Drake, Paul, ed. *Money Doctors, Foreign Debts, and Economic Reforms in Latin America from the 1890s to the Present.* Wilmington, Del.: Scholarly Resources, 1994.

Furtado, Celso. *Economic Development of Latin America: A Survey from Colonial Times to the Present.* Cambridge: Cambridge University Press, 1970.

Harrison, Lawrence. *Underdevelopment Is a State of Mind: The Latin American Case.* Cambridge: Harvard University Press, 1985.

Hirschman, Albert O. *A Bias for Hope: Essays on Development and Latin America.* New Haven: Yale University Press, 1971.

Klarén, Peter F., and Thomas J. Bossert, eds. *Promise of Development: Theories of Change in Latin America.* Boulder, Colo.: Westview Press, 1986.

Lang, James. *Inside Development in Latin America: A Report from the Dominican Republic, Colombia, and Brazil.* Chapel Hill: University of North Carolina Press, 1988.

O'Brien, Thomas F. *The Century of U.S. Capitalism in Latin America.* Albuquerque: University of New Mexico Press, 1999.

Park, James William. *Latin American Underdevelopment: A History of the Perspectives in the United States, 1870–1965.* Baton Rouge: Louisiana State University Press, 1995.

Prebisch, Raúl. *The Economic Development of Latin America and Its Principal Problems.* New York: United Nations, 1950.

Sanderson, Steven E. *The Politics of Trade in Latin American Development.* Stanford: Stanford University Press, 1992.

Sklar, Martin. *The United States as a Developing Country: Studies in U.S. History in the Progressive Era and the 1920s.* New York: Cambridge University Press, 1992.

Soto, Hernando de. *The Mystery of Capital: Why Capitalism Succeeds in the West and Fails Everywhere Else.* New York: Basic Books, 2000.

Stallings, Barbara. *Banker to the Third World; U.S. Portfolio Investment in Latin America, 1900–1986.* Berkeley: University of California Press, 1987.

The Americas of Roosevelt and Martí, c. 1850s to World War I

Bederman, Gail. *Manliness and Civilization: A Cultural History of Gender and Race in the United States, 1880–1917.* Chicago: University of Chicago Press, 1995.

Collin, Richard H. *Theodore Roosevelt's Caribbean: The Panama Canal, the Monroe Doctrine, and the Latin American Context.* Baton Rouge: Louisiana State University Press, 1990.

Gilderhus, Mark T. *Pan American Visions: Woodrow Wilson in the Western Hemisphere, 1913–1921.* Tucson: University of Arizona Press, 1986.

Kaplan, Amy, and Donald F. Pease, eds. *Cultures of United States Imperialism.* Durham: Duke University Press, 1993.

Knight, Alan. *The Mexican Revolution.* 2 vols. Cambridge: Cambridge University Press, 1986.

LaFeber, Walter. *The American Search for Opportunity, 1865–1913.* New York: Cambridge University Press, 1963.

———. *The New Empire: An Interpretation of American Expansion, 1860–1898.* Ithaca: Cornell University Press, 1963.

Langley, Lester D. *The Banana Wars: United States Intervention in the Caribbean, 1898–1934.* 1983. Reprint, Wilmington, Del.: Scholarly Resources, 2002.

Limerick, Patricia. *The Legacy of Conquest: The Unbroken Past of the American West.* New York: W. W. Norton, 1987.

Martí, José. *Our America: Writings on Latin America and the Struggle for Cuban Independence.* Edited by Philip S. Foner. Translated by Elinor Randall. New York: Monthly Review Press, 1977.

McCullough, David. *The Path Between the Seas: The Creation of the Panama Canal.* New York: Simon and Schuster, 1977.

Meinig, D. W. *The Shaping of America: A Geographical Perspective on 500 Years of History.* Vol. 3, *Transcontinental America, 1850–1915.* New Haven: Yale University Press, 1998.

Munro, Dana G. *Intervention and Dollar Diplomacy in the Caribbean, 1900–1921.* Princeton: Princeton University Press, 1964.

O'Brien, Thomas F. *The Revolutionary Mission: American Enterprise in Latin America, 1900–1945.* New York: Cambridge University Press, 1996.

Pletcher, David M. *The Diplomacy of Trade and Investment: American Economic Expansion in the Hemisphere, 1865–1900.* Columbia: University of Missouri Press, 1998.

Slotkin, Richard. *The Fatal Environment: The Myth of the Frontier in the Age of Industrialization, 1800–1890.* New York: Atheneum, 1985.

Stephanson, Anders. *Manifest Destiny: American Expansionism and the Empire of Right.* New York: Hill and Wang, 1995.

Takaki, Ronald. *Iron Cages: Race and Culture in 19th-Century America.* New York: Oxford University Press, 1990.

Tenorio-Trillo, Mauricio. *Mexico at the World's Fairs: Crafting a Modern Nation.* Berkeley: University of California Press, 1996.

Wiebe, Robert. *The Search for Order, 1877–1920.* New York: Hill and Wang, 1967.

Wilkins, Mira. *The Emergence of Multinational Enterprise: American Business Abroad from the Colonial Era to 1914.* Cambridge: Harvard University Press, 1970.

The Americas from World War I to World War II

Barclay, Glen St. John. *Struggle for a Continent: The Diplomatic History of South America, 1917–1945.* London: Whitefriars Press, 1971.

Conn, Stetson, and Byron Fairchild. *The Western Hemisphere: The Framework of Hemispheric Defense* and *Guarding the United States and its Outposts.* Vol. 12, pts. 1 and 2,

U.S. Department of the Army, Office of the Chief of Military History, *United States Army in World War II*. Washington, D.C.: Government Printing Office, 1960.

Frye, Alton. *Nazi Germany and the American Hemisphere, 1933–1941*. New Haven: Yale University Press, 1967.

Gellman, Irwin F. *Good Neighbor Diplomacy: United States Policies in Latin America, 1933–1945*. Baltimore: Johns Hopkins University Press, 1979.

Green, David. *The Containment of Latin America: A History of the Myths and Realities of the Good Neighbor Policy*. Chicago: Quadrangle Publishers, 1971.

Haglund, David G. *Latin America and the Transformation of U.S. Strategic Thought, 1936–1940*. Albuquerque: University of New Mexico Press, 1984.

Humphreys, Robin A. *Latin America and the Second World War*. 2 vols. London: University of London Athlone Press, 1982.

Munro, Dana G. *The United States and the Caribbean Republics, 1921–1933*. Princeton: Princeton University Press, 1974.

Quintanilla, Luis. *A Latin American Speaks*. New York: Macmillan, 1943.

Smith, Robert F. *The United States and Revolutionary Nationalism in Mexico, 1916–1932*. Chicago: University of Chicago Press, 1972.

Spykman, Nicholas J. *America's Strategy in World Politics*. New York: Harcourt, Brace, 1942.

Wood, Bryce. *The Making of the Good Neighbor Policy*. New York: Columbia University Press, 1961.

The Americas in the Cold War, c. 1948 to 1989

Ameringer, Charles D. *The Democratic Left in Exile: The Antidictatorial Struggle in the Caribbean, 1945–1959*. Coral Gables: University of Florida Press, 1974.

Barber, Williard F., and C. Neale Ronning. *Internal Security and Military Power: Counterinsurgency and Civic Action in Latin America*. Columbus: Ohio State University Press, 1966.

Carothers, Thomas H. *In the Name of Democracy: U.S. Policy Toward Latin America in the Reagan Years*. Berkeley: University of California Press, 1991.

Duggan, Laurence. *The Americas: The Search for Hemispheric Security*. New York: Henry Holt, 1949.

Goldhamer, Herbert. *The Foreign Powers in Latin America*. Princeton: Princeton University Press, 1972.

Haines, Gerald K. *The Americanization of Brazil: A Study of U.S. Cold War Diplomacy in the Third World, 1945–1954*. Wilmington, Del.: Scholarly Resources, 1989.

Johnson, John J. *Political Change in Latin America: The Growth of the Middle Sectors*. Stanford: Stanford University Press, 1958.

Latham, Michael. *Modernization as Ideology: American Social Science and "Nation Building" in the Kennedy Era*. Chapel Hill: University of North Carolina Press, 2000.

Levinson, Jerome, and Juan de Onís. *The Alliance That Lost Its Way: A Critical Report on the Alliance for Progress*. Chicago: Quadrangle Publishers, 1970.

Lowenthal, Abraham F. *Partners in Conflict: The United States and Latin America*. Rev. ed. 1987. Reprint, Baltimore: Johns Hopkins University Press, 1990.

Middlebrook, Kevin, and Carlos Rico, eds. *The United States and Latin America in the 1980s: Contending Perspectives on a Decade of Crisis*. Pittsburgh: University of Pittsburgh Press, 1986.

Rabe, Stephen G. *Eisenhower and Latin America: The Foreign Policy of Anticommunism*. Chapel Hill: University of North Carolina Press, 1988.

———. *The Most Dangerous Area in the World: John F. Kennedy Confronts Communist Revolution in Latin America*. Chapel Hill: University of North Carolina Press, 1999.

Radosh, Ronald. *American Labor and United States Foreign Policy*. New York: Random House, 1969.

Rockefeller, Nelson. *The Rockefeller Report on the Americas: The Official Report of a United States Presidential Mission for the Western Hemisphere.* Chicago: Quadrangle Publishers, 1969.

Schoultz, Lars. *Human Rights and United States Policy toward Latin America.* Princeton; Princeton University Press, 1981.

Smith, Gaddis. *The Last Years of the Monroe Doctrine, 1945–1993.* New York: Hill and Wang, 1994.

Weis, W. Michael. *Cold Warriors and Coups d'Etat; Brazilian-American Relations, 1945–1964.* Albuquerque: University of New Mexico Press, 1993.

Wesson, Robert G., and Heraldo Muñoz, eds. *Latin American Views of U.S. Policy.* New York: Praeger, 1986.

The Contemporary Americas

Buchanan, Patrick J. *The Death of the West: How Dying Populations and Immigrant Invasions Imperil Our Country and Civilization.* New York: Thomas Dunne, 2002.

Castañeda, Jorge. *Utopia Unarmed: The Latin American Left After the Cold War.* New York: Alfred A. Knopf, 1993.

DePalma, Anthony. *Here: A Biography of the New American Continent.* New York: Public Affairs Press, 2001.

Domínguez, Jorge I. *The Future of Inter-American Relations.* New York: Routledge, 1999.

Earle, Robert L., and John D. Wirth, eds. *Identities in North America: The Search for Community.* Stanford: Stanford University Press, 1995.

Farer, Tom J., ed. *Beyond Sovereignty: Collectively Defending Democracy in the Americas.* Baltimore: Johns Hopkins University Press, 1996.

———. *The Future of the Inter-American System.* New York: Praeger, 1988.

Fishlow, Albert, and James Jones, eds. *The United States and the Americas: A Twenty-First Century View.* New York: W. W. Norton, 1999.

Green, Roy, ed. *The Enterprise for the Americas Initiative: Issues and Prospects for a Free Trade Agreement in the Western Hemisphere.* Westport, Conn.: Praeger, 1993.

Guillermoprieto, Alma. *Looking for History: Despatches from Latin America.* New York: Pantheon Books, 2001.

Haar, Jerry, and Edgar Dosman, eds. *A Dynamic Partnership: Canada's Changing Role in the Americas.* New Brunswick, N.J.: Transaction, 1993.

Harrison, Lawrence E. *The Pan-American Dream: Do Latin America's Cultural Values Discourage True Partnership with the United States and Canada?* Boulder: Westview Press, 1998.

Hartlyn, Jonathan, Lars Schoultz, and Augusto Varas, eds. *The United States and Latin America in the 1990s: Beyond the Cold War.* Chapel Hill: University of North Carolina Press, 1992.

Hufbaer, Gary Clyde, and Jeffrey J. Schott. *Western Hemisphere Economic Integration.* Washington, D.C.: Institute for International Economics, 1993.

Langley, Lester D. *MexAmerica: Two Countries, One Future.* New York: Crown Publishers, 1988.

Leiken, Robert S., ed. *A New Moment in the Americas.* University of Miami North-South Center. New Brunswick, N.J.: Transaction, 1994.

Lipset, Seymour. *American Exceptionalism: A Double-Edged Sword.* New York: Norton, 1996.

Lowenthal, Abraham F., ed. *Exporting Democracy: The United States and Latin America.* Baltimore: Johns Hopkins University Press, 1991.

Mitchell, Christopher, ed. *Western Hemisphere Immigration and United States Foreign Policy.* University Park: Pennsylvania State University Press, 1992.

Ramos, Jorge. *The Other Face of America: Chronicles of the Immigrants Shaping Our Future.* Translated by Patricia Duncan. New York: HarperCollins, 2002.

Randall, Stephen J., Herman Conrad, and Sheldon Silverman, eds. *North America Without Borders? Integrating Canada, the United States, and Mexico.* Calgary, Alberta: University of Calgary Press, 1992.

Reimers, David. *Unwelcome Strangers: American Identity and the Turn Against Immigration.* New York: Columbia University Press, 1998.

Rochlin, James F. *Canada as a Hemisphere Actor.* Toronto: McGraw-Hill Ryerson, 1992.

Smith, William C. *Latin American Political Economy in the Age of Neoliberal Reform: Theoretical and Comparative Perspectives for the 1990s.* University of Miami North-South Center. New Brunswick, N.J.: Transaction, 1994.

Weintraub, Sidney, *Integrating the Americas: Shaping Future Trade Policy.* Miami: North-South Center, 1994.

Wiebe, Robert H. *Who We Are: A History of Popular Nationalism.* Princeton: Princeton University Press, 2002.

Index

Acheson, Sec. of State Dean, and U.S. policy toward Latin America, 160–61, 164–65
Act of Havana (1940), 134
Adams, Brooks, on U.S. empire, 34
Adams, Henry, on Populist revolt in United States, 32
African Americans: in late nineteenth century United States, 28; and Spanish-American War, 60; and U.S. relations with the British West Indies during World War II, 141
Afro-Cubans: and *Cuba Libre*, 60; colored revolt of 1910–12, 89
Alba, Víctor, opposes U.S. aid to Latin America, 211
Alberdi, Juan: 39; on immigration to Argentina, 41
Alemán, Pres. Miguel, and Mexico's relations with the United States in late *1940s*, 162
Alessandri, Pres. Jorge: and Chile's policy toward Cuba (1959–62), 180; and 1970 Chilean presidential election, 227
Allende, Pres. Salvador: applauds Cuban revolution,177; heads socialist government in Chile, 227–31
Alliance for Progress: Latin American origins, 171–73; Pres. John F. Kennedy proposes, 181; accomplishments in early years, 193–95; problems, 195–97, 210–15
Almazán, Juan Andreu, in 1940 Mexican presidential election, 128

Alvarado, Gen. Juan Velasco, and 1968 military coup in Peru, 215
Amador, Manuel, first president of Panama, 84
American Popular Revolutionary Alliance (APRA), 110
American Treaty of Pacific Settlement (or Pact of Bogotá, 1948), 155.
Americanization: in Puerto Rico after the Spanish-American War, 64; in Cuba in the early twentieth century, 86–87; North American corporate culture in Latin America in the *1920s*, 109–10; in the circum-Caribbean in World War II, 143; North American consumer culture in Latin America and the Caribbean in the *1990s*, 268
Americas. *See* Western Hemisphere
Anderson, Sec. of the Treasury Robert D., at OAS economic conference (1957), 172
Angell, Norman, *The Great Illusion* (1911), 90
Arbenz, Pres. Jacobo, Guatemalan politics and relations with the United States (1950–54), 166–69
Arévalo, Juan José: 167, 198; and overthrow of Guatemalan government in *1944*, 144
Argentina: political and economic development in late nineteenth century, 41–43, 74; at 1889 Pan-American Conference, 81; role of European immigrants in Argentine development, 81–82; political reforms of *1912*, 91; in the 1930s, 123; and fears of German